THE FLOATING UNIVERSITY

The Floating University

Experience, Empire, and the Politics of Knowledge

Tamson Pietsch

THE UNIVERSITY OF CHICAGO PRESS

CHICAGO AND LONDON

The University of Chicago Press, Chicago 60637
The University of Chicago Press, Ltd., London
© 2023 by The University of Chicago
Published 2023
Printed in the United States of America

32 31 30 29 28 27 26 25 24 23   1 2 3 4 5

ISBN-13: 978-0-226-82516-8 (cloth)
ISBN-13: 978-0-226-82517-5 (e-book)
DOI: https://doi.org/10.7208/chicago/
9780226825175.001.0001

Library of Congress Cataloging-in-Publication Data

Names: Pietsch, Tamson, 1978– author.
Title: The floating university : experience, empire,
and the politics of knowledge / Tamson Pietsch.
Description: Chicago ; London : The University of Chicago
Press, 2023. | Includes bibliographical references and index.
Identifiers: LCCN 2022040054 | ISBN 9780226825168 (cloth) |
ISBN 9780226825175 (ebook)
Subjects: LCSH: Lough, James E. (James Edwin), 1871–
1952. | New York University—History—20th century. |
Transnational education—History—20th century. |
Education, Higher—United States—History—
20th century. | Ocean travel. | Voyages around the
world. | United States—Civilization—1918–1945.
Classification: LCC LC1095 .P54 2023 |
DDC 378.747/10904—dc23/eng/20220824
LC record available at https://lccn.loc.gov/2022040054

♾ This paper meets the requirements of
ANSI/NISO Z39.48-1992 (Permanence of Paper).

For Mum, and Ruth, and Vita

Contents

Introduction

How to Know the World?

In mid-September 1926, five hundred people from across the United States boarded a ship in New York for an eight-month cruise around the world encompassing forty-seven ports of call. They met some of the major figures of the twentieth century, including Benito Mussolini, the king of Thailand, Mahatma Gandhi, and Pope Pius XI, while visiting countries in the midst of change: Japan in the process of industrialization, China on the cusp of revolution, the Philippines in agitation against US rule, and Portugal in the aftermath of a coup. In an era of internationalism and expanding American power, the leaders of the voyage believed that travel and study at sea would deliver an education in international affairs not available in the land-based classroom. It was through direct sense experience in and of the world, rather than passive, indirect engagement via textbooks and lectures, that students would learn to be "world-minded." The trip was promoted as an "an experiment in democratic theories of education," and New York University lent the venture its official sponsorship.[1] Yet the undertaking, known as the Floating University, has all but disappeared from our history books.

My initial encounter with the Floating University was an accident. While working on an entirely different research quest, I came across a yellowing pamphlet from the mid-1920s that had been slipped into the back of a book.[2] Printed on two sides of a single sheet, the pamphlet described an enterprise led by NYU's professor of psychology, James E. Lough, in which students would receive university credit for travel abroad. It promised that the venture was designed "to develop the ability to think in world terms, to interest students in foreign affairs and to strengthen international understanding and good will" through "first hand contact with places, peoples, and problems."[3] I wanted to know more about this intriguing initiative and its origins. But I found that although it dominated the contemporaneous press coverage, historians of internationalism, education, and American history alike have had little to say about it.[4]

What was the Floating University? What does it tell us about the history and politics of knowledge in the 1920s? And why—given the huge amount of attention it attracted at the time—does it not appear in our histories? Those are the questions this book sets out to investigate. The story it tells concerns some of the keynotes of US and global history during the twentieth century. With origins that lie in the wake of the American Civil War and the flowering of the philosophic and intellectual movements that followed, the Floating University emerged from the aftermath of World War I and the tectonic economic and geopolitical changes that the war had set in motion. Coming to fruition in the rapidly expanding urban context of New York City, it sailed along the expanding tentacles of US global power during the interwar period, riding the waves of imperialism, anticolonialism, and international jazz culture. But the creation of US newspaper syndicates, the expansion of academic expertise, and the emergence of a very different kind of international politics in the shadow of another war brought on the initiative's demise. Uncovering the history of the Floating University not only reveals much about the entangled world of internationalism, American empire, and education in the 1920s but also has implications for how historians understand the legitimization of knowledge during the twentieth century.

Universities derive much of their social standing (not to mention their income) from their claim to have authority over knowledge. They are the institutions that undertake the research, distill the learning, and provide the training that enables the specialized expertise so crucial to multifaceted economies and societies. This book troubles the naturalization of this assumption. It reveals a 1920s contest over the kind of knowledge that should underpin university education in which academically authorized expertise came into conflict with an emphasis on direct personal experience. As old authority structures were shaken after World War I, the question of how to know became an urgent priority for a variety of actors, from modernist artists and writers to quantum and atomic physicists, theologians, anticolonial and revolutionary leaders, and liberal internationalists. New, popular technologies such as photography, film, radio, inexpensive novels and newspapers, as well as cheaper transatlantic travel, jazz, and the latest improvised forms of dance, seemed to offer direct, embodied, and experiential ways of knowing that were at once deeply personal and widely accessible. Although it was academically authorized expertise that came to underpin the business model of universities during the twentieth century, at the start of the 1920s the issue of what legitimized knowledge was by no means settled.

The Floating University world cruise serves as a microcosm through which this politics of knowledge can be discerned. By focusing on the contours of this politics in the United States, this book shows that experts' claims to authority over knowledge are not neutral, natural, or timeless, for they, too, have a history. And it is a history that cannot be understood without attention to broader power relations. Despite lobbying by W. E. B. DuBois, the Floating University's student body reflected the color line of Jim Crow–era America. It sailed along routes protected by the US military, enabled by US commerce and finance, and legitimated by US networks of moral empire. What those on board ultimately experienced during their nearly eight-month voyage was not so much "the world" as the reach of their own nation's culture and power. What they learned were lessons in empire.[5] As well as revealing a history of knowledge and its legitimation, the story of the Floating University shows how the uneven geopolitical terrain of the postwar era was already beginning to emerge in the 1920s.

◆ ◆ ◆

In the last two decades, international and intellectual historians have turned to questions of expertise, information, knowledge, and education. They have pointed to the rise of internationalist culture during the twentieth century and the role played by nonstate actors, civil society groups, and institutions such as universities in fashioning it.[6] Visions of world order advanced by specific thinkers have been a central focus for many, as have the surveys and statistical projects that sought to describe the world and the communications technologies, educational institutions, and international communities facilitating cross-border interaction.[7] More recently, public opinion has become a key concern.[8] Yet for all their attention to expertise and ideas, these accounts of the history of interwar internationalism and ideas tend to take for granted the more fundamental question of knowledge itself. By what methods could the world be known? How was such knowledge verified? Questions about the production, foundation, and legitimation of knowledge claims have been central to the work of historians of science and to scholars working on gender, postcolonialism, Black history, and US empire for decades. However, they have been less prominent in the work of intellectual historians focused on visions of world order, international historians interested in knowledge exchange, and educational historians concerned with specific institutions during the interwar period.[9] *The Floating University* places these questions at the center of its analysis.

This emphasis in turn has significant implications for the history of higher education. For historians of American educational institutions, the parallel growth of liberal arts colleges and universities with graduate professional and research schools in the decades after the Civil War stands as a key turning point in the development of the modern university. Some scholars go so far as to argue that it was the establishment at Harvard in the 1880s and 1890s of the bachelor's degree as a prerequisite for admission to graduate school that "brought into being the system of elite education that the United States maintains today."[10] The dramatic increase in student enrollment during the first three decades of the twentieth century and the expansion of professional vocational degrees are usually understood as part of the story of rising social mobility, growing institutional marketization, and increasing stratification.[11] The Floating University's pedagogic approach could be cast as part of the reaction of liberal culture to mass education that took place during this period, but that would capture only part of its meaning.[12] As David Labaree notes, discussions of American higher education "tend to focus much too heavily on a few institutions at its very pinnacle."[13] And very rarely do they concentrate on administrative concerns, such as extramural studies departments or academic credit. The Floating University cannot be understood without attention to these dimensions of institutional life. In equating university learning with the accumulation of hourly units of study, the system of academic credit established in the first decade of the twentieth century opened the door to fundamental issues of recognition. For what sorts of activities would credit be awarded? Who counted as an educational authority? What place would extramural learning be accorded? This book suggests that attending to how these questions played out at an aspiring mid-tier institution reveals the claims to power and priority that US universities were making in the 1920s.

The production of these claims within the context of broader power relations has ramifications for historians of US foreign relations during the interwar period. Questions of knowledge and power have, of course, long been a focus for historians of science, medicine, and US empire. Public health, race relations, policing, and educational institutions in places like Hawaii, Puerto Rico, Panama, and the Philippines (and their influence on the national project at home) have attracted significant attention.[14] More recently, the established focus of US diplomatic historians on financial and commercial, cultural and religious, and official forms of foreign relations has joined with intellectual history to stimulate new discussion not only of the United States as an imperial power but also of how global and imperial connections shaped domestic life and politics.[15] Although there is now a significant body of scholarship that brings these literatures together and considers the relationship between higher education and power in the context of the Cold War, with some notable exceptions the period between World

War I and World War II remains underexamined.[16] From the American international alumni who hosted the Floating University's students in China, Egypt, and Japan to the University of Missouri graduates running newspapers across the globe, college ties and US expertise abroad are a central part of this story. Following historical work focused on American imperial education projects, this book reveals the entangled relationship between domestic US higher education institutions and the making, policing, and naturalizing of US power relations—not only in insular possessions but at home and across the globe.[17]

Key to the projection of US power abroad was the sea. Since the 1990s, the rise of global and environmental history has led to a rejuvenation of the traditional field of maritime history. From the New Thalassology to the Blue Humanities, this new maritime scholarship has sought to move beyond the sea as a space to be traversed, beyond a focus on arrivals and departures, to an approach in which journeys at sea are connected to lives on land; in which the ocean itself is a subject of study; and in which maritime infrastructures, from labor relations to coaling depots, are crucial to understanding global power relations.[18] Building on the "global history of science," which has increasingly centered on the entanglement of Western science in the imperial project (and its limits), some scholars have focused on the knowledge-making voyages of figures such as Charles Darwin, the seafaring racial science of Americans in the Pacific, or the National Science Foundation's "floating laboratory," the R/V *Alpha Helix*.[19] But most studies of higher education remain terrestrial. This book examines learning aboard the Floating University and the complex relationship between the idea of an around-the-world voyage, the space of the ship, the localities that the students visited, and land-based politics and educational norms.

In drawing together these four usually disconnected fields of scholarship, *The Floating University* shows how the story of a long-dismissed educational experiment in the mid-1920s can shed light on the history of knowledge and power during the twentieth century, presenting a challenge to historians of the United States, intellectual and educational historians alike.

◆   ◆   ◆

The Floating University came to fruition as one of the many proposals to renew American higher education that emerged after the demise of the prescribed classical curriculum of the traditional nineteenth-century college and the advent of mass higher education.[20] Taking advantage of the exploding 1920s transatlantic travel industry, Professor James Lough's innovation—with its focus on direct personal experience in and with the world—was to recognize travel experience with university credit. This, however, put it at odds with another approach that at the same time was increasingly being advanced by US universities eager to position themselves as crucial to the nation's political and economic life. Although initially prepared to sponsor Lough's commitment to experience as the basis of learning, in early 1926 NYU withdrew its support, having concluded that only lessons learned in class from an approved university instructor should be granted credit. As far as NYU was now concerned, it was academic expertise, not direct experience, that should underpin authorized knowledge during the twentieth century.

The tensions between these two approaches were revealed when Professor Lough's Floating University set sail, claiming both the status of the university and the thrill of adventure on the high seas. As well as offering more than seventy-three subjects, a full extracurricular program, and arranged shore excursions and visits to foreign universities, the voyage introduced the traveling students to the hotel bars and back alleys of the world's port cities. Alcohol was a constant attraction, and the coeducational nature of the voyage provoked panics about gender and sexual promiscuity that sparked an explosion of coverage in the US domestic as well as international press. "Sea Collegians Startle Japan with Rum Orgy," read one Detroit newspaper's headline.[21] The voyage that had been so widely championed as an experiment in modern education was resoundingly pronounced a failure—by both US higher education institutions, which followed the lead of NYU, and the US mass media, which was convinced that student antics were incompatible with educational attainment. Lurking behind their condemnation was perhaps also a latent fear that the spectacle of ungoverned youthful bodies betrayed a lack of national readiness for the new global role the United States was rapidly assuming. By the time the Floating University returned to New York at the start of May 1927, the cruise had become an object of ridicule.[22]

Yet many of those who traveled on board the ship told a very different story about the nearly eight-month voyage. What was at stake for its protagonists in 1927 when the Floating University returned to New York, only to be branded a failure? And what is at stake for historians and educationalists today if they continue to take that judgment at face value? Nearly a century after the Floating University sailed, this book argues that it is time to take a different approach, one that forces historians to examine the conventions that underpin our own knowledge claims. In this, it is potentially the "failed" nature of Professor Lough's project that might be its most instructive legacy. Perhaps one of the reasons academic historians have not attended to the story of the Floating University is because they have, in many respects, inherited the rules of knowing that deemed it unsuccessful. Thinking with failure might help historians better see how legitimate knowledge was and is produced, the institutions that normalize it and profit by it, the sanctions that reinforce it, and the other ways of being it exiles.

The Floating University makes sense of the 1926 voyage, its delegitimation, and its historical neglect by drawing on concepts central to both the pragmatist philosophy that so influenced Professor Lough and work from the history of science and the sociology of knowledge in recent decades.[23] It analyzes different ways of warranting or justifying knowledge claims (Lough emphasized direct experience, but universities traded on the authority of experts and "book knowledge"); the systems of social acknowledgment that conferred or withheld legitimacy (such as university endorsement and press approval); and the background assumptions that all actors took for granted (like the growing power of the United States abroad). In focusing on a single educational initiative and following a dozen or so characters who made their way around the world aboard a ship, it exemplifies global microhistory and embraces the nuance, attention to primary sources, and place-based specificity of that approach.[24] But as a study of an around-the-world cruise, it is also a book that spans many regions of the globe, focusing (to paraphrase Thomas Cohen) on the large things as well as the small.[25] Although this risks prioritizing the movement of a handful of privileged actors and riding roughshod over local context, the conjunction of these scales brings to the surface questions of whose world, whose mobility, whose knowledge, and whose forms of authorization that go to the heart of this study. While focusing on individual experience, *The Floating University* reveals the broader power structures that studies attending to the complexities of specific institutions, sites, or subjects can sometimes obscure.

The sources on which this book is based are hugely diverse and drawn from nearly fifty archival repositories. The view from the ship is conveyed using the personal papers, letters, diaries, and memoirs of passengers; course outlines; shipping company and organizational records; and the ship's onboard newspaper. The view from the United States is explored through domestic news coverage, State Department records, NYU and other university archives, court and immigration records, published works, and personal correspondence. Apprehending how the ship was understood in the localities where it docked is a harder task, but local vernacular newspaper records, an oral history, diplomatic correspondence, and the students' own letters and reports open a window on what the Floating University meant to those who encountered it.

◆　◆　◆

The book begins by exploring the Floating University's origins in the experimental psychology of William James and the new educational thinking of John Dewey. Although later derided as little more than a "new style tourist agency," the undertaking had serious intellectual foundations.[26] The first chapter argues that James Lough's efforts to launch the voyage grew out of his psychology studies at Harvard and his innovations in experiential education at New York University during the period before and after World War I. It shows just how fully the university initially backed his plans. But on the eve of departure, NYU withdrew its sponsorship of the voyage. The second chapter follows the machinations that led the university to revoke its sanction and places the venture within the wider context of US higher education in the 1920s and the changing business model of universities. It ends with the ultimatum NYU gave Professor Lough—he could go on the voyage, but only if he found a new job.

Yet go on the voyage Lough did. Despite NYU's withdrawal, in September 1926 his dream became a reality. Chapter 3 examines life aboard the Floating University and the attempt to implement Lough's educational philosophy in classes, shore trips, and the "extracurriculum." However, as the ship made its way around the world, divisions surfaced between and within the various groups on board that revealed tensions inherent in the project: Was there a difference between students and tourists? How much latitude should passengers be given to "experiment" onshore? What constituted an education anyway? These questions became acute when the students' behavior in port attracted the attention—and judgment—of the US and foreign press. Reports of drunkenness and romantic liaisons were seized on by American newspapers, which cited them as evidence of educational failure. With the endorsement of NYU already withdrawn, it was in their pages that the battle for the Floating University's educational legitimacy was waged. The fourth chapter traces the evaporation of the voyage's social standing as newspapers across the United States seized on events in Cuba, Japan, Rome, and Paris: in their view, students' misbehavior in the port cities of the globe did not equate with a university education.

Meanwhile, it was becoming clear that the "world" the Floating University students were encountering was one that assumed the existence of expanding US power. Chapter 5 traces the military, commercial, and cultural geographies along which the ship sailed. Shadowed by the comforting reach of the United States' military presence, the students' experiences of "the world" were conditioned by the networks and informal embassies of their nation's growing commercial and cultural reach. If Professor Lough had wanted to teach students to be "world-minded," what they were discovering was the meaning of the United States' place in the world. The sixth chapter explores how those aboard made sense of what they were seeing. It examines how acceptance of the United States' emerging role as an imperial power was produced over the course of the voyage through lectures and reading materials, shipboard debates over US colonization in the Philippines, comparisons to British, Dutch, and Japanese rule, and racial constructions of global order. It then follows the students to Palestine, Paris, Abbotsford, and Stratford, where they read US history into the landscape, finding in these places abroad the cultural antecedents of their national story. But every now and then, other ways of knowing did force their way onto the ship, surfacing anxieties about American cultural limitations. Chapter 7 inverts the perspective on the Floating University to reveal some of the alternative systems of authorization to which it was recruited. It explores how the ship and its passengers were understood and employed by those belowdecks and on the docks, whose concerns were quite different from those of the Americans traveling in the staterooms and tourist cabins. Making the world their playground, the Floating University's members only occasionally perceived that they, too, were sometimes being played.

Returning to New York in May 1927, the Floating University was greeted by cheering crowds on the pier, but the fight for its legacy was only just beginning. Chapter 8 considers the various grounds on which the "educational experiment" was judged. Although supporters of the cruise advocated sober scientific principles, the press coverage ensured it was the students' conduct that was the measure of evaluation. Although Professor Lough won a court case for unfair dismissal from NYU, his successive attempts to relaunch the Floating University attracted the suspicions of the US State Department, which even deployed a special agent to report on him. By the 1930s, it had become clear that the Floating University's claims of the academic possibilities of situated and embodied knowledge presented just too much of a challenge to the emerging epistemic and social order. The conventions for knowing the world during the interwar period were determined by Professor Lough's detractors.

But are their terms the criteria against which the voyage should continue to be assessed? The final chapter attends more closely to the legacies of the voyage and the question of its failure. It considers the influence of the trip on the lives and careers of a selection of students and staff, several of whom were active in attempting to relaunch the floating university idea in the 1960s, including in the form of Semester at Sea, a program that operates to this day. With university study abroad growing exponentially during the twenty-first century, tensions between experience and expertise have reemerged, and the ways educational success or failure is framed have once again come to the fore. Thinking about failure, this chapter suggests, is important, because it draws attention to the social and political processes by which knowledge claims are supported, the forms of recognition they rely on, and the assumptions underpinning them.

◆ ◆ ◆

In the telling of this story, some usual suspects are absent. Elite universities and the growth of research—a feature of so many US higher education histories—play a relatively minor role. Major philanthropic institutions like the Carnegie, Ford, and Rockefeller Foundations appear only briefly, and major figures in the nascent discipline of interwar international relations as well as the growing number of interwar think tanks, the League of Nations, and the interwar ecosystem of international conferences and organizations are rarely mentioned.[27] Although the State Department appears now and then, states and municipalities more generally hardly feature, although their crucial role as funders, regulators, and legislators of American secondary as well as tertiary education and the requirements they introduced for professional registration help shape the context of this story.[28] The political convulsions associated with labor, race, and economic relations within the United States at this time, and the contested visions of American democracy and freedom associated with them, also echo only on the sidelines of the narrative. Instead, a set of less prominent though still quite privileged actors, both individual and institutional, are at its heart. The endeavors of middle-class men and mid-tier (and often midwestern) institutions to navigate and shape the changing landscapes of their interwar world offer a fresh insight into the importance of a period in which, as historians such as Barbara Keys, Frank Costigliola, Emily Rosenberg, and Robert Dean have variously shown, the foundations for post-1945 US foreign relations were laid.[29]

The account presented here is limited by available sources, space constraints, and its perspective. Coverage of the students' experience of onboard classes, for example, is conditioned by the content of their accounts; and Professor Lough, who is so central to the opening chapters, disappears from the middle ones, both because of a lack of firsthand material and because he was marginalized by his colleagues. Some locations are dealt with more fully than others, with Portugal, Spain, the Netherlands, Scandinavia, Sri Lanka, and Algeria in particular receiving only cursory coverage.

The view presented is a white, American-centric one. For the most part, it approaches the port cities of the world through the eyes of a handful of privileged staff and students. Not only does this sideline other ways of seeing, but worse, its invocation of the tropes of bright lights and jazz could obscure what made the decade important and particular in different contexts across the globe, detracting from such issues as franchise reform and its consequences (in the United Kingdom and Japan, among other places), the growth of print culture in the port cities of Southeast Asia, and the expansion of long-standing struggles against colonial rule.[30] Awareness of the limits of this shipboard perspective is important. Not only did it tend to homogenize cultures that were dynamic and diverse, but the temporary arrival of a shipload of five hundred rich Americans may or may not have presented a momentous event for those who lived and worked in the places the *Ryndam* visited. For those who did engage with the traveling students, chapter 7 only gestures toward hinterlands of possible motivation and purpose.

There is a danger too that in casting the fate of the Floating University as one settled by the contest between different ways of authorizing knowledge in the 1920s, this book overstates both that conflict and its resolution. Professionalized knowledge in the form of social surveys helped shape notions of self and nation, as Sarah Igo has shown, blurring the lines between experience and expertise. Moreover, many of the early twentieth-century progressive social reformers who kept company with John Dewey were chief among the new experts eager to mobilize their authorized knowledge, with repressive as well as enabling effects.[31] Travel experience was, of course, a crucial aspect of US higher education from the colonial period onward, and as chapter 8 outlines, it continued in various ways throughout the twentieth and into the twenty-first century.[32] Experiential approaches to learning also have endured beyond the 1920s, from the progressive critique of conventional schooling mounted by Dewey's followers in the 1930s and 1940s to David A. Kolb's development of the Experiential Learning Model in the 1970s and 1980s, the quite separate traditions of Montessori and Steiner schooling, and recent initiatives such as Barnard College's "Reacting to the Past."[33] In different ways, pedagogic innovations such as problem-based learning, work placements and design thinking, and the explosion of study abroad programs in the first two decades of the twenty-first century have all sought to embed "experience" within the university curriculum.

And then there is Constantine Raises. A member of the Floating University's cruise management team and later a travel agent, he told a story of the origins of the 1926–27 world cruise different from that presented here. His centers on a chance meeting with Professor Lough at the University of Athens in the summer of 1920 and a dinner five years later hosted by Captain

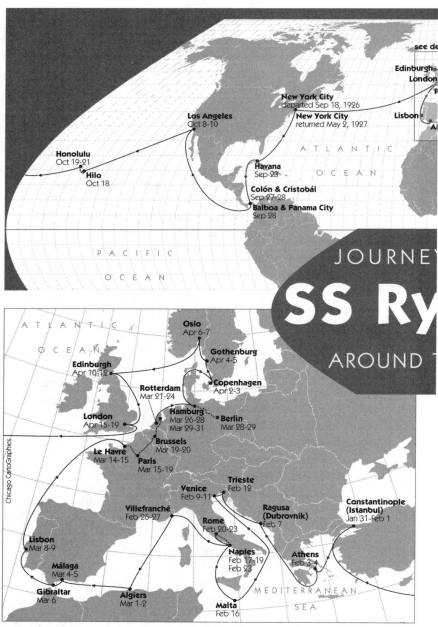

The Floating University's 1926–27 around-the-world voyage on the SS *Ryndam*. Dates reflect the days actually spent in port, rather than when the ship docked (which was sometimes the night before). Chicago CartoGraphics.

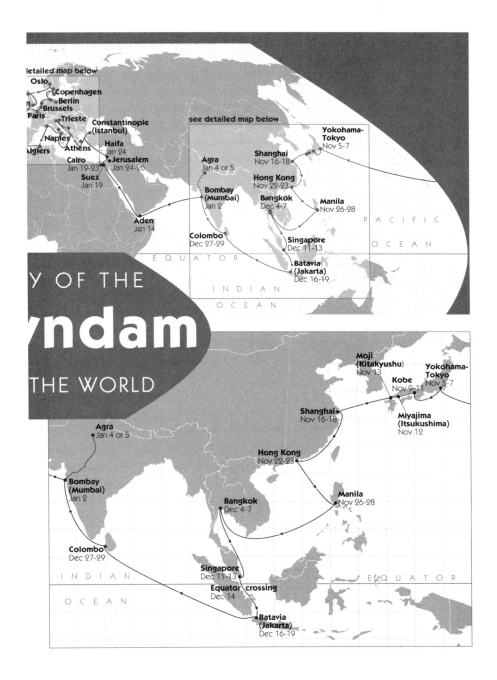

detailed map below

Oslo
Copenhagen
Berlin
Brussels
Paris
Trieste
Constantinople
(Istanbul)
Naples
Athens
Algiers
Haifa
Jan 24
Cairo
Jan 19-23
Jerusalem
Jan 24-26
Suez
Jan 19

see detailed map below

Agra
Jan 4 or 5

Shanghai
Nov 16-18

Yokohama-
Tokyo
Nov 5-7

Hong Kong
Nov 22-23

Aden
Jan 14

Bombay
(Mumbai)
Jan 2

Bangkok
Dec 4-7

Manila
Nov 26-28

PACIFIC

OCEAN

Colombo
Dec 27-29

Singapore
Dec 11-13

EQUATOR

Batavia
(Jakarta)
Dec 16-19

INDIAN

OCEAN

Y OF THE

ndam

THE WORLD

Agra
Jan 4 or 5

Moji
(Kitakyushu)
Nov 13

Kobe
Nov 9-11

Yokohama-
Tokyo
Nov 5-7

Shanghai
Nov 16-18

Miyajima
(Itsukushima)
Nov 12

Bombay
(Mumbai)
Jan 2

Hong Kong
Nov 22-23

Manila
Nov 26-28

Bangkok
Dec 4-7

Colombo
Dec 27-29

INDIAN

Singapore
Dec 11-13

EQUATOR

OCEAN

Equator crossing
Dec 14

Batavia
(Jakarta)
Dec 16-19

Felix Riesenberg on board the New York Maritime Academy's training ship, the (SS) *Newport* (for a full version of Raises's story, see the appendix).[34] In presenting the account I have, which privileges the archival trail over Raises's oral testimony, I am in many respects enacting the very forms of warrant and mobilizing the same structures of recognition that I otherwise seek to historicize. Archives are themselves unreliable and problematic creations that work to select, categorize, normalize, and erase.[35] They are not natural or neutral, and in mobilizing them I must recognize that I, too, inhabit the city of legitimate knowledge built by Lough's detractors.

Social and institutional recognition will always be central to how human communities validate the knowledge they make about the world and each other. This book shows that these forms of recognition have a history and politics that were (and are) structured by unequal relations of power. One hundred years after the Floating University set sail, and in the context of the need for rapid and transformative societal change to meet the challenges of the environmental crisis, the stakes of securing anew that social recognition could not be higher. How will it be done? Thinking about why the Floating University was deemed a failure in the 1920s highlights the failure in our own times to ground knowledge in ways recognizable to those outside the community of academically authorized experts. In seeking alternatives, perhaps Professor Lough's vision of personal and embodied experience as linked to institutional authority is a good place to begin.

1

Professor Lough's Big Idea

At 4:25 p.m. on the afternoon of September 18, 1926, a long whistle sounded, and the SS *Ryndam* pulled away from the Dutch-owned Holland America Line's Hoboken, New Jersey, pier. The flags of thirty-five countries flew from bow to stern as the ship made its way down the Hudson River, UNIVERSITY WORLD CRUISE painted on its side. Over 1,000 friends and family members stood on the shore, waving handkerchiefs and hats and blowing tearful kisses from the gangway. They were there to bid farewell to more than 500 excited and slightly trepidatious passengers—306 young men, 57 young women, and 133 adults who were combining travel with education—and 63 faculty and staff who had signed up to join the Floating University: an eight-month around-the-world "educational experiment" in which travel abroad would count toward a university degree at home. By 10:00 p.m., the lightship stationed off the coast of Cape Hatteras, North Carolina, could be seen on the starboard side, and the work of establishing a university-at-sea had begun.[1]

Where had this seemingly madcap notion of taking hundreds of young American college students on a worldwide cruise come from? Riding the wave of postwar internationalism and American prosperity, the Floating University had firm intellectual foundations in the experimental psychology of William James and the educational philosophy of John Dewey. It was the realization of more than twenty years of one man's thinking about experience as the foundation of learning.

ED BECOMES JAMES

Professor James Edwin Lough had been trying to launch the Floating University since 1923, but the intellectual foundations of the project had been laid many years before, during his time as an undergraduate. Named for a dead uncle who had fought for the Union army, Ed (as he was known to his family) had grown up in the shadow of the Civil War in a home marked by grief and dashed ambitions. At age sixteen, he had left the small farming community of Eaton in western Ohio, borrowing money to enter Miami University, a small scholarly community in the nearby town of Oxford. And it was there, in the courses taught by Roger B. C. Johnson, that he discovered the philosophy and psychology that would later shape the Floating University cruise.[2]

Johnson's philosophical interests tended toward metaphysics, British idealism, and the social (as opposed to the individualist) understandings of the self he gleaned from the early writings of James and Dewey, and he passed these ideas on to the serious young man from Eaton. Graduating with honors in philosophy in 1891, Ed returned to his hometown to take up a series of teaching posts in various public schools. Perhaps he wanted to be near his family, but he also needed to earn an income to pay off his loans. His academic ambitions were far from over, however. According to his younger brother, William, Ed had already "made up his mind that he intended to head for something bigger." He even talked of going to Harvard. "You must realize," wrote William many years later, "that from the viewpoint of a small farming community in western Ohio, Harvard looked as remote and inaccessible as the moon."[3]

But go to Harvard Ed Lough did. Applying for graduate entry in 1893, he borrowed more money and took on as much teaching work as he could get, tutoring students at Radcliffe and Wellesley Colleges and later earning an assistant professorship in the university's psychology division. Harvard introduced the young man from Ohio to new social circles, and the extra courses he took suggest he was conscious of the cultural limitations of his background and was working hard to fit in. No longer "Ed," he now called himself James E. Lough (fig. 1.1).

HARVARD AND EXPERIMENTAL PSYCHOLOGY

At Harvard, Lough gravitated toward the psychology courses of William James, the founder of the discipline in the United States, and the philosophy subjects taught by George Santayana and Josiah Royce, the latter a friend of his old professor, Roger Johnson. This was a dynamic time to be arriving in Cambridge, Massachusetts.[4] Only three years before, James had published his highly influential two-volume *Principles of Psychology* (colloquially referred to as "the James"), followed by a condensed version released two years later (known as "the Jimmy").[5] These books—which Lough had read in Ohio—were a reaction against the approach being developed in Leipzig

FIGURE 1.1. James Edwin Lough, ca. 1896 while a student at Harvard University. UAIII 15.88.10, Harvard College Student Folders, ca. 1890–1968, box 3026, Harvard University Archives.

by Wilhelm Wundt. Known already as the "founding father" of experimental psychology and the "laboratory method," Wundt and his followers contended that it was possible for the introspection of the conscious mind to separate and identify thoughts and sensations and analyze their constituent elements. But James, who had for a time worked under Wundt, repudiated this view. Consciousness, James argued, was personal, selective, constantly changing, and continuous. It could not be segmented for analysis: "Consciousness . . . does not appear to itself chopped up in bits. Such words as 'chain' or 'train' do not describe it fitly as it presents itself in the first instance. It is nothing jointed; it flows. A 'river' or a 'stream' are metaphors by which it is most naturally described."[6]

For James, the notion of discrete sensation was an abstraction: "From our natal day," he wrote, consciousness "is of a teeming multiplicity of objects and relations, and what we call simple sensations are results of discriminative attention, pushed often to a very high degree."[7] Above all, he understood consciousness as practical—its purpose was "that of the functional and dynamic adjustment of the organism to its environment."[8] This was an articulation of one of the key tenets of the specifically American philosophical tradition that became known as pragmatism.[9] For James, conscious and bodily events were deeply intertwined: "What we esteem the highest is at the mercy of what we esteem the lowest" was how he put it in a lecture delivered in 1878.[10] His notion of habit flowed from this. Arguing that over time, "currents pouring in from the sense-organs make with extreme facility paths which do not easily disappear," James saw habit formation as a process mutually constituted by both consciousness and bodily sense perception. The crucial thing, in his view, was to choose which habits to form.[11]

These ideas were attractive to a clever and ambitious young man carrying the hopes of his family and the name of a dead soldier. In the wake of the Civil War and the destruction caused by its opposing ideological certainties, American families like Lough's were left reeling. Louis Menand and others have argued that Gilded Age thinkers such as James were driven by the desire to avoid the potential for violence they saw as inherent to the notion of an external, discoverable truth.[12] Influenced by Charles Darwin's ideas about a universe made by dynamic and random variation, they moved away from the notion of certainty and toward what became known as a pragmatic theory of knowledge. For James and his friend Charles Saunders Pierce, and for those who looked to them, knowledge was "an instrument or organ of successful action."[13] Ideas were not like external truths waiting to be discovered, but rather tools that people devised "to cope with the world in which they find themselves."[14] When Lough entered the Philosophy Department of Harvard in 1893, he went to the very place these concepts were being developed, and James was emerging as one of their greatest proponents.

But 1893 was also the second year of Hugo Münsterberg's initial stay at Harvard. Like James, Münsterberg had studied in Leipzig under Wundt, eventually becoming his research assistant. He, too, had been critical of Wundt's voluntarist notion that free will could be consciously experienced as a separate element of the mind, instead arguing that what humans experience as free will is a product of bodily behavior.[15] Over time, Münsterberg turned to the many practical applications of psychological principles, including forensics, industry, and education, and in the United States he became known as the founder of applied psychology.[16] In the early 1890s, however, his ideas and his interest in laboratory experiments seemed to make him an ally to James, who was looking to move away from experimental psychology to develop his interests in philosophy. After a considerable lobbying campaign, in 1892 James finally persuaded Münsterberg to move to Harvard, initially for a three-year trial period. Despite his lack of English at first, the German professor quickly became a popular figure among the psychology students. He taught the laboratory part of the systematic psychology course in which Lough enrolled in 1893 and assumed responsibility for supervising the graduate students and directing their research.

Although James's and Münsterberg's thoughts would come to differ considerably, in the early 1890s they were united by a shared interest in sensation, perception, and the connection between physiology and the mind, concepts that framed James Lough's doctoral research project. It focused on the intensity of sensation, which Lough sought to measure by experimental means.[17] For James, understanding the intensity of sense perception was crucial to understanding the formation of habits. For Münsterberg, understanding sense perception was also important because it helped establish the relationship between free will and bodily behavior.

But in the middle of Lough's studies, Münsterberg returned to Germany. Although he continued to advise his PhD students "by correspondence" and was back in time to see the completion in 1898 of Lough's dissertation, it is likely that much of the supervision of Lough's doctoral research was in fact provided by James. And during Münsterberg's absence, it also fell to Lough to teach many of his supervisor's experimental psychology and laboratory courses, including one that ran at the Harvard Summer School of 1898. It was at this summer school that James presented a hugely popular lecture course on psychology for an audience of teachers. It would help mark out the path of Lough's future career.[18]

EDUCATION AND EXPERIENCE

In the last decade of the nineteenth century, pedagogy was emerging as a new field within universities. The growth of secondary schooling in the decades after the Civil War created a huge demand for trained teachers, and although courses in teacher education were offered by state normal schools, increasingly universities, too, began to establish departments of education.

Educational psychology and experimental methods were subjects taught in many of these new university schools, and the popularity of James's 1898 lectures, which Lough almost certainly attended, reflected this bourgeoning interest.[19]

James, however, was somewhat skeptical about the applicability of his subject to the classroom. "You make a great, very great mistake," he told the 1898 audience at his first lecture, "if you think that psychology, being the science of the mind's laws, is something from which you can deduce definite programs and schemes and methods of instruction for immediate schoolroom use." Perhaps, he conceded, a general knowledge of psychology might narrow "the path for experiments and trials." Particularly useful might be an understanding of habit. The "teacher's prime concern," James suggested, was "to ingrain into the pupil that assortment of habits that shall be most useful to him throughout life." And here, the greatest asset to the teacher was the student's own experience: *Begin with the line of [the student's] native interests*," James advised, "*and offer him objects that have some immediate connection with these.*"[20]

These were themes that at the time were being developed in much greater depth by one of William James's early admirers. As professor of psychology and philosophy at the University of Chicago in the mid-1890s, John Dewey was fascinated by education and the learning process. In an influential article published in 1896 (while Lough was still at Harvard), Dewey put forward his notion of the reflex arc.[21] An act is an organic circuit, he argued; knowledge does not flow from experience but is rather made through experience itself. Dewey explored the implications of this position in the Laboratory School he established the same year in Chicago. It followed a model of experimental and experiential education that worked with the interests and desires of children, an approach that gained wide circulation after the 1899 publication of Dewey's *The School and Society*. Education needed to unify the curriculum, Dewey argued in this book, and the only way to do this was to connect it to the world outside the classroom: "We do not have a series of stratified earths, one of which is mathematical, another physical, another historical, and so on. . . . We live in a world where all sides are bound together. All studies grow out of relations in the one great common world. When the child lives in varied but concrete and active relationship to this common world, his studies are naturally unified."[22]

For Dewey, both the Laboratory School, run by the University of Chicago's Department of Psychology, and the students' method of learning and instruction were experimental: it was by doing things in and with the world that students (and the Chicago psychologists) would best learn. Like James, Dewey accorded a central place to habit. He wanted education to foster critical inquiry, experimentation, imagination, independent thought, and sympathy with others, equipping the child and the adult with habits that would enable them to respond to change. *School and Society* was hugely popular, and Lough certainly read it soon after it was published in 1899.

By that time, Lough had begun teaching educational psychology himself. While still a student, he taught the subject at the newly opened Teachers Institute in Richmond, Indiana, and soon after completing his PhD he accepted a post as professor of psychology at the state normal school in Oshkosh, Wisconsin. Although the Oshkosh post was not an ideal appointment in that it was not at a university, it did afford Lough the opportunity to make his own mark in the emerging field, with the added benefit that it was near his family. Although he was back in the Midwest, the young boy from Eaton, Ohio, had come a long way.[23]

Yet despite his achievements, Lough was anxious. While at Harvard, he had met Dorothy A. Bailey, whom he called Dora. His love letters to her from Oshkosh carry the echo of his motherless childhood. They speak of his feelings of inadequacy and his fear of abandonment as well as his longing for love and security. After a year of nervous correspondence in which Dora reassured him repeatedly of her affections, Lough finally plucked up his courage and proposed. In June 1900, they were married on the Bailey estate in Sommerville, Massachusetts, in a ceremony displaying the social distance between the two families. In gardens illuminated by Japanese lanterns and decorated with the college colors of Harvard and Tufts (where Dora had studied), two hundred guests, including many alumni and several of the Harvard Philosophy Department (including Josiah Royce), were in attendance. James's younger brother, William (who himself had entered Harvard in 1899), was there, but the rest of his family was not.[24]

It is perhaps unsurprising that Dora, who after the wedding joined Lough in Oshkosh, did not take to small-town life. She missed her family and the densely networked social world of the East Coast. So Lough began to look for a new appointment more fitting to the couple's aspirations. The resignation of Charles Hubbard Judd from New York University's School of Pedagogy in 1901 provided an opportunity. Judd had trained under Wundt and was one of the leading exponents of the German professor's experimental methods in the United States. But only three years into his NYU post he had resigned, frustrated at the lack of support for his ambitions to develop the school. Lough's training in the rival tradition of James and Münsterberg, together with his experience as a teacher in Ohio and an educator in Oshkosh, perhaps gave him an advantage. In 1901, he was appointed professor of experimental psychology and method, and he and Dora packed up and relocated to New York, moving to a place on 115th Street in the Morning-

side Heights neighborhood—a halfway point between NYU's Washington
Square and Bronx (University Heights) campuses.[25]

NEW YORK UNIVERSITY

In moving to NYU, Lough was joining the first university department of
education in America. The university's School of Pedagogy had been established in 1890, and from 1903 onward it accepted only graduate students
seeking to train for "the higher positions in the field of elementary and
secondary education"—those who would be principals, supervisors, and
superintendents of public schools or professors of pedagogy in colleges.[26]
It therefore catered to teachers already in post rather than those seeking to
enter the profession, and most of its courses were offered in the evenings
as a consequence. Based at the university's Washington Square campus, it
offered a curriculum that from its beginnings included educational psychology. By 1910, 25 percent of the school's program consisted of psychology
courses, and it was from the School of Pedagogy that all the university's
psychology teaching, including the courses listed under the Department of
Philosophy and in the Graduate School, were run.[27]

For the first decade of the twentieth century, all this teaching was delivered by Lough and his only other disciplinary colleague, Robert Mac-
Dougall, the professor of descriptive psychology. Both men had trained under William James and Hugo Münsterberg, and the influence of the Harvard
school was clearly evident in the NYU curriculum. Its functional outlook
emphasized practical laboratory work focused on classical experimental
problems, such as sensory thresholds, space perception, memory, association, and accuracy of movement.[28] While MacDougall taught the courses
in social and developmental psychology and some philosophy subjects,
Lough took charge of the laboratory and experimental courses in addition
to those in logic, educational psychology, educational research, and systematic psychology.[29]

Lough continued to be influenced by the work of John Dewey, who in
1903 had moved to nearby Columbia University.[30] Lough's Methods in Geography course, for example, examined "the general principles . . . scope
and educational value" of the subject.[31] This emphasis drew directly from
Dewey, who in *School and Society* had written that "the unity of all the
sciences is found in geography. . . . It is through what we do in and with the
world that we read its meaning and measure its value."[32] While his own research work stuttered, Lough's earlier interest in experiment, bodily sensation, and habit was beginning to extend to a wider interest in environment,
experience, and the classroom.

Along with his heavy teaching load, Lough took on several administrative posts. From 1902, he was secretary of the School of Pedagogy and director of the Summer School, and from the end of 1903 he was also secretary of the Washington Square Collegiate Division.[33] The NYU Summer School had been established by the School of Pedagogy in 1895, largely to meet the requirements of "continuation study imposed upon teachers in the city schools."[34] Unlike the School of Pedagogy, its courses were open to all teachers, and largely thanks to Lough, it became an enormous success.[35] By 1907, over five hundred students were attending, and it was this demand that in 1904 led the School of Pedagogy to create a Collegiate Division based at Washington Square to provide instruction for teachers throughout the year, mainly during the late afternoons and on Saturday mornings. In 1908, Lough took on yet another role. In response to demand from the community in Newark, New Jersey, the university created a new Extramural Division, with Lough as its founding dean. Distinguishing itself from "extension" teaching, which sought to "popularize for the general public the teaching of the University," usually without credit or entrance criteria, the new division offered credit-bearing "instruction given by college officers to the same type of students as those whose whole instruction is given in the University itself, the only distinction . . . being a distinction of locality."[36]

Indicative of Lough's intellectual interests and academic ambitions, this somewhat frenetic administrative activity in his first decade in New York also reflected his need to support a growing family. In 1905, Dora had given birth to a son, Edwin Bailey, and in 1908 a daughter, Barbara Esther, had followed. Their family would eventually expand to include two more children: Richard Colburn, born in 1912, and Dorothea Wesson, born in 1914.[37] By 1910, Lough was also paying for a new house, built at University Heights near the NYU campus in the Bronx, and he had several additional money-making plans on the go. With his brother-in-law, he was running a business venture growing and importing grapefruits from Puerto Rico, and he was beginning to seek opportunities for writing articles for the popular press.[38] Perhaps the extra payment received by NYU faculty who taught courses for the Extramural Division was attractive. Yet there was also an intellectual coherence to Lough's administrative roles. They all focused on finding new contexts for university education.

THE CITY LABORATORY

It was therefore a rude surprise when, on Christmas Eve 1913, via an article in one of the city's newspapers, James Lough learned that the NYU Council had abolished the position of secretary of the Collegiate Division.

He understandably saw this as "serious impeachment of" his leadership of the division and wanted either an impartial investigation or an explanation. The chancellor, Elmer Ellsworth Brown, attempted to mollify him but nonetheless implied that Lough had been spreading himself too thin. The reorganization of the division was intended, Chancellor Brown wrote, to make it possible for Lough to "effect somewhat more of concentration on administrative attention and effort upon three important divisions of the University instead of four."[39] He also made clear that Lough's pay was to remain the same. Noting the demand for higher education among the immigrant families populating the Washington Square surrounds in the early decades of the twentieth century, the council had decided to convert the Collegiate Division into a fully fledged undergraduate College of Arts to be known as Washington Square College (to distinguish it from the campus at University Heights).[40] Its courses quickly proved attractive to large numbers of recent high school graduates, who displaced the teachers and differed from those students at the University Heights Bronx campus only in that they were coeducational and came from what the official history called "the newer social strata."[41] Lough was left to channel his considerable energies into the Extramural Division.

One way of understanding Lough's activities during this period is to see him as a teacher of experimental methods who turned the university's extramural classes into his laboratory. Chancellor Brown, in his annual report of 1914, seemed to understand Lough's work in precisely these terms. In sharp contrast to the still-semirural setting of NYU's college at University Heights, the Extramural Division, Brown wrote, was "an advance guard." In trying out new undertakings, it "must be sufficiently venturesome to undergo the risk of occasional failure for the sake of the larger success," for by doing so it would be "an agency for the continuous and rather rapid readjustment of the University to its changing environment."[42] That changing environment was the city of New York, with its urban population and industrial and commercial businesses. Extending the logic of William James and John Dewey, Lough wanted to connect university education to those contexts. In Chancellor Brown's words, his method was to "project the training for any occupation in life as far as possible into the workshops of that occupation, and to utilize to full measure whatsoever teaching ability may have appeared among those engaged in the actual direction of those workshops."[43] Brown, himself a former school principal and commissioner of education, might as well have quoted Dewey, who in *School and Society* had written that "there should be a natural connection of the everyday life of the child with the business environment about him, and . . . it is the affair of the school to clarify and liberalize this connection . . . not by introducing special subjects . . . but by keeping alive the ordinary bonds of relation."[44] For Lough, this meant offering extramural courses in context, on location.

In 1913, the Extramural Division began negotiations with various firms on Wall Street to give on-site instruction in commerce. Lough was well placed to perceive the growing demand among the commercial firms for instruction in aspects of business and management, thanks to his younger brother, William H. Lough. After several years teaching in the NYU School of Commerce, in 1909 William, together with the dean, Joseph French Johnson, had left the university to found the Alexander Hamilton Institute as an avenue for professional information about business principles.[45] James Lough's Extramural Division secretary, Stuart Cameron McLeod, also an instructor in the School of Commerce, was the perfect man to lead the initiative. In 1914, he launched extramural courses in accounting, foreign trade, investment, and finance in the Financial District, some inside the stock exchange itself and others in the rooms of various banks or the Merchants Association.[46] With the cooperation of the American Institute (for the Encouragement of Science and Invention) and teaching assistance from NYU's lecturer in economics and statistics, Edward Ewing Pratt (who will become relevant later in this story), the immediate popularity of these courses signaled their potential. Lough remained closely connected with them through his membership of what became the Advisory Board of the Wall Street Branch, in this capacity working with William M. Kingsley of the United States Trust Company, a man who in 1926 as member of the NYU Council would turn the course of Lough's career. But in 1914, this was all in the future. After only a year of operation, the university celebrated Lough's new educational approach. Through it, Chancellor Brown told the *New York Tribune*, the School of Commerce and the Extramural Division "aim[ed] to make the City of New York its laboratory department and to make of itself an educational agent—as it were, a scientific branch—of the city."[47]

Lough sought to extend this principle to other departments of the university as well. In 1914 Milton E. Loomis, also from the School of Commerce, established classes for city government employees in the Manhattan Municipal Building. The following year, art appreciation courses were held on-site at the Metropolitan Museum of Art, an extensive program of engineering courses was offered to railway men in Grand Central Station, and travel courses in geology were authorized to regional parts of the state of New York.[48] Further initiatives followed, and like the rest of the courses offered by the Extramural Division, all these courses carried college credit.[49]

These initiatives were part of NYU's quest to expand its professional offerings and draw new constituencies into the university.[50] Such moves were characteristic of universities' broader expansionary aims during this period and created a significant new income stream for them. But the Wall Street classes at NYU also had intellectual foundations in the developing field of educational psychology, one in which Lough had been trained and was eager to make a mark. Over his fifteen years at NYU, he had shifted the focus of his interest in experiment from the laboratory to the classroom. This was a shift that followed William James's own intellectual progression, and it was clearly articulated in a book that Lough himself later coauthored with his NYU colleagues:

> Most of the early experiments on the learning process were conducted in the psychological laboratory. They are now also being carried on in the classroom with pupils under school conditions. Many teachers are acquiring experimental techniques and taking an experimental attitude for the purpose of discovering the ways in which pupils learn. . . . The development of methods is a never-ending process. No one procedure may be considered as forever fixed. [But enough is known to be certain that] . . . the closer these classroom activities are related to life experiences the greater will be the spread of improvement.[51]

Offering university graded courses on location was a kind of experiment in educational method in which the city became the university's laboratory. But it was an experiment based on the well-established psychological principle that connecting education to the environment, experiences, and interests of students enhanced their learning while fashioning their habits. And, following John Dewey, this also meant stimulating the active participation of both students and teachers.

THE SCHOOL OF FOREIGN TRAVEL

Lough then reasoned that if the city could furnish laboratory material, so, too, could foreign countries. University travel parties from the United States to Europe were a recent but growing phenomenon in the decade and a half before 1914. One such trip had been conducted in the summer of 1912 by Lough's part-time colleague, Edward Pratt, at that time also head of the Industrial Bureau at the New York City Merchants Association. He had taken a private party to look at industrial developments in Germany and upon his return had joined NYU as a lecturer in statistics.[52] With reports of his trip's success in the press, Pratt persuaded the university and the School of Commerce to sponsor a follow-up tour in the summer of 1913, arguing that the work of "higher institutions" in business and social science must come "from a first-hand study of the most approved methods sanctioned by experience and in practical operation."[53]

While there was a long tradition among elite Americans of traveling to Europe for higher education and cultural formation, what was remarkable about Pratt's 1913 European tour was that NYU recognized it as contributing toward a degree—making that university perhaps the first in the United States to grant credit for travel abroad.[54] Extending the principle that underpinned the Summer School and Extramural Division, the School of Commerce awarded "credit for sixty hours" upon the completion of each course and the submission of "a satisfactory thesis on some phase of the subject of the trip." The school brochure clearly stated the university's recognition of "the educational value of travel" and its belief "that no better means could be adopted to bring [to Americans] . . . fresh viewpoints, a storehouse of information and a wealth of suggestion for future work." But it also made clear that travel was not educational on its own. Only when combined with guidance from lecturers who outlined "the principles underlying the things to be seen" was it more than mere tourism.[55] This NYU-sponsored European trip led by Pratt in 1913 was considered so successful that another series of tours to Europe were planned for the summer of 1914, this time under the aegis of Lough's Extramural Division.[56]

Running an international educational tour was complicated. While faculty members could provide academic instruction, taking a party to Europe also required financial and practical organization. It entailed making advanced bookings, receiving funds, and paying expenses; it meant securing visas, booking steamship passages, and arranging hotel accommodations and ground transportation on the other side of the Atlantic. None of this was university work. So, to take care of "business management," in early 1914 Chancellor Elmer Ellsworth Brown gave his support to the formation of "a corporation" called the Institute of Educational Travel. Its stockholders were Pratt and the wonderfully named Royal Ramson Miller (who acted as treasurer and tour manager), with Charles W. Gerstenberg (secretary of the School of Commerce and assistant professor of finance) representing the university.[57] The institute was to assume the financial risk and engage McCann's Tours as its agent to organize the travel practicalities. It was under this arrangement that in July 1914, two NYU travel courses left New York, one headed to Britain to study economic conditions and industrial organization, and the second to Germany to examine municipal planning. They went equipped with formal letters of introduction from Chancellor Brown to various universities, and their courses of study were organized by the Extramural Division in conjunction with the School of Commerce.[58]

The summer of 1914 was not, as it turned out, a particularly good time to be in Europe. While Philip B. Kennedy's tour of Britain was considered successful despite being interrupted by the outbreak of war in August, Pratt's trip to Germany faced certain other "regrettable difficulties." Sixteen people had abandoned the trip midway, leaving the university to foot the bill.[59] According to Mr. Miller, the "difficulties" consisted of "a certain lack of old-fashioned honor and honesty on the part of Dr Pratt." Miller accused his business partner of financial "irregularities," including spending large sums on personal purchases. But Miller did not want to see the project abandoned. He had been nurturing his "splendid educational enterprise" for more than three years, he claimed, and was keen to pursue it with NYU, which had "made such a creditable beginning in various lines of extra-mural instruction."[60] But Pratt told a different story, and the university refused to take sides between them. Pratt's teaching contract with NYU was, however, not renewed, and the tours were—unsurprisingly—suspended for the duration of the war.

Edward Pratt had no trouble securing another appointment. In fact, in 1914 he was hired by the president of the United States, Woodrow Wilson, as head of the Bureau of Domestic and Foreign Commerce in the Federal Department of Commerce. But he maintained his connection with James Lough through Lough's brother, William. Both Pratt and William Lough moved in the somewhat amorphous world between universities, governments, and consultancies, trading in business information and advice. In 1916, the two men even formed an entity called the Foreign Trade School.[61] Although this venture fizzled, Pratt remained active in the emerging field of foreign commerce and business education; and his actions, or rather inactions, would help determine the Floating University's relationship with NYU.[62]

Meanwhile, there was a war on. Legislation passed in May and June 1916 by state and federal governments sought to stimulate a college-level training program for the Officers' Reserve Corps.[63] Sensing an opportunity, James Lough argued that NYU was particularly well prepared to conduct nontactical courses in various war-related fields, including engineering, sanitation, logistics, international law, and hospital work. He lobbied the chancellor to allow the Extramural Division to offer courses in military science, approved by a former Chief of Staff of the US Army, General Leonard Wood.[64] These courses were crucial to supporting the university's finances during the conflict. They also showed Lough beginning to think about the contribution that educational psychology and the Extramural Division might make to national and international politics.[65]

In this, he was by no means alone. During the war, President Wilson had articulated a vision of liberal internationalism that, rejecting the balance-of-power politics he saw as associated with imperialism and economic nationalism, instead combined a prewar emphasis on free trade with a sense of his nation's moral mission to advance democracy and self-determination along with a system of international law. These found expression in his Fourteen Points, which he outlined in a speech before Congress in January 1918. Although the points set the tone for the Paris Peace Conference a year later, they came into conflict with Wilson's loss of domestic authority at home and opposition from France's vision of a "just peace," as well as the postwar realities of exhausted economies. In the end, opposition in Congress meant that the United States did not join the League of Nations, but the country did go on to cooperate with a variety of international agencies throughout the 1920s and 1930s. This took the form of official involvement in disarmament treaties aiming to reduce military strength in Europe and limit it in Asia; reparations and war debt negotiations as outlined in the Dawes Plan (1924); and the signing of the Kellogg-Briand Peace Pact (1928), which sought to avoid conflict. International cooperation was also advanced in the United States via the diverse activities of a host of private, commercial, and philanthropic organizations concerned with both building international connections and trade, including through an emphasis on "dollar diplomacy," and the fostering of public opinion at home. This latter objective was progressed through educational programs run not only by universities and schools (where students treated internationalism with only mild interest) but also through International Mind Alcoves in public libraries and Armistice Day radio programs, conferences, and publications, as well as a host of other initiatives.[66] All this took place in the context of a booming postwar economy, which meant increased consumer spending as well as expanded credit.[67]

THE TOURIST THIRD-CLASS TRAVEL BOOM

These forces combined in the rapid growth of student travel across the Atlantic. The early years of the 1920s were a moment of crisis for the transatlantic shipping companies.[68] Whereas before 1914 between 750,000 and 1 million passengers had traveled in steerage from Europe to the United States each year, after the introduction of immigration restrictions, first in 1921 and then with the Johnson-Reed Act in 1924, these numbers collapsed.[69] With their old market all but gone, the shipping companies desperately needed to find a new one. The creation of "tourist third" was central to their response. They "upgraded their steerage accommodation to include passable dining rooms, salons, lounges and smoking rooms—a move which served to lower the class barriers to transatlantic travel."[70] But despite these efforts, the American market eluded them. American travelers continued to associate "third class" with "poor migrants from Europe, packed together in unsanitary conditions and subject to the indignities of Ellis Island."[71] The shipping companies quickly realized that for an affordably priced ticket, American college students would not only tolerate the conditions of the new tourist third but in doing so would help launder its reputation and make it acceptable to the rest of the American middle class. The relative strength of the US dollar in postwar Europe, combined with the soaring rates of college attendance, stoked students' desire to see and experience the cultural wonders of the Old World. And for anxious parents who, influenced by the contemporary American image of Europe (and particularly France) as a pleasure ground, worried about what independent travel would mean for their daughters, many of these tours promised (although did not always deliver) measures designed to allay such fears, including female-only accommodations, chaperones, and prebooked hotels.[72] The shipping companies began actively targeting the student market, placing advertisements in college newsletters, touting support from college faculty, and even establishing dedicated student travel associations. By 1930, as many as 127,835 "tourist class" passengers were sailing east from the United States and Canada every year, spending annually as much as $650 million in Europe and $200 million in France—"a sum greater than the ordinary exports of France to the United States."[73]

Lough took advantage of these possibilities and in the summer of 1923 relaunched the Extramural Division's summer study tours. Travel in "one class boats" (aboard the Cunard Lines' SS *Saxonia* and on the way back on the SS *Columbia*) was justified not only for the money saved but also for the student "comradeship" fostered and the more leisurely pace the slower ships afforded. With three instructors drawn from the university faculty as well as a counselor of women (the wife of one of the professors) and business management by the American Express Travel Department, all courses carried the possibility of credit at NYU.[74] Chancellor Brown himself wrote to the secretary of state, Charles Evans Hughes, notifying him of the tours and requesting a suitable liaison from the foreign office. Leading one of the trips was Brown's secretary, Harold O. Voorhis, who was also a member of the economics staff.[75]

With these summer tours, Lough carried his prewar educational philosophy into the postwar period. According to his own account, "the technique of field work, common in a subject such as geology, was applied more broadly," with the instructors finding that "the distractions were more than compensated for by the advantage derived from first-hand contact with the art galleries of Europe, and with the people and places of educational signif-icance."[76] These NYU tours ran again in 1924, this time in cooperation with the Institute of International Education. And for the first time, James Edwin Lough, accompanied by his wife, Dora, was among those who sailed.[77]

The NYU professor from the Midwest had hit upon a formula that was well calibrated to meet the growing demand from middle-class Americans keen to acquire some of the cultural credentials that had traditionally been the preserve of the elite. With prices pitched at the budgets of American students and teachers, these educational tours also met their desire for con-venience. For the large number of female travelers, they offered the promise of safety too. This was a significant market: according to a contemporane-ous *New York Times* article, by 1925 as many as 60 percent of American summer tourists to Europe were likely to have been women.[78] Including all accommodation and transport costs (including the ocean passage), visas, admission to museums, transfer of baggage, and taxes, the escorted program protected the prospective traveler from the unpleasant and unpredictable aspects of contending with foreign systems and practices. It also packaged up meaning, offering essentialized and highly scripted itineraries that told travelers what to see and how to feel when they saw it. If the luxury around-the-world tours of the period catered to an audience that, in historian Joyce Chaplin's words, "wanted to step onto a global stage that had been carefully cleaned of any dirt, strife, and toil, even when they had caused it," Lough's more affordable educational summer tours achieved much the same thing.[79] What travelers made of their experiences, however, was often another mat-ter. Although the glosses and guides of the travel industry served to elevate certain places in the American imagination and ascribe importance to some sites over others, they were also rewritten and contested by individuals whose engagement with them was far from passive.[80]

This new type of travel was big business, and by 1925 the travel courses offered by NYU instructors had grown into an extensive program of nine tours, with practical arrangements made by an entity called the School of Foreign Travel.[81] Like the prewar Institute of Educational Travel, this or-ganization was run by someone familiar to NYU—Edward Ewing Pratt. Although Lough was listed as president, it was Pratt who as vice president undertook most of the practical work, with Neals Becker (who had also previously been involved with the Institute of Foreign Travel) acting as sec-retary and treasurer. Despite Pratt's clouded history with the university, relations with the chancellor seemed to be cordial.[82] But while for Pratt the summer tours were clearly a commercial opportunity, for Lough they were also the product of twenty years of thinking about ways to extend the labo-ratory method of learning to new contexts.

THE LABORATORY METHOD MADE MOBILE

Lough articulated the principles underpinning his philosophy in a book he published with his NYU departmental colleagues in 1926. Entitled *Psychology for Teachers*, its aim was to "set forth the psychology that teachers need for the specific work of teaching and of guiding the development of the mental life of growing children," and each of the authors took responsibility for the chapters that fell within their particular expertise.[83] Lough wrote the sections on sensation, perception, habit, the learning process, and possibly others, and they show the direct influence of William James and John Dewey on his thinking.

"All knowledge can be traced directly to sense experience," Lough wrote in the chapter on sensation. "Objects and ideas should be presented through as many different senses as possible and should be carefully associated in all their relationships."[84] These sense experiences came from a learners' active engagement with their environment. "If the child's experience with any subject is limited to his textbook, he then has only a book knowledge of the subject."[85] For example, "to have a knowledge of the metric system the child must actually measure objects with these units of measurement."[86]

"Learning is an active process," Lough told teachers. "The child learns to do a thing by doing that thing, not by memorizing the rules or by watching others"; "to see and to handle is far better than merely to listen."[87] This was an approach to education that engaged the learner, as well as the teacher, in experiment: "The study of every subject calls for laboratory methods whereby the learner establishes first-hand contact with his subjects." "Learning should be self-initiated," he continued. "The learner should trace his own progress and criticize [the] results."[88]

These ideas were brought together in the chapter on thinking and learning. "Perceptual thinking is basic. It furnishes the concrete experiences out of which all other forms of thinking are derived." Such "thinking always involves a problem and an effort to solve it," and "the vital thing to bring about a response is that the person must use his experiences for the purpose of discovering the solution." That process involves trial and error.[89] In this respect, traditional educational methods were considered wanting: "Highly formalized teaching frequently fails in this respect, with the result that the real thinking of the pupil is done outside the schoolroom."[90] Instead, the chapter concluded with a statement on educational method that directly described what Lough was trying to do with the Extramural Division's travel courses: "It is not too much to say that every subject studied from the kindergarten through the college and the university must be founded on perceptual thinking—either directly as in the case of laboratory courses and courses involving field work, or indirectly as in the case of mathematics, literature, philosophy, or history. In all these courses thinking must be based on those forms of thought which have been derived ultimately from sense experiences."[91] For Lough, taking students out of their classrooms and giving them firsthand experiences of the world through travel was a way of enabling them to form habits that would equip them for life.

AN AROUND-THE-WORLD EDUCATIONAL CRUISE

Toward the end of 1923, James E. Lough produced a plan that took these ideas about habit formation, sense experience, and the laboratory method one step further.[92] If summer travel courses could work, why not a whole year at sea? As Lough himself wrote to Admiral Leigh C. Palmer, a ship could be fitted out "for educational service . . . to conduct extensive tours, during which, courses in collegiate and professional subjects [would] be conducted by members of different university faculties."[93] Courses would be offered in "English, geography, foreign languages, history, geology, contemporary civilization, economics, comparative government, mathematics," and also in "certain professional subjects—foreign trade, navigation, marine engineering, naval architecture, and oceanography." But the "principal value of the tour" would consist "in bringing American students in closer touch with world problems."[94]

Lough was not the first to come up with the idea of an around-the-world educational cruise. Similar plans had been advanced before World War I by the US Navy, and Yale and Harvard Universities had both made attempts, although none of these had been realized.[95] The rise of around-the-world cruises in 1922 run by major commercial luxury liners stimulated new interest in the idea.[96] In the context of the United States' new sense of its international commercial power, these educational travel initiatives were conceived as ways of culturally as well as commercially equipping the rising American elite. In fact, Lough's notion of buying a vessel from the US Shipping Board was identical to that of Asa G. Candler Jr., heir to the Coca-Cola fortune. Candler's purchase of the former army transport SS *Logan*, with a plan to carry a full university faculty and four hundred "rich men's sons" around the world on the premise that this would be good preparation for their future business careers, had received some news coverage earlier in 1923.[97] According to one of these reports, the plan was in the end scuppered, because the task of reconditioning the ship was much greater than anticipated. It is not clear whether Lough had read any of this coverage, but as he traveled to Washington, DC, in the spring of 1924 for a meeting with the

US Shipping Board, he must have been confident he would not be similarly caught out.[98]

Despite its initial reservations, the Shipping Board was taken with Lough's idea and accepted his offer to purchase the SS *President Arthur* for $100,000, with 10 percent to be paid in cash and the remaining balance by letter of credit maturing over two years. Upon hearing the news, Lough must have been ecstatic. Yet by the end of March, the deal had fallen through due to a lack of capital.[99] Lough was not deterred. He had gathered a group of academics and businessmen that included Charles T. Mcfarland, controller of the [Columbia] Teachers' College, Dean Albert K. Heckel of Lafayette College, Captain Grafton B. Fish of the US Navy Reserve, and L. E. Raymond, a financier from Stamford, Connecticut, and they had done the sums on the operating costs.[100] If evidence of public interest could be demonstrated, Lough was hopeful of finding financial backing.

At the 1924 National University Extension Convention, Lough took his plan public. "An educational institution on water, making an around the world excursion, is the latest innovation of university extension courses." was how his friends at the *Oshkosh Northwestern* newspaper in Wisconsin reported his talk, noting that plans were under way "to secure an unused ship from the US Shipping Board." Positioning himself as an educational innovator, Lough told the assembled audience of university professors and administrators that this was the way of the future: "The time is not far distant," he predicted, "when extension travel courses of this kind will be common."[101]

The story was quickly picked up by news agencies and soon made its way across the country. Even the *Nanaimo Daily News* in Canada's British Columbia carried reports of the proposal. The newspapers were taken by the combination of adventure and education the venture promised, with one paper likening it to a modern-day Grand Tour.[102] Still trying to make a bid for the SS *President Arthur* by appealing to the Shipping Board's mission of supporting the merchant marine, Lough emphasized that the 450 (all-male) prospective students would be enrolled in the Naval Reserve and kept under strict naval discipline. The Rochester, New York, *Democrat and Chronicle* even announced that as assistant secretary of the Navy, Theodore Roosevelt had personally "signified the navy's interest in the proposal."[103]

A new language of internationalism also emerged in Lough's accounts. The cruise would make students "world-minded," he told the papers. It would foster the habit of international thinking, making "them better citizens of [the United States] through being citizens of the world."[104] The students would be "Ambassadors of Friendliness," traveling "in all humility, in the spirit of learning, with the main purpose of studying the customs, the appearance and the background of the strange peoples of the world."[105] But all this was still tentative, Lough was careful to point out. A ship still needed to be purchased.

These caveats turned out to have been well placed. While in November 1924 negotiations with the Shipping Board were still being reported as "in progress," by then the SS *President Arthur* had disappeared from Lough's reach. It had been bought in October by the newly formed American Palestine Line steamship company to run a direct passenger service between New York, Naples, and Palestine.[106]

At the end of 1924, Lough had no ship and no practical plans for putting his idea for a floating university into action. But what he had succeeded at doing was positioning himself as "the moving spirit in the enterprise," the man who, after "some years . . . evolving the details," would "inaugurate the movement for the first '30,000 miles college course.'" His insistence that his university ship would be an educational experiment had also been noted. The outcome, predicted the *Tampa Bay Times* of Florida, would be "be watched with interest."[107]

. THREE MEN AND A SHIP

By April 1925, things were looking more promising. Lough had approached Elmer Ellsworth Brown with a proposal that the Extramural Division of NYU should initiate the cruise, and the chancellor was sympathetic. Brown took the proposal to the university's Executive Committee, expressly stating that he presented the plan in an informal way, "anticipating the possibility that it might assume acceptable proportions at an early date, and thereby call for official action." The motion was passed, and detailed consideration of the project was handed to the dean of faculties, Marshall Brown, with power to act.[108] NYU would sponsor the cruise.

Lough announced the venture to the press. Leaving New York City in September 1925 on an eighteen-thousand-ton vessel, the "S.S. University" would return eight months later.[109] Although naval discipline was no longer invoked, the plan remained largely the same. Students would undertake a range of courses appropriate to "study under cruise conditions" for which they could receive college credit, although they would need to make arrangements for this with their home institutions.[110] This time the cruise— still advertised as Lough's idea—would be organized by an incorporated entity called the University Travel Association (UTA). It was principally composed of three men.[111]

It is not clear how Professor Lough (fig. 1.2) met Andrew J. McIntosh (fig. 1.3). McIntosh himself described his business as "selling ships," al-

FIGURE 1.2. Professor James Edwin Lough, 1926. 1DD6 Thwing Papers, box 48, folder 4, the *Binnacle*, September 17, 1926, Case Western Reserve University Archives.

FIGURE 1.3. Andrew J. McIntosh, 1926. 1DD6 Thwing Papers, box 48, folder 4, the *Binnacle*, September 17, 1926, Case Western Reserve University Archives.

though he was mostly a yacht broker. Given the difficulties Lough had faced in his attempt to purchase the SS *President Arthur* the previous year, the need to enlist "the cooperation of competent shipping people" was obvious. McIntosh confessed that as a Quaker, the project appealed to him, because it would "incidentally be of benefit in International Relationship," and he began to "investigate the subject thoroughly from a business standpoint."[112] By May, the UTA, with McIntosh as president, had been established to "[carry] out in a practical way the ideas put forward by the Universities" and to take care of the business management of the cruise.[113] If the Floating University was Lough's idea, it swiftly became McIntosh's baby.

McIntosh immediately took steps to enlist "steamship people who are competent and financially responsible." The firm he chose was Phelps Brothers and Company. Through its international network, it would take care of the practical arrangements and provide the financial backing. Moreover, McIntosh contributed some of his own funds.[114] Eventually, Phelps Bros. engaged the United America Lines' SS *Mount Clay* to serve as the "S.S. University." While Lough was negotiating for NYU to "[take] over the entire educational program by which [the university] would issue scholastic credits in the same way as if a student were in his classroom," McIntosh brought in a third man, Charles F. Thwing (fig. 1.4), to take charge of "the educational and welfare part of the work."[115]

FIGURE 1.4. President Charles F.
Thwing, n.d. Image 06573, Case Western Reserve University Archives.

In 1925, Charles Franklin Thwing was president emeritus of Western
Reserve University in Cleveland. Throughout his thirty-one-year tenure
(during which he was also a trustee of the Carnegie Foundation for the
Advancement of Teaching), Thwing had overseen the institution's growth
from a liberal arts and medical college to a fully fledged university with
seven professional schools. Ordained a Congregationalist minister, Thwing
was a proponent of coeducation and the author of several books about
higher education that had earned him a degree of national recognition.
They mapped out his commitment to student interest and experiment.[116]
Thwing was clear that progressive educational methods brought definite
results, and among his papers on the Floating University is a list that sum-
marizes them: students had greater interest in their work, greater power
to think, greater self-control, greater consideration for others, greater accuracy, greater ability to occupy themselves, and greater reading ability.[117]
He was attracted to Lough's traveling university project, precisely because
it enacted the methods he had long championed but on a new and wider
scale, and his participation in the Floating University project elevated its
standing considerably.

In addition to Thwing, who would serve as president of the "Steamship
University," and Lough, who was to be its dean, faculty appointments were
reported as having been made from several of America's leading universi-

ties, including Harvard, Princeton, Swarthmore, Chicago, and Michigan. The cost to students was advertised as $2,200 each, including all expenses and tuition. Although certainly expensive, given that it included a tour around the world, it bore some comparison with one year's tuition, rent, board, and textbooks on land; at the University of Pennsylvania in 1927, these costs came to a little over $1,200.[118] In addition, only young men were eligible to apply. "It will not be a pleasure trip," Thwing was careful to point out, and the students would "take up studies just as if they were matriculating in a university." Rather than the distractions of college life, they would have "the globe for a campus."[119]

James Lough's notion of the laboratory method made mobile soon caught the imagination of the popular press. "When Roman history is to be studied, the ship will cast anchor off the Italian coast, and a landing party will go ashore" was how the *Cleveland Press* put it in July 1925.[120] But not all the newspapers were convinced that the "new kind of college" would go off without a hitch. "Regardless of the serious purpose manifested," ran one such piece in the *New York Journal*, "something tells us that President Thwing and his colleagues are going to have their hands full, especially in port."[121] The author was tapping into a popular understanding of undergraduate life as dominated by football, proms, fraternity gatherings, and homecoming celebrations, all of which featured alcohol.[122] The "college woman," too, was cast as a socialite alongside flappers and "new women," titillating audiences with the suggestion "of promiscuity on campus."[123] If this was the behavior of college students on American soil, reasoned the writer at the *New York Journal*, how much more fun might they have in the port cities of the world?

By the start of June 1925, McIntosh had claimed to have received applications from "several times the number" of students the Floating University could take. But he felt that only a fraction of those were "of such character" that they should be considered for the trip; he did not want "to run any risks." McIntosh did report some "minor differences of opinion with the different Universities." But it was "nothing serious," he told Thwing; they all had different views "as to the way the educational part should be carried out." While some "caught the idea instantly and . . . cooperated enthusiastically," another group "thought it was a tourist trip and ignored it." So McIntosh proceeded "extremely slow[ly]." He and Thwing agreed that it was "very secondary" whether they "put the project through this year or not." If standards could not be maintained, they would "cancel it [for 1925] . . . and keep at it and endeavor to do it next year."[124]

In the end, this is what happened. First the sailing date was pushed back until October 1925, and then November. Finally, the UTA was forced to defer the voyage until 1926. This was disappointing, but it gave Lough and McIntosh and Thwing time to get properly organized.[125] With NYU agreeing to credentialize the courses, and Chancellor Brown's 1925 annual report speaking of the forthcoming cruise in glowing terms, Lough's long-planned "educational innovation," with its intellectual foundations in the new psychology and educational movements of the early century, was finally coming together. As the winter of 1925 closed in on New York, everything seemed in place for the first university-sponsored around-the-world educational cruise, scheduled to depart from New York in autumn 1926.[126]

2

The University Flexes Its Muscles

It was only the second week of January 1926, and already Chancellor Elmer Ellsworth Brown had a problem. Personally, he liked Professor James E. Lough, who had done a great deal to build up the Extramural Division and the Summer School at New York University and whose Floating University project was an innovative, if slightly eccentric, proposal that appealed to Brown's own interests in international education. In fact, only twelve months before, Brown had appointed Lough full professor with tenure. But in the last week, all that had changed. Strong words had been exchanged at the meeting of the NYU Council on January 7, particularly by General Charles H. Sherrill, who had spent a good amount of time detailing what he considered to be Professor Lough's improper and embarrassing, if not illegal, behavior in operating the Extramural travel courses.[1] The situation was difficult, not least because Sherrill was far from a disinterested party when it came to the running of overseas programs. Given the university's precarious financial situation, Brown could not afford to provoke the ire of his council, which was developing serious concerns about the risks of endorsing Lough's university cruise.

What lay behind NYU's reluctance to endorse the cruise it had agreed to sponsor? Although Professor Lough's education experiments celebrating the value of direct experience had previously been seen as beneficial, by the mid-1920 this approach was becoming incompatible with the university's expanding claims to authority over knowledge. The fate of the Floating University's relationship with NYU was ultimately determined by the university's desire to maintain control over its credentials.

THE UNIVERSITY FLEXES ITS MUSCLES   >   41

TROUBLE FOR CHRISTMAS

Chancellor Brown (fig. 2.1) had first learned there might be a difficulty in early December 1925, when the dean of faculties, Marshall Brown, had told him that the company Lough had hired to organize his summer trips to Europe was in fact run by none other than Lough himself. The professor was happy to admit as much, not thinking he had done anything wrong. But some of the council members felt that the matter amounted to "a serious indiscretion . . . tending to compromise the reputation of the University."[2] So, with a heavy heart, Chancellor Brown commissioned a "fact-finding committee" to investigate. He made sure, however, to fill it with long-serving council members he knew he could trust: Judge Edwin L. Garvin, Mr. Alexander S. Lyman, and Dr. William M. Kingsley.[3] They proceeded at once with their task, consulting with Lough and his old friend and collaborator Edward Ewing Pratt (who by 1925 had left the Federal Department of Commerce and was running the School of Foreign Travel alongside a Mr. B. Becker). They also consulted Dean Marshall Brown and members of the NYU teaching staff who had been involved in the summer travel courses.[4] In the meantime, Chancellor Brown attempted to keep General Sherrill and other increasingly irate council members at bay.[5] He hoped for a quick decision from Garvin's committee and was relieved when its report landed on his desk early in the new year.

The report's contents initially seemed to offer a way through the mess. There was no question that Lough was president of the School of Foreign Travel and that, as dean of the Extramural Division, he had contracted the company to take care of travel arrangements for the NYU summer travel courses, much as the Institute of Educational Travel and School of Foreign Travel previously had. What was at issue was whether Lough had misled the university by not disclosing his involvement. Garvin's committee established that Lough had asked Pratt to send details of the company's leadership to the dean of faculties, but they also found that this request seemed never "to have been clearly complied with." Nonetheless, the committee was "of the unanimous opinion that there [was] no proof that Dean Lough ever had it in his mind to conceal from the University authorities his connection with the School of Foreign Travel, Inc." The committee concluded that no person connected with the university had been guilty of wrongdoing, and it recommended that the council take no action.[6] This seemed clear enough.

The problem was that in its fact-finding mission, Garvin's committee had made another explosive discovery. In addition to employing the School of

FIGURE 2.1. Chancellor Elmer Ellsworth Brown, n.d. Image courtesy of the Lillian and Clarence de la Chapelle Medical Archives, New York University.

Foreign Travel to take care of the practical arrangements of the summer travel courses, Professor Lough had contracted the company to act as business managers of the Extramural Division's European travel courses. This did not mean simply the planning of itineraries: it also involved employing instructors. The contract provided for Lough as dean of the Extramural Division (or someone appointed by him) to accompany the trips as "Educational Director" and for the name of the university to be associated with the courses.[7] Chancellor Brown knew that these revelations would raise serious questions in the council about who was delivering NYU's credit-bearing courses. So before presenting Garvin's report to the council, he had come up with a plan.

Brown called Lough into his office, conveyed to him the contents of the report, and suggested that it might be time for the Extramural Division to be reorganized. The interview had not been an easy one, but Lough had agreed to resign as dean "as soon as he had received a copy of the report exonerating him."[8] Brown then appointed another committee to undertake a full-scale review of the workings of the Extramural Division.[9] It wasted no time in finding a replacement for Lough. Their choice was Rufus D. Smith, professor of politics, whose appointment was to begin on January 6, the date from which Lough's resignation became effective.[10] With this plan in hand, Chancellor Brown had thought he was in a good position to confront the council at its regular meeting on January 7.

But the council members were unimpressed. Sherrill led the charge, laying out his own version of the story: Lough had "affected a construct with a company organized for profit . . . to conduct the business management of Extramural foreign travel courses, [a] company of which he himself was president, a director, and a stockholder, and had by that arrangement realized a profit of some $500."[11] He succeeded in getting the council to strike any suggestion that Lough was "exonerated" from the university executive's minutes. He also persuaded the group to pass a "general resolution condemning an act of this character" and stating specifically its disapproval of "any officer of the University making a concealed profit from an official connection with an outside organization with which he represents the University."[12]

Sherrill was a formidable enemy for Lough to have made. Only a recent appointment to the council, he characterized the new breed of men with corporate and political experience who were making their way onto university boards during this period.[13] Having studied at Yale, he had practiced law in New York City before being appointed by President Taft as the United States' ambassador to Argentina in 1909. He was an ardent and active Republican who during World War I had served as brigadier general in the National Guard of New York, where he oversaw the federal draft. Sherrill was also interested in internationalism. He was a member of the International Olympic Committee and had published several volumes on "Stained Glass Tours" of the cathedrals of Europe and Britain.[14] Since 1922, he had been honorary director of the university's new Department of Fine Arts and, somewhat ominously for Lough, in that capacity was planning his

own Paris Summer School. The program was to be under the business management of American Express and would be taught by NYU professors with
the cooperation of the French Ministry of Fine Arts.[15] Like Lough's Extramural tours, his art courses carried official credit toward NYU degrees. But
Sherrill was also a university donor. When concerns about Lough's dealings
were first raised, Chancellor Brown had been quick to make clear that Sherrill's Paris plans would not be affected.[16]

General Sherrill had skin in the game when it came to NYU's foreign
courses. But the university's turn against James Lough in the first week of
January 1926 was about much more than the hobbyhorse of a particularly
obstreperous council member. Professor Rufus Smith, Lough's successor
as dean of the Extramural Division, struck at the heart of the matter when
a few months later he argued that educational travel presented "financial,
educational and moral risks" to the university.[17] Far from a marginal concern, it challenged the social and economic status that, in the mid-1920s,
NYU was attempting to establish.

A SERIES OF FINANCIAL CRISES

The university's finances were certainly at the forefront of both the chancellor's and his council members' minds at the meeting on January 7. Elmer
Ellsworth Brown gave an update on the financial health of the university,
and it did not look good.[18]

This was the third financial crisis of Brown's relatively short tenure at
NYU. The first had greeted him when he took office in 1911.[19] Since 1894,
the university had been running both an undergraduate campus uptown in
the more spacious and relatively secluded surrounds of University Heights
in the Bronx as well as professional and graduate schools at Washington
Square. But in 1911, the costs of building the new Bronx campus were still
outstanding, and the undergraduate colleges could not financially support
themselves. Brown had estimated that $5 million in additional revenue plus
$30 million in endowment funds would be needed over the next twelve
years. Unsuccessful in his attempt to receive funding from the John D.
Rockefeller–funded General Education Board, the chancellor had judged
that the only way forward was to generate revenue through tuition.[20] He
turned the Collegiate Division at Washington Square into a fully fledged
undergraduate college offering a four-year liberal arts degree while he introduced undergraduate preparatory courses for medical students at University Heights. These decisions remedied the crisis. Students streamed in,
and the university's enrollment doubled in the space of five years, growing
from 4,300 students in 1912 to about 9,300 in 1917.[21] As long as the increase

of students continued and maintenance work was deferred, the university could meet its costs. But living off student tuition was not a sustainable business model: NYU's debt continued to mount, and its endowment hardly grew at all.[22]

Brown was therefore not entirely surprised when financial trouble struck again following the US entry into World War I in 1917. NYU, like many other education institutions across the country, offered its services to the cause. Red Cross volunteer units were established at both its campuses, and when the United States declared war on April 6, hundreds of students as well as faculty and staff sought to enlist, dramatically affecting enrollments. The student population at the University Heights campus halved, and the university faced a huge deficit for 1917–18. Financial collapse for NYU was a real possibility.[23] But salvation had come, paradoxically, from the US Army. In fact, it was Professor Lough who in 1917 led the establishment of courses in military science through the Extramural Division, and in March 1918 the university began to offer courses of technical instruction to units of the National Army Training Detachment for the Department of War. The establishment of a Student Army Training Corps later in 1918 for the training of an officer class further expanded these offerings. The University Heights campus came to resemble a military barracks, complete with physical training and drills in addition to lectures, laboratory courses, and a mandatory "War Issues" course.[24] The income derived from this venture into military training, together with a private bequest, saved the university from ruin. Its having trained 1,223 soldiers in the NATD courses alone turned a projected deficit of $165,000 for 1918–19 into a modest surplus.[25]

The university's financial situation had stabilized in the immediate postwar period as yet more students—some funded by US government support for veterans—again flooded onto its campuses in even greater numbers than before. While the University Heights campus grew modestly, Washington Square College expanded from 504 undergraduate students in 1916 to 895 in 1921, with total enrollment reaching more than 7,000 by the end of the decade. But the real growth came from enrollments in the professional schools: Law and Medicine, but also Commerce, Engineering, and Education. In fact, the School of Commerce nearly doubled in size, from 4,396 in 1916 to 8,174 in 1921.[26] Its massive expansion was in keeping with the general growth in higher education across the United States. According to the US Census, while in 1910 American institutions of higher learning conferred 37,199 bachelor's degrees, by 1930 this number had risen to 122,484, with the proportion of female graduates jumping from 23 to 40 percent.[27] These dramatic increases were in turn a reflection of the growing number of people completing high school, thanks in large measure to state investments in public education systems. The new students were often the children of immigrants, and they brought new challenges to higher education institutions that had hitherto taken for granted the racial and social character of their campuses. By 1925, 35 percent of the Washington Square College students were women.[28] Their arrival in the 1920s turned Chancellor Brown's university into one of the largest in the country.

The influx of these new students dramatized a problem that had long been latent within the growing university. Was NYU an education institution focused on the acquisition and expansion of knowledge, as per the ideals of the research and professional university? Or was it about social reproduction, as per the ideals of traditional collegiate life?[29] Columbia, Harvard, Yale, and Princeton were also confronting this question. Advocates of "social homogeneity" had been increasingly taking issue with what they perceived to be the growing numbers of Jewish students entering college as "merit candidates." In the early 1920s, all four institutions infamously instituted forms of selective admission.[30] The same issue erupted at NYU in 1919, when eighty students from University College of Arts and Science petitioned Chancellor Brown in protest of the large numbers of Jewish students enrolling in medical preparatory classes. The university responded by introducing a selective admissions policy "in order to modify the composition of the student body to permit Americanizing influences to work more freely." Consequently, the number of Jewish students dropped significantly.[31]

But this policy held only in the wooded setting of the uptown campus at University Heights, where NYU provided—at great cost—a small and exclusive collegiate education to a limited number of students. Meanwhile, downtown in the urbanized surrounds of Washington Square, a very different institution had developed, one that more closely resembled the developing land grant universities (fig. 2.2). Contemporary journalists Heywood Broun and George Britt described NYU's city campus as a "non-restricted, non-collegiate, profit-earning knowledge factory" with graduate schools, research institutes, and "the world's largest numerical group of undergraduate Jewish students." In the 1920s NYU was, in Broun and Britt's words, "a house divided against itself" that squared the circle of collegiate and university values by effectively running two very distinct operations.[32]

The consequence for Chancellor Brown was yet another acute financial situation. Expansion downtown cost money, and the Heights campus continued to drain the budget. The university was running an annual deficit, and despite "constant paring in every direction," the situation looked likely to continue. To make matters worse, NYU was rapidly nearing its borrowing capacity, with a debt of approximately $2.5 million.[33] Tuition

FIGURE 2.2. New York University, Washington Square campus, 1926. Photographer Henry J. Sihler. Image courtesy of New York University Archives.

income was strong, but insufficient to cover expenses. By January 1926, it had become clear that a new approach was needed.[34] Brown initiated the professionalization of the fundraising office and hired marketing staff. In addition, he created the Centennial Fund with the aim of raising $47 million before 1935 and putting the university budget back in balance by 1931.[35] Its campaign involved some unorthodox initiatives, including the School of Education Realty Corporation, a private corporation that purchased new properties on Washington Square and held them for university use until NYU had sufficient funds to take them over. Bonds were sold to former students and faculty, with NYU Council members making particularly significant contributions. But the success of the fundraising campaign really relied on attracting the support of New York's businessmen. "It is obvious," read the Centennial Fund's planning document, "that it will be necessary for us to prove to the men whom we approach . . . that New York University occupies a unique position in the educational field and is very closely affiliated with the business and professional interests of this city."[36]

Demonstrating this affiliation depended on another educational revolution that had been gathering momentum, both at NYU and across the country. And it wasn't so much about who should be admitted to college but rather how far the reach of university authority might extend.

EXPANDING UNIVERSITY AUTHORITY

The period before and after World War I was one during which higher education institutions drew new professional and vocational fields into their domain. At NYU, this expansion of the university's reach began in earnest in 1889 with the establishment of the School of Applied Science. It offered professional degrees in engineering, chemistry, teaching subjects such as geology, drawing, hydraulics, surveying, and carpentry.[37] The following year, the School of Commerce, Accounts and Finance was founded, expanding NYU's reach to include courses in advertising and marketing, economics, journalism, languages, commercial law, and management, many of which were taught in the university's Wall Street building at 90 Trinity Place.[38] These new professional schools joined the Law School, which began awarding the graduate Master of Law degree in 1892, and the Medical College, run since 1898 in conjunction with Bellevue Hospital.

In the years after the war, NYU's credentialing reach increased even further. A master in business administration degree program was launched in 1917, and a fully fledged Graduate School in Business Administration followed in 1920. In 1921, a School of Retailing was established, offering courses in salesmanship, ethics, and merchandising, and in 1922 the School of Pedagogy became the School of Education, offering a series of graduate degrees. General Charles Sherrill's Department of Fine Arts launched the same year, and in 1925 a bequest from aviation enthusiast Daniel Guggenheim enabled the establishment of a Department of Aeronautics.[39] The university's 1926 merger with the New York College of Dentistry resulted in a new dental program. During the period before Elmer Ellsworth Brown's tenure as chancellor, entry requirements for these professional degree programs had been minimal. Gradually, however, prerequisites were increased to one and then two, three, and, by the mid-1920s, often four years of prior undergraduate study, effectively making them graduate schools.

Such an expanded range of course offerings represented a profound shift in who got to claim authority over what kinds of knowledge. It was also, of course, beneficial to NYU's balance sheet, widening the market for possible enrollment as well as increasing the number of years students were required to spend in undergraduate study. But business, engineering, journalism, retail, and teaching were all fields closely connected to vocational or professional work. Before the war, a student seeking knowledge and training in any of these fields would have been much more likely to seek out an apprenticeship or cadetship or just obtain work in the lower ranks of an organization than they were to enroll in a university degree program. Knowledge came from on-the-job experience and the guidance of practitioners, not from the pages of a book or the lectures of a professor. Learning had came from doing. When universities began to establish schools in these fields and offer courses in them, they were staking a claim for their own institutional authority: over how mastery in these domains might be acquired as well as the grounds on which claims to knowledge could be made.

James Lough's own field, education, was at the forefront of the revolution at NYU. The establishment of Washington Square College in 1913, together with the rise of the free City of New York colleges and the intrusion of the war, had sapped the numbers of schoolteachers taking courses in the School of Pedagogy. By 1919, the school's total enrollment was only 168, and its graduate numbers were tiny.[40] After muddling through with an interim dean for two years, the NYU Council in 1921 appointed John W. Withers, at that time superintendent of schools in St. Louis. He introduced changes that dramatically transformed the departments in which Lough worked.[41]

Withers began by abolishing the School of Pedagogy and establishing the new School of Education. Its purpose was to prepare "men and women for educational service, both locally and in the wider field of national and international education."[42] Not only would the new school continue to train higher-level superintendents and principals, but now it would also produce "research toward the solution of practical problems of school administration," for schools and for municipal and state authorities. Additionally, it would render "expert assistance to school officials" in solving immediate problems. This included assistance with school surveys. Further, it would work with NYU's other schools to offer undergraduate degrees in education for high school teachers, and it would work with the Graduate School to offer courses in teaching methods for college professors. Finally, it would develop close cooperation with the officials of the school systems of the New York metropolitan region, wherein were to be found, as Withers put it, "every type of educational problem and every variety of public or private-school condition to be met with elsewhere."[43]

With these moves, the new School of Education extended the university's authority into the city and all the branches of the teaching profession. It positioned its own undergraduate and graduate degrees as appropriate qualifications for teaching practice and management and the expertise of its faculty and graduates as the solution to the education problems of the city and the nation. This emphasis on university expertise was further facilitated by Withers's establishment in 1924 of the Institute of Education as an arm of the school expressly dedicated to offering professional education and consultancy services.[44]

The resulting growth was enormous. By 1930–31, NYU's School of Education could boast an enrollment of 7,493 students.[45] Each year, the demand for the expert services of its faculty through the Institute of Education was more than it could meet.[46] The rise of the survey method proved to be a boon to university social scientists like those in the School of Education; through it, they asserted their ability to know and describe life in a mass society.[47]

In the early years of the century, NYU's School of Pedagogy, Extramural Division, and Summer School—all led by Professor James Lough—had acted as the "advance guard" of the university's expanding reach. In 1914, Chancellor Brown had loudly celebrated them as such.[48] Under their protection, the university had fostered constituencies in education, retailing, and banking and finance on Wall Street. The Extramural Division had gone out into the communities in which work in these fields was taking place and utilized the skills of practitioners to establish the relevance and credibility of the teaching it offered. But in the 1920s, the university shifted gears. The on-site courses that had grown up under these umbrellas were turned into professional academic schools. The "advance guard" became a settlement, and modes of operating that had worked on the frontier were forced to give way to those befitting the new order. No longer would the experience of practitioners be recognized as a form of knowledge that could be credentialized. The university had come to stay.

ACADEMIC CREDIT AND THE EMPIRES OF EXPERTISE

This expansion of epistemic reach was not unique to NYU, which in many ways was late to the party. Uptown at Columbia University, President Nicolas Murray Butler, himself once a lecturer in the NYU School of Pedagogy, had remade his institution into a flagship of this new kind of university. By the 1920s, it embodied a distinct set of beliefs about how the world might and should be known. Butler was committed to asserting what historian Thomas Bender has described as "the authority of university expertise in the city and the nation."[49] If for Butler the job of the college was to build moral character, the purpose of the university was "to bring society closer to truth of all sorts" through the development and application of sophisticated research methods.[50] The recruitment of high-profile appointments (including John Dewey's) was therefore central to Butler's agenda, as was expanding the number of Columbia's professional schools. He turned the existing Schools of Law and Mines into graduate programs and added new

Schools of Political Science, Journalism, Architecture, Business, and Dentistry; the Institute of Public Health; and the Columbia-Presbyterian Medical Center, as well as the Teacher's College (of which Butler himself was the first president).

This transformation was by no means a seamless process, confronting as it did a range of established and entrenched knowledge communities.[51] Expansion required huge sums of money, and that in turn meant convincing both potential donors and the public of the necessity of the new mission of universities.[52] Butler was an excellent self-publicist, and although he was roundly criticized by many as vacuous and long-winded, he succeeded in securing a significant number of bequests that transformed the fortunes of his institution and associated his own name, as much as Columbia's, with universities as centers of expertise.[53] President Butler was, however, less concerned with consulting with his faculty members. Professors who taught Columbia's undergraduate college students, as well as those concerned with protecting academic freedom, did attempt to resist changes that concentrated power in the president and the trustees, but they were largely unsuccessful.

This shift toward expert knowledge had influential backers, notably richly endowed philanthropic foundations. Noting the extent to which governments were willing to draw on outside expertise during the war, after 1919 the Carnegie Endowment for International Peace began to actively cultivate ties to the US State Department.[54] It turned away from its prewar focus on peace advocacy and began to actively support the production and dissemination of knowledge about international relations, funding new foreign affairs institutions, universities, and other initiatives overseen by its Division of Intercourse and Education—of which none other than Nicholas Murray Butler was the director. At about the same time, the General Education Board moved away from its support of endowment fundraising, which supported college attendance and teaching, and increasingly focused on funding science and research.[55] The Rockefellers, too, had come to realize that their strategy of directly funding institutes was perceived as too closely connected to their commercial interests, so their foundation began to professionalize in order to pursue their goals by supporting the work of other independent institutions.[56]

From the start of the 1920s, the new emphasis on university-sanctioned expertise, together with the huge philanthropic support behind it, accorded to academic experts increasing influence and authority over how the world was known, both in the United States and internationally. As evidenced by NYU's Institute of Education, many universities actively embraced this new role. The decade witnessed an ever-increasing number of professors offer-

ing their services to municipal and federal governments, international organizations, and industrial and commercial enterprises, including through
secondments.

Academic credit was the chief currency of this new empire of expertise.
When in the last decades of the nineteenth century US colleges and universities moved away from the prescribed classical curriculum and began to
offer electives, they needed to find a new way to determine students' progress toward the attainment of their degree. With many academic pathways
now possible, the traditional measure of the completion of a prescribed
course of study no longer made sense. In the 1890s, Harvard began granting
degrees based on a student's accumulation of a set number of individual
courses (which were advertised as corresponding to different quantities of
"credits," depending on how much study time each course required). By the
time of World War I, this "credit system" had become widely established.
"Credits" served as a standardized and transferable national "educational
currency" that was enforced by the Carnegie Foundation and the General
Education Board as a "calculus" of efficiency and productivity.[57] It took a
little longer, however, for universities to realize the implications of this new
system. In introducing a new measurement for knowledge, it opened the
door to issues of recognition. Whose knowledge, exactly, would universities credentialize?

The stakes in this changing politics of knowledge were high, and not just
because it promised to radically expand the power and reach of American
universities. The question of the political relationship between professional
expertise and democratic citizenship in increasingly complex industrial
capitalist societies was one that dominated public as well as scholarly debates in the 1920s United States and beyond.[58] It enlivened a range of potent
issues, such as intelligence testing, public opinion, educational practice,
and race policy, engaging commentators such as economist Carter Good-
rich, political scientist Charles Merriam, John Dewey, and journalist and
political thinker Walter Lippmann, among others. The so-called Lippmann-
Dewey debate has, as Tom Arnold-Foster pointed out, long served as "an
influential heuristic device" for understanding American political thought
during this period as "an opposition between the technocratic power of
expertise and the deliberative promise of democracy," though this opposition distorts both thinkers' concern with the relationship between them.[59]
While very much a national (and international) conversation, many of the
chief protagonists in this debate—including Dewey and Lippmann—were
based in New York. The city, with its millions of migrant citizens and many
financial, commercial, and municipal enterprises, as well as many popular
and elite print platforms, was also home to the major philanthropic founda-

tions. And it was amid all these influences that both President Butler and Chancellor Brown worked to secure the future of their respective academic institutions.

This was the heated context in which Professor Lough was attempting to expand his credit-bearing foreign travel courses. Elmer Ellsworth Brown had initially been an enthusiastic supporter of Lough's ideas. He himself had come to higher education after working as a teacher and had experienced the benefits of education abroad, having completed his PhD at the University of Halle in 1890. He shared an interest in fostering international education and since before the war had been attempting to establish a school of international affairs at NYU.[60] And when Lough first proposed the summer travel courses, Brown clearly saw their financial advantages. But the School of Foreign Travel scandal underlined to the chancellor and his council that the professor's travel courses also risked upsetting the status and authority that his university was in the process of claiming for itself and its degree programs.[61] If the university's role was to produce and authorize knowledge, then it was imperative that NYU maintain control over its credits. Lough's travel courses, which not only outsourced teaching but also celebrated the educational value of direct experience, dangerously muddied those waters.

THE PROBLEMS OF EDUCATIONAL TRAVEL

One of the first people to realize the implications of the new class of travel for universities was Stephen Duggan, director of the Carnegie-funded, New York–based Institute of International Education.[62] In May 1924, he had written a circular letter to American university presidents, including Chancellor Brown, with a warning about the advent of student third-class passage. "Properly organized and directed," it had the potential to be of "immense advantage to the travelling college public," Duggan wrote. But he worried that students would not be provided good accommodations in Europe. Citing figures that were merely speculative, Duggan warned that ten ships would leave in the coming summer, with a total capacity between them for eight thousand third-class passages. The arrival of this many Americans in Europe was, he feared, a situation that "might have unhappy consequences especially for women students."[63]

Overseas experience of American women students differed from that of their male counterparts.[64] At the postgraduate level, they were in the minority but nonetheless eager to study abroad, and they were prepared to overcome all sorts of obstacles to do so. By the 1920s, the American Association of University Women and the International Federation of University Women had established an international infrastructure of travel scholarships and housing, although these largely supported postgraduate students and women who were already working as professors, university librarians, and curators.[65] At the undergraduate level, women studying abroad actually outnumbered men, at least in France. Studying there was likely to have been attractive for the cultural credentialization it offered, in a context in which teaching remained one of the only certain career options for the growing number of female graduates who still were excluded from the economic and professional rewards of higher education.

Gendered national stereotypes profoundly shaped these women's travel experiences, as Whitney Walton has shown. Spending time in France carried associations of moral laxity that were viewed as potentially dangerous to girls, and while overseas, women students were frequently subjected to restrictions on mobility and behavior not imposed on their brothers.[66] At the same time, women students in the 1920s were seen by many as archetypes of what Eve Weinbaum and colleagues have called the "modern girl"—a figure reproduced in advertising and popular culture both in the United States and internationally and associated with fashion and cosmetics, independence, and sexual, economic, and political emancipation. Women students traveling abroad had to negotiate these tropes, but they did so in light of their lived experiences. Even as they sometimes played on the popular cultural image of the modern girl for effect, they constructed their own versions of national identity and cultural encounter.[67]

These gendered anxieties were evident in Duggan's 1924 circular letter, but alongside them was also an educational concern. "In the interest of international goodwill, I should be delighted to have 8,000 American students visit Europe this summer," he wrote, "but if their visits were not properly planned, they might return less interested in international goodwill than before their departure."[68] What was at stake was how traveling students were to learn about international politics and culture and who was to teach them. As far as the Institute of International Education (IIE) director was concerned, impressionable American students careering around Europe made for neither good education nor good international relations. He wanted something more regulated that US institutions could control.

Stephen Duggan had initially been captivated by the promise that educational travel held for international relations. Founded in 1919 and funded by the Carnegie Endowment, the IIE was one of an array of international organizations established during a period that regarded knowledge and cultural exchange as the basis for more peaceful relations between nations. As historian Akira Iriye has argued, this was a "cultural internationalism" based on the belief that knowing more about people from other places and having firsthand human contact with them would help develop goodwill and friendship.[69] The movement was concretized in 1926 with the establishment of the International Committee on Intellectual Cooperation by the League of Nations. But a host of nongovernmental associations surrounded and anticipated it, from the International Federation of University Women (1919) to student organizations such as the Confédération Internationale des Étudiants and the National Student Federation of America, as well as the Rockefeller-funded International House in New York (1924) and the Cité Universitaire in Paris (1925) that were built to accommodate them.[70] These initiatives figured young people (and those who taught them) as crucial actors in a global project: education and international experience would help fashion the sensibilities of a generation who would in turn forge a more peaceful world.[71]

Like many of these organizations, Duggan's IIE was premised on the notion that national education had resulted in irrational nationalism that had then led to war, and his goal was to "develop international good will by means of educational agencies." In practice, this meant circulating regular bulletins containing information on conferences, employment, and visiting scholars to the United States who would be keen to lecture at American universities, as well as bringing distinguished foreign scholars to the United States and providing information to foreign students coming to study in the country.[72] In 1922, the institute had also experimented with extending the transformative experience of international travel to American undergraduates.[73] It lent its auspices to the International Students' Tours that ran summer education courses in the United Kingdom, France, Italy, and Scandinavia, thanks to partnerships with the English-Speaking Union, the Fédération de l'Alliance Française, the Italy America Society, and the American-Scandinavian Foundation. As the promotional brochure put it, "Nothing contributes more to education and to an intelligent interest in international affairs than does a contact with the larger world and a personal acquaintance with the history, the traditions, the resources and the problems of other nations."[74]

In sponsoring these tours, the IIE and Duggan were conscious of the potential dangers of unregulated student behavior and took very deliberate steps to actively manage it. Because the touring students would "in a certain sense be unofficial representatives of the United States," the trips were to be surrounded "with every safeguard necessary to protect the name of the group and of its members individually." Chaperones were to accompany students, who would be carefully selected, and all student excursions would be guided by the "interpretative leadership" of professors and host institutions.[75] Notably—and unlike the trips that James Lough was at the same time running through the NYU Extramural Division—these study tours and summer courses of the early 1920s did not carry any official college credit in US institutions. However, the nascent Junior Year Abroad programs did, bringing different risks.[76]

Begun by war veteran Raymond Kirkbride at the University of Delaware in 1923, at its inception the program was intended to create what Delaware's president, Walter Hullihen, called "a great reservoir of college trained businessmen upon whom commerce and government may draw for work that involves a knowledge of the language and customs of other countries." But Hullihen knew that young American men of business did not want to "lose a year" in postgraduate study abroad, so his ambition of reaching significant numbers of students meant that the program must be "available for *undergraduates* and must *not* depend upon scholarships or fellowships."[77] Delaware's solution was to substitute one of the four years of an American liberal arts degree for a year enrolled at an institution overseas, initially the Cours de Civilisation, taught through the University of Paris as a course for foreigners.[78] The students' studies overseas would count toward their Delaware degree. To safeguard against any "difficulties," great emphasis was placed on the selection of "appropriate" junior-year students who were also required to stay either with a local family or in approved accommodations.[79] Even so, the program was opposed by Delaware faculty on the basis that the French Department could provide all the education required at home.[80] Personal experience abroad was educationally advantageous, but extending American college credit for foreign travel had to be premised on rigorous selection criteria, the direction of European universities, and the oversight of an accompanying American professor.[81] In any case, the numbers involved in this program between the wars were tiny.[82]

European universities were certainly very willing to take advantage of the booming American student market. By 1927, the Universities of Madrid, Florence, Paris, Rome, Geneva, Oxford, Liverpool, Cambridge, Vienna, Berlin, Heidelberg, Hamburg, Athens, and Jerusalem all had courses designed for foreigners.[83] In 1921, the rector of the University of Paris initiated the construction of the Cité Universitaire as an international village for students.[84] In the wake of World War I, the French government also sponsored scholarship and exchange programs for graduate students, and a variety of US private initiatives for "international education" were launched.[85] And—amid a host of proposals for an international university—two summer school initiatives were created: the Geneva Institute of International Relations, led by English classical historian, internationalist, and deputy director of the League of Nations' International Committee on Intellectual Cooperation, Alfred Zimmern, and the international summer school established by Paul Otlet and the Union of International Associations at the Palais Mondial in Brussels.

Alongside these initiatives, and less remarked on in scholarly literature, a whole new for-profit commercial industry was developing, with off-shoots in both Europe and the United States.[86] In addition to travel company agents selling tickets and the creation of student departments in travel agencies such as American Express and Thomas Cook, a host of smaller providers emerged selling guided tours. Styled as "summer study tours," at their more respectable end these trips were affiliated with a US university and featured coursework or research and a stay of three or so months. At their less respectable end, they were a glorified package tour, perhaps led by a professor or other guide but comprising little formal education or assessment and lasting as little as four weeks. As far as the shipping and travel companies were concerned, this was a perfectly legitimate business venture. According to the National Educational Council for Foreign Travel, there was "always a profit made on student tours."[87]

This meant that, as NYU was finding out, it was not always easy to tell where the commercial undertaking ended and the educational provision began. While sympathetic to the notion of international education (especially when it was backed by the weighty funds of the Carnegie and Rockefeller Foundations), by the mid-1920s, US universities had grown wary of this emerging educational travel industry. Just how much money was being made on such tours? Who was teaching them? And how "educational" and rigorous were the courses being offered?

PROTECTING CREDENTIALS

When Chancellor Elmer Ellsworth Brown and the NYU Council met in the first few months of 1926 to discuss Professor Lough's financial dealings with the School of Foreign Travel, much lay in the balance. Not only did Lough's travel projects potentially threaten the credibility of the university's fund-raising push, but his granting of university credit for travel experience challenged a business model that depended on the tuition fees students paid for education in a wide range of professional fields delivered on campus and taught by academic authorities. In fact, in the 1920s NYU's status, like that of its competitors, increasingly rested on a claim to authority over knowledge that was completely incompatible with Lough's ventures. If the professor's education experiments beyond the university's walls had seemed desirable during the period before World War I, by early 1926 it had become clear to Brown and his Executive Committee that it must be the university and its qualified faculty members that stood as the source of authoritative knowledge about the world—not the direct, personal experiences of sundry travelers.

At the end of January 1926, the members of the committee Brown had appointed to investigate the Extramural Division delivered its report. It recommended a series of significant policy changes designed to protect the integrity of the university's credentials. It believed that the university should immediately break relations with the School of Foreign Travel and cancel the forthcoming summer tours. But existing contractual relationships made these actions both financially and legally impracticable, so a series of compromises were proposed. First, the university would focus only on "residential study, as distinguished from itinerant study," with courses at all times under the exclusive educational control of NYU.[88] There were to be no more courses of the type Lough had been running: tours moving from one center to the next, albeit with a lecturer, for which neither the conditions of study nor its content could be assured. Second, no travel courses were to be offered in Paris. This was to be the exclusive domain of General Charles H. Sherrill's Department of Fine Arts. Third, the name of the university could not be used in association with any programs other than those the university sanctioned. And fourth, college credit for travel courses was not to be guaranteed, and the conditions for acquiring it had to be made explicit in all promotional publications. Whether travel courses would count toward an NYU degree was "the exclusive prerogative of the respective faculties of the University," and students would need to satisfy both residential and academic requirements to be eligible.[89]

University secretary Harold O. Voorhis was particularly clear on this last point. It had become evident that members of the Washington Square College faculty had been teaching summer courses advertised as earning NYU credits that were being run not only by the School of Foreign Travel but also by other independent travel agencies, including Thomas Cook and Son along with the American Institute of Educational Travel.[90] This could no longer continue. Only work conducted under "University auspices" would receive its credits. Only by directly controlling the content of students' courses and grounding them in place could the "position of the University academically" be "fortified" and the extramural summer courses be made "compatible" with the "other interests" of the university abroad.[91]

The committee's choice of Rufus Smith as Lough's replacement was itself telling. Since 1922, Smith had been part of the process by which the credit-bearing courses of the Extramural Division and the Summer School were brought back within control of the relevant schools.[92] In the first months of his new role, he ensured that the Extramural Division's nonmatriculated students would be taught by instructors from Washington Square College and were financially within its jurisdiction.[93] Five months later, he recommended that the division change its name altogether: the Extramural Division became the University Extension Division.[94] While the old distinction between extramural (credit-bearing) and extension (noncredit) teaching had long been blurred, and while the new Extension Division did continue to deliver a limited number of courses for credit at some sites off campus, this name change was significant. It signaled NYU's desire to separate matriculated students (who were working for credit) from nonmatriculated students (who were not).[95] It located the ability to award credit firmly within the walls of the university's colleges and schools and took it away from the dean of the Extramural/Extension Division.

The adoption of these changes in early 1926 signaled a major shift away from the basis on which, for the past twenty years, Professor Lough had advanced his educational innovations. No longer was New York City the university's laboratory, with courses offered on location, credentializing the experience of its diverse population and utilizing a wide array of teachers wherever they could be found. Now the city was merely the backdrop to study and the site for students' social activities, what NYU's centenary historian in 1932 described as "the cultural and social background of the New York College student."[96] Protecting the authority of the university meant protecting the integrity of its credentials, and this meant rendering its walls much less permeable than Lough's initiatives had made them.

Such concerns determined the fate of the Floating University's relationship with NYU. The original arrangement had been based on the university's preparedness to issue certificates for courses taken aboard the ship that might then "be credited toward a degree in New York University or in other institutions under local regulations governing the transfer of credits."[97] But in the course of its investigations, Chancellor Brown's committee had discovered that the only way the project's organizers—James Lough, Andrew J. McIntosh, and Charles F. Thwing—were going to get the number of students they needed to cover the costs was to "let down the bars and take all comers, without much respect for educational or moral qualifications." It was not confident in Lough's ability to maintain NYU's academic standards while the cruise was in progress.[98] This was a major problem if the university was to award credit for courses taken during the cruise. If NYU's name was to be associated with the venture, the university had to have "complete control" not only over admissions but over the entire "academic side of the operation."[99] As far as possible, the traveling students would need to be brought within the authority of the institution in New York and Thwing himself would need to accept an official appointment at NYU. The university would need a financial guarantee from Phelps Bros., and Thwing and McIntosh would have to agree that Lough would have no part at all in the academic organization of the cruise.

Chancellor Brown had little choice but to accept these recommendations from his committee. He asked Voorhis to break the news to Professor Lough.[100] The security of NYU's academic authority was no longer compatible with Lough's participation in the cruise he had conceived and initiated.[101]

THE UNIVERSITY TRAVEL ASSOCIATION GOES IT ALONE

The ensuing negotiations between NYU and the University Travel Association (UTA), the entity organizing the cruise, did not go well. The primary objective of Lough's successor, Rufus Smith, was to protect the university's interests along the four lines laid out for him by the chancellor's review committee. McIntosh, however, did not see the force of the university's arguments. As far as he was concerned, Phelps Bros. was a reputable shipping agency; more than two hundred registrations had already been sold based on high selection standards, and more were coming in. For his part, Thwing was not prepared to be a "passive figurehead" and turn control of admissions over to NYU.[102] At an impasse, Smith became "more and more convinced" that continuing to sponsor the cruise was a bad idea.[103] In the end, it was McIntosh who suggested that NYU was "not quite around to visualizing the necessities" and that the university might retire from sponsorship.[104] For Smith, this was a very welcome suggestion, and by mid-March 1926, NYU and the UTA had formally agreed to end their relationship.[105]

The university's withdrawal was completed "under friendly and satisfactory circumstances," with Smith promising "passive co-operation" in making the cruise a success.[106] Neither he nor McIntosh wanted negative attention from the newspapers.[107] NYU was to have no further financial obligations to the cruise. Its name was not to be used in any connection with the undertaking. The university would henceforth be only one of many institutions at which students might be eligible for credits for the onboard courses, and Smith had been careful to make clear that regarding NYU, the ultimate decision about eligibility would be made case by case by the university's various faculties.[108] The participation of NYU faculty members as instructors on the floating cruise would be subject to the approval of their dean and the University Council. This arrangement was officially ratified by the university executive on April 13, 1926.[109] From that moment on, everything NYU found out about the Floating University it learned through the UTA's publicity and the press.

In March, the newspapers began to carry notices that a ship had been secured.[110] The students of the world cruise would be traveling aboard the Dutch-owned Holland America Line's (Holland-Amerika Lijn's or HAL's) SS *Ryndam* (or *Rijndam*).[111] Built in 1901 in Belfast by Harland and Wolff, the ship had worked the transatlantic passenger route until it was damaged in January 1916 by a German mine in the North Sea. Requisitioned by the US government in March 1918 and converted into a troopship, the *Ryndam* was released in 1921 to resume the transatlantic route. McIntosh boasted that it would be refitted to include a gymnasium, swimming pool, library, and other rooms appropriate to a college-age party. But readers of the shipping columns would have noted that two weeks before the Floating University's scheduled departure, the *Ryndam* had still been in Europe.[112]

The press articles also indicated that despite McIntosh's earlier confidence about numbers, the UTA was continuing to register students right up until August. The entrance requirements were initially the same as those for the aborted 1925 voyage: the cruise was open to currently matriculated students at any American college or university as well as to graduates of high schools or preparatory schools who could meet college entrance requirements.[113] McIntosh sought to ensure the "highest standards" by requiring applicants to detail their scholarship record, leadership qualities, and physical fitness.[114] Additionally, they needed to provide character references in the form of letters from their schools or colleges.[115]

An astute observer, however, would have noted that the UTA had begun to adjust its admission criteria. Initially, the cruise was advertised for men only.[116] But by early 1926, some of the UTA's promotional materials had begun to note that faculty members' wives and daughters might also join. Reflecting the gendered notions that still underpinned even coeducational campuses, McIntosh and Thwing judged that "there would probably be no objection" to the young ladies sitting in on the lectures or becoming involved in music and art. But with "<u>actual</u> registrations" at the start of June still numbering only 245 paid and a further 105 sure, McIntosh decided to issue a "purposely ambiguous" bulletin that opened the voyage to "men and women with educational inclinations, of all ages."[117] By August, the papers were noting that the cruise was to be coeducational.[118]

James Lough, meanwhile, was seeking to ensure he could still participate. As soon as Rufus Smith had made it clear that NYU staff wishing to serve on the voyage would need to obtain the approval of the University Council, Lough put in an application for leave.[119] When the matter came before the council on April 26, it generated considerable discussion. In the end, the council did agree to grant the professor a leave of absence for the 1926–27 academic year at half salary, but it would do so only on two conditions. First, he could not "undertake any educational activity in which the name of the University shall be connected with his own"; and second, he must "do everything possible to make another connection which will enable him to leave the University at the end of his year's leave."[120] Lough could go on the Floating University world cruise, but if he did, he would need to find a new job upon his return.

3

A Shipboard Education

The evening before the Floating University's scheduled departure, a crowd of more than fifteen hundred people, all wearing colorful identification badges, gathered at New York's Waldorf Astoria.[1]

Miraculously, seventeen-year-old Charles Ladd and his mother, who had made the long journey to New York from Missouri, managed to bump into several people they knew from Kansas City. Together, they listened to speeches that celebrated the venture as a unique "experiment in modern education" and paid tribute to its founder, Professor James Edwin Lough.[2] Taking the stage, Lough himself had told the assembled audience that those traveling aboard the Floating University would experience "a method of study which actually brings the student into living contact with the world's problems about to be realized." The difference between it and what was ordinarily served up to students was, as he put it, the difference "between reading a menu and eating the full course meal."[3]

Could Lough's fine educational ideas be implemented and operationalized amid the realities of traveling with hundreds of college-age students on a 560-foot Dutch steamship? What would education as experiment and experience mean as the *Ryndam* made its way around the world? In the face of New York University's ultimatum, Professor Lough had nonetheless decided to go on the trip, taking his wife and youngest daughter with him. But launching a seagoing college was a major undertaking and one for which he was spectacularly ill prepared.[4] In the end, it was Andrew J. McIntosh who had appointed most of the faculty and the Phelps Bros. shipping agency, which undertook the practical work of establishing liaison with the Holland America Line and managing the voyage. As their efforts to actualize Lough's vision were put into effect, what counted as education, and the means through which it might be acquired, emerged as a significant source of contention.

On the day of departure, Charles Ladd was eager to find the cabin that would be his home for the next seven and a half months.[5] But confusion reigned as he and his mother made their way up the gangplank and attempted to navigate the ships' five decks. At the very top they found the bridge, with the wheelhouse, chart room, and observation platforms used by the captain and his crew. Beneath it was the hurricane deck, which contained lifeboats for use in emergency and spaces outfitted for games and sports. The next level down was the promenade deck. It was home to a limited number of first-class staterooms, known as deck cabins, where the senior members of the cruise, the deans, and the president were accommodated. It also featured writing, reading, and smoking rooms as well as the captain's desk. Below that was A deck, where a good deal of activity was taking place: along with some better-appointed staterooms, they found the main dining room, the kitchen, the cruise manager's office, and the infirmary. And on the expanse of this deck, Ladd spied two outdoor canvas saltwater swimming pools and an open-air gymnasium.

Descending the stairs again, the Ladds reached B deck, where they found another dining room and kitchen as well as a bakery, the barber's shop, and many cabins allocated to students. These rooms were fitted out in the manner of "tourist" class, with two or three people to a room. Mother and son descended yet further to C deck, where there were yet more student cabins in addition to the newspaper office, the press room, baggage rooms, and assembly rooms.[6] The student library and reading room was also located here, although Ladd noticed that its books were still in boxes and its shelves in the process of construction.[7]

It was here on C deck that Ladd and his mother finally managed to find his assigned room. Upon opening its door, they looked at each other in dismay. The student accommodations on this floor were spartan, having been converted from steerage class. As a result, the space was tiny and located right next to the coal bunkers, with a bed that was far too short.[8] Ladd and his mother could hear the firemen with their shovels through the wall, and coal dust was already seeping into everything. Even worse, it was extremely hot, and together B and C decks were provided with only a small number of shared bathrooms, supplied with salt water pumped directly from the ocean. For a moment, it seemed to Ladd that his mother might call the whole trip off, so outraged was she that her son would be traveling in steerage. But the complaints of one of the female students assigned to one of the "good" rooms on A deck saved the day. His mother then saw the funny side of the situation, and as the sirens sounded, she scurried off the ship along with all the other visitors. The depression Ladd had initially felt upon seeing his room was swept away. He and his roommate, William S. Worthington, resolved to make the best of their circumstances.[9] They "borrowed" wood from the carpenters' supplies and built a study desk, above which they tacked up a world map for tracing the ship's progress.

Amid the crowds looking for their lodgings on C deck was Charles Gauss from Michigan.[10] He was perfectly happy with his room, as was James S. McKenzie, from the small town of Cottonwood Falls, Kansas. Meanwhile, DeWitt Reddick of Fort Worth, Texas, was counting his blessings.[11] He had been assigned a cabin with four bunk beds but only one roommate—a fellow journalism student from Iowa named Ellis H. Dana, with whom he immediately struck up an amicable friendship.

One level up on B deck, the members of the faculty were also finding their lodgings. At one end of the deck was the *Ryndam*'s instructor for the Art of Design course, Holling C. Holling, and his wife, Lucille; they had traveled up to New York from Chicago, where Holling had been working alongside McIntosh's son-in-law, Ralph Linton, at the Field Museum of Natural History.[12] Not far away from them was Tom Johnson of Vermont, who for the last twelve months had been teaching at Williams College in Massachusetts. He was on board as the English lecturer and had been provided a shared stateroom with Thomas K. Urdahl, the professor of economics from Wisconsin.[13] Like Reddick, Johnson was aware of how much better off he was than many of the other passengers, who, having been promised rooms for two, found themselves unexpectedly bunking with a third. Lillian McCracken was one of these. A sixty-year-old high school teacher from Boulder, Colorado, she and her sister (Mary Grimes) had signed up for the trip after it was opened to women. They were surprised to find themselves sharing a room with a nurse from New Mexico.[14] Yet, much like Charles Ladd, the sisters embraced their predicament with good grace, and the three women soon became fast friends.

Mrs. Pearl Bash Heckel was not subjected to these indignities.[15] Together with her husband, Albert K. Heckel, who was the Floating University's dean of men, she had been provided with one of the more luxurious first-class staterooms on A deck. But while surveying the crowds waving handkerchiefs and shouting farewells to their family and friends, she soon found a different cause for concern.[16] Most of them were, in her estimation, "fine appearing stalwart young men, eager and wholesome looking," and there were "about forty just as fine appearing girls, already lighting their cigarettes." But as the ship prepared to depart, to her surprise Pearl Heckel also noted forty preparatory school students, a handful of parents, "a few dozen middle aged women interested in educational travel," and "a few more or less distant relatives of students—men or women of mature years, some of these obviously setting out for a cheap form of sport." These passengers were definitely not the college-age students she and her husband had been led to believe would form the company of the world's first Floating University. As the *Ryndam* pulled away from the dock, she began to wonder what was in store for them all.[17]

THE STUDENT BODY

The University Travel Association had promoted the cruise as one that, in keeping with its pseudodiplomatic mission, would be "representational" in character.[18] Correspondingly, the shipboard newspaper, the *Binnacle*, encouraged the students to see themselves as "represent[ing] the American youth of the present to the peoples of the countries visited."[19] Applications had initially been received on a pro rata basis from the different states, and the cost of the voyage had been fixed so as "to prevent its being used as a trip for rich men's sons."[20] But, as Pearl Heckel had already learned, the exact number of "students" on board was difficult to pin down. The *Panama Canal Record* recorded a passenger list of 570 (including students and faculty), with an additional 239 in the crew.[21] James McKenzie reported that 363 of these passengers were students (47 of whom were in the "preparatory" or precollegiate division), with an additional 133 "older people" eligible to take instruction.[22] Unable to sell enough tickets to male collegians, first McIntosh and then Phelps Bros. had been forced to open up places not only to women but to nonstudents as well. Of the 316 college-level students aboard the *Ryndam*, only 14 percent were currently enrolled at or had attended an Ivy League institution, 25 percent were associated with a private or liberal arts college, and 35 percent were associated with a land grant or public university (and the affiliation of 28 percent was unknown).[23] But, with a price tag of $2,500 per berth, "wealth and power and culture and good breeding" were, in Charles Ladd's approving words, "observable everywhere."[24]

New York State had the largest group of passengers, with Missouri and Kansas following closely behind. California, Ohio, Pennsylvania, New Jersey, Texas, Michigan, and Massachusetts all had significant representation.[25] The student body did, however, draw its members from virtually every state of the union, with a handful of students from Hawaii, Puerto Rico, Canada, and Cuba as well.[26] The ship layout accentuated these geographies. Students from the same state were accommodated together, and street

FIGURE 3.1. Floating University students from Kansas. In Walter Conger Harris, *Photographs of the First University World Cruise* (New York: University Travel Association, 1927), no. 358.

signs appeared in the corridors, pointing the traveler to "Broadway" or to midwestern towns.[27] Many passengers had never left their state before, let alone met so many of their fellow countrymen. As Tom Johnson, whose life so far had straddled only the borders of Vermont, put it, "I have never been with a group of people who have been so truly representative of the whole country as this group is."[28] What the *Ryndam*'s passenger list represented, however, was not so much "the whole country" as the power relations that shaped it. Not only was the Floating University's student body dominated by the well off; it was entirely white (fig. 3.1).

The University Travel Association's correspondence from 1927 suggests that a deliberate policy of racial exclusion was at play. At the end of May of that year, in response to advertisements for the second college cruise, a young African American from Wichita, Kansas, named W. H. Leonard sent a letter of application to the UTA. He received a reply from Charles A. Phelps Jr. telling him it would not be considered.[29] Leonard was not prepared to accept this rejection at face value. He wrote again, seeking more information. Was it that the cruise was full? Or that bookings had closed? Or did the UTA have a policy not to take colored students?[30] This time, Phelps's reply was direct: colored students would "not be eligible."[31]

"W. H. Leonard" was in fact a false name assumed for the purposes of this correspondence by W. L. Hutcherson. He was a board member of the Wichita Branch of the National Association for the Advancement of Colored People (NAACP) and executive secretary of the city's Young Men's Christian Association. In May, he had written to former Kansas governor and member of the 1926 cruise, Henry J. Allen, to ask whether it would be possible for one of his "very fine young men" to attend the cruise. But Hutcherson had received such an indefinite response from Allen that he had made follow-up inquiries under the guise of an interested student. Outraged at the reply he received from Phelps, Hutcherson forwarded the rejection to W. E. B. DuBois, director of publicity and research at the NAACP. DuBois wrote to the *New York Times*, denouncing the UTA's race prejudice. The paper, however, never published his letter.[32]

This 1927 UTA policy is difficult to square with the publicly expressed views of the cruise president, Charles F. Thwing, a founding member of the biracial National Negro Committee (a predecessor organization of the NAACP). Western Reserve University, of which he had been president, had admitted African Americans since the mid-nineteenth century.[33] Yet there were no Black students on the 1926 voyage, and as Hutcherson's inquires attest, it was not as if there weren't any who were eligible. In the 1920s, significant numbers were attending colleges and universities in the South, such as Fisk, Howard, and Shaw, with a much smaller number enrolled in predominantly white colleges in the North, and a well-developed network of Black Greek-letter societies was in operation.[34]

When it came to the admission of Jewish students, the UTA was a little more accommodating; there were at least a handful aboard. Ben S. Washer Jr. was one. Studying at the University of Michigan, he was from Louisville, Kentucky, where his father was the president of the local synagogue. The Copenhagen-based *Politiken* newspaper no doubt displayed a double prejudice when it judged the "majority of the women students" on the *Ryndam* to be "Jewesses, unmistakably even if the Rachel tints had been applied less carefully," and described the men as "generally of the Nordic type," some of them "real giants."[35] Far off the mark in its racialized caricature, the *Politiken* had been right about one thing: the Floating University *was* produced as an imagined version of rising America. It projected an image of a largely white and wealthy, healthy, and "modern" society to the world.

THE SHIP'S COMPANY

The *Ryndam* was white in another sense as well. The agreement that the UTA signed in March 1926 with the Holland America Line stated that the

FIGURE 3.2. The officers of the SS *Ryndam*, with the captain seated in the center. In Walter Conger Harris, *Photographs of the First University World Cruise* (New York: University Travel Association, 1927), no. 629.

hired ship would come with a captain, officers, engineers, firemen, and crew.[36] Unlike many other ships (particularly British but also European) that employed African and Asian seafarers, or lascars, on lower wages to undertake the dirty and demanding work associated with steam travel, the *Ryndam* had an almost wholly Dutch crew.[37] Many had been in the service of the HAL for several years.[38]

Captaining the ship was Jan Klaas Liewen (fig. 3.2). Born in Amsterdam in 1875, he had joined the Netherlands-America Steamship Company (which later became the HAL) at age nineteen and worked his way up from the position of apprentice mate until his appointment as captain in 1909.[39] With Liewen, the HAL had selected one of its most experienced sailors. He was "not without a sense of humor" and was happy to participate in the costume balls and other entertainments of the voyage.[40] But he established quickly that his word was law. The HAL-UTA contract outlined his "right to deviate [from its terms] on account of actual or apprehended quarantine, obstructions, riots or civil commotions, [or] war."[41] It was he who imposed a nightly curfew on the *Ryndam* and charged his crew with surveillance of the students.[42] On one occasion, he made clear that anyone bothering him with "fool questions about the position the ship, of their room . . . or calling [him] 'steward'" would receive "a punch in the jaw."[43] Unlike that of the professors, Liewen's authority was embodied and absolute.[44]

The staff with whom the American students had the most interaction were the stewards and the men in the purser's office. The latter was presided over by H. J. Pascal Souren. Much like the manager of a large hotel, the purser was responsible for the smooth running of the ship and the soothing of passengers and crew alike. He paid the crew and managed the traveler's checks, purchased all supplies and provisions, and oversaw visas, transfers, and customs.[45] Souren had worked on the *Ryndam*'s transatlantic passenger routes for five years and was fluent in English. Many of the stewards, however, were not—and this, together with the unmet service expectations of wealthy Americans, became the source of considerable tension on board.

Only a few weeks into the voyage, passengers were already making complaints, with at least seven abandoning the cruise at Colón, Panama, and at Los Angeles because of their dissatisfaction with meals and accommodations.[46] The Phelps team telegrammed the HAL to report that the Steward's Department was understaffed. At least 10 more men were required, they said. Evidently, 36 table stewards, 18 room stewards, 13 general service stewards, 6 mess room stewards, 7 bathroom stewards, 3 deck stewards, 1 smoking room steward, and 3 stewardesses were not enough to keep five hundred American passengers in the manner they expected.[47] Pearl Heckel was sure that the crew was not only overworked, with their numbers reduced to cut down on costs, but also bad tempered, because they were receiving fewer tips, owing to an arrangement by which the UTA would pay a lump sum to the shipping company for gratuities at the end of the voyage.[48]

Initially, the HAL had been unmoved by Phelps's objections. In its view, some of the passengers seemed to "have the mistaken idea that [HAL was] operating a luxury cruise," when all they were actually entitled to was third-class service.[49] Even Phelps thought the trouble with the food lay with the predominance of unfamiliar Dutch cuisine on the menu, not poor quality. But by the start of November, the complaints from students had become enough to force HAL to respond. The shipping line was as eager to avoid bad press as was the UTA, so it agreed to put on more staff. But HAL headquarters in Rotterdam stressed that not only were any new recruits to be paid the same rate as the existing staff, but "orientalen" must not be hired.[50] The management wanted to avoid difficulties with the rest of the crew. This had not, however, stopped the *Ryndam* from taking on seven additional Filipino laundrymen in Los Angeles.[51]

Another class of crew member remained all but invisible, only entering the students' consciousness because of an article in the *Binnacle*. It described anonymous firemen, stokers, and coal pushers: men who undertook the sweltering and dirty work of shoveling black coal into the red light of glowing fires, laboring two shifts of four hours a day in a tiny room reached only by narrow corridors and hot ladders. The only signs of the existence of this world to the students on deck were the ventilators, whose purpose, the reporter revealed, was to pour a stream of fresh air down to the workers.[52] In all, 58 men toiled in the engine room, while 34 worked the bridge and decks as sailors.[53] In the bakery were more anonymous men, working each night from 6:00 p.m. to 6:00 a.m. baking bread, with special pastry chefs replacing them during the day.[54] In addition, there was a kitchen team of 15 cooks, 2 butchers, 18 pantry men, and 4 pantry boys.

In the 1920s, a global labor and race politics pitted sailors' unions eager to exclude nonwhite workers, who they thought stole their jobs and undercut their wages, against shipowners seeking to drive down prices by hiring low-waged African and Asian seafarers who themselves were struggling to navigate the color lines of a racialized world.[55] But on the *Ryndam*, the "Nordic" America above deck was largely mirrored below it. Rather than being understood as a constitutive element of the nation-at-sea, the concept of race was projected onto the places and peoples the Americans would meet.[56] The contract Phelps Bros. had negotiated with HAL, the type of ship Andrew McIntosh had procured, and the students and passengers Phelps Bros. had assembled to travel on it were heavily shaped by commercial considerations as well as race and class prejudice. The Floating University that sailed in 1926 reflected the social, political, and economic contexts of Jim Crow–era America, and it was within their constraints that James E. Lough's "pedagogical experiment" took place.

AND THEY ARE OFF

It took several days for everything to get organized on board. Teaching spaces needed to be allocated, and the various academic departments had to meet before classes could start. Charles Ladd ended up fishing his own bags out of the storage area in the ship's hold. The passengers, too, needed some time to get their sea legs. Ladd managed to avoid seasickness, but Tom Johnson struggled to adjust to the "great hunks of flat waves that tip with a sickeningly steady motion."[57] At least the *Binnacle*, the shipboard student newspaper, was in operation. President Thwing used it to underline once again the pedagogical philosophy of the cruise. There were two methods of education, he told readers: one centered on book learning and the other on direct experience. The student of the world had hitherto found it "easier to study from the works of men who have gone before him over the same ground," yet the "only way seriously to study most subjects [was] at first hand."[58] Everyone on board knew that the Floating University was a new way of pursuing an education; nothing like it had ever been tried. But as Thwing's comments to the *Binnacle* made clear, the Floating University was experimental in a second sense as well. Onboard learning was to be "practical" and experiential, with field trips in ports and enterprises such as the student-run newspaper serving as "laboratories" on the ship. It was through student-led experiment in and with the world that learning was to take place.

This experimental approach made room for a good deal of messiness and also accommodated the making of mistakes. Indeed, in the minds of those leading the voyage, such mistakes were an intrinsic part of the learning process. "There are two kinds of people in this world" was how Dean George Edwin Howes put it: "those who are always ready to join a successful venture and those who prefer to be on hand at the working out of an original problem, something new and untried." "The bite of a mosquito is annoying," he continued, alluding to things that might go wrong, "but by no means a tragedy."[59]

With the South Carolina coast slipping out of sight, the students who would participate in this experiment began to enroll in their courses.[60] They could choose from seventy-three subjects offered by sixteen "departments." The subjects included government, English composition, economics, foreign languages, geography and geology, English literature, journalism, public speaking, classics, art, mathematics, navigation, philosophy and psychology, foreign trade, music, astronomy, botany and biology, history, sociology, and physical education.[61] English composition was the most popular subject, with journalism, geography, languages, economics, and government not far behind. Some students signed up for as many as seven courses. Professor Lough was delighted. "I have never before, in all my experience, found students so [eager] to take more than the required number of studies," he told the *Binnacle*.[62]

Formal teaching was to be conducted while the ship was at sea and complemented with shore excursions. Each day was to begin with compulsory calisthenics, followed by breakfast at 7:30 a.m. Classes would then commence, and they would be interspersed with breaks for snacks at 11:00 a.m., lunch at noon, and tea at 4:00 p.m. Following afternoon tea, there were to be more compulsory exercises. Dinner was at 6:00 p.m., although sometimes night classes were also held, as were independently organized evening discussion groups. Only Sundays were rest days.[63]

This rosily timetabled vision of order masked the more complicated reality that quickly emerged. To begin with, there was a lack of clear academic leadership, with power divided between a president and three deans. As

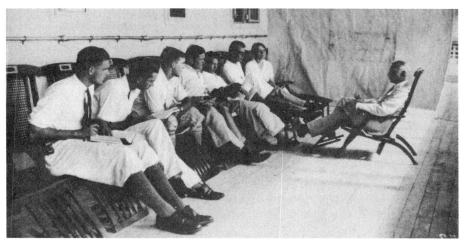

FIGURE 3.3. Dean George Edwin Howes and his first class. In Walter Conger Harris, *Photographs of the First University World Cruise* (New York: University Travel Association, 1927), no. 9.

McIntosh later acknowledged, the educational work "was not prepared in advance and the educational heads did not co-ordinate at first nor have a policy or program."[64] Making matters worse, the ship itself had not been well prepared to serve as a college, with little provision made for classrooms or equipment in the hasty refit. However, according to Pearl Heckel, the faculty swiftly "began to work towards salvaging the ideal." Despite the deans' very different personalities, "an effort was made to parcel out the work" among them.[65] Howes took charge of academic work, Heckel was responsible for student discipline, and Lough took on the educational side of shore excursions. The promenade deck was sectioned off into classrooms by canvas dividers, which were pulled across the thoroughfares to create some sense of separation, and students and teachers alike lounged in chairs (fig. 3.3). DeWitt Reddick described the instructors' voices mingling with the rush of the wind and churn of the water against the side of the ship.[66]

Even the library needed to be constructed.[67] It was presided over by Miss Alida Stephens from Williams College, and Tom Johnson spent his first few days at sea helping her set it up.[68] Demand for books was high.[69] By Christmas, "so many books [had] been taken out and not returned that the work of the college [had] become seriously handicapped."[70] Miss Stephens's pleas for students to return missing volumes grew more desperate as the voyage progressed. Soon she was facing even greater challenges. In one corner of her room was a grand piano that "never seem[ed] to get a rest," and in another there was a Victrola record player, ensuring that the students would never need to sit in silence.[71] By the time the ship was approaching Japan, Miss Stephens, evidently not used to such behavior, was threatening to close the room in the evenings.[72]

If the space of the ship had to accommodate all the requirements of college life, it also provided plenty of diversions. Certainly a diligent student, Charles Gauss attended all his classes, but he found it "hard to study under crowded conditions" and hard to "get started again" after stops in port.[73] Within a few days of leaving New York, students had dragged their mattresses out onto the decks in order to escape the increasingly tropical heat.[74] Just before Christmas, in the Indian Ocean, even the faculty were sleeping on the deck: "Sheeted form after sheeted form, there lie the brains of universities from all over America. Not so brainy looking when asleep," wrote instructor Holling C. Holling.[75] Conditions at sea were sometimes less than conducive to study. "Be glad you're not trying to whip a class into some semblance of shape in the tropics in the rainy season," he wrote to his sister from the Caribbean, with "the boat rolling like a whale."[76] Officially organized tours during the stops in India and in Aden (in what is now Yemen) made fieldwork impossible, and although earlier in the cruise he had described his students as "all interested and all hard at work," Holling's notes suggest some of them had stopped attending class halfway across the Arabian Sea.[77]

For many, being at sea itself constituted a learning experience. Reddick described with wonder the changing shades of the water in the Gulf Stream and the porpoises and flying fish that traveled alongside the ship. Lying on the deck at night and gazing up at the stars as the *Ryndam* sailed further south, he had "a queer feeling" that something was not quite right. He'd never paid much attention to the stars before, but the Big Dipper seemed to have dropped out of the sky, and the Milky Way was stretching halfway to the horizon.[78] Some students seized on opportunities to engage with the crew. Gauss even became friendly with one of the table waiters, who taught him German in exchange for English lessons.[79] The geology and geography students undertook a series of experiments with the *Ryndam*'s officers in cooperation with the Hydrographic Office of the US Navy. Every day at noon, they threw overboard numbered bottles, some intended to track the currents (loaded with sand to make them float erect) and some the winds (empty to make them lie flat on the water).[80] And crowded decks became more crowded, thanks to periodic fads that captivated the student body. These included a walking cane craze, a mustache craze, and a sticker craze, the latter causing students to rush to secure hotel stickers at each port for plastering onto their baggage. At Hong Kong they all bought wicker chairs, and at Colón they purchased live pet monkeys, marmosets, and parakeets, all of which had to be "chloroformed" at Los Angeles and dropped over-board because of quarantine restrictions.[81]

Yet for all the organizational complications, and amid the thrills and dis-tractions of shipboard life, the space of the *Ryndam* seemed, on the whole, conducive to formal education. Charles Ladd, who was far from diligent, was among those noting that "while on the 'bounding main' there was little else to do [but study]."[82] According to Reddick, once teaching began, a "col-legiate atmosphere" had enveloped the ship.[83] But it fell largely to the indi-vidual instructors to attempt to put the classroom side of Professor Lough's idea into practice.

BOTANY

From small-town Kansas, James McKenzie signed up for the Botany course. He was drawn to the prospect of being taught by the Harvard-trained in-structor Oran Lee Raber. Originally from Indiana, Raber had interrupted his PhD studies to serve as a lieutenant in the US balloon service during the war. He'd already been to Japan and had also spent time at the University of Paris, returning to the United States to take up the position of assistant professor of botany at the University of Michigan. Most recently, he had taught at the University of Arizona.

Raber's course description was particularly attractive to McKenzie, who looked forward to the field trips it promised as well as the special visits to the "great" botanical gardens along the cruise route.[84] Raber's enthusiasm for his discipline must have been appealing as well. "Is it possible to separate science from life?" Raber asked, "and who would want to?" Like McKenzie, he was clearly thrilled at the prospect of seeing the botanical riches the voy-age offered, and he had even resigned from his post at the University of Arizona to join its faculty. Most of all, Raber was excited that the *Ryndam* would cover "some of the territory which Darwin traversed in the 'Beagle' [giving] . . . abundant opportunity to see many of the facts which led the father of modern thought to his illuminating epoch-making conclusions."[85]

Raber's students visited some of the premier botanical gardens of the globe. In Hawaii, they toured the Maunalua Gardens with Professor Berg-man, head of the Botany Department at the University of Honolulu, and vis-ited Kapiolani Park, known for its tropical and semitropical beauty. There, the students were asked to collect species so that they could study them on the journey from Honolulu to Japan.[86] In the Philippines, they were hosted by Professor José Kabigting Santos, the first Filipino head of the Depart-ment of Biology at the University of Manila, who took them on a three-hour field trip around the city and the university. Santos had in fact produced many of the drawings for one of the textbooks Raber was using, and James McKenzie was thrilled to be able to examine the living material alongside the original studies.[87] In Singapore, the class went to the botanical gardens, where they saw collections of palms and tropical gymnosperms as they roamed the grounds for two and a half hours.[88] On the island of Java (now part of Indonesia), McKenzie was impressed by the world-famous Buitenzorg Gardens, which he and the class toured with a guide. The boy from Kansas was learning to see the world in botanical and evolutionary terms, and his account of his stop in Java was filled with descriptions of the terraced rice fields and banana and coconut groves, details of their cultivation, and explanations of their importance to Javanese economic life.[89]

In Algiers, Raber, along with Professor Maire of the University of Algiers, took the students to the Jardin d'Essai du Hamma. By 1927, it had occupied 150 acres and combined a park with a botanical garden and experimental farm. Established by the French colonial government in Algeria, it was the source of trees and other plants provided to European settlers and the site of experimentation with cultivation techniques. From it, according to the *Binnacle* report, plants were selected that could be grown profitably in the Algerian soil and climate.[90] The central place of the Jardin d'Essai in legitimating and advancing both colonial rule and the subordination of nature was a function fulfilled by all the botanical gardens the students visited, including those in Havana, Los Angeles, Bombay (Mumbai), and Gothenburg—and, of course, Kew Gardens in London, "the most famous of [its] kind in the world."[91] It is entirely possible that Raber's lectures celebrated this aspect of botany's place in "improving" the world, but without any transcripts or class notes, it is hard to say for sure. Though full of reassurances to his parents that he was hard at work, McKenzie's letters focused on the sights seen on land rather than his course curricula.

Holling C. Holling was a little nervous about teaching the Art of Design course.[92] Although he had graduated from the Art Institute of Chicago in 1923 and had been writing and illustrating children's picture books as well as producing material for advertising agencies since then. Unlike Frederick Wellington Ruckstull, the *Ryndam*'s lecturer in the Art Appreciation and Art History courses, he was hardly an expert. An Alsatian-born sculptor who had grown up in St. Louis, Ruckstull had studied sculpture in Paris before returning to the United States to teach at the Metropolitan Museum of Art schools in New York. He had become a member of the National Institute of Arts and Letters and a founding member of the National Sculpture Society. He had just published *Great Works of Art and What Makes Them Great*—and he felt no compunction about making this the class text. A figurative sculptor in the Beaux Arts tradition, Ruckstull's classical approach contrasted markedly with Holling's, whose realist and Romantic style would later become associated with American regionalism, although some of his work from the 1920s shows the stylistic influence of art nouveau. Ruckstull's forthright lectures with titles such as "From Sanity to Insanity in Art" highlighted his and Holling's very different approaches. Holling thought Ruckstull was "an old fossil" who wanted to "tear down all modern ideas [of] design."[93]

Ruckstull's course guide for his Art Appreciation course promised that students would experience a "first-hand study" of the art of the world, with "special reference to the cultural and physical environment that produced it," and his Art History course undertook to "treat art from an historical standpoint," including through views of works via lantern slides and visits to art museums.[94] Holling's Design course, by contrast, offered "practical" training in design and drawing. It reflected his own practice of engaging directly with his subject matter and promised that through individual supervision and fieldwork ashore, students would "collect original material" that they could then "work up" at sea (fig. 3.4).[95] Ruckstull's courses were extremely popular, with the History of Art attracting 131 enrollments in the first semester (no doubt some of them "tourists").[96] Holling's enrollments were more modest: he had thirty people in his class, about half of whom were three-hour (three-credit) students and half six-hour (six-credit) students.[97] While at sea, he taught mornings from ten to eleven o'clock and afternoons from three to four o'clock on Monday, Wednesday, and Friday.

Although Holling was very amused to be given the title Professor, he took teaching his class seriously and worked hard to integrate the *Ryndam*'s experiential philosophy into his course design.[98] He decided to divide his semester-long course into ten sections. First, the students would find out what interested them personally and learn how to make the portfolios in which they would keep their work. Then they would move to discussions of design itself, what was meant by the term, and its history and development, placing special emphasis on the relation of forms and space and the use of ornament. Holling decided to plunge his students into practical work after these introductory sessions. Each would be provided with art materials, ordered before the ship's departure. These included paper, pencils, brushes, thumbtacks, inks, watercolors, and other items Holling deemed essential. He gave them the task of drawing ship objects, focusing on light, shade, and composition. He then put the students to work applying these lessons to

FIGURE 3.4. Sketching class onshore in Singapore. In Walter Conger Harris, *Photographs of the First University World Cruise* (New York: University Travel Association, 1927), no. 304.

sketching "in the field," inviting them to experiment with different mediums: charcoal, pencil, pen and ink, watercolors, pastels, and oils.

Holling also integrated organized field trips into his teaching. "Before entering a country," he told his family in a December letter, "I have [the students] all primed to get certain things, some get costumes, some architecture, some landscapes. Then in port we usually have one field trip."[99] In Singapore, the whole class rose early, went to the city, and sat down on the canal side for a few hours, sketching the ships, sampans, and junks. Then they headed to the museum, where they made drawings of its models of Malay houses and seacraft. These sketches provided the material that the class would later analyze. "Not hard," wrote Holling, "and I think I am learning more than my students," though clearly his students were learning too.[100] The novice teacher kept detailed notes tracking their practical work across the first three weeks of semester two, and Irene Haines was among those who showed great progress. A student at Smith College, she went from never having worked with a pencil held in charcoal fashion to completing a design Holling judged as "light and subtle" with "very good color."[101]

The final parts of Holling's course turned explicitly to the surroundings the students were encountering. He examined design in the material culture of everyday life and in the buildings and industry of "diverse races." He paid particular attention to commercial design: magazine covers, newspapers, book illustrations and layouts, and printing methods, asking the students to examine the publications they were finding en route. Articles in the *Bin-*

nacle discussing the intricacies of Javanese batik or Japanese lacquerwork give a sense of his enthusiasm for these items, which, as Kristin Hoganson has shown, had become a feature of well-to-do American domestic interiors of the time, even though his letters reveal he knew little about them and boned up for the general talks he gave in the *Ryndam*'s library on two days' notice.[102] But this section of Holling's course also reveals the romantic and racialized notions that shaped his sense of foreign peoples. The "primitive mind," read his course plan, had a "love of design" and an "urge" to incorporate it into all aspects of life.[103]

JOURNALISM

DeWitt Reddick signed up for the Journalism class. He already had considerable experience in the field, having supported himself and his younger brother by working as a reporter for newspapers in Fort Worth and Austin while completing a bachelor's degree at the University of Texas.[104] Journalism was still a relatively new discipline in universities, with the first school devoted to the field having been established at the University of Missouri in 1908. Many newspapermen opposed the move, arguing that journalism required talent and could be learned only through on-the-job practical experience. But that was of little matter to ambitious US universities seeking to expand their empires of expertise. In 1909, NYU started offering journalism courses at the undergraduate level through its School of Commerce (indeed, James Lough's brother, William, was one of the inaugural teachers), and throughout the 1910s and 1920s many more universities extended their credentializing reach into the newspapers' domain.[105]

The Floating University's course guide promised Journalism students plenty of firsthand experience. Students would "participate in every phase of the practical newspaper work through the daily newspaper," the *Binnacle*.[106] The editors (fig. 3.5) felt it necessary to explain—for the benefit, they maintained, of the landlocked students from Kansas, Missouri, and Texas—that the shipboard paper was named for "the brass instrument [on a ship] which houses the compass and keeps it steady." Like the brass binnacle, their paper would be "the most important single unit in navigating [the] ship" along the high seas of international experience. But if the *Binnacle*'s editors had noble and somewhat grandiose notions of the role of their publication, their speculating student readers had other ideas. Wasn't a binnacle the snail growing on the ship's hull? Or perhaps the smokestack?[107]

Those enrolled in Journalism I (News Writing and News Reporting) were to undertake assignments on shipboard and onshore trips, and those taking Journalism II (Magazine Writing and Features Work) would develop

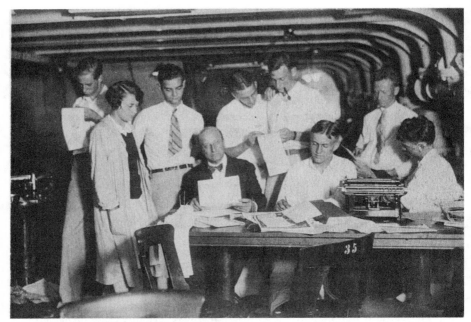

FIGURE 3.5. Editorial staff of the *Binnacle*, with the ex-governor of Kansas, Henry J. Allen, seated in the center. In Walter Conger Harris, *Photographs of the First University World Cruise* (New York: University Travel Association, 1927), no. 146.

"experiences from the cruise into articles adapted to different types of publication."[108] As the *Binnacle*'s own editorial put it three days into the voyage, the *Ryndam*'s student newspaper was to be "the laboratory of the school of journalism."[109] The night before arrival in a new port, students would be given "assignments," and these were printed in the paper in the days that followed. They would also report on American and world news, thanks to the paper's connection to the Associated Press. "No reporters in the world have had so wide and so alluring a field in which to search for that which is fit to print," boasted the paper.[110]

Thomas G. Brown was the Journalism lecturer, and he was also the *Binnacle*'s managing editor.[111] Brown had both practical experience in journalism and academic qualifications. He had worked at the *Philadelphia Public Ledger* and as the war news editor at the *New York Tribune* before serving in the American Expeditionary Forces in France, studying at the Sorbonne, and returning to the United States for a post as assistant professor of English at Dartmouth College.[112] Initially, it was Brown who gave the students their shore assignments and Brown who in all likelihood marked them.[113] But as the ship crossed the Pacific, Henry J. Allen began to take over issuing instructions to the Journalism students.[114]

Allen was the former governor of Kansas and the owner of several of that state's newspapers. His role as editor in chief of the *Binnacle* had been advertised in the lead-up to the *Ryndam*'s departure from New York, and he was later listed as its head of Journalism. Andrew McIntosh had selected him because he thought the *Ryndam* needed a "thoroughly practical man," but the intention had always been that these would be largely honorary roles.[115] Yet Allen's commitment to the *Ryndam*'s promise of pioneering a new method of international education was genuine. He had been a key protagonist in the establishment of the School of Journalism at the University of Missouri and had already traveled widely in Europe. He became a commanding and divisive presence on the ship. Pearl Heckel thought his influence was unhelpful and dangerous, because it was "wielded secretly and most adroitly under the guise of friendliness."[116] Yet the students mostly loved him.

The Journalism class members took to their subject with relish. The *Binnacle* is full of their adventures, with reports of students sneaking backstage at the Princess Theatre in Honolulu; going down to the docks at Pearl Harbor to talk with the US submarine servicemen; investigating the nightclubs of Shanghai; attending cockfights in Manila; witnessing swift justice at the police courts in Singapore and attempting to extract information from the British colonial undersecretary there; and talking their way past the guards at the palace of the sultan of the Malaysian state of Johore (Johor).[117] The student journalists met with the editors of various newspapers in the ports they visited, including the *Star-Bulletin* in Honolulu, the *Asahi* in Tokyo, and the Commercial Press Printing works in Shanghai. And they turned the *Ryndam* and its passengers into "the daily grist of news," interviewing even the night crew, the bakers, the stewards, and the stokers.[118] They profiled the faculty and paraphrased their lectures and filled the pages of the newspaper with in-jokes and letters to the editor—stoking controversies associated with students' antics as well as issuing editorials imploring them to engage in better behavior.[119]

DeWitt Reddick quickly impressed his teachers, so he was among the chosen few whom former governor Allen deemed "promising" enough to be given the responsibility of editing the paper, as were Charles Ladd's friends John Killick and Paul Robinson. In this capacity, the trio wrote the editorials that, sometimes with hectoring, sometimes with humor, both reflected and helped fashion student opinion on board the ship. As day editors, they also oversaw the hot and dirty work of actually printing the paper, assisted by the official linotypist, Arthur R. Blakely, who hailed from Fort Scott, Kansas.[120] Cramped in the ship's hold, they hammered type into place and stripped down to their underclothes to work on the rollers.[121] When the *Ryndam* departed New York, however, it had swiftly become clear that the original press would not be able to keep up with the demands of printing the daily paper, so an order for a new "vertical Miehle" was cabled to Los Angeles, where the ship would collect it. It proved to be a huge improvement and enabled a radically expanded print run. Capable of working on a restless foundation as well as hanging on a wall for storage, the Miehle was well suited to sea conditions.[122] Yet even it struggled to cope with bad weather in the Pacific. With the rolling of the ship, the "ink-roller carriage swung savagely on its hinges until the Texan-ranger day editor [i.e., Reddick] lassoed and tied it up," while the "Mergenthaler linotype, unable to stand the thirty-five-degree tilting, began to spit up slugs [as] . . . whole galleys of type cut loose and ran all over the shop."[123]

In selecting his editors, Allen gave clear preference to the male students. But his Journalism class was also full of women, as the bylines in the *Binnacle* attest.[124] They tended to be assigned writing tasks that focused on things like dress styles in Shanghai or arts and culture. Yet not all the women were prepared to be restricted to genteel pursuits. Laura Yaggy was particularly tenacious.[125] She was a nineteen-year-old from Hutchinson, Kansas, and a student at Smith College who was traveling on the *Ryndam* with her brother, Edward, a student at Yale University. She was active in the *Ryndam*'s Women's Council as well as other shipboard activities. Honolulu's *Star-Bulletin* described her as a "young lady of brisk and resolute manner" who "laid down a barrage of questions."[126] Like many of the *Ryndam* students, she was not only writing for the *Binnacle* but also sending articles back to the hometown paper, in her case the *Hutchinson News*.[127]

In their courses, Raber and Holling, Brown and Allen engaged seriously with the Floating University's professed educational philosophy of making student experience central to the learning process. While some lecturers, no doubt, gave less heed to these foundations, the *Binnacle* contains other examples of those who did.[128] Despite the initial academic disorganization, the predilections of individual faculty members, and the issue of student engagement, for the most part the academic side of the Floating University's program was effectively delivered. It was, however, only one element of the educational experience the Floating University had promised.

THE "EXTRACURRICULUM"

Like many of his contemporaries, President Charles Thwing believed colleges were sites not just of knowledge creation but also of character formation. That colleges remained highly competitive, gendered, and socially exclusive worlds was something frequently celebrated by their advocates.[129] Student "democracy" in the form of communal living and student-run activities was seen as crucial, because it stimulated both individual responsibility

FIGURE 3.6. The Globe Trotters jazz band entertaining aboard the *Ryndam*. In Walter Conger Harris, *Photographs of the First University World Cruise* (New York: University Travel Association, 1927), no. 988.

and the bonds of collective experience. This philosophy also informed the Floating University. For President Thwing, religious worship was a central part of this communal life, and the nonsectarian morning chapel service (where attendance was voluntary) was held on deck every Sunday at 7:30 a.m.[130] But for most students on the *Ryndam*, communal living meant student clubs, and these swung into gear soon after the ship left New York.

Charles Gauss started a jazz band called the Globe Trotters (fig. 3.6), in which he played the saxophone alongside a cornet, banjo, drums, and piano.[131] Their principal activity was, along with the *Ryndam*'s traditional Dutch orchestra, to provide music for the students' deck dances.[132] To begin with, Gauss thought his musicians "all were rotten."[133] But by the time the *Ryndam* reached Japan, the group had become good enough to play at the Oriental Hotel in Kobe, earning twelve dollars each for their troubles. On this occasion, the crowd was mostly from the ship, but the group's reputation soon spread, and they received several advance bookings from hotels along the *Ryndam*'s route.[134]

In 1926, jazz was still a relatively new phenomenon in the port cities of the world. Its potency was connected to how it made concrete the otherwise ambiguous notion of modernity. Associated with a paradoxical entanglement of emotional and social liberation, Black music, political change, American culture, and Old World decline, jazz—and the dancing that went with it—stimulated anxiety as well as excitement.[135] Along with other cruise ships of the interwar period, the *Ryndam*, with its crowd of well-heeled patrons and its own dance orchestra, both met and fed an international phenomenon already created by the distribution networks of the American music and film industries. The Globe Trotters took the Floating University's "extracurriculum" onto the shore at the same time that it brought the global tentacles of US commerce and culture onto the ship.

Gauss also signed up for the men's Glee Club. It, too, was formed in the first week of the voyage, and eventually it was judged sufficiently good to perform for 150 Japanese university students in Yokohama.[136] Gauss and his fellow singers had worked hard for the privilege, rehearsing three times a week at 8:00 p.m.[137] Their next performance was at the invitation of His Majesty, King Rama VII of Siam (Thailand). Offering a program of British folk and college songs, the Glee Club, sweating in their tuxedos, "did their best" in a hall with terrible acoustics. But in Holling's judgment they gave "the best interpretation of a cats' wedding on a dark night" he'd ever heard.[138] A Women's Chorus was also started, and both groups appeared in the program of shipboard Christmas entertainments (the women's group as the angels of the Heavenly Chorus), but they both folded during the second half of the voyage.[139]

The Planet Players were a more enduring group. Led by Mrs. Beatrix Prior, whose main qualification was that her son-in-law was the Hollywood actor Theodore von Eltz, it attracted many of the older women "tourist" passengers, including six in the production department and five in the costume committee.[140] Lucille Holling was among them, and she worked feverishly on costumes and set design. Her husband, Holling C. Holling, described with some relish the group's first production, *The Very Naked Boy*, which was staged as the ship made its way from Panama to Los Angeles. James McKenzie took the starring role, appearing suspiciously unclothed, half hidden behind a curtain with his head and bare arm and shoulder poking out.[141]

If this play dramatized a loosening of moral strictures as the *Ryndam* passed through the tropics, the script Holling wrote as the ship approached Panama explicitly mobilized racial caricature. As the *Ryndam* passed Honduras and the Yucatan, he had apparently been inspired by "a vision of russet-skinned people moving stealthily" through the forest. He set his play in a ruined Aztec temple in the overgrown jungle, where "black shapes break away from blacker shadows." A delirious American youth staggered to the top of an ancient pyramid and collapsed. Before him rose a scene of pageantry and human sacrifice that ended with the youth's own death. Titled *Aztec Fantasy* and performed as the Floating University crossed the Pacific, it was a thin proxy for the fears and excitement of Americans at sea.[142]

Blackface and racial caricature were similarly a feature of the various costume competitions included on the *Ryndam*'s calendar of entertainments. There was a Christmas pageant, a Halloween masquerade, and a Crossing the Line (of the equator) ceremony, as well as a farewell ball hosted by the captain.[143] Such events gave members of the cruise the opportunity to don costumes and masks and assume identities that loosened the usual codes of conduct. Cross-dressing was a favorite among the male students, and "many boys enjoyed dancing with their roommates and side-kicks who turned clinging vines and gold diggers for the evening in exotic feminine attire."[144] Common to the luxury cruises of the period, these events inverted the usual ordering of white, middle-class American life on land and pointed to a troubling of racial and gender categories en route.[145]

While several fraternity groups emerged, as did various state associations, a chapter of the DeMolays, a camera club, and various discussion groups, it was sports that most consumed the students' extracurricular energies.[146] By the 1920s, they had assumed an institutionalized place on most American college campuses. On the *Ryndam*, participation in physical activity was a requirement, and there were lots for the students to choose from, including deck tennis, golf, rowing machines, quoits, soccer, boxing, basketball, and wrestling.[147] Swimming lessons (fig. 3.7) were organized by Mrs. Bryant, dancing lessons by Miss Peters, and fencing classes were held by none other than Holling C. Holling.[148] And in various ports along the way, the "SSU" (for SS *University*) fielded baseball and football teams in games against local universities.[149] The program of compulsory physical exercise reflected both the contemporary belief that sports cultivated the physical and moral qualities of (white) American citizens and the anxieties about the bodily discipline and health of American youth on tour. In the inaugural issue of the *Binnacle*, an article with the somewhat alarming title "Regular Program to Guard Health of Students on Voyage" evidenced this clearly.[150] Mirroring the racial concerns that were finding expression in some of the theatrical productions, there was an early attempt to effect gender segregation, especially in the swimming pool.[151] But this was difficult to police: "in the warmer weather [the students] move about all over the ship in bathing suits and gym clothes," wrote McKenzie to his parents.[152] The program of physical exercise was short lived. When the *Ryndam* reached the tropics, it was impossible to enforce, with regular shore trips further disrupting the schedule. It wasn't until the ship left London and began to make its way across the Atlantic that serious athletic activity resumed.[153] Charles Gauss

FIGURE 3.7. One of the two swimming pools on the A deck. In Walter Conger Harris, *Photographs of the First University World Cruise* (New York: University Travel Association, 1927), no. 11.

was among those who returned to daily exercise in an effort, as he put it, to "get a little . . . surplus fat off" before arriving back in New York.[154]

OFF THE SHIP AND ONTO THE SHORE

The third component of the Floating University's experiential education was its shore program. The idea was that students on the cruise would "establish first-hand contact with places, peoples and problems, and . . . meet the leaders of thought and action in many significant centers of culture and of social and political development."[155] This was the dimension of the trip for which Professor James Lough had assumed official responsibility. In the second part of 1925, he and Andrew McIntosh had written to the Department of State, requesting its assistance.[156] After some consideration, it had told them it couldn't offer special help for what seemed to be a commercial undertaking, albeit one with educational claims. Undeterred, Lough and McIntosh contacted US diplomatic missions directly, notifying them of the Floating University's visit and requesting suggestions for local points of interest and "possibly means of taking care of so large a party."[157]

In some places especially, this generated an enthusiastic response. When the *Ryndam* students disembarked in Yokohama Harbor, for example, several hundred people greeted them on the dock.[158] English-speaking students from Japan's universities were assigned to guide the Americans during their visit, with forty even agreeing to sleep on the *Ryndam*'s deck while it was in Japanese ports. The US commercial attaché, it turned out, had written to the presidents of the local universities and chambers of commerce. At many ports, however, the official receptions hosted by municipal, governmental, or university bodies were combined with commercial sightseeing tours.[159] It was not Lough who organized them but rather the Phelps Bros. team, which, according to both Pearl Heckel and McIntosh, had seized control of "the management of entertainment and contacts on shore."[160] In turn, the shipping agency usually employed a locally based American Express or other tourist agent, the consequence of which was that the Floating University shore tours often followed a standard tourist program.[161]

The spectacle must have been astonishing: five hundred Americans pouring off the *Ryndam* and into various modes of transport, leaving in convoy for tours around the region (fig. 3.8). In Singapore, tenders carried the students from the ship anchored in the bay to the quay, where the group divided into two: half leaving in a train and half in the eighty or so cars waiting on the pier. Lillian McCracken got into a car with two of the other women students, and in convoy they drove "along beautifully paved streets in a good motor with [a] Malay chauffer" through the Chinese quarter and over the bridge into the European business district.[162] As they went, Mc-Cracken checked off the landmarks of the colonial port city: "beautiful municipal Bldgs. YWCA Hotels along the ocean front. Big clock tower. Statue of Sir Stanford Raffles . . . China town . . . native quarter where life from all

FIGURE 3.8. Motorcade carrying Floating University students through Havana Cemetery. In Walter Conger Harris, *Photographs of the First University World Cruise* (New York: University Travel Association, 1927), no. 42.

Asia is seen."[163] They passed the hotels and swung up Orchard Road through the residential section, where the green lawns and gardens of the colonial houses "were as luxuriously beautiful as were the homes themselves." Stopping briefly in the botanical gardens, where McCracken was taken by the "Snake Charmers in flowing white linen, turban and silken sash," the convoy continued north, driving for thirty miles through rubber plantations until it finally stopped at the factory of Nee Soon and Sons.

The smell hit them before they arrived. "Atrocious fumes," wrote Charles Ladd, "familiar to anyone who has been in a vulcanizing plant."[164] McCracken was fascinated, describing the tapped rubber trees and rubber production process and noting the participation of Chinese women in the sorting and drying of the rubber. The students were taken through the buildings and, after assembling for a photo, were allowed to wander among the rubber trees.[165] The printed shore program explained to the students that Nee Soon and Sons was among the largest shippers of rubber in the colony, and a few days later the *Binnacle* would make the connection between the process the students had witnessed and the tires that cushioned the ride of many American cars.[166] Before they left, they were treated to some of Lim Nee Soon's famous iced pineapple.

These commercial tours offered sightseeing as well as some prospects for adventure and new experiences, but they were hardly designed to facilitate firsthand contact with local people, and little attempt was made to integrate them into the curriculum. General lectures were, however, given to the students in advance of the ship's arrival at a new port. They covered the history, economy, geography, and people of the country about to be visited.[167] These were generally very well attended and were complemented by advance articles published in the *Binnacle*. The officially issued *Ryndam* logbook, in which the Hollings kept their journal, also contained short introductions to each port. Hilo on the island of Hawaii, for example, was described as offering "glimpses of primitive life," Singapore was the "Charing Cross of the East," and Leith in Scotland was the "headquarters of the Scotch whisky business."[168] As these excerpts reveal, efforts to prepare the students for what they were about to see frequently replicated the tropes of tourist scripts. James McKenzie acknowledged that it was through generalist books, pamphlets, and newspapers, as well as the professors' talks, that his knowledge and expectations were mostly shaped.[169] As Pearl Heckel put it, "The students [were] first prepared for what they [were] to see and, later, helped to an interpretation of what they have seen." Yet, as chapters 4 and 6 show, the students' own activities and ways of making sense of their experiences were often far more diverse than their teachers imagined.[170]

EXPERIENCE AND EDUCATION

The official shore program was not always popular. Ladd was unimpressed with the scheduled activities in Shanghai. It didn't help that the weather there was awful—drenching rain mixed with sleet and hail greeted the students' arrival.[171] As *The Student Magellan* (the *Ryndam*'s student yearbook) later put it, for the "movie-educated young American," it felt like a stage set for murder.[172] Ladd and his friends John Killick and Paul Robinson spotted what they called "a bad omen" before the ship had even docked: two Chinese students boarding the *Ryndam* with a greeting of welcome. Ladd thought this meant that "while in China [they] were to be close-herded by a body of these peripatetic questionnaires."[173] And he was right. Following the pattern of the ship's arrival in Japan, "thirty-seven leading Public Bodies and Educational Institutions" along with a brightly costumed brass band and a fireworks display greeted the *Ryndam* at the China Merchants' Lower Wharf. Ladd and the rest of the cruise members were then bundled into cars waiting at the dock and conducted to Nanyang University, where they were treated to what Ladd described as "some longwinded Chinese and American speeches."[174] These were followed by a reception and an art exhibition, and then an eleven-course lunch at the Oriental Hotel, which Ladd described as "rank tasting stuff."[175] He and his friends far preferred to skip the formal program and experiment on their own.

The stop in the Philippines had revealed what happened when the *Ryndam* students weren't "close-herded." Although they all piled into automobiles for a tour around Manila, many had peeled off before the official visit to the Legislative Building and the reception at the university that followed. McCracken attended and made friends with the local students, but the Hollings were both embarrassed that so few of the other Floating University members had come. Instead, the students had poured out across the city, where they were to be found on dance floors and in dining rooms. Little wonder, then, that the following day few of them were interested in attending the university's program of lectures, which had to be "condensed to short talks" due to sparse attendance.[176] Even the interuniversity sports competitions were often poorly attended. In Hawaii, for example, the local university had organized a program of events that included a military review, University of Hawaii versus SSU baseball, shooting and swimming competitions, and an exhibition soccer match.[177] But only four *Ryndam* students turned up to meet the one thousand assembled local students. The swimming and rifle competitions had to be canceled, and only seven members of the ship's baseball team presented themselves.[178] Most of the *Ryndam* students, it turned out, had preferred to go to the beach.

These incidents kicked off a debate about education and experience that would resurface again and again throughout the voyage. The term *tourists* had emerged early in the cruise as a means of classifying the members of the voyage who were not working for credits and who, as the *Binnacle* put it, had "reached a maturer age than that attained by those who, more by reason of youth than by reason of fact, are called students."[179] Tensions between the two groups erupted after the stop in Hawaii. "A tourist is out to see things," the editor of the *Binnacle* had written, whereas "a student desires to study objects and people." Which did the *Ryndam* passengers want to be? "You may travel around the world seeing things and learning little . . . or you may study civilization through [meeting] people and come back . . . an intelligent citizen of the globe."[180] The letters section of the paper erupted. "Don't you think that actual contact with the peoples of a country will give you a better understanding of their peculiar traits, of their ideals and ambitions, than ethnological study in a museum?" asked one correspondent, who signed as "One of Them." "You say yourself, 'The widest education may be obtained through intercourse with the people.' Surely you don't mean the kind of intercourse you'd get from looking closely for two hours at a stuffed bird or a pickled python?"[181] The writer had a point. The students had been promised firsthand contact and direct personal experience, not museum visits and official handshakes.

In many ways, this distinction between travel and tourism made by those aboard the *Ryndam* resonates with Harvey Levenstein's notion of the rivalry between cultural tourism aimed at personal uplift versus recreational tourism directed at pleasure. While the two overlapped, it was the latter, he argues, that transformed the former into something quite different from the high cultural immersion of the Grand Tour. The rise of mass transatlantic travel by the 1920s was a big part of this process, as was the increasing participation of women and, of course, students. Indeed, Levenstein argues that the explosive surge of touring college students in the 1920s helped preserve American cultural tourism, albeit in a mutated form.[182] However, while the *Ryndam*'s tourist-versus-traveler debate drew on, and in some ways helped produce, the phenomenon he describes, it did not map directly onto it. What was at stake for the student participants in the Floating University was what counted as "an education" and the means through which it could be acquired. Mobilizing the cruise's own distinction between firsthand experience and book learning, many argued that it was the experience of exploring off the ship that provided the very education in foreign culture the Floating University had promised them (though none noted that these explorations were themselves frequently structured by the contents of guidebooks). Having fun, by this logic, did not stand in opposition to cultural engagement. Rather, it was a means to achieving it.

Professor Oran Raber was a member of the committee appointed to deal with these tensions. Initially, he felt that the distinction being drawn between the two groups was an erroneous one. "A student is one who studies," he said. "Many of the so called tourists . . . study more than half of the young fellows who call themselves students."[183] But by the end of the voyage, he, too, had drawn a much clearer division. One of the results of the Floating University "experiment," he wrote as the ship approached New York, was that everyone learned "there is a difference between college travel and educational travel." One group "wishes to be able to display its knowledge before Harvard professors," while the other group "will be quite content to satisfy the ladies of Hutchinson, Kansas. And they have very nice ladies there, too."[184] The problem with the *Ryndam*, Raber felt, was that it was attempting the impossible task of reconciling these two different kinds of learners. Yet reconciling them was part of the voyage's pedagogical promise, and part of what not only the passengers but also the American public had come to expect.

Formal assessment was held in the lead-up to Christmas as the ship sailed from Java to Ceylon (Sri Lanka).[185] The faculty were certainly rigorous in its standards: no re-sits were permitted, and makeup examinations were to be granted only at the discretion of the instructor.[186] The results were published in the *Binnacle* toward the end of April. Of the 395 students who had enrolled in college-level courses, 281 (or 71 percent) were working for credit in one or more subjects, with 114 (29 percent) attending only for interest. This suggests that virtually all the college-age students aboard the *Ryndam* were taking the academic side of the cruise seriously enough to enroll for credit, at least in the first semester, although 15 percent of marks awarded were fails and 6 percent were for "incomplete work."[187] Full-year results were released after the *Ryndam*'s return to New York, and they told a similar story.[188] According to the *Binnacle*, the exams had passed off "with a surprisingly small number of casualties," although it also made clear that the conditions had not been ideal and that not everyone had been equally studious.[189] According to Dean George Howes, those who were "negligent in their work on board" the *Ryndam* were no doubt also negligent in their college studies onshore.[190]

The flamboyant antics of college students were in fact a familiar trope of interwar popular culture, and the American public seemed relatively tolerant of them.[191] Historian David Levine has argued that going to college had become part of a "culture of aspiration" to the extent that that youthful transgressions were accepted as part of a desirable process of network formation and upward social mobility.[192] As Ellwood Griscome, the *Ryndam*'s Public Speaking lecturer, later put it, "The student of a floating college is at heart essentially similar to one on land," and their stunts were "not unlike those occurring daily on many an American campus."[193]

Yet the Floating University students were not attending a land-based American campus. They were participants in a traveling "educational experiment" that had been launched with great fanfare and behind-the-scenes controversy. If the student body and the ship's company reflected the racial and social divisions of Jim Crow–era America, the student-versus-tourist debate highlighted a fundamental problem facing the venture as it traced its westward route. It was one thing to build excursions to botanical gardens and "practical" training into course design, to utilize the spaces of a ship for instruction and extracurricular activities and arrange for visits to local dignitaries in ports along the way. It was another thing entirely to formalize and regulate student explorations onshore. Dean Howes might have talked about the "mosquito bites" that were part of the Floating University's bold new pedagogical experiment, but the attempt to operationalize Professor Lough's idea on board the *Ryndam* in 1926 revealed unforeseen tensions inherent in the project. What exactly constituted "an education"? As students embraced the pleasures and possibilities of onshore experimentation, this would become a question that brought the Floating University into the spotlight of the American reading public in ways that threatened to further undermine its educational legitimacy.

4

Scandal and the Press

As the *Ryndam* sailed through the Red Sea, H. Dupree Jordan and DeWitt Reddick were hard at work at their typewriters. Back in their home states of Georgia and Texas, they each had been editor of their college newspaper, and both had paid their way through their undergraduate studies by working for commercial publications.[1] Now, the two of them were systematically writing to more than one hundred newspapers across all forty-six states represented in the membership of the Floating University.[2] Surely American readers would be impressed to learn that Joseph A. Taylor had undertaken a bicycle tour of Java? Or that David Inglis had been elected to the Student Council? Or that the whole Michigan contingent had been personally hosted by King Rama VII of Siam (Thailand)? The Floating University had been caught up in a series of scandals that were beginning to tarnish the reputation of the voyage. With the ports of Europe and the Mediterranean approaching, Dupree and DeWitt knew that the students would soon meet plenty of overseas correspondents eager for salacious accounts, so they were keen to offer good news alternatives.[3]

How would the Floating University's legitimacy be determined? If it was an educational experiment, what proposition was it testing? The official sponsorship of New York University had stood as verification of its educational character. But when NYU withdrew its support, it also withdrew one of the cruise's chief social warrants. Andrew J. McIntosh, Charles F. Thwing, and James E. Lough had not been especially worried by this. In lieu of credentialing from NYU, they had arranged for course credit to be given by the students' home institutions and increased their publicity efforts both across college campuses and in national papers. But in doing so, they had called on another form of social sanction, that of public opinion—or, more accurately, the American press. This meant that instead of academic peers or even the students themselves, it would be the newspapers that determined not only what counted as evidence in the Floating University's pedagogic experiment but also the criteria against which that evidence would be assessed.

SEARCHING FOR SOCIAL RECOGNITION

The American press had readily absorbed the Floating University's message that education on board the *Ryndam* was to proceed via the experimental method. Colleges had been "too bookish," relying too heavily on textbooks and lectures, the *Dayton (Ohio) Daily News* reported Professor Lough as saying in September 1926.[4] In laboratories, students could observe and discover things for themselves. The Floating University was to be a new kind of laboratory, one that would show rather than tell students about international history, economics, arts, trade, and politics.[5] Many reporters were attracted to what seemed to be a self-evident proposition: it was "easier for most persons to remember what they see than what they hear."[6]

Yet in some press reports, another note crept into this predeparture coverage. How would student discipline work under cruise conditions? The Floating University not only employed an experimental pedagogy but had styled itself as a pedagogic experiment. Several of the papers picked up on this. The *Hartford Courant* (and other newspapers subscribing to the Associated Press) called it "an experiment in democratic theories of education."[7] And, as the *Brooklyn Daily Eagle* noted, it would be via the newspapers that "educators throughout the country" would follow the experiment's progress and "check up on the results."[8]

McIntosh was not taking any chances. Understandably, many parents were anxious about saying goodbye to their children, and he had been careful to ensure that the students-at-sea could remain connected to their parents onshore. Letters from home would be forwarded to the ship en masse from two US addresses, regular "publicity scrapbooks" would provide updates on the voyage's progress, and copies of the *Binnacle* would be mailed home from ports along the way.[9] And for those in a hurry to get in touch with their families, there was the radio.[10] Radio at sea was still a developing technology in 1926, and it caught the imagination of many journalists covering the cruise: "The itinerant students," noted one slightly breathless reporter, "will be in daily contact with the folks at home, if they so desire, though the twain be separated by the diameter of the globe."[11] All these mechanisms ensured that the ship would remain connected to the shore.

On the eve of departure, McIntosh also took steps to ensure that the shapers of public opinion remained well disposed toward the voyage, inviting several newspaper editors and other "friends of the cruise" to dine with President Thwing and Professor Lough immediately before the farewell gala at the Waldorf Astoria.[12] Among those who had attended were Adolph Ochs, editor of the *New York Times*; Senator Hiram Bingham from Connecticut; Clyde Furst, secretary of the Carnegie Foundation (for the Advancement of Teaching); William N. Jardine, secretary of agriculture and recently retired president of Kansas State University; Willis J. Abbott, editor of the *Christian Science Monitor*; and John N. McCracken, president of La Fayette College. Also present was Henry J. Allen, ex-governor of Kansas, owner of the *Wichita Beacon*, and head of the Floating University's Journalism Department.

Courting the attentions of the American mass media was a perilous thing to do in the 1920s. Newspaper circulation boomed during the decade, jumping from 27 million readers in 1920 to almost 40 million by 1929.[13] But as readership increased, the number of papers declined as national newspaper chains began buying up and consolidating local papers across the country. With a central office, these chains provided syndicated news services to their papers, including stories and features written for a national audience. Consequently, many local and regional papers increased their coverage of national and international news as well as of Hollywood, sports, and finance.[14] At the same time, tabloid papers flourished. Often referred to as yellow or jazz journalism, their stock in trade was sensational celebrity gossip, crime stories, and accounts of sex scandals accompanied by illustrations and (often edited) photographs. The Floating University sailed at exactly the moment when the infrastructure for the national distribution of news developed, feeding a readership hungry for gossip and scandal. With students and faculty members signing up from colleges and universities in virtually every state of the union, the Floating University presented US newspapers with an attractive local angle on a national story. It proved to be one that had immediate and wide appeal.

HAVANA AND THE HONOR CODE

The *Ryndam*'s first stop was in Havana, where, according to the *Detroit Free Press*, the Floating University was to be "given its first test."[15] Would the city's reputation as a playground for visiting Americans seeking to escape the strictures of Prohibition prove just too tempting for the touring students? The inaugural issue of *The Binnacle* had announced that the campus-at-sea would feature the same form of student government "as prevails at many American schools and colleges."[16] Initially at least, there was to be "only one rule practiced, the rule that each man should act in a manner be-fitting honor and good breeding."[17] In place of punishments and regulations, it was to be "self restraint and student opinion" that would "discourage self indulgence and anti-social conduct which would bring either discredit or personal inconvenience upon this newest experiment in education." De-spite the rule of Prohibition in the United States, Dean Albert K. Heckel did not feel that the consumption of alcohol should be totally forbidden, only that the students should "practice a form of government based on self restraint."[18] It was overindulgence and the lack of self-discipline it reflected that he did not countenance.

As the *Binnacle*'s article recognized, an honor code relied on social sanc-tions of shame, loss of status, tarnished personal integrity, and lost pride. Heckel saw it as an expression of the Floating University's commitment to a form of learning that would allow the students to work out their own limits in relation to one another and the world. The discredit of causing damage to the Floating University's reputation would, in his mind, be sufficient disin-centive for potentially renegade students and sufficient punishment for mis-behaving ones. He did not, however, think that such misbehavior was some-thing that could delegitimize the entire venture. Indeed, President Thwing anticipated that the honor system was itself an experiment that would need "considerable time in which to prove itself" before it was either adopted or substituted for another plan. Obstacles would in all likelihood appear, but as Thwing put it, "new problems, as they emerge, will be solved."[19] In his view, student (mis)behavior was not automatically an invalidation of the wider project but rather an effective means of learning, both for those lead-ing the *Ryndam* and those traveling on it.

This distinction between experiment-as-method and ship-as-experiment was, however, lost on US newspaper reporters. In covering events in Ha-vana (fig. 4.1), they printed verbatim the statements about the success of the honor system made by Dean Heckel to the Associated Press. "I doubt very much if at any college in America with equal numbers of students there were as few cases of delinquency," he said. "The students gave the ordinary American tourist a lesson in dignity and self-control and they gave to the people of Havana an exhibition in which Americans could take pride."[20] US newspapers were certainly prepared (and even quite keen) to invoke the possibility of student ill-discipline, but—with just the wire messages from Havana to work with—in this instance, they could do so only by referencing its negation. "Only Few Fall for Lure of Bars," wrote the *Detroit Free Press*.[21] "Faculty [had] feared the worst," read the article carried in a Nevada paper, "but the results . . . were so splendid that every one on board the ship was happy and proud."[22]

FIGURE 4.1. Students lining up for beer at the reception in Havana. F. Gano Chance, Photograph Albums and Diary, 1926–27, Personal Collection of Garrison Chance, Columbia, Missouri.

The Floating University therefore left Havana with its reputation intact. As it passed through the Panama Canal and sailed up the West Coast of North America, it continued to be cast in the US press as a serious educational enterprise. An article carried by the *Christian Science Monitor* in mid-October, soon after the ship docked in California, judged that "the floating school seemed assured of success."[23] Its "collegiate atmosphere" was offered as proof: with sports activities, a Men's Glee and Ladies' Choral Club, a theater group, and above all the "clicking typewriters . . . heard in all parts of the ship," the *Ryndam* "picture[d] [a] Unique Campus Scene," admittedly novel yet also (crucially) recognizable.[24] At the end of October, as the *Ryndam* began the long voyage across the western Pacific from Hawaii to Japan, the *New York Times* published a piece situating the Floating University as one of a range of new educational developments in international education, placing it alongside highly respected initiatives for graduates such as the Rhodes Scholarships, Rockefeller Foundation grants, and National Research Council Fellowships; organizations such as the Institute for International Education and the Geneva School of International Studies; and programs for undergraduates such as the Open Road travel initiative and study abroad scholarships.[25]

So far, the University Travel Association's communicative strategies were doing a good job at managing its public image. But the way the US newspapers had reported the stop in Havana established an important principle. There, the Floating University had been measured against a form of moral conduct and was, for the most part, judged to have performed appropriately. But what was more important for the legitimacy of the undertaking was that the newspapers had established a behavioral standard of success. That it was one regularly breached on college campuses across the United States in the 1920s would prove largely irrelevant. It was a standard the contravention of which was crucial to the newspapers' business model and one they knew would attract their readers' attention.

THE "CONSTRUCTIVE MERITS OF MODERN DISCIPLINE"

Events, moreover, had not gone quite as smoothly in Havana as press reports suggested. James McKenzie recorded that "several students came on board so 'tight' that they had to be helped to their rooms."[26] And in Colón, Panama, the same thing happened, but this time one of the faculty members was "in almost as 'tight' [a] condition as the others."[27] By the time the ship reached Los Angeles, the *Binnacle* had reported that "the honor system does not work upon those who have no honor in their systems," referring elliptically to "a young man" who "had three times broken his word."[28] Pearl Heckel indicated that more than one student had "shown themselves to be un-equipped for the cruise."[29]

Recognizing a potential problem, upon reaching Los Angeles Dean Heckel attempted to take certain steps. He felt that quietly putting ashore seven of the most disruptive students before the ship left the United States would be easier to organize and would attract less public attention.[30] But despite Heckel's "strenuous arguments," Phelps Bros. cruise managers were not interested in his suggestions for managing a group of college students. They were more worried about the profitability of the voyage than its respectability, judging that the financial loss of refunding the tickets could not be borne. So the miscreants stayed on board. Pearl Heckel was convinced that this decision had the effect of making it known to the students that, whatever the academic administration said, "the cruise office was opposed to drastic discipline," and the captain had an "indifferent attitude . . . toward misconduct so long as it did not interfere with his own nautical regulations."[31]

Dean Heckel was forced to resort to other disciplinary measures. He insisted that one student be vouched for by six of his classmates to both provide a bond "indemnifying the ship's company from any responsibility" if it became necessary to send him home, and tell his father about these terms. The *Binnacle* backed him. While the student in question had an opportunity to "redeem himself in the atmosphere in which he lost his standing," read its editorial, the "members of the Cruise have an opportunity to become acquainted with the constructive merits of modern discipline such as Dean

FIGURE 4.2. The all-male Student Council. In Walter Conger Harris, *Photographs of the First University World Cruise* (New York: University Travel Association, 1927), no. 526.

Heckel advocates."[32] Heckel framed these conditions as "safeguards," but they represented a significant "modification" of the honor system. Upon the ship's leaving Los Angeles, he took further steps to establish a student council as a means of enabling what was elliptically called "intelligently directed self government."[33] Elections were held by a general ballot of the male students and three candidates ran for president, all advocating some form of honor code.[34] McKenzie judged Jim Price from Kansas to be the "best suited for the office," and in the end, it was Price who was elected. He was joined by ten other council members, who were to meet weekly when the ship was at sea (fig. 4.2).[35] All of them were men. Reflecting the gender-exclusive student associations that characterized the coed campuses of the time, a separate election for the women's council was held, though this group dissipated early in the voyage.[36]

But the disruptions on board continued as the *Ryndam* sailed west toward Hawaii. A handful of students colluded to conceal the identity of a stowaway who hid in full view, lounging about on the desk and eating alongside them. Neither the officers, nor the faculty, nor the cruise management seemed aware of his presence until they were told he had left the ship in

Honolulu.[37] Between Los Angeles and Hawaii, it also became evident that someone was stealing items from the staterooms. While castigating the culprits, the editors of the *Binnacle* reprimanded members of the cruise for leaving out their valuables: "You have been on this boat long enough now to discover that one of the educational opportunities of the trip is in the necessity it forces upon the student that they should learn how to do a few things for himself."[38] Although straining under the pressure of these disruptions, the language of the educational experiment still could accommodate them. But the faculty was increasingly prepared to institute rules. While Dean George E. Howes made clear he did not think "disciplinary methods" were desirable, he also made it known he was prepared to enforce them.[39] Little did anyone on board anticipate the events that were to follow.

"SEA COLLEGIANS STARTLE JAPAN WITH RUM ORGY"

On the afternoon of Thursday, November 4, the students and faculty of the Floating University gathered on the *Ryndam*'s hurricane deck, shivering in their woolen coats and peering out into the heavy haze that hung about Tokyo Bay, hoping to catch a glimpse of Mt. Fuji as the ship sailed toward Yokohama Harbor.[40] After nearly two weeks at sea, the American students were eager to go ashore, but it was 5:00 p.m. by the time the health inspection at Yokohama was complete, so cruise management decided to keep them all on board until the next morning. However, this measure failed to stop as many as sixty-five young Americans (according to one diarist) from climbing down the side of the ship on ropes to see Yokohama by night.[41]

A day later, readers of the *Detroit Free Press* woke to a sensational front-page headline: "Sea Collegians Startle Japan with Rum Orgy."[42] "More than a hundred students, among whom six girls were to be noticed, were doing intensive laboratory work this evening, in the bar of the Imperial Hotel," continued the article, cabled to the *Detroit Free Press* and the *New York World* from Tokyo on November 5. The notice itself was relatively short, but the *Detroit Free Press* took the opportunity to gather all the cable notices it could find: not only about the Floating University but about the iniquitous behavior of college students more generally on US campuses—the smoking of women and the drinking of men—to piece together an article about corrupt student morality.[43]

Soon the story had spread nationwide. While some papers echoed the sensationalist tone of the *Detroit Free Press*, the *New York Times* sounded a more measured note. "Denies Wild Drinking by Students Afloat," read its headline on November 8.[44] Speaking with the paper's correspondent in Tokyo, Henry Allen had "expressed surprise over the stories cabled to

America," noting that the general standard of the students' behavior was high while admitting that a few irresponsible members brought discredit to the whole ship. The *Winona Daily News* of Minnesota dismissed the escapade as "a minor incident on a so far most successful cruise."[45]

Correspondents for the *Chicago Tribune* and the *New York World*, it later turned out, as well as representatives of the United Press wire service stationed in Japan, had been at the bar of the Imperial Hotel in Tokyo and the Tent Hotel in Yokohama the night of the *Ryndam*'s arrival. There, they met some of the aggrieved students who had slipped overboard and loosened their tongues with a drink (or three).[46] Knowing promising copy when they saw it, the correspondents had fed the news back to the United States, where it had ricocheted around the wire networks. Two weeks later, further details filtered through to the *Honolulu Advertiser* via a dispatch from Tokyo to the Honolulu-based Japanese-English language paper, the *Nippu Jiji*. Not only had the *Ryndam* students had "a drinking party" but they had also stolen an automobile and driven to "the underworld districts of the city."[47] Somewhat more decorously, *Time* magazine called it a "drinking and 'necking' spree."[48]

Pearl Heckel was appalled, both by the behavior and by the attention it was attracting locally and back in the United States. She blamed the Phelps Bros. team, which had refused to accede to the faculty's requests to let the students off the ship in Yokohama.[49] The spectacle that their nocturnal drinking had created was exacerbated the following day: the Phelps office allocated most of the culprits to the group traveling to Nikko, and at the train stops they drank the sake offerings left at shrines along the way (fig. 4.3).

The repercussions aboard the *Ryndam* were immediate and significant. "Prominent Americans," wrote the *Binnacle* on November 15, "including those in official as well as those in the business and educational circles, declared that the exhibition by the delinquent minority had severely discredited us in Japan."[50] The American ambassador sent a notice to the ship stating that "the vandalism had done more to hurt the relations between the two countries than anything that had happened for fifteen years."[51] With the Floating University's social respectability called into question, the *Binnacle* acknowledged that "something would need to be done, not only to atone for the past so far as was possible, but to secure the future."[52] Finally, wrote Pearl Heckel, the "reluctant policy of the cruise office had to give way." Her husband expelled five boys immediately and turned fifteen others over to the Student Council.[53] Initially, the council voted only to curtail their shore privileges, but Heckel demanded it reconsider this verdict, warning that either some of the students be expelled or the council would be dissolved. It

FIGURE 4.3. The sacred red lacquer bridge at Nikko, Japan. Note the guards telling the student to get down from the raised area on the left. In Walter Conger Harris, *Photographs of the First University World Cruise* (New York: University Travel Association, 1927), no. 169.

was, in his wife's understated words, "a somewhat strenuous time."[54] In the end, four additional students were dismissed and the rest put on probation, with the unfortunate nine sent home in disgrace aboard the next available ship. The audiences for this disciplinary response were multiple. It was intended not only to reform student behavior and show appropriate contrition to wronged Japanese hosts, but also to appease an American public that was now following the *Ryndam* with a great deal of attention.

STUDENT LETTERS

Reading all these accounts from his desk at the *Flint Daily Journal* in Michigan, Joseph R. Taylor, whose son was a student on the *Ryndam*, definitely wanted some appeasing. On November 16, he sat down and wrote a letter to President Thwing, reporting the damaging stories in the *Detroit Free Press* as well as the "editorial matter criticizing the trip, based on cable reports" that had been sent out by the Newspaper Enterprise Association.[55] Taylor had, it turned out, been publishing in his *Journal* letters from the *Ryndam* written by his son Joseph Jr. as well as receiving regular cabled updates from him. Taylor sought assurance that discipline would be imposed.[56]

The return of the expelled students to San Francisco on December 1 set off another round of intrigue. First the story was picked up by West Coast papers. The *Los Angeles Times*, having interviewed the students, told how they were "not at all downcast about the situation" and "talked freely of the parties they say constituted an almost continuous program aboard the *Ryndam*."[57] The following day, the *New York Times* and other papers carrying the item via the Associated Press went so far as to name and shame the culprits (also reporting that two had jumped overboard in Honolulu and swum to shore).[58] Although noting the stories circulating in Asian newspapers with headlines such as "Floating University Lads in Rickshaw Wreck" and "Cut-Ups Powder Buddha's Nose," a jocular tone continued to characterize the report, with the students described as "almost as good space getters as the Harvard Lampoon staff."[59]

But when the first letters from *Ryndam* students began to arrive in the United States at the start of December, the American reading public soon had another story to titillate it. Taylor Jr. and DeWitt Reddick were not, it turned out, the only cruise members whose correspondence en route was being published by American newspapers. Laura Yaggy was writing for the *Hutchinson (Kansas) News*, James McKenzie's letters were being published by the *Chase County (Kansas) Leader*, and Margaret B. Lum wrote for the *Chatham Press* (New Jersey).[60] The size of the *Ryndam*'s mailbag conveys a sense of the sheer volume of correspondence traveling between the ship and the United States. Upon arrival in Manila, about fifteen thousand letters were delivered, just about matching the number received in Hawaii.[61] Although the University Travel Association continued its attempts to shape the image of the Floating University in the American press, its version was only one of many circulating in the newspaper columns and along the wire networks.

It was one of the student letters, forwarded to Henry Allen's own paper, the *Wichita Beacon*, and published there on December 2 that finally presented to the American reading public the juicy details of what had supposedly happened in Japan. Circulated widely across the country by the Associated Press, the letter told how drunk students had "insisted in [*sic*] visiting the royal suite of the Imperial Hotel, carried off an image of the Buddha from a temple and engaged in a free-for-all fight with Tokio policemen."[62] Newspapers like the *Chicago Daily Tribune* soon connected the dots between the expelled students' return and the new tales of vandalism, with *Time* magazine adding that "the U.S. consul, irate, had thereafter refused to receive Dean Lough."[63] Meanwhile, the *Brooklyn Daily Eagle* turned all these events into doggerel verse.[64]

In the face of this coverage, the cruise leadership attempted to mount a counteroffensive.[65] The Floating University's "friends of influence" were mobilized to reassert the *Ryndam*'s educational identity. True to its commitment to eschewing scandal, in mid-December the *Christian Science Monitor* carried a long piece by the professor of geography, Douglas C. Ridgley, which spoke of the "promptness and effectiveness of the organization for serious college work" on board the ship. Not mentioning the events in Japan, he described the relationship of classwork to shore trips and concluded that the "educational experiment [was] developing along promising lines."[66] And in early January, the *New York Times* published a three-page article by the president of Vassar College, Henry Noble MacCracken, that described the challenges facing American colleges and universities under the pressures of a 700 percent increase in college attendance since 1901. Experiment was needed, MacCracken maintained, but experiment would not come from the associations of professors and research councils. Rather, it was being "initiated by courageous spirits . . . who have faith in their own convictions and have built up groups of disciplines around them."[67] The "University Afloat" was one of these. Although "attended by unfortunate publicity" and "perhaps not fully organized," MacCracken judged it an idea that was "certain to bear fruit in the future."[68]

This publicity strategy was somewhat successful. Newspaper accounts, while mentioning the problems in Japan, frequently also cited Heckel's expulsions. But the students' antics had seized the imaginations of both US newspaper editors and their readers, and the broad coverage they had attracted ensured that the issue of student behavior was now closely associated with the reputation of the ship.

NEW YEAR'S EVE OFF THE INDIAN COAST

By Christmas, those aboard the *Ryndam* had realized this too. "The newspaper clippings from home began to overtake us," wrote Pearl Heckel, "and we felt very helpless."[69] Cables and parental letters from the United States had made their way back onto the ship, and their message was clear.[70] On the afternoon of December 24, as the *Ryndam* sailed between Java (now part of Indonesia) and Ceylon (Sri Lanka), Dean Heckel called a meeting of the male students, stressing "that the reputation of the Cruise [was] precarious, and that nothing must be done to aggravate the present situation."[71] Roused to action, the Student Council announced that an open forum would be held on January 9 after the stop in India to "discuss the Cruise in all its phases."[72] But in the meantime, New Year's Eve intervened.

It was just as well for the reputation of the cruise that on December 31 the *Ryndam* was at sea, making the three-day voyage between Colombo in Ceylon (Sri Lanka) and Bombay (Mumbai) on the west coast of India. Charles Gauss's diary recorded only that "a big New Year's dance was given by Mr. Phelps" and that "everyone had a good time and enjoyed it very much."[73] Naturally, Gauss's jazz band, the Globe Trotters, played. Lillian McCracken was equally succinct: "dance—frolic—gayeties (wine)—fun—more fun—Orangeade with the Smiths."[74] Full details of the evening's events only became apparent the following morning.

A group of boys, it turned out, had set off giant firecrackers in "the most combustible section of the boat deck"; others had climbed into the crow's nest; several others paraded around the promenade decks sounding "home-made ticklers and horns"; and still others engaged in "a wild party" involving a jar of peanut butter and Ping-Pong until dawn. Not surprisingly, a large number of the revelers had gotten drunk.[75] The *Binnacle* editorial of January 2 contained a full-throttled denunciation of this behavior:

> The most heart-breaking thing about the present-day youth in his cups is that he becomes a disgusting animal without even the sense of decency which belongs to the cleaner animals. He wobbles about bleary-eyed and witless, with drooling mouth and filthy person, a spectacle to make those who love him weep, because they know they will never forget him as he appeared in that moment of his loss of self-respect. We know of nothing so grotesquely out of harmony with every thing a gentleman should do as getting drunk. They sometimes call it "beastly drunk" without reference to the fact that the adjective slanders the better beasts when used in that connection.[76]

Reminding the *Binnacle*'s readers that the ship would soon be sailing back into the reach of the US press, the editorial warned that the Floating University project would "be ripe unto the harvest and our American friends, literally thousands of them, who have been reading about us at home, will be giving us the appraising eye."[77] Or, as DeWitt Reddick's roommate and fellow *Binnacle* reporter, Ellis H. Dana, wrote, "This is not time for pussy-footing either in words or actions. The crisis has arrived."[78]

In this light, the forum meeting scheduled for January 9 took on a new urgency. Cruise members of all kinds aired their views in "the American vernacular" during a discussion that continued until midnight.[79] Their recommendations included improving cooperation among "the various elements of government on board the ship"; a few days later, the front page of the *Binnacle* announced that student discipline would "Undergo Complete Change."[80] The Student Council was putting the whole ship on probation, with "any case of drunkenness . . . sufficient grounds for immediate dismissal of the offender." That the announcement came from the Student Council helped maintain the fig leaf of student control, but it was really operating at the direction of Dean Heckel and the executive committee of the faculty.[81]

Both groups were acutely aware that the legitimacy of the cruise now turned on how it was getting reported in the American press. "We cannot afford to run the risk to have this cruise again flouted before the eyes of the American public in unfavorable, disquieting and exaggerated headlines," ran the announcement in the *Binnacle* as the ship approached Aden (in what is now Yemen) in mid-January. "One unfavorable report may be enough to permanently establish for our venture a bad reputation and mark our effort as a failure."[82] The paper commended Reddick and H. Dupree Jordan on their efforts to send home positive articles that might provide an "effective antidote for the unhappy and somewhat sensational accounts" resulting from the stop in Japan.[83]

ET TU, BRUTE? ROME AND NEW YORK

But reports of even the best-behaved students could not counter a new set of rumors that by February had begun to circulate in US papers. On the twentieth of that month as the Floating University students explored Rome, the Rochester, New York, *Democrat and Chronicle* reported that plans were being made by an organization called the International University Cruise Inc. for a second around-the-world student trip, scheduled for that September aboard the Cunard Line's SS *Aurania*. Citing the "success" of the *Ryndam* cruise, still in progress, the organizers of this venture announced that on their trip, women would be admitted.[84]

That same day, the Associated Press carried an announcement from the University Travel Association in New York that was widely published in newspapers across the country. It stated that a second Floating University cruise would depart in 1927 and be male only. Although there was "no dissension on the present tour"—which, according to the UTA's new secretary, C. W. Lowack, was "working nicely"—parents had demanded a trip strictly for boys.[85] Two days later, the *Brooklyn Daily Eagle* was reporting the obvious—that the question of coeducation had "split the organization now running the floating university."[86] If Lowack and the Phelps Bros. group at the UTA were on one side of this argument, it was rapidly becoming clear that Andrew McIntosh, now back in New York, was on the other.

McIntosh had left the *Ryndam* in Hawaii; "matters of a business nature" were cited in the *Binnacle* at the time as the reason for his departure.[87] But his own explanation to ex-governor Henry Allen pointed to events much more colorful. "Some time before the trip started," he wrote, "the Phelps people obtained control of the organization." They were "over anxious in regard to registrations and insisted on taking some who had better not been taken."[88] The Phelps team did indeed have anxieties about recruitment, and these were well founded. They had written to the Holland America Line at the end of July to negotiate a cost reduction if the ship sailed under capacity.[89] But McIntosh alleged that six weeks before the trip, Theodore (Theo) Phelps quite suddenly announced that he, too, would be joining the students on the *Ryndam*. McIntosh offered to withdraw but was "induced to continue . . . under the faithful promise" that Phelps would not interfere. According to McIntosh, this promise was not kept. Only two days into the trip, the Phelps group "took charge of everything, including faculty," sidelining McIntosh, Charles Thwing, and James Lough as well as Deans George Howes and Albert Heckel. Thwing had always intended to leave the ship at Havana to return to the United States for a Phi Beta Kappa conference. But at Hawaii, McIntosh decided to return home too. He didn't tell anyone why he was leaving, "so that no one could start an agitation" in his favor.[90] That left Lough to continue as the nominal leader of the cruise. In practice, however, his influence was very limited. Despite being the "Father of the project," in Pearl Heckel's opinion, Lough "was <u>not</u> an organizer or an executive."[91] With power already divided between three deans, the Phelps Bros. running shore excursions, and Allen asserting his forceful personality, Lough became a marginal figure on his own cruise.

Upon McIntosh's return to the United States, and unbeknownst to those still aboard the *Ryndam*, he started a new organization, which he called the International University Cruise. Garnering financial support from the parents of one of the students on the cruise-in-progress, he set about arranging new faculty, brokering a relationship with the Cunard Line, and placing advertisements in the newspapers. In planning this second and rival voyage, McIntosh sought to correct some of the problems he thought were besetting the *Ryndam*. A recently built modern ship powered by oil rather than coal would provide better accommodations and service. One academic leader—the president of Kansas State Normal School, Dr. Thomas W. Butcher—would take charge of organizing an integrated teaching program, and only students who agreed not to drink would be accepted. No "free time" would be permitted, and all shore excursions would be guided.[92] But McIntosh was insistent that the cruise would take both men and women students. He was "absolutely convinced that the time is ripe for co-education on a trip of this kind."[93]

News of the organizational split swiftly made its way back to the *Ryndam*, which at that moment was in Rome, where the students had just spent the day in audience first with the pope and then with Mussolini. Allen shot back a response via the Associated Press, aligning himself firmly with the UTA. He listed three principal objections to coeducation: first, the presence of "companionable young women distracted the young men from their studies"; second, it had started "many courtships to varying degrees of intensity"; and third, "residents in foreign ports . . . not having reached American ideas of the emancipation of women, misinterpreted the meaning of the venture." And Allen's conclusion? "After five months of this experiment we are forced to the opinion that it would have been more effectual if the cruise had been confined to men."[94]

Allen's comments drew on the shifting logic of exclusion that had emerged in discussions of women and higher education in the United States. Although the percentage of women enrolled at colleges and universities increased significantly in the 1920s, women remained, in historian John Thelin's words, "second class citizens in the campus community."[95] They were frequently denied academic honors, excluded from student government, and prevented from taking on roles in campus life, such as editors and reporters on student newspapers. No longer was it their biological unfitness that was being cited by opponents, but instead the harm their presence brought to their male contemporaries. Allen's comments invoked not only the dangers that coeducation on the Floating University posed to the men on board, whom the women distracted, but also the dangers to the women themselves in the form of the sexual relations (and possible pregnancies) implied in those courtships of "varying degrees of intensity."[96] Off the ship as well, the women students were cast as agents of harm, endangering the legitimacy of the venture itself because of the misunderstandings their appearance (and indeed existence) generated in the places they visited.

This latter notion of the women students, with their cropped hair, makeup, dancing, and modern clothing, as vehicles or vectors of confusion and misrepresentation was common to the discourse on "modern girls" in the 1920s, both in the United States and abroad. As Madeleine Yue Dong wrote of Chinese women, there "was no sure way to tell the class of a young woman sporting the Modern Girl look, nor was there any guarantee of her high moral standing."[97] Upon landing in the port cities of the world, the dress, speech, and hair of those aboard the *Ryndam* drew local comment, both positive and negative. While a Shanghai reporter for the English-language *North China Herald* celebrated the "gorgeously apparelled youths and flappers . . . [who] contrasted very pleasantly with the [usual] rather liverish type of tourist," in the Netherlands Indies (Indonesia), *De Indische Courant* was highly critical of "the little maidens: [with] a bob or Eton haircut . . . [wearing] a lot of powder and lipstick, sports dresses and no knickerbockers at all."[98] The Floating University's female students were made to carry the weight of a set of associations that connected modernity with the United States and consumption.[99]

As the American papers picked up on these disagreements about coeducation, the *Ryndam*'s passengers also learned that McIntosh had resumed publication of his "bulletins." These contained excerpts from *Binnacle* editorials and accounts from students' letters, forwarded to him by their parents. Upon receiving copies of these bulletins, the *Binnacle* lampooned the "rich imagination" they evidenced, particularly when it came to the supposed studiousness of the students and the harmonious relations on board: "Meals are often neglected so that certain lectures will not be missed," read its hyperbolic summary of McIntosh's reports. "It has never been necessary to make rules about early retiring"; "Social distinctions do not exist."[100] Allen—already annoyed—took umbrage at being misquoted by McIntosh and fired off another angry telegram. In reply, McIntosh attempted to explain that he was trying "to boost the trip for your [Allen's] good and that of everyone on the vessel."[101] McIntosh recognized that the "editorials and those letters were exceedingly optimistic and in a way expressed the hopes of the trip rather than the actual facts, but . . . was not aware until the last ten days that many of the things that the students wrote about did not permanently materialize."[102] In an attempt to establish friendly relations, he explained his plans for a second cruise. But it was to no avail. Allen maintained his opposition to coeducation and his loyalty to the UTA. Meanwhile, McIntosh turned his bulletins into a lavish magazine, *The Floating University*, complete with photographs and student accounts of the voyage-in-progress. It became the platform for the promotion of the International University Cruise Inc.'s planned voyage.[103]

From the beginning of March, American newspapers began carrying notifications of two rival organizations, both claiming the legacy of the in-progress *Ryndam* voyage and both planning to launch a second cruise in September 1927. On the one hand, McIntosh, heading the newly formed International University Cruise, was advertising a coeducational trip, "the University Afloat," that would sail on the SS *Aurania*.[104] On the other hand, the UTA, now led by C. W. Lowack, was advertising a men-only cruise that would again sail on the Holland America Line's SS *Ryndam*, also leaving in September 1927.[105] Professor Lough was no longer mentioned.

MOONLIGHT ON THE SEA

Unsurprisingly, the American press pounced on this public disagreement, and Allen's February dispatch from Rome quickly made its way into papers nationwide. "There isn't a newspaper in the United States that hasn't car-

FIGURE 4.4. Students dancing on deck. In Walter Conger Harris, *Photographs of the First University World Cruise* (New York: University Travel Association, 1927), no. 981A.

ried [it]" was how McIntosh put it.[106] The story combined not only the thrill of betrayal but also the whiff of scandal, youth, travel, and romance: "Can it be that the learned gentlemen discovered for the first time that thing known as sex attraction?" read one widely circulated version (fig. 4.4). "Had they never heard or read that this same sex attraction functions more strongly on sea than on land?"[107] The presence of women in the context of other environmental factors—"moonlight on the sea, the wind from the palm trees, the temple bells around Mandalay"—made it easy to understand how study could seem unappealing, reported the *New York Times,* tongue only lightly in cheek.[108] The *Philadelphia Inquirer* came to a similar conclusion, judging that "anyone familiar with the intimate connection between romance and the sea might have foreseen the result."[109]

In this new round of reporting, the Floating University's high-minded beliefs in experimental pedagogy and environmental experience were beginning to be turned against it. As the *Ottawa (Ontario) Journal* reported on February 26, the cruise had promised that the "unique environment" of the ship and "the contact with the learned minds of many countries" would give "a cosmopolitan charm" to the *Ryndam*'s "rugged American intellects."[110] Yet in the hands of the reporters, environmental conditions were proving to be the venture's greatest problem. The presence of women and the influence of the moon and tropical winds sent studious minds sex mad, so ran the line. What could the sober educationalists really expect? As the *Journal* went on to point out, sentimental relations were not the only feelings fostered by the confined space of the ship; enmity, too, could result.[111]

Enmity, certainly, was being widely evidenced as former *Ryndam* shipmates turned against each other in the newspaper columns. The nationwide coverage of Henry Allen's Rome comments prompted what the *Brooklyn Daily Eagle* described as "a smashing retort" from Andrew McIntosh in New York. "This is a co-educational world," McIntosh told the paper, and the "verdict of modern educators in the majority of American institutions has been that contact with women working along the same lines of thought is normal and healthy, whereas contact with 'outside girls' may be more distracting."[112] The *Los Angeles Times* agreed: coeducation made "American life wholesome," while "unnaturally suppressed and segregated, sex becomes abnormal."[113] McIntosh even wrote to *School and Society,* the progressive education journal, arguing that "parents were willing to register their sons" for his second cruise, "knowing that they would be associated with women students of their own class and standards rather than seeking the companionship elsewhere of those not under the environment of the family group."[114] This was a thinly veiled reference to the imagined dangers that port city prostitution posed to wholesome American manhood. It made clear that although Allen feared sex on the ship, McIntosh was equally troubled by the possibilities of sex on the shore. Despite their disagreement, both men invoked tropes that played into broader anxieties about sexual morality in American colleges in the 1920s—what Paula Fass called the "frantic fear of sexual promiscuity, of the upheaval in social relationships and the destruction of definitions and limitations."[115] Same-sex relations were not even mentioned.

PROBLEMS IN PARIS

The *Ryndam* docked at the northern French port city of Le Havre on the morning of March 14, and its passengers made their way to Paris by train, arriving at Saint Lazare station and spreading out to more than a dozen different hotels across the city.[116] The US papers reported that many of the older cruise members had in fact arrived a week earlier, having traveled overland from Nice.[117] With the American press already making arguments about the dangerous effect of romantic environs on the hearts and bodies of young people, the story it ran about the Floating University's time in Paris was predictable. Certainly, the account was fueled by the many American journalists residing in Paris who eagerly interviewed ex-governor Allen, faculty members, and students, feeding their "exclusives" back via cable to the waiting editors in New York, Chicago, and Los Angeles. "Ship Students Reported Wed," ran the story's headline on March 16 in the *Los Angeles Times*; "Faculty Oppose Sea Co-Education," read its counterpart in the *New York Times*.[118] Now three cruises were brought up for discussion for 1927: one for men only, one for women only, and maybe one for both. But of course, what the papers were really interested in were the details. The numbers were spun in different ways: "12 Troths on the Ryndam"; "Trip Nets Two Marriages"; "the total might reach twelve, but . . . six the best for publication purposes."[119]

Newspapers in the United States exploded with Floating University news. Alongside this story about romance was another told by the students to the Paris correspondents: how members of the supposedly dry cruise had become intoxicated in Granada when the labels on the wine bottles got switched.[120] Also circulating were reports of poorly attended roll calls in Paris and students who preferred "night classes" in Montmartre to the scheduled tours of World War I battlefields.[121] "Floating University's Classes Thinned by Lure of Paris Cafes," read the headline in the *Tampa (Florida) Times*.[122] As one student told a reporter, "The only possible punishment was being sent home, in which case the Floating University had to defray our expenses and also make a refund. We knew they couldn't afford that much."[123]

While the students frolicked in Paris, the largely empty *Ryndam* sailed toward its home port of Rotterdam. Before it got there, yet another story erupted in the pages of the domestic newspapers. "Bubonic Plague Found on 'Floating University,'" read the front-page headline of the *Indiana (Pennsylvania) Gazette* on March 18, neatly wrapping up its coverage of this leg of the cruise with some political scare mongering: "the Socialist press is strenuously protesting against the admission of the Americans to the country, on the ground that they might cause the disease to spread."[124] The *Ryndam* had been forced to anchor at Waalhaven, flying the black quarantine flag.[125] Across the United States, the ship's "bath" was announced with varying degrees of hype.

Both Theo Phelps and Henry Allen, still in Paris, learned of these events via the American news correspondents who stopped them on the streets. The interviews they gave in return provided yet more fodder for articles reporting "denials" of illness and quarantine.[126] They also added to anxieties about the sexual and bodily health of Americans abroad. That the *Ryndam* was empty of students when it arrived in Rotterdam, and that it was two "coal trimmers" who had left the ship in Venice who were found to be sick, was immaterial to the American press. The Floating University continued to serve as good copy for reporters for weeks.[127]

Amid the cacophony of the newspapers' focus on the students' bad behavior, the glimmer of another approach could still be found. When the reports from Japan first made their way back to the United States, the *Harvard Crimson* had placed them in the context of contemporary college campus culture:

> The ports visited along the primrose path to higher education [are] not only opportunities to examine bizarre architectures and to pass off foreign language requirements, they are to be compared with the nocturnal diversions of big game weekends when everything but a desire to submerge dry and musty knowledge in the enjoyments of wine, women and song or at least song—is cast to the winds. And when those winds are of the seven seas the celebrations may last longer than a weekend and may be slightly more bacchus.[128]

The *Los Angeles Times* agreed: "Pranks of college boys in Yokohama, Harvard or Rome . . . make good headlines. However, they keep the world from going to seed. And what real American would have it different!"[129] In the 1920s, unruly student behavior was an established aspect of the popular image of American college life.[130] Although such antics were perhaps most strongly associated with elite private universities like Harvard, Yale, and Princeton, where the social side of college life was seen as central to liberal culture, they were also a feature of state universities, where fraternities and sororities provided means of performing and reproducing social stratification.[131] As the *Crimson*'s article suggests, by the 1920s sports had assumed a major role in university life, and athletic competitions against other schools were occasions for students to travel together in large groups. And at single-sex colleges, the practice of "weekending," or visiting between the men's and the women's colleges, became popular too.[132] From this perspective, the students' behavior on the *Ryndam* was unremarkable. "There was a certain amount of necking on board," explained George T. McClure to Camden, New Jersey's *Courier-Post* in March, "but not more than I saw at the University of Colorado last year."[133]

Yet all possibility of positively influencing the Floating University's image in the US press was rapidly receding from view. By March, the *Ryndam* had become an object of ridicule. Indiana University's musical revue lampooned the "activities of a group of college students on a world tour on a floating university."[134] The ship's reputation was now so well established that it featured in humor columns: "No co-eds on the floating university this year," joked the *Dayton (Ohio) Herald*. "The first cruise gave too much attention to the Romance languages."[135] Even support from the Floating University's "friends of influence" was beginning to wane. By the end of February, the *New York Times* was describing the "educational tour" as one that had "failed."[136] Only the *Christian Science Monitor* remained loyal.[137]

LOSING CONTROL

When, back in September 1926, on the eve of the *Ryndam*'s departure from New York, Professor Lough had referred to the Floating University as an "experiment in modern education," he understood it to be one that would test the viability of a particular "method of study": could experiences gained during travel be used as laboratory material?[138] Neither the merits of co-education nor the suitability of the honor system had been his concern. But Lough had not made clear how his pedagogic innovation should be assessed. In the context of NYU's withdrawal of its sponsorship and the commercial pressures that led to the influence of the Phelps Bros. team, and despite the founders' and others' best efforts to influence the press, thanks to the newspaper coverage that the Floating University received, it was the students' behavior that came to be seen as the measure of their learning. If students were drinking in bars, skipping lectures, and romancing with coeds, then they were neglecting their studies, or so the story ran. By this logic, the Floating University was found wanting. Or, to put it another way, the newspapers were unconvinced by the Floating University's educational legitimacy because it did not appear serious enough.[139]

The paradox, of course, was that the direct student experience (albeit in the bars) that was seen by the press as evidence of educational failure was the very thing the founders of the Floating University had initially championed as key to education (though they, too, might have preferred that not so much of it happened in bars). After all, it was through experiment in and with the world that Professor Lough thought students would learn, and certainly what the students were doing, even in bars, was experimenting. But by the end of the trip, the newspapers' focus on the ship-as-experiment seemed to have distracted even the faculty leadership from the experimental methods they had once championed. Perhaps Botany professor Oran Lee Raber was exactly right when he noted toward the end of the voyage that the trip had often "seemed like 550 different experiments not to mention the several major ones conducted by 'the Big Four' [the deans and president], the Cruise Management, the Captain, and (let us not forget) the Student Council."[140] For Dean Heckel's part, his experiment with student discipline at sea had taught him that it "demanded firmness without obstinance, conciliation without softness." With no college traditions to guide them, the students needed more than "mere educational theory."[141] And if Pearl Heckel blamed Allen's unwelcome interventions, the Vermont-born lecturer in English, Tom Johnson, judged Professor Lough's leadership to be at fault. "Lough is a pothering old idiot" was Johnson's opinion. In explaining why Lough had become a marginal figure once the *Ryndam* set sail, he thought there was "really nothing in his character or make-up that is worthwhile, except that personally he is harmless and represents the middle-class virtues well, and is an honest citizen and devoted parent, but what has that to do with the job in hand?"[142]

The newspapers' insistence on studiousness as the measure of the Floating University's success reflected a shift taking place more broadly in US higher education. According to historian Roger Geiger, the "peer culture of the 1920s placed greater value on one's associates than what one learned," and this was celebrated as an aspect of elite liberal culture as against the mass or professional education.[143] But at the same time, university leaders across the country were beginning to turn against the excesses of the "extra-curriculum" and the perceived hedonism of campus culture. As University of Chicago President Rupert Maynard Hutchins put it in 1931, "College is not an athletic association . . . [it] is an association of scholars."[144] In arraying the *Ryndam* students' (mis)behavior in opposition to the possibility of learning, the newspapers' reports served to reinforce US universities' increasingly monopolistic claims that it was their degree programs, rather than student experience, that authorized knowledge of the world.

5

America's Classroom

On the morning of November 22, 1926, Lillian McCracken awoke to find that the Floating University had arrived in Hong Kong. Sampans were gathered around the *Ryndam*, salesmen were climbing onto its decks via rope ladders, and beggars were waiting on the dock below. After breakfast, and under a brilliant sun, she and her fellow passengers were ferried across to Victoria (Hong Kong) Island, where they were met by automobiles that drove them along the bay and through the hills before depositing the party at Hong Kong University. After a reception by the president, Lillian was placed in the hands of two of the twenty female students who attended the university: an East Indian girl who had completed her schooling in "the French Orient" and a Chinese girl who was about to head to Columbia University in New York for graduate studies. McCracken enjoyed their company immensely, but after only an hour the visit ended, and she was bundled back into one of the waiting cars to return to the ship. Captivated by what she had seen of Hong Kong so far, she asked her driver not to go to the docks but instead to take her to the American Express offices so she could get some money, "and thence to the Lane Crawford Department Store tea rooms"—a "lovely place" where she was served sandwiches, fancy cake, and coffee "by little Chinese men" dressed in white jackets and trousers.[1]

The Floating University had promised that it would teach American students to be world-minded. But what "world" were they learning to know? Although the ship's emphasis on experience came into conflict with both the universities' and the newspapers' ways of authorizing knowledge, all three institutions operated within a set of background structures and assumptions about the expanding footprint of US global power. As McCracken's exchange with the students at Hong Kong University suggests, the routes along which the *Ryndam* sailed, the people its passengers met, and the activities they undertook were shaped by the cultural, military, commercial, and epistemic geographies created by the United States' emerging dominance on the world stage.

GOING WEST

The *Ryndam* followed a route that had only recently been popularized by the advent of around-the-world luxury cruises. In 1922, not one but four luxury liners had sailed from New York to great fanfare and publicity.[2] Leaving at the end of the popular—and for the shipping companies, highly profitable—summer season of Atlantic crossings, their westbound journey enabled American passengers to head south just as the weather in the United States was cooling. Stopping first in Cuba and then traveling through the recently opened Panama Canal, the ships visited Los Angeles before crossing the Pacific to Hawaii. They caught winter in Japan and China but soon returned to the tropical climate of the Philippines, the Dutch East Indies (Indonesia), Singapore, Siam (Thailand), and India. Traveling through the Suez Canal into Egypt and Palestine, the cruises delivered their American passengers to the Mediterranean and Europe with the spring weather before heading home across the Atlantic in time for the shipping companies to free the vessels for the next transatlantic summer season. As the pressures of US immigration restriction forced these companies to innovate, such tourist routes became increasingly important to their business models. In leasing the *Ryndam* to the University Travel Association in 1926, the Holland America Line was hoping for a publicity splash that would help it cash in on the new and growing student cruise market. For the Floating University, however, this Panama-enabled route had other consequences. Sailing west meant that before they visited foreign countries, the *Ryndam* students encountered the United States' own national and imperial footprint—or one version of it.

During the first few days of the voyage, America's coastal southern states slipped unseen past the starboard side of the ship as the Floating University's passengers struggled to compose their seasick bodies, find their luggage, and make themselves at home.[3] The *Binnacle* reported that a terrible storm had ravaged Florida, killing more than a thousand people and making as many as thirty thousand homeless.[4] Otherwise, with only white southern students on board, the contemporary divisions of the American South did not appear on the ship's horizon.[5] But the politics of racial segregation and technological mastery in the United States' peripheries quickly did.

Coming immediately into range was Cuba, shrouded in a "tropical blanket of heat."[6] The stop there was brief, but it was long enough for an automobile tour of Havana and a reception in the tropical gardens. From the window of her car, Lillian McCracken noted the "mottled citizens: jet black West Indians, Cubans of a light chocolate, Americans, Spaniards etc."[7] Tom Johnson found the city itself dirty and old, the streets narrow, and the houses crowded together. This he put down to the influence of Spanish rule.[8] But he, like Holling C. Holling, was also struck by the flowers everywhere and by the "Color! Color! Color!"[9] Occupied by the United States following the Spanish-American wars (1898–1902), and then again from 1906 until 1909, Cuba had suffered an economic collapse in 1921 that forced it to turn to the United States for financial assistance. The number of American tourists, who had been visiting the island since the 1910s, had increased rapidly thanks to Prohibition, and whole industries had grown up around them. This made it easy for the *Ryndam*'s passengers to navigate the shops, improve their wardrobes, or purchase tobacco.[10] Some of them certainly enjoyed the hotel bars. But there is no evidence that anything in this short, frictionless stop challenged their sense of themselves or the role of their country in the region.

At the end of their day in Havana, the students reboarded the ship, ready for the trip through the Panama Canal. This was an eagerly anticipated event. The canal had opened in 1914 after a costly, complicated, and drawn-out construction process, during which relations between an interventionist United States and the Panamanian government had grown increasingly fractious. Celebrated as a strategic as well as a technical achievement, it dramatically shortened the sea journey between the East and West Coasts of the United States and reduced its cost.[11] As the *Ryndam* made its way slowly through the canal's three locks, students covered the ship in search of a vantage point.[12] They clung to the rigging and the ladders, and some even perched in the crow's nest. Sitting on the hurricane deck, his legs hanging over the side, DeWitt Reddick was as eager as any of them. He marveled at the water fifty feet below him, "surging and eddying around" the ship and carrying it "into the air at about 1 foot a second."[13] On the shore, the soil was red, and Tom Johnson noticed that every inch that was not cultivated or cleared was "a mass of tangled vines, trunks, roots and leaves, whose names [he had] no idea about." He admitted to being "much more impressed than [he] would have imagined [he] could be by the magnificent feet [*sic*] of engineering."[14]

Although Charles Ladd found the canal a little disappointing after all the hype, he, too, understood clearly that this massive construction project was very much an extension of US power. He also noticed the racial division of labor that enabled it: in Colón, Panama, the whites were in the minority, and most of the commerce was carried out by "Hindu, Japanese, and Chinese venders," while the "natives [were] very poor."[15] This hadn't escaped Tom Johnson's attention, either. While the engineers were mostly white Americans, the canal workers were "West Indians, negroes," Chinese and "natives."[16] These workers were not, of course, permitted to enter the Balboa Club in Panama City, where the sign above the swimming pool read, "America Needs Healthy Children."[17] Reddick drafted a newspaper article on the "gold" and "silver" classifications that demarcated spaces for whites and "coloureds."[18] At only their second stop, it was clear to these students that the canal's technological triumph over nature was reinforced by white American claims to civilizational superiority.[19] This seemed to be a timely reassurance given that on the *Ryndam*, white bodies were vulnerable to the heat. Leaving Balboa, Panama, it was almost the only thing Lucille Holling could think about. Everyone slept on the decks in an attempt to survive it, but even that brought little respite.[20]

Escaping the tropics, the *Ryndam* steamed toward Los Angeles, where an additional thirteen students and faculty members were to join the ship's company. For many of the passengers, this was their first encounter with the American West. The *Binnacle*'s writers portrayed Los Angeles as a technocratic triumph of American engineering much like the canal, a place where "man's conquest of nature is exemplified." The development of San Pedro Harbor, the suction dredges filling up the flats toward Long Beach, the guaranteed water supply, and the newly opening oil fields and orange groves were the signs of "civilization" brought to the desert by American ingenuity.[21]

And of course there was Hollywood, through whose motion pictures the Floating University's passengers had already come to know themselves and the world. They took a guided tour of the studios' simulacra, stepping from the Orient to a Russian tavern, to a suburban backyard, and then into a London street, delighting in the dramatic shift from "the land of make-believe to the everyday traffic of Hollywood."[22] Nothing encapsulated the sense of human triumph better than the recently completed city library. The students "looked in wonder at the large cream-colored pile of windows and stucco that rose from the head of Hope Street."[23] Topped by a pyramid decorated with a colorfully tiled image of the sun and with plinths featuring idealized figures, it projected the confidence of the city and its inhabitants in a way that seemed alien to those from the East Coast and Midwest.

Dominion over the environment was the keynote in the students' accounts of California. None of their stories made any mention of the people who had long inhabited the region and on whose backs the nation was continuing to be built. The population of Los Angeles tripled in the 1920s, with migrants pouring in from the Midwest and Mexico.[24] By 1930, the city had the largest Mexican American population in the United States, and although the African American community was small, it was steadily increasing.[25] Although racial-exclusion laws governed where these communities could live and go to school, their members were nonetheless visible on the city's streets. American First Nations people were present too (and being subjected to assimilationist policies and indentured-labor laws), regardless of what was seemingly implied by films such as *The Vanishing Native* (1925) and the "Mayan" architectural and design motifs that publicly invoked their disappearance.[26] And then there were the Japanese. Despite immigration restrictions, their numbers in Los Angeles were growing, and in California anxiety about their presence was acute. But for the affluent white students of the Floating University, LA was simply the furthest extension of a supposedly white nation.

NOT A FOREIGN COUNTRY

With these examples of the apparent civilizational triumph of white America behind it, the Floating University sailed for Hawaii. In advance of the ship's arrival, the *Binnacle* had presented its readers with an account of the islands' history, proceeding from "discovery" by Captain James Cook in 1788, through unification by King Kamehameha in 1791 and constitutional monarchy in 1840, to revolution and Hawaii's subsequent proclamation as a republic in 1894. This Whiggish trajectory culminated in peaceful annexation to the United States in 1900.[27] Facts about the islands' exports were given—they were the leading sugar center in the world and annually shipped more than thirty million US dollars' worth of pineapples—pointing to a modern economy now animated by the United States.[28] For Dean Albert K. Heckel, the Hawaiian Islands were not only an extension of manifest destiny: "without conscious policy [t]he United States has carried her flag continually westward," he told the students in a lecture, first as the *Ryndam* sailed across the continent and now as it traveled over the seas. They were also a strategic link in an emerging geopolitics. The coming century would be the "Pacific Era," Heckel concluded, and in that century Hawaii would be of vital importance.[29] He was alluding, of course, to the rising power of Japan.

Before the *Ryndam* even docked in Honolulu, the *Binnacle* had decided that Hawaii had a "race problem." Of a total population of 275,884 in 1921, it listed 42 percent as Japanese, with significant communities of Chinese (8 percent), Filipino, Portuguese (27 percent), "American" (13.5 percent), Asian-Hawaiian, and Caucasian-Hawaiian people. The "native" community was the smallest, at just under 8 percent of the total population.[30] With the "steady increase of the Japanese . . . this American territory will eventually be controlled by an electorate of an alien race," warned the student paper. There might even be a "Japanese governor" of the forty-ninth state![31] Meanwhile, the newspaper's guide to Hawaiian customs and language evoked a population of colorful and exotic locals, and a meeting of the male students to discuss a subject "of interest only to the men of the Cruise" alluded to the possibilities of sexual allure.[32]

As the ship rounded the Hilo breakwater, DeWitt Reddick could not quite believe his eyes. It was seven o'clock in the morning, and in the distance he could see Mauna Loa, the highest peak in the Pacific, lit up "like a field of glowing copper." Before him lay Hawaii, "a painting in green." As the *Ryndam* drew into the dock opposite the US Naval Radio Station, a group of Hawaiian girls, dressed in white and carrying leis made from orange flowers, began singing for them. Still eating his breakfast, Reddick poked his head out of the dining room porthole so as not to miss a thing. After disembarking, he and his classmates rode in a long motorcade through the main streets of Hilo and up Kilauea Avenue. Just outside town, the convoy pulled into the gateway of what turned out to be the Kapiolani School.[33] As the cars slowed to a stop, they were greeted by lines of singing children waving American flags. The boy from Texas was astonished: "Here, was a mingling of races such as [he had] never seen before—Chinese, Japanese, Filipinos, Hawaiians, part-Hawaiians and Americans—all mingling together, attending the same school." A grinning student went from car to car with a basket of native fruit. Then the cars started their engines, and they were off again, driving up toward the crater of the volcano, passing fields of cane that grew past a man's head.[34] This was a sight very different from what Reddick had so far seen, either at home in Texas or in the territories of US colonial rule. Here, too, were unmistakable signs of American economic and technological development, but what was the status of these mixed-race and seemingly happy people, waving their American flags and singing?

Various activities were organized for the students during their stay. The Geography class visited a twelve-thousand-acre sugar plantation, and Economics students watched the unloading of goods on the docks under the guidance of the University of Hawaii's instructor in commerce, Cecil C. Tilton, who made sure they understood that the islands' trade with the United States was not classified as foreign.[35] Then they proceeded to the production line of the Hawaiian Pineapple Company, "one of Hawaii's most modern organisations." But as soon as they could, most of the *Ryndam*'s passengers "hastened to the Waikiki beach."[36] Actually, many of them then hastened elsewhere, finding Waikiki itself "disillusioning," being too shallow and insufficiently sandy.[37] Two students hitched rides around the island of Oahu from "natives" and spent the night sleeping on the beach, breakfasting with a "gang of Philippine road-builders."[38] Others lounged in the cafeterias.

On the second day, the Floating University was invited to a reception hosted by Hawaii's governor, Wallace Rider Farrington (a former newspaper editor appointed to the post by President Warren Harding). "We have no more race problem than does Kansas," he told the visitors, dismissing the "mainland papers" that "grabb[ed] up anything even mildly startling about the Japanese and blaz[ed] it forth in scare heads and extra editions." "The only disturbing factor in the Japanese situation in Hawaii is the presence of the alien language schools," Farrington had said, and "the antidote is found in the American schools which every Jap youngster is required to attend."[39]

Albert Taylor, the librarian of the islands' state archives, was equally on message. "Hawaii is the one place on the face of the earth where our western civilisation has come in contact with the aborigines and has . . . raised them to equality with the whites"; it is "the finest example of the ideals of American expansion."[40] For settlers like Farrington and Taylor, the visit of the *Ryndam* was an opportunity to showcase the close relation between Hawaii and "the mainland" and advance the cause of official statehood. For them, the uncertain border between outside and inside could be fixed through the logic of cultural and economic development. "The American civilisation and religion offers a much higher type of living," pronounced Farrington, and young Japanese want "modern opportunities and modern good times."[41] This was the same message Reddick had seen presented at the Kapiolani School: it was culture and economic development, not biology, that was the defining characteristic of national belonging.

Yet it was clear, even to the *Ryndam* students, that all was not quite as Farrington and the brief stop at the school had made it seem. The Japanese consul spoke of the difficulty that "the educated Japanese" faced in finding work.[42] The Sociology class visited a Honolulu school in which racial ordering was obviously in evidence, and two members of the faculty witnessed a Korean immigrant committing suicide.[43] Nonetheless, Farrington's robust statements prompted a mea culpa from the editors of the *Binnacle* and an opportunity for them to acknowledge the benefits of the laboratory method. They had been "too cocksure," they confessed. The paper had "honestly believed that it knew all about this problem" from having "read about it in the grave books of . . . profound gentlemen" and having "studied it in California." But, confronted with "actual experience" in Hawaii (and the forceful presentation from the governor), the editors had been "unlearning what California and the guide books had taught us to believe." There was no

Japanese problem in Hawaii. Through education and access to "American standards of life," the Japanese there were becoming Americans and "losing their taste for Japanese ways." Hawaii, they had discovered, was "a foreign land," but it was "not a foreign country."[44]

With such temporal and spatial framings, the students of the Floating University sailed across the shifting and permeable borders of nation and empire, home and away, past and present, self and other. The stop in Hawaii showed them that education and culture, as well as technological improvement and territorial rule, were tentacles along which US influence extended. "American civilization" was the means through which "foreign" peoples, otherwise cast as "backward," could be incorporated into a "modernizing" twentieth-century world, and perhaps also into "America." Perhaps that was part of the reason the Planet Players gave a minstrel show as the *Ryndam* sailed toward Japan, seeking to restage the racial categories that in many ways had been troubled in Hawaii. The End Men ("Buttercup," "Snowball," "Bones," and "Tambo") wore blackface, and ukulele playing as well as hula dancing featured in the program.[45] Veiled comments in letters to the *Binnacle* as well as the ship's official photographs suggest that the cross-dressing hula dancers may have been a little too risqué for some of the cruise members, but there was little critique of the crude stereotypes on which the show relied.[46]

ARMS OF THE STATE

As the Floating University made its westward progress around the nation's past and present territorial holdings, it did so in the company of the US military. Navy airplanes buzzed the *Ryndam* as it approached Colón's Limon Bay, thrilling the students by flying alongside the ship, only a few yards above the water (fig. 5.1). Nearby, three submarines were periodically visible as they emerged from and then disappeared beneath the water.[47] Indeed, the whole Panama Canal Zone operated as a military-civilian community overseen by a governor who had been a senior officer in the Army Corps of Engineers.[48] Approaching Los Angeles, the *Ryndam* encountered yet more of the US Pacific Fleet, this time at target practice: huge battleships "belched great columns of black smoke" and gave off deafening roars as they shot leaden missiles at floating targets, while the *Ryndam* "steamed serenely through the gauntlet."[49] Hawaii, too, was full of members of the US armed forces, who had welcomed the students with a military band on the pier, given them rides in their cars, and taken them on tours of the radio station at the naval base.[50] And when the *Ryndam* arrived in Hong Kong, it

FIGURE 5.1. Airplanes buzzing the ship as the Floating University passes through the Panama Canal. In Walter Conger Harris, *Photographs of the First University World Cruise* (New York: University Travel Association, 1927), no. 73.

found one of these warships (the USS *Huron*) stationed in the harbor. The *Binnacle* reported that yet others were steaming toward Shanghai to provide protection to the foreign trading concessions there.[51]

Nowhere, however, was the US military presence more evident than in the colony of the Philippines. Upon disembarking from the ship, James McKenzie was offered a lift by a woman driving a Hudson coupe. She turned out to be Mrs. McClellan, the wife of one of the captains in the US Air Force, and she drove James and his friends out to the airfield to inspect the planes and talk with the men. The next day, the cruise visited Fort McKinley, where the Filipino troops paraded for them, and also the Malacanag (executive building), where they heard a stirring address by Admiral Kitelle of the US Navy.[52] Without planning it, the Floating University had sailed into Manila on "the big social night of the year," the one that eclipsed New Year's Eve and Christmas.[53] It was the night of the US Army–Navy football game, and servicemen had gathered in Manila to hear the final score, cabled in from halfway around the world.[54] Charles Ladd was lucky enough to be invited to the Army and Navy Club, where wine flowed freely all night and the rivalry between members of the two military branches was intense. The final score finally arrived at seven o'clock the next morning—a tie.[55] More than one student noted the contrast between the military personnel making their way home and the hundreds of thousands of devout Filipinos streaming toward La Luneta Park to witness the crowning of the Virgin of Antipolo.[56] The next place the students would encounter the reach of the US armed forces in such numbers would be in Europe, in the war cemeteries of the western front.

The footprint of the United States' consular and diplomatic corps was even more extensive than its military one.[57] In planning the voyage, Professor James E. Lough and Andrew J. McIntosh had asked for the support of the State Department. They had even managed to enlist C. Bascom Slemp, a former Republican congressman from Virginia and (until March 1925) secretary to the US president, to help them seek visa waivers by writing directly to various American embassies abroad.[58] Lough had also attempted to interest the emerging international organizations of the period, sending a copy of the University Travel Association's bulletin to the League of Nations' International Committee on Intellectual Co-operation (which in 1926 became the International Institute of Intellectual Co-operation, or IIIC).[59] But the committee did not reply, and the State Department had declined to give the voyage its official assistance on the grounds that it would have to do so for all similar trips. Reports of the Floating University's antics in Japan had only added to the latter's reluctance to lend formal assistance to the venture.

All this changed, however, in the second part of the Floating University's trip, thanks largely to the representations made by Addison E. Southard, the US consul general in Singapore.[60] He had met Mrs. Elizabeth Lippincott McQueen (one of the *Ryndam*'s "tourists"), the Hollings, and other members of the cruise at a luncheon hosted by the British governor, Sir Laurence, and his wife, Lady Ella Guillernard (to whom Mrs. McQueen had a personal introduction).[61] At that lunch he'd learned more about the nature of the student trip and resolved to use his influence to correct the negative impression it had generated by writing to all members of the US Foreign Service at the ports it was to visit and "giving them such information" as to open their previously closed doors.[62] The students were mightily impressed by the official hospitality that resulted, and by the efficacy of what Southard had called "an intelligence system by which the State Department in Washington keeps a finger on all parts of the world."[63] Owing to his interventions—and revealing the role informal networks played in enabling access to official diplomatic support—the Floating University students were hosted by US ambassadors and diplomats at receptions in Jerusalem, Cairo, Malta (near Sicily), Athens, Rome, Naples, Algiers, Málaga (Spain), Berlin, and London, among other places, and some of these events were quite large-scale affairs (fig. 5.2).

FIGURE 5.2. Reception for the Floating University hosted by US Minister to the Netherlands Richard M. Tobin. In Walter Conger Harris, *Photographs of the First University World Cruise* (New York: University Travel Association, 1927), no. 827.

INFORMAL EMBASSIES

For all their reach, however, the US military and diplomatic services played a minor role in the passengers' experience of the Floating University's voyage. Much more significant were the "European" hotels—the informal embassies of Americans abroad. After the *Ryndam*'s passengers arrived in port, the first thing they did was make their way to the nearest such hotel, turning, as *The Student Magellan* (the *Ryndam*'s student yearbook) later put it, "respectable hostelr[ies] . . . into a college pow-wow, with students in the lobby, students in the dining room, students at the desk seeking stickers, and a few more affluent students in the rooms."[64] At the Seville-Biltmore in Havana; the Washington in Colón; the Moana in Honolulu; the Imperial in Tokyo, the Tent Hotel in Yokohama, and the Kaihin in Kamakura, Japan; the Majestic in Shanghai; the Hong Kong Hotel; Raffles in Singapore; the Hotel der Nederlanden in Batavia (Jakarta); the Grand Oriental Hotel in Colombo, Ceylon (Sri Lanka); the Heliopolis Hotel in Athens; and the Excelsior Hotel in Rome, the pattern was the same.[65]

With imposing frontages, capacious rooms, and the latest technologies (such as the electric light and the electric fan), these hotels offered the material and cultural comforts of home in foreign settings (fig. 5.3). The familiar food they served provided a welcome break from the "monotony of cruise lunches" while their English-speaking staff were greeted with relief by the Americans.[66] In the hotels' luxurious spaces, the *Ryndam* passengers found an easy sociability that offered the thrill of new environments moderated by a familiar mode of exchange. "We stretched our legs in comfortable chairs and ordered the bell-boys around" was how Charles Ladd put it.[67] As sites of racialized labor and stratified sociability, the hotels stood as microcosms of the interwar colonial and commercial world.[68] For those on the *Ryndam* who could afford to rent a room, the space "in which to spread out without bumping into the narrow sides of the stateroom, [and the pleasure] of bathing in fresh water" were doubtless also welcomed.[69]

When evening fell, the students flocked to the hotels' dance floors.[70] In Hong Kong, Lucille Holling headed out to dance in the company of the vice-consul and one of his friends, only to find other members of the cruise already there "in full force."[71] The evening had been intended as a formal affair, but it did not remain so for long. With all the swagger of youth, Ladd and his friends "tagged" girls away from their partners (a practice of interrupting or cutting in without an introduction).[72] "The British gasped" and "not a few frowned," resenting the Americans for "hogging the show," but Ladd and his countrymen "went merrily on." The Americans were bested at the Raffles hotel, however; several students were "elbowed off the dance floor" by a local couple, and others suffered unpleasant remarks from

FIGURE 5.3. View from the door of Queen's Hotel, Kandy, Ceylon (Sri Lanka). In Walter Conger Harris, *Photographs of the First University World Cruise* (New York: University Travel Association, 1927), no. 389.

"supercilious English men and women." "It's Dance or Die," ran a headline in *The Binnacle*. The student reporter had interviewed a resident American girl, and this had been her assessment, not of dance-floor diplomacy, but of the Singaporean social scene: "If you can't dance there is no social life."[73]

The US diplomatic service might have provided the Floating University with one entry point to foreign cities, but the expanding reach of American culture and commerce offered another. Like the American films that by the 1920s were being distributed widely across Southeast Asia, American jazz preceded the ship across the Pacific. It had been carried by, among other agents, African American musicians seeking opportunity and escape from the racial violence of their homeland. Ladd and his friends encountered this in Hilo when, upon settling down to a meal of "chop suey" in a Chinese restaurant, they heard familiar sounds wafting in from outside. Looking at one another in amazement, they rushed to the windows to see a big bus driving up the street "with streamers along the running board telling everyone that the 'Original California Minstrel Show' was in town." Leading the show was a "big negro in shining silk top-hat" who, it turned out, was not from California but Alabama.[74]

The global prevalence of jazz did not, however, simply represent the obliteration of local cultures by the new foreign forms. Local traditions were already diverse, and jazz, too, had been hybridized and creolized.[75] In Japan, Russell Wertz had been surprised when, escorted by the Japanese reporter from the *Osaka Herald*, he arrived at "a glistening marble shanty on the Times Square of Osaka." There, he found foxtrots and kimonos, men clad in suits, and a Japanese jazz band singing "Show Me the Way" in a perfect American accent. This was a cosmopolitan culture he understood. To his mind, the faces, sparkling with good humor, "did more to assure one of the non-existence of a yellow peril than a thousand public addresses on either side of the question."[76] At the Silver Bell nightclub in Tokyo, meanwhile, Jack Eakin of New Jersey was dancing the Charleston for a group of geisha.[77] In fact, the dancing services of Eakin and his partner, Mary Eikel of Texas, were in high demand.[78] The craze for the Charleston, which had only just run its course in the United States, was being taken up abroad, and almost everyone wanted to see it—even the king of Siam (Thailand).[79]

It was a hot tropical night in Bangkok, and all the cruise's male passengers were sweating in their tuxedos in the Thai Royal Theatre ("whoever invented the Tuxedo was a northerner," cursed Holling), even as they gaped at the loincloths (*chong kraben*) worn by the members of the court.[80] They were gathered for an evening in which, somewhat incongruously, the *lakon* and *khon* dramas would be performed alongside various acts by the American students.[81] Having been presented with the dubious efforts of the Glee

Club, King Rama VII was keen to see the dance about which he had heard so much. Jack and Mary were asked to do the honors, to the sounds of the Globe Trotters' saxophones. "It wasn't bad," judged Holling. Irene Haines kept a close eye on the king's face. From his "pleased expression," she was "sure he enjoyed it," and Laura Yaggy described him "nearly fall[ing] out of his royal box" with enthusiasm.[82] Holling, however, said the King had later intimated quite the opposite.[83] In the port cities of the world, jazz and the Charleston served as the Floating University's cultural calling cards, with the Globe Trotters playing for the visiting Americans and locals alike.

It was on these dance floors, and in the hotels' lobbies and dining rooms, that the American passengers met a cosmopolitan set of circulating European and American officials, international tourists, and local elites. Some of these fellow travelers were glamorous: at the Majestic Hotel in Shanghai, the students bumped into the crown prince and princess of Sweden, and at the Hotel Principe de Asturias in Málaga, they met the queen of Spain.[84] But more often than not, they met people who were very much like themselves. At the Kaihin Hotel in Japan, Glendon H. Roberts and his friends bumped into "Mr. Fuller," an American also undertaking a tour around the world whom they had already encountered in LA.[85] At Shanghai's Majestic Hotel, Charles Ladd and his friends met a writer named Phil Harrison, who had spent many years in China; he proceeded to show them the city's nightlife.[86] Like these Americans, the *Ryndam* students made the hotels their unofficial headquarters. Following escapades into the markets or the countryside, they inevitably retreated to these places, assured of finding a comfortable chair, a good meal and a dance, the possibility of gossip, and the likelihood of a meeting with their own countrymen.[87]

AGENTS AND EXPERTS

In places such as Singapore, the grand hotels were actually where most of the resident Americans lived. Employed by the Standard Oil Company, rubber companies, or international banking houses; running insurance firms, banks, and English-language newspapers, or commodity and agricultural export agencies; or dealing in agricultural products from sugar mills or cane fields, these Americans were the agents of US commerce and culture abroad.[88] The *Binnacle* was careful to underline just how important these US companies abroad were in the production of the commodities that by the 1920s had become increasingly central to American consumers.[89] The rubber that provided cushioned comfort to American cars came from the estates of the Malay forests, where it was harvested by "Coolie labour" before being sorted and rolled in Singapore.[90] The graphite that filled American pencils was mined in Ceylon (Sri Lanka) and pounded into a coarse grain in Colombo by "native" women who received three-quarters of a rupee a day.[91] The tin for the cans that had become ubiquitous in US food preservation was produced in British Malaya (states on the Malay Peninsula and the island of Singapore) and the Dutch East Indies (Indonesia) as well as China and Siam (Thailand). As Elmore Peterson, the Floating University's economics professor, told the student newspaper, the United States' consumption of these items relied on a global system of production in which manual work was done by people from "the lands of the brown, the yellow, and the dark-skinned races" and the executive work by men from the United States and Europe. Peterson called it "the romance of the trade of one great division of the world called the Orient and the Far East."[92] Although the *Binnacle* noted the paltry pay of the workers who re-coaled the *Ryndam* by hand in the port of Moji (Kitakyushu), Japan, and of the "coolies" who, in the factories outside Shanghai, pounded sulfur on a rock to make firecrackers, it also reported that these workers were happy for the money.[93] The paper's reporters and editors seemed not to understand that the factories and plantations supplying US markets with rubber and tin and oil (many owned and run by US citizens) were reliant on mostly Chinese but also Japanese, Tamil, and Filipino indentured or otherwise unfree labor. Their vision of a global system of capitalist production was mostly in keeping with the model of civilizational development they had seen in action in the Panama Canal Zone.

American experts and advisers were as much a part of this system as were executives and owners.[94] Nowhere was this more apparent to the students than in Siam (Thailand). Although independent and never formally occupied by a European power, the country had, much like China, been subjected to unequal treaties for decades. According to King Rama VII's American adviser on foreign affairs, R. B. Stevens, "modernization" in the form of centralization, the establishment of a privy council, the abolition of slavery, and the construction of railways had been a way for the kingdom to "make a nation out of herself."[95] Many of those offering counsel to Rama VII in this ongoing process had "been taken from American universities," including several members of the royal family who had themselves studied in the United States as well as in Britain.[96] For the fresh-from-the-Philippines students on the Floating University, there was a real sense in which the much-lauded "enlightened" rule of the House of Chakri was both recognizable and admirable. It was a sense that was no doubt enhanced by the thrill of English-speaking Asian royalty who, to American minds, lived and dressed like movie stars.

The *Ryndam* and its passengers were very much part of these networks of expertise. Albert Brunson MacChesney had in fact already met King Rama VII when, as Prince Prajadhipok, the monarch stayed with the MacChesney family in Chicago during a 1923 visit to the United States. It was on this visit that Prajadhipok had made Albert's father, Nathan W. MacChesney—a lawyer, special attorney general for Illinois, and trustee of Northwestern University who was well connected in Republican circles— his country's consul general in Chicago. And Albert was not the only one who arrived in Bangkok with a connection to its royal family. Several cruise members from Kansas carried letters of introduction from Mrs. Kittel (Lucy Goldschmid), who had lived there with her first husband, a mining expert. Professor Peterson and Mr. A. Bishop Chance had already made personal acquaintance with Prince Pra-ong Chao (Phra Ong Chao) Dhani, the recently appointed Oxford-educated minister of education, whom they had met at a Rotary Club dinner in Kyoto.[97] Not only in Siam (Thailand) but across Asia, preexisting connections to American experts abroad gave students on the Floating University a point of entry into international life in foreign cities. Charles Bagnall spoke Japanese, because he had grown up in Japan while his father worked for the General Electric Corporation installing the first electric lights in Tokyo.[98] Professor Carl W. Rufus (the Astronomy professor, also from Michigan) and Mrs. Rufus had spent ten years at the Chosen Christian College in Korea, teaching mathematics and music, respectively, and William Edwin Haigh (head of the medical staff) had served as a military surgeon in the Balkans during the Great War and was epidemic commissioner for the League of Nations.[99]

Schools, churches, Rotary Clubs, Masonic associations, Eastman Kodak branches, newspaper offices, banks, shops, movie theaters, ice cream parlors, and other outposts of US culture and commerce helped produce this world of Americans abroad. The *Ryndam*'s passengers called in on all of them. And almost everywhere they went were offices of the American Express. Not only did the company "accommodate the students in the exchange of money," but its travel agencies organized many of the Floating University's shore excursions, which in turn included visits to American-owned or -operated sites.[100] An American Express agent even sailed on board the *Ryndam* between Colombo and Bombay (Mumbai).[101] In many ports, the company's branches functioned as a central social hub for visiting Americans. Nowhere was this more the case than in Paris. While there, Charles Ladd made a habit of regularly "repair[ing] to the American Express Company's office." Between 10:00 a.m. and noon, "everyone goes" there, he discovered, "especially after a night spent in sightseeing and revelry."[102]

As Paul Robinson knew, American college ties were crucial links in this world, joining the US heartland to the edge of Asia and beyond.[103] One of the first things Robinson did after arriving in Tokyo was look up A. M. Mizzlewitz, the editor of the *Japan Advertiser* and his former classmate at the University of Missouri. "Mizzie" also turned out to be an old friend of two other Floating University students—Jack English and Bob Dalmeyer—the three having belonged to the same fraternity.[104] He organized a Japanese dinner for them all at the Imperial Hotel with several "distinguished Americans" resident in the city, and the following night he conducted them to the Silver Bell nightclub. It catered directly to a foreign clientele, serving fried eggs and ham and hosting geisha dancing. There, the young Americans spent the evening eating, dancing, and picking up and tossing the women "from one boy to another, to the accompaniment of [their] excited screams and laughter."[105] The *Ryndam*'s passengers could so easily navigate the United States' cultural and commercial empire in Asia precisely because they shared the class and race background, the gendered sociability, the college ties, the fraternity networks, and the geopolitical imaginary that underpinned US "dollar diplomacy" during this period.[106]

EDUCATION AND MORAL REFORM

As Lillian McCracken's encounter with the students at the University of Hong Kong revealed, by the 1920s these college ties ran in two directions. Sailing from Hawaii to Japan to China, the Floating University traveled along a set of long-standing educational connections linking the world to the United States and the United States to the world. Local universities en route often hosted the visiting students, arranging lectures and formal receptions as well as sports competitions. In Japan, Shanghai, Batavia (Jakarta), and Egypt, they also provided English-speaking student guides, forty of whom in Japan had even agreed to sleep on the *Ryndam* while it was in port.[107] These were the eager students that Ladd dismissed as "peripatetic questionnaires," yet they knew a great deal more about the United States than the *Ryndam*'s students knew about them, as a formal discussion staged in Shanghai revealed.[108] "The manner in which those Chinese students caused us to look like school children . . . made me fairly sick," a *Ryndam* student was overheard to say about the debate held aboard the ship on November 16.[109] Laura Yaggy was shocked to find that one of her English-speaking guides in Bangkok was a Princeton graduate.[110]

If the Floating University students displayed their ignorance in such encounters, its Public Speaking professor knew better. Lionel Corker had taught English at Waseda University in Tokyo, and he was well aware that many of the Japanese professors welcoming them had themselves studied in the United States. The official lecture program at the Methodist Episcopal Church in Kamakura included Jiro Haranda, who had studied at the University of California before becoming a curator at the Imperial Household Museum; Yusuke Tsurumi, who had made several trips to the United States to study its railways and had only just returned from a lecture tour promoting Japanese-American relations; Yasaka Takagi, who had spent time at Amherst College before becoming professor of American government and history at Tokyo University; Dr. Tatsunosuke Ueda, who had completed his doctorate at the University of Pennsylvania and returned to teach at the Tokyo University of Commerce; and Dr. Riichiro Hoashi, who became professor at Waseda University after completing his PhD in Chicago.[111]

Like Professor Lough, Hoashi was a follower of the educational ideas of John Dewey, which he had first encountered through his own teacher, Tanaka Ōdō, who had studied under Dewey at the University of Chicago.[112] Hoashi translated Dewey's works into Japanese and published books arguing that the Japanese education system should do more to foster students' individual development. Those *Ryndam* students who attended the reception hosted by President Yoshinao Kozai of Tokyo Imperial University at the Sanjo-Kaigisho (Faculty Club) might also have heard echoes of Dewey's philosophy in his address.[113] In an era of rising tensions between the two nations, Kozai told the Americans he hoped that cooperation and contact among college-educated people across the "wide world" might open their "mental eyes" and that seeing "various peoples face to face" would facilitate "a better understanding of the races, nations, and individuals."[114]

Despite being one of the "tourists" on board the *Ryndam*, McCracken loved this dimension of the Floating University's shore program. She went to virtually all the university events, took diligent notes, and attended the associated receptions hosted by local branches of the Young Men's Christian Association.[115] In Japan, the National Committee of the YMCA had helped organize the Floating University's program, offering the services of its hostels to the students throughout their visit.[116] Even Ladd had cause to avail himself of them one night when, having attempted to ride bicycles from Kobe to Osaka, he and his friends had gotten lost in the dark. Taking pity on them, a local policeman led them not to a hotel or even a police station but rather to "a beautiful modern building," on top of which glowed a neon triangle—the emblem of the YMCA.[117]

Like missionary-led educational undertakings such as the Christian colleges in Canton and Shanghai, the YMCA was one of the institutions of cultural and moral reform that had been projecting American values across the Pacific and into Asia since the end of the nineteenth century.[118] In these international contexts, its more "democratizing" agendas came into tension with the British YMCA's traditional focus on serving resident European and Eurasian communities. Perhaps unsurprisingly, the American approach was much more attractive to local populations, and by the mid-1920s the well-resourced North American YMCA had funded and helped run an extensive network of branches in India, China, and Japan. For the most part, the branches were locally led, racially integrated, and more concerned with "uplift" and social work than religious conversion. Their approach did not, of course, make them any less a vehicle for the spread of American influence.[119]

This was abundantly evident in the Philippines, where the YMCA's work of "uplift" was very much aligned with the imperatives of colonial rule.[120] However, in Manila the American students found not one but six YMCA buildings, together claiming over five thousand members. Unlike the branches in China and Japan, the YMCA in the Philippines was still segregated in 1926. There was an American-European Y, a Filipino Y, a Chinese Y, an Army and Navy Y, a students' Y, and a city Y—all, in the words of the *Binnacle*, "serving the class of members for which they are designed." "We are trying to make men out of the boys of the Philippines," Mr. Turner, the local secretary, told the *Binnacle*.[121] Much as in Hawaii and in the Philippines too, education (and with it, public health, legal regulation, and economic development) was a key branch of the "civilizing mission" of the United States' progressive rule (fig. 5.4).

Rising early one morning, McCracken traveled south with a Mr. Archie Woods to Cavite Province to see their nation's progressive rule in action.[122] As they drove, they passed "villages & villages of the thatched houses . . . all set apart 6 ft from ground." After climbing a shaky ladder made of bamboo, they visited the home of a local Filipino teacher of domestic science.[123] She would have attended one of the American- or European-led medical, research, and educational institutions that by the mid-1920s were operating across the globe.[124] From the Estación Experimental Agronómica in Cuba and the Culion Leper Colony in the Philippines to the American universities of Beirut and Cairo, these institutions were both sites in which American and European obsessions concerning disease, race, gender, and public health were advanced and incubators for national independence.[125] They drew in foreign teachers, professionals, and missionaries such as Archie Woods, who contributed to the uneven exchange. In the process, they produced the English-speaking graduates who consumed the "modern" products, staffed the junior schools, and served in, and contested, the administration of government; in some cases, the graduates also traveled to the United States and elsewhere to continue their studies. Very often, it was students from these institutions who greeted the *Ryndam* in port,

FIGURE 5.4. Filipino teachers. In Walter Conger Harris, *Photographs of the First University World Cruise* (New York: University Travel Association, 1927), no. 242a.

"close-herded" its passengers, and—as discussed in chapter 8—sometimes also pushed back against the traveling Americans' expectations. Although McCracken seemed only dimly aware of this complex infrastructure that underwrote her encounters, she endorsed what she understood as its developmental effects. Sitting down with the Filipino teacher and her "good-looking" brother in Cavite Province, she reported eating "delicious cakes" and bananas. "Both well educated," she noted approvingly; "—speak good English." And, invoking the temporal logic so common to civilizational discourses, she noted that, displaced onto the landing, their "<u>old</u>" mother sat, wearing "two very meagre garments one dark and <u>not</u> pretty," clutching her "knees drawn up closely" to her chest.[126]

In launching the Floating University, Professor James E. Lough had wanted to use travel experience as his students' laboratory material. But the "world" his students experienced was one produced by the power relations both shaping the United States at home and extending its influence abroad.[127] This was a world that US universities and their graduates helped fashion. Their social networks structured commercial and cultural exchange, and their specialized knowledge built systems of governance and trade, laying foundations for the uneven terrain that would dominate the postwar world.[128] The expanding university empire of expertise worked to extend the empire of Jim Crow and the unequal exchanges of dollar diplomacy, and this was as true for the Floating University, which cited the centrality of direct experience, as it was for the land-based institutions that championed authorized knowledge.[129] DeWitt Reddick wrote for the American press, the Globe Trotters played on the dance floors of port-city hotels, and at every port in which it stopped, the *Ryndam* temporarily altered the local economy.[130] These exchanges were by no means one-sided, as the hybridization of jazz shows (and as chapter 8 discusses further); but they were unevenly structured, and the experiences the voyage presented to the students both reflected and helped reproduce these geographies of power. By projecting an image of the United States as white, well bred, and well heeled, not only did the Floating University sail along the currents of interwar power relations, it was deeply entangled in making the world it was learning to know.

6

Students of Empire

Leaving Lisbon, the Floating University's lecturer in English, Tom Johnson, was surprised at just how far "behind the United States and England" most of the southern European countries he had visited seemed to be concerning their capacity for self-government. They all had the same start in the sixteenth century, he wrote to his mother, but only England had been able to maintain its colonies, "because only England ha[d] the sense of Evolution— that is the capacity to suit her polices to her changing needs." Of course, England had lost the American colonies, he acknowledged, but "after all, they were of the same race as England herself."[1] The Floating University trip had given Johnson "a feeling far more nationalistic than [he had] ever had before." Certainly, he believed that the "international attitude [was] very necessary," but he thought the blame being heaped on the United States for its wealth and economic success was largely unjustified. Although he knew that the nation had its own version of government corruption, he really did not think it could be compared with what he had seen in Portugal. Frankly, the rising tension in Europe made him glad he "happen[ed] to be an American and a member of one of the really powerful nations of the world."[2]

The world that the Floating University encountered was one shaped by US culture and power, but how did those on board make sense of it? What were the lessons drawn from the voyage? As the *Ryndam* traced its westward route, they learned a version of world-mindedness that was more about their nation's emerging place in the interwar international order than it was about friendliness and goodwill.[3] Encountering European colonies in East and South Asia, they embraced the United States' role as an imperial power, albeit one that was on the rise, animated by modern methods and ambitions. What they then found in the ancient and European worlds served as the antecedents of this national story. For most of the Americans on board the *Ryndam*, these lessons in the imperial underpinnings of interwar internationalism were what the Floating University's experiential education ultimately affirmed.

LITTLE IMPERIALISTS

At the time of the *Ryndam*'s sailing, the *York (Pennsylvania) Daily Record* wrote that "three great experiments in colonial administration [would] be studied on [the ship's] visits to the Philippines, the Dutch East Indies, and India."[4] However, even before the Floating University left New York, the students had fitted themselves out in the dress of white men in the tropics. The recommended clothing list for men included a tuxedo, two linen suits, two white drill suits, a couple of pairs of white "duck trousers" (no flannels), eighteen white shirts (with collar attached), eight pairs white socks, two (washable) white belts, twenty-four handkerchiefs, and one pith helmet.[5] The official photographs taken by cruise photographer Walter Conger Harris show the students gleaming in their matching white uniforms, looking for all the world like Europeans anxious to protect themselves from the harmful effects of tropical climes.[6]

The Floating University's students soon learned to behave like little imperialists too. Although on their first encounter with rickshaws in Japan they found it strange to be pulled by men working "like animals," the Americans swiftly embraced a mode of transport that enabled them to navigate Asian cities on their own (fig. 6.1).[7] In a harebrained ascent of Mt. Fuji without guides at the beginning of winter, eight of them staged their own version of heroic imperial masculinity.[8] Another group went tiger hunting in Ceylon (Sri Lanka).[9] Furthermore, DeWitt Reddick and his friends poked fun at "the natives" who did not speak English, shouting made-up greetings at them ("Kalamazoo" was a favorite) and asking nonsensical questions.[10] The Floating University's students moved through the world with the racial privileges inherited from European empires.[11]

They also moved through the world with British imperialists as their guides. Lord Northcliffe's *My Journey round the World*, published in 1922, proved to be a particular favorite in the ship's library.[12] As Alfred Harmsworth, Northcliffe was a hugely influential British press baron whose newspapers included the London-based *Daily Mail* and the *Times*. Acting as the director of British propaganda during World War I, he had traveled to the United States in 1917 as head of the British war mission. However, because of declining health, in 1921 he embarked on a seven-month world cruise, the diary of which was published shortly after his death in 1922. In his

FIGURE 6.1. Cruise manager Theo Phelps in a rickshaw in Colombo, Ceylon (Sri Lanka). Note the sign for "American Hairdressers." In Walter Conger Harris, *Photographs of the First University World Cruise* (New York: University Travel Association, 1927), no. 372.

traveling west from London, Northcliffe's route was broadly similar to that followed by the *Ryndam*, and his direct prose and elite access—often, he stayed in Government Houses of the British Empire—appealed enormously to the American students. Sometimes, the *Binnacle* excerpted whole sections of his accounts.[13] Northcliffe was a proud imperialist, and his diaries painted portraits of many of the British officials the students would meet.[14]

Rudyard Kipling's Verse was also in great demand.[15] In it the students found, along with other imperial-themed pieces, Kipling's 1899 poem "The White Man's Burden," which exhorted the United States to join the project of conquest and take up the civilizing mission. James McKenzie sought out the Raffles hotel as a place "made famous by Kipling and other noted writers in books and stories," and in India *The Jungle Book* was a constant reference.[16] Upon stepping off the quay in Bombay (Mumbai) and finding snakes coiled in baskets, the students knew "at once that they were descendants of Nag, the king cobra in 'Riki-Tiki-Tavi.'" On the way to Agra, they "saw some of the Bandarlog tribe" swinging in the trees, and at the Taj Mahal they described the Mina birds "living up to the reputation Kipling endowed them with as to their inherent curiosity."[17] Kipling's 1901 novel *Kim* was one of the texts recommended as preparatory reading alongside those of other British authors, including Elizabeth W. Grierson (*Things Seen in Edinburgh*), Gilbert Murray (*Legacy of Greece*), and J. H. Longford (*Japan of the Japanese*).[18] In addition, popular in the library of the *Ryndam* were generalist travel accounts such as Harry A. Franck's *Vagabond Journey around the World* (1910) and, recently published, Fred Elmer Marble's *Round the World Travel Guide* (1925).[19] If Northcliffe and Kipling taught the students to see through British imperial eyes, Marble offered a more American perspective. An ordained Baptist minister, after serving congregations in New England Marble turned to travel education, becoming in 1919 the American Express agent in charge of the Far East and director of education for the company's around-the-world tours of the 1920s.[20] The aim of his book was to "give sufficient data for anyone to plan a trip Round the World."[21] It provided maps, hotel recommendations, and itineraries that, like the route of the Floating University, followed a westward path—first crossing the American continent or sailing via Cuba and Panama before traversing the Pacific to Hawaii and making many of the *Ryndam*'s other ports of call. Though less of a narrative account, it nonetheless provided glosses that framed stops along the way in terms similar to the *Ryndam*'s own special-issue logbook: Hawaii was a "melting pot," Japan a rising power "keeping pace" with Western nations, and India a land under British rule whose nationalism had been animated by "the principle of self-determination uttered by President Wilson."[22] Each country was superimposed on a map of the United States for context.

McKenzie acknowledged that these generalist volumes, together with the *Binnacle* and the professors' talks, were what primarily shaped his knowledge and expectations of the places and people he was visiting.[23] Produced by student journalists and editors and overseen by the Floating University's Journalism Department head, Henry J. Allen, in addition to the

Forum Club (see below), the *Binnacle* was one of the chief means for shaping and disciplining how the students made sense of what they were seeing and experiencing. Upon the *Ryndam*'s approach to a port, it published potted guides of what to expect, book recommendations, and summaries of the lectures being given by professors. The editions published immediately after a stop were full of student news items and accounts of onshore antics, together with sometimes moralizing editorials about behavior. Read issue by issue, its pages reveal how a kind of "house line" was progressively produced from a range of possible interpretations.

RISING JAPAN

Although in Havana the *Ryndam*'s passengers had contrasted the remnants of the Spanish conquest with the animating force of US power, the Floating University's first sustained encounter with other empires was in Japan.[24] The *Binnacle* had initially presented the relationship of the United States with Japan as an extension of manifest destiny: "American contact with this oriental people was but one of the logical steps in our progress of westward expansion," read the editorial written as the *Ryndam* made its way across the western Pacific.[25] The special logbook issued by the University Travel Association framed its summary of Yokohama with an account of the arrival there of the US Navy's Commodore Matthew C. Perry in 1854, and the *Binnacle* carried a piece by Albert Heckel that cast Perry's arrival as the act that "broke the ancient seclusion" and "started that country on a career of modernization."[26]

Nevertheless, Japan was also a rising and rival imperial power in its own right, as the students quickly came to realize. The industrial factories, printing presses, and railways they visited, the migrants and workers they had seen in Hawaii, and the presence of the "Mitsuma Maru" (likely the *Katori Maru*)—a Japanese steamer that shadowed the *Ryndam* on its journey through Asian waters—forcefully underlined this.[27] In Japan, the United States had not only a rival, but a rival that seemed to be "modernizing" on terms that would—potentially—bring it into conflict with the United States' own ambitions in the region. The *Binnacle* framed this as an "international problem" created by the "irrepressible expansion of two of the most virile races on earth," but it was just as much about empires in competition.[28]

Much was made in the *Binnacle*'s special Japanese supplement about the spiritual origins of the country's nationalism.[29] Confronted by Japan's industrial development, the Americans sought out "traditional" Japanese culture.[30] They bought kimonos and lacquer boxes and ate in local restaurants. Charles Ladd, John Killick, and Paul Robinson went out into the

countryside and got lost attempting to cycle from Kobe to Osaka.³¹ Staying
at a "real" Japanese inn seemed to be the ambition of many members of the
cruise, who had read about them in the *Japan and Korea* volume of Frank
G. Carpenter's *World Travels*, held in the *Ryndam*'s library.³² At Nikko, they
walked among the cryptomerias, great two-hundred-year-old trees 150 feet
high, and marveled at the shrines, set amid maple trees heavy with colored
leaves. To Lillian McCracken, it was all "marvelous" and "gorgeousness,
but not gaudiness."³³ Tom Johnson could not believe it was drunkenness
alone that had led to the students' misconduct in such places. He attributed
it instead to the corruptions of modernity: an inability among the Americans to feel "for holiness of beauty" and, perhaps, a discomfort with the
place accorded these qualities, not only at Nikko but more broadly in Japanese culture. "With money and machinery and desire to experiment," he
wrote home from Moji (Kitakyushu), "does not necessarily come wisdom
or sense of responsibility or regard for the rights of others."³⁴ The visit to
Japan served to simultaneously establish a standard for "modernity" and
"development" in Asian countries and a desire for cultural "authenticity,"
which became a point of reference as the *Ryndam* sailed south and encountered the colonies of older European empires.

TREATY PORT SHANGHAI AND BRITISH HONG KONG

After the independence of rising Japan, Shanghai was a sharp contrast. As
Johnson put it, "Shanghai seems to be a sort of international territory, about
as Chinese as Chinatown, New York."³⁵ The United States was one of the
many "foreign" powers vying for China's riches, but the *Ryndam*'s passengers placed the blame for what they thought they saw (and did not see)
in Shanghai at the feet of the British. Having been turned away from their
scheduled stops in Canton (Guangzhou) and Peking (Beijing) because of
conflict in these regions, the Floating University's students were fully aware
of the movement to boycott British goods as well as the popular nationalism
targeting foreigners.³⁶ And they struggled to reconcile the modern city they
saw in Shanghai with their desire to experience an "authentic" China, just as
they felt they had found an authentic Japan. "The fact remains," wrote Johnson, "we saw [international] exploitation at its worst . . . and have not seen
the real China at all."³⁷ For Lucille and Holling C. Holling, the responsibility
for both the political discord and perhaps their unmet expectations lay with
the British and their mode of rule: "There are the American, French and
Russian colonies too, but England has put her stomp on it and the Chinese
feel the <u>oppression</u>."³⁸ They liked to think that the United States' combination of trade and education in China was less repressive.

Hopes for Hong Kong, therefore, were not high. The *Binnacle* warned that of all the cities the cruise would visit, "Hong Kong [would be] the least interesting, because it [was] a British port."[39] After three days of uneventful sailing, the *Ryndam* made its way into the harbor on the evening of Sunday, November 21. Like so many travelers who arrived at night, McKenzie was wowed by the lights that "seemed to almost completely cover the slopes of the mountain . . . mingling with the stars."[40] It was not the only way in which Hong Kong would surprise the *Ryndam*'s passengers.

The *Ryndam*'s passengers went ashore the next morning, and after a drive that the Hollings thought "equal[ed] or surpass[ed] Hawaii," they ended their tour at Victoria Peak, traveling first on the "tram cog," which McKenzie felt was like riding a big dipper, and then onward via sedan chairs carried by "coolies."[41] In contrast to rainy, urban, and dirty Shanghai, Hong Kong shone below them in the sunshine. Only the "murmur of people's voices" and the noises of traffic from two thousand feet below "made us realise," wrote McKenzie, "that this was not a painting before us, but that it actually contained life."[42] Besides, the students had all been reading Lord Northcliffe's travelogue and, as McCracken noted in her diary, he judged Hong Kong harbor to be "one of the finest in the world."[43] Lucille Holling spent the rest of her day shopping, ordering some dresses, and having her hair washed before returning to the *Ryndam* for an on-ship black-tie dinner attended by over one hundred notable guests.

This was an event of high diplomacy.[44] Along with the vice-chancellor of Hong Kong University, W. W. Cornell, it included Sir Shou-son Chow, the former Chinese ambassador to the United States, and Lady Shou-son Chow; US Consul-General Roger Culver Treadwell and his consul and vice-consul; and Lieutenant Commander Godwin and Captain Williams of the USS *Huron*, which was stationed in the harbor. But there were also several officials from other imperial and commercial constituencies: Lieutenant Commander Leeds of the British Navy and Mrs. Leeds; Quarrels van Ufford, the general agent of the Java-China Japan Line, and Mrs. Ufford; Mr. Methoven, the vice-consul for the Netherlands; Mr. Harold Shantz, aide-de-camp to the British governor; and Mr. Robert Kotewall, a Chinese-Parsi-European businessman and member of the Hong Kong Legislative Council. The United States in 1926 was not as major a commercial player in Southeast Asia as it would later become, but its interests in the region were growing, and it was quickly replacing Britain and the Netherlands as their colonies' primary trading partner. Imperial collaboration and competition went hand in hand.[45]

The Americans' experience of British Hong Kong, with its grand houses, magnificent views, expatriate nightlife, collaborative imperial

diplomacy, and buzzing international trade, was set against their visits to
the Kowloon Walled City, whose residents they had already learned to call
"Kowlunatics."[46] Located across the bay in the New Territories (leased to
Britain for ninety-nine years in 1898), the Walled City was a kind of diplomatic void between the British and the Chinese, its indeterminate status
useful to both parties. For McCracken, who had admired the University of
Hong Kong and the well-presented students she had met there, the version
of China she saw in Kowloon was shocking: "Ye gods!" she wrote. "Such
filth, poverty, crowded quarters, horrible markets I had never imagined.
Revolting hogs, feeding everywhere—chickens & babies & cats & dogs &
pigs all wallowing together."[47] McKenzie was not a fan either. "Most of the
Chinese live no better than animals" was his assessment. Lucille Holling,
meanwhile, found the "narrow and winding streets," fat pigs, fishing junks
on the harbor, "deliciously Chinese rooms and buildings" (which Holling
sketched), and markets with "food stuffs in a weird variety of forms" all
"picturesque."[48] Both these versions of the Walled City—the degenerate
and the romantic—seemed to provide the Americans with what they had
been looking for in Shanghai but failed to find (fig. 6.2). Kowloon did not
stand as a challenge to Western influence but rather legitimized it by providing a setting against which visitors could draw a contrast between "native"
lawlessness and British order.[49]

Against their expectations, Hong Kong had impressed the Americans.
McKenzie thought it "very evident that the coming of Great Britain to

FIGURE 6.2. Near the old town wall, Kowloon. In Walter Conger Harris, *Photographs of
the First University World Cruise* (New York: University Travel Association, 1927), no. 226.

Hongkong has been a great blessing." Its "law, efficiency, and permanence" had turned a region "infested with pirates" into one of the great world centers of trade.[50] Tom Johnson put it succinctly: "Hong Kong itself is completely safe, because it is completely British."[51]

What the students learned in Hong Kong was a new enthusiasm for British rule. After experiencing the developing power of Japan and witnessing the ruptures rippling out from China and the international treaty port of Shanghai, Johnson endorsed the English practice of holding on to "decently acquired possessions," seeing them as "an essential benefit to the sustaining of influence and protection." However, setting British rule in Hong Kong against what he had seen in Shanghai and Kowloon had also hardened his views on racial and civilizational difference. The Chinese hated change, he wrote home to his mother. Theirs was a country that had "always been the same; [and] would always be the same"; the "mass" were "a different people; completely different." Unlike Japan, which had self-modernized, it was "the West" (including the United States) that had developed Shanghai and Hong Kong. Nevertheless, Johnson was clear that it had not been done out of altruism: "she [the West] has done it for herself and has reaped a rich reward."[52]

The Japanese were building their own empire, which was reaching out across the region, and the leaders of Republican China were struggling to tread a path between the exploitation of the international concessions on the one hand and the warlords on the other. Hong Kong presented to the students another model of rule in Asia; one that in 1926 impressed the young Americans. It was what they carried at the forefront of their minds as they sailed toward the Philippines at a moment when the US presence there was coming under increasing challenge from a people anxious to realize promises of self-rule.

THE AMERICAN PHILIPPINES

The American students arrived in Manila well aware that they were about to encounter "a controversy . . . worthy of educated thought."[53] During the journey from Hong Kong, the *Binnacle* had provided them with a potted history of US rule over the islands and appraised them of the current standoff between the US governor-general, Leonard Wood, and the president of the Filipino Senate (Manuel L. Quezon) and Speaker of the House of Representatives (Manuel Roxas).[54] The dispute was a crucial one, the paper argued, because it would "perhaps determine whether American or native control is the stronger" in the islands. Independence was acknowledged to be inevitable, "but the time at which that independence should be granted has been a sore spot among the statesmen of both countries."[55]

FIGURE 6.3. President of the Filipino Senate, Manuel L. Quezon, addressing the Floating University. In Walter Conger Harris, *Photographs of the First University World Cruise* (New York: University Travel Association, 1927), no. 239a.

Arriving at pier 7 in Manila Harbor on the morning of Friday, November 26, some of the Floating University's passengers evidenced more interest in this tense political situation than others. Dispersing across Manila, many seized the opportunity for shopping, while others visited the American warships arrayed in the harbor. Charles Ladd and Paul Robinson called on Carson Taylor, the owner of the *Manila Daily Bulletin*, a newspaper widely regarded as carrying the views of the American community; they ended up driving with him into the middle of Luzon Island to inspect his coconut mills.[56] On Saturday, the entire student group piled into automobiles for a two-hour trip to points of interest, including key sites of American governance such as Fort Santiago, San Lazaro Hospital (where they toured the segregated leprosy and insanity wards), the mint, the governor-general's palace, and the prison. The tour ended at the Legislative Building, where the students had the opportunity of gaining firsthand experience of the political crisis in the form of a meeting with Senate President Quezon and his staff and a "scholarly speech" by Speaker of the House Roxas (fig. 6.3).[57] Sports competitions, lectures, and a reception featuring folk dances and music were held at the University of the Philippines.[58] However, much to the embarrassment of the faculty, only a few students attended. The rest had hit the town instead. At the Manila hotel, the Globe Trotters played to a dancing crowd; others flooded the segregated dance floors at the Santa Ana cabaret, Tom's Dixie Kitchen, or the Army and Navy Club until the early hours of the morning.[59]

Conflicting opinions about the political situation, as well as headaches, were evident the next morning as the *Ryndam*'s passengers reboarded the ship and prepared to sail out of Manila harbor on their way to Bangkok. With questions being raised about the legitimacy of US rule in the islands, Kansas ex-governor Henry Allen took control and instituted the Forum Club, aimed at giving "thorough going student attention" to every angle of "the controversy now raging in the Philippine Islands."[60] Ostensibly a platform for "exchang[ing] experiences which will help us gain a better understanding of the people and their problems in the countries visited," it also served as a stage for Allen to exert his influence, much to the annoyance of other faculty members.[61] According to the Hollings, "The whole ship turned out to hear [arguments that] were hot on either side."[62] Students and staff alike gave "full expression of [their] feeling."[63]

Rev. W. W. Youngson advanced the radical view. On Friday night, he had dined with Bishop Charles Mitchell of the Methodist Episcopal Church, a long-standing friend and fellow Freemason, and Mitchell had made clear his support for independence.[64] For the *Binnacle*, Ben S. Washer Jr. had interviewed vice-governor Eugene Allen Gillmore and questioned the American official about the rights of the Filipino people.[65] The Hollings, too, were drawn to appeals for independence. They did not like the idea of the United States as an imperial power and were critical of "the unpleasant spirit on the part of the Americans living" in the Philippines. The "disgusting" attitude reflected in the speech given by a naval officer at the reception at the governor-general's palace infuriated them.[66]

However, (Albert) Brunson MacChesney, whose father had managed Leonard Wood's (unsuccessful) 1920 campaign for nomination as the Republican Party's presidential candidate, was among those who held the opposite view. Together with a few friends, he had piled into a car on Saturday and turned up at the governor-general's country house in Baguio. Wood was sick, but he discussed the US Exclusion Act with the enterprising students and announced his disapproval of "the mixing of colors." In Wood's opinion, it would be a long time before the Philippines would "be ready for independence and that the United States really ought never to give them up." Corruption, money wasting, and lack of education were cited as reasons.[67] James McKenzie was also convinced that "the Philippines must under no consideration be given their independence *now*." He had been shocked by what seemed to him to be "terrible conditions" and thought folks in the United States had "no idea what is going on" or "how near a big crisis the problem of governing these people has reached."[68]

There was little doubt about which position Allen favored. He took the Forum meeting in hand and, with what the Hollings described as "magnificent calm," defined the terms of debate and assessed the position as he saw it: "The Filipinos must have their freedom" was Lucille Holling's summary of his argument, "but they want it now—and there are many things that make them not ready to take it now." The shipboard discussion had changed the Hollings' minds, and they cited Wood's views on racial mixing as one reason why. In the hands of the authoritative ex-governor, the Forum Club had been an effective device for managing potentially dangerous student opinion. "We went away knowing quite a bit more about the Filipino problem than those in America do," as the Hollings put it.[69] Pearl Heckel took a dimmer view of Allen's involvement. She wrote, "It is very simple for a man of large experience and engaging personality and plausible, friendly manner, to influence young people."[70] The *Binnacle*, certainly, was under his influence. In its judgment, the feeling "of the majority" at the Forum was that "no harm is being done to the Filipino people." Rather, the United States was bringing improvements to the country and its preparedness for complete independence, and the establishment of "a conscious middle class" would require more years yet.[71]

Tom Johnson, however, was not convinced by Allen. He did not think that the islands could be held by the United States "indefinitely on the grounds they are not 'ready.'" In his view, the country would achieve independence after a "<u>definite</u> number of years" but continue to be "a kind of illegal child of the United States—in some manner much as Cuba is: that is, extending the Monroe Doctrine to the Philippines."[72] Yet both types of relationship, Johnson implied, were undesirable forms of foreign control.

THE NETHERLANDS INDIES AND THE COLONIAL POLICIES FORUM

The island of Java (now part of Indonesia) presented another mode of empire to the traveling Americans. The Dutch colonial government there had taken seriously the University Travel Association's invitation—issued to all the countries the ship was to visit—to send an educational official to assist the cruise. Consequently, A. T. Keen—director of the Prins Hendrik School in Batavia (Jakarta) and minister of education in the Dutch East Indies government—had joined the students in Singapore, and as the *Ryndam* made its way south, he delivered preparatory lectures on board.[73] The Official Tourist Bureau of the Netherlands Indies took charge of the official program. Upon arrival at Tandjong Priok dock, the cruise split into two parties, each of which visited three destinations. One trip was to Buitenzorg (Bogor), where the Americans were met by a brass band playing the rousing John Philip Sousa march "The Stars and Stripes Forever"; they were required by their uniformed hosts to assemble in rank order, "from

FIGURE 6.4. Leaving the Station at Buitenzorg (Bogor), Java (Indonesia). In Walter Conger Harris, *Photographs of the First University World Cruise* (New York: University Travel Association, 1927), no. 335.

the Deans down to the most humble member," and to march to the botanical gardens (fig. 6.4). Then followed a trip to the zoological museum and the governor-general's palace.[74] Another trip was to Batavia, where they boarded automobiles for sightseeing at the fish market, aquarium, museum, Kali Besar canal, and Portuguese church. The third trip was a five-hour journey to Bandoeng (Bandung), where the students traveled by automobiles on loan from the US War Department to a tea plantation and to Dago waterfall (Curug Dago) for a picnic. Also, by courtesy of the War Department's air service, about twenty students were taken for airplane rides over the inland.[75]

The Student Magellan (the *Ryndam*'s student yearbook) later described what the group saw from the windows of their special trains: "flat barges manned by half-clad natives" moving slowly along the canals and brown-limbed women "clad in bright colored sarongs" standing knee-deep in water washing their clothes.[76] McKenzie employed a common developmental trope when he called the scene "a veritable 'Garden of Eden' with a lot of sparsely clothed 'Adam and Eves.'"[77] Holling C. Holling, too, was entranced by the lush plants, plants, the ubiquitous bamboo, and the giant rice fields.[78] The Americans contrasted this verdant landscape with the order of the main urban centers. Johnson thought "Batavia was as Dutch as Singapore was English," and Ladd described it as "a commercial city, modern and sanitary," containing the "steep gabled houses and walled canals of old Holland."[79] Dutch "cleanliness is seen everywhere," noted Holling, comparing it favorably to China.[80]

On the evening of the first night, Batavian students from the STOVIA medical school (School tot Opleiding van Inlandsche Artsen) came aboard the *Ryndam* and gave a performance of the *serimpi* (*srimpi*) and the *wayang wong* in elaborate costumes. If these dances impressed Holling and Lucille, they made less of an impact on most other students, who promptly fell asleep.[81] On the other nights, the Americans, led by the Globe Trotters, hit the dance floor of the Hotel der Nederlanden. The crew, too, made the most of their stop. Having been paid part of their salary, a handful had too much to drink and got into fights that left one with a broken arm and another with a broken leg. One of the firemen disappeared into the water and in the morning was found to have drowned.[82]

For the *Binnacle* staff, "Java was a surprise." "Instead of the jungles and swamps with wild, uncivilized natives that had been expected, students found paved roads and automobiles, great bridges and trains that ran along at a rate rivalling that of trains in America."[83] As the *Ryndam* left the Netherlands Indies (Indonesia) and made its way toward Colombo, Ceylon (Sri Lanka), Henry Allen convened another forum meeting for the entire group to discuss "the colonial policies of the United States in the Philippines and of Holland in the East Indies."[84] Its conclusion was perhaps equally surprising. Although the views differed, the "prevailing opinion" (stated forcefully by Allen) was that the "Dutch colonial policy, which is frankly one of benevolent exploitation . . . is producing better results than the more sentimental colonial policy of the United States."[85] Charles Ladd agreed. He thought "the Dutch surpass[ed] both the Yankees and Englishmen in successful colonization," citing the islands' profitability: "Relatively one-fifth the size of Texas, Java, under Dutch rule, has developed its native resources to a greater extent than any like colony of any other nation in the world."[86] John Killick thought the "modern highways, the well paved streets, the dial telephones, the fast express railroads, and the use of all the modern conveniences" far exceeded "the progress that has been made in America's colonies."[87]

Allen determined that the diverging education policies of the two colonial powers were the chief cause of the difference. Whereas in the Philippines, the United States "enforced mass education by making school attendance compulsory" and aimed to "educate the Philippines until its people could understand freedom," the Dutch "[did] not encourage the education of the native."[88] According to the *Binnacle*, the Netherlands Indies government was frank in its opinion that the US policy

of so-called mass education in the Philippines has not achieved good results. They say we have made a people restless without making them more
useful to either themselves or to us. . . . There is in the Dutch attitude no
conscious feeling apparently that these brown and yellow people have any
right to self-government. They believe that the Dutch will give them better
government than they could give themselves. They say so quite frankly and
they do not moan over self-determination. . . . In Java, they probably would
send Senator Quezan [*sic*] to the new convict colony to which they sent the
disturbers in the recent uprising.[89]

The Dutch "understand the psychology of conquered islanders better than
the Americans" was Killick's conclusion.[90] In the Dutch East Indies (Indonesia), the people may not be free, but they were happy and prosperous.
In this opinion, Killick followed Lord Northcliffe, who in his own exercise
of imperial comparison had rated the Dutch as good at colonization as the
British but less prepared to give freedom to "the natives"—"in which," he
judged, "they are wise." "Free natives are ungrateful natives" was Northcliffe's assessment.[91]

Sarah T. Palmer, one of the older "tourists," disagreed. After nearly three
hundred years of occupation, only 10 percent of the native population was
literate, which she found appalling.[92] Although education had improved in
the last fifteen years, she gave credit for this not to the example set by the
Americans (as stated at the Forum) but rather to the Chinese, who had demanded and initially also funded educational opportunities for their children, inspiring the Malays also to press for schools. Sarah Palmer, however,
was very much a minority voice on the *Ryndam*. Ellen Day did not think
that the laborers in the sugar estates of Surabaya were either especially
prosperous or very educated. But it was this, she judged, that would protect Java from "a labor problem such as Hawaii [had] made for herself." Importing workers from China, Japan, Portugal, Puerto Rico, and the Philippines, Hawaii then "force[d] free education upon [them]," only to find that
when their children finished school, they wanted something better than the
drudgery of the plantations.[93] If most of those aboard the *Ryndam* had left
the Philippines endorsing the United States' doctrine of "uplift," they sailed
from Java with a much firmer commitment to occupation and control.

BRITISH INDIA, "NATIVE LIFE," AND FALLEN KINGDOMS

Still to come were the British colonies of Ceylon and India, and the *Ryndam* passengers sailed toward them with a framework for understanding
colonial rule firmly in place. At these stops, the trips ashore were organized

by the American Express Company, not local governments. Rather than university lectures and official receptions, the excursions featured stays in the cities of Colombo and Bombay (Mumbai) and train trips to tourist sites such as Peradeniya and Kandy, Agra, and the Taj Mahal. Moving through these sites, the *Ryndam*'s passengers mapped the economic prosperity and urban infrastructure they had learned to see as markers of "modern" civilizational development against what they understood as the timelessness of "native life."

Frederick Daggett, a student from Brown College, praised the British for making Ceylon the "Pearl of the Indies," but he judged that "for the most part the natives are as near if not nearer the soil than they ever used to be."[94] Bombay, according to *The Student Magellan*, was a "typically English city," with planned gardens and "broad, paved streets, ponderous buildings, massive and impressive," and "street cars clanging noisily, uniformed traffic policemen, [and] stores with neat displays behind plate-glass shop windows."[95] But turn a corner, wrote H. R. Baurmann, and the "scene shifts from 1927 to 927." "The hum and bustle of the modern day seem to have been a dream, like a forgotten glimpse into an impossible future—for here is life, life as it was a thousand years ago."[96] The trip from Agra's train station to the Taj Mahal in two-wheeled horse-drawn carts was one that took the students "from the present into the far off past of the Arabian Nights," where "all about [was] primitive, dusty, grassless, desolate" (fig. 6.5).[97]

This trope of a temporal shift into a world of timeless "native life" was exactly what the Americans really wanted to see.[98] Followed by "the various races and racial problems" and the variety of religions, the "native life" was voted in a shipwide survey to be the chief attraction of the stop in India. Tom Johnson, therefore, spoke for many when he judged "the real interest" of any country to be "in the interiors and away from the cities where the races are so mixed and have so little unity, controlled by a European power, that you do not know the people themselves."[99] This quest for "the people themselves" cast an exotic light over some local populations (usually the rural and the poor), while framing others (usually the urban) as deceitful and suspicious. The brown bodies glimpsed from the windows of trains, standing in rice fields or guiding bullocks, were celebrated as authentic. However, the beggars and salesmen of Colombo were too canny by half, and the "over-estimated and over-advertised" "sad-eyed sons of the desert" who picked the cruise members' pockets in Algiers were "disappointing," dirty, and in need of a bath.[100] In the context of what historian Robert Vitalis has called "an era of increasing mobility and mobilization of colored peoples," both constructions served to reassure the white Americans on the *Ryndam* of their own leading place in a world of racialized instability.[101]

FIGURE 6.5. The Taj Mahal. In Walter Conger Harris, *Photographs of the First University World Cruise* (New York: University Travel Association, 1927), no. 433.

If in Shanghai at least some of the passengers on board the *Ryndam* had been prepared to see the United States' foreign presence as different from the repression of British rule, by the time the ship left Manila they had changed their minds.[102] Not only did Johnson recognize economic dependence as a form of informal empire, but his fellow passengers had learned to see the United States as part of what historian A. G. Hopkins calls the "Western imperial club."[103] Led by Henry Allen, after the stop in Netherlands Indies they even came to think that perhaps the United States might have something yet to learn from its European progenitors. In measuring modern colonial cities animated by Western powers against what they cast as simple "native life," their commitment to "uplift" and their belief in progressive colonial rule also waned. "Generally speaking," concluded Daggett following the stop in Ceylon, "East and West may never intermingle," echoing Kipling as well as contemporary US prohibitions against interracial marriage.[104]

In India, the students had seen the architectural legacies of past empires. Agra Fort, the "marvelous palace of the old Moghuls," was an unexpected revelation. The cruise members delighted in its "morbid torture chambers with their tales of blood" and the stories of Akbar and Shah Jahan that "haunt[ed] the empty halls."[105] They compared the carvings at the Elephanta Caves to those of the Grecians and celebrated the Taj Mahal as "something unreal [and] fairy-like."[106] However, like the remains of the Spanish rule in the Philippines, these were the remnants of fallen empires and vanished kingdoms—great in their day, but their day had passed. As the *Ryndam* sailed toward Europe, the Pyramids in Egypt, the Acropolis in Greece, and the Doge's Palace in Venice were all made to fit into this frame. Although the United States might have things still to learn in the way of colonial rule, the *Ryndam*'s students were confident that their country was a power in the ascendant.

The performances the Planet Players staged as the ship was en route to Europe reflected this. They included *The Idol's Eye*, a thriller by the Anglo-Irish playwright Lord Dunsany, whose stories and plays were very popular in the United States and Britain during the periods before and after World War I; *Spring* by the young American playwright Colin Campbell Clements; *His Aunt-in-Law* by the *Ryndam*'s own Dupree Jordan; and *In the Net* by Percival Wilde.[107] As the students left East and South Asia and entered the war-scarred lands of Europe and the Middle East, the theatrical troupe was occupied less with racial and sexualized tropes and more with familial and political ones. These two approaches to world order—the temporal and the familial—came together in the Floating University's approach to Palestine and Europe.

PALESTINE AND THE HOLY LAND

"These Are Our Ancients" was the title of DeWitt Reddick's editorial in the January 19 edition of the *Binnacle* as the *Ryndam* sailed through the Red Sea: it "is almost impossible to realize . . . that we are come to the land which has provided so much of the background of our everyday consciousness in our far western land." Reddick drew a genealogy of his fellow students' cultural inheritance that was intimately connected with the places they were about to see in the Mediterranean and Europe:

> Here were born the great leaders of the Christian era. Not far away Christopher Columbus saw the light of day and grew to manhood before he carried Spain's adventure to the unknown continent of America. Here in this Mediterranean area and its neighboring smaller seas were fought out the earlier battles of theology. . . . It is the land of more ancient beginnings of the things which concern us than any other we shall see.[108]

But first came Palestine. "Every child who goes to that most numerous of all American institutions, the Sunday School, knows this land," he wrote. For Reddick, the *Ryndam*'s visit was to be a kind of direct physical communication with the foundations of their own religious and political culture.[109] "Yesterday we passed Mount Sinai, where Moses got the law and the commandments," and "before a week is spent we shall be in the ancient kingdom of Solomon and David"; "Jesus was born here, and Oriental though he was, he led the Occidental world into its modern conception of the brotherhood of man."[110]

This way of thinking traced the manifest destiny of Protestant America to an ancient place of origin in biblical Palestine. It exemplified an approach to the Holy Land that—by the 1920s—had become well established in the United States. American pilgrims had begun traveling to the region in the mid-nineteenth century, searching for religious renewal.[111] With the reduced costs of steam travel, the opening of the Suez Canal, and the decline of the Ottoman Empire, from the 1880s onward their numbers increased significantly, leading to the development of a robust tourist industry. In Palestine, they sought a "fifth gospel" that might counter the uncertainties of modernist historicism.[112] However, they were frequently disappointed that what they found did not match the world they had imagined, so they sought to make Palestine more "biblical." They achieved this vision by creating Protestant sites more familiar to Americans and increasingly arguing that Palestine should be Israel—a Jewish nation—just as it was in the Bible.[113] By the 1920s, the travel narratives, biblical illustrations, pictographs, and archeological accounts this pilgrimage industry produced had brought the places of Palestine into "the center of the American theological landscape."[114]

This Protestant "rediscovery" of the Holy Land was attached to an Anglo-American millenarianism to which the British occupation of Palestine during World War I seemed to give fresh justification. One of its greatest proponents was Elizabeth Lippincott McQueen, who was traveling on the *Ryndam* as one of the middle-aged educationally minded "tourists." A follower of Mary Baker Eddy, the founder of Christian Science, McQueen had previously traveled to Jerusalem just after the war, impelled by her belief that the British presence there was a fulfillment of the biblical prophecy that foreshadowed the coming of the Christian millennium. Like Eddy, she subscribed to a version of Anglo-Israelism that saw the English peoples— including those in the United States—as one of the ten lost tribes of Israel. Their joint action in Palestine thus had a biblical mandate and, in her mind, heralded the beginning of a new historic era.[115] *The New Palestine*, by McQueen's friend W. D. McCrackan, outlined these views. It was set as recommended reading for the *Ryndam* students, and McQueen delivered lectures on the Holy Land in advance of the ship's arrival there.[116]

After the ship dropped anchor at Haifa on January 24, the students boarded a train to Jerusalem. "Mount Carmel, Elijah," wrote Lillian Mc-

Cracken in large letters at the top of her diary, complete with the corresponding Bible verses. Peering out her window on the train, she described a beautiful journey through rocky mountain passes, often rugged, bare, and desolate, followed by terraces with rock fences at the top and olive orchards, orange orchards, and almond trees in full bloom, and then more rocky "desolation." Then, suddenly, there it was: "Jerusalem!"[117]

McCracken and her fellow Americans poured off the train and into "motors directed by fez-topped officials," which took them not into the old city but to a series of nearby sights relevant to the Protestant visitor—the Well of Mary, the Tomb of the Magi, the Mount of Olives, and the Church of the Nativity. Only then did they enter Jerusalem itself, where, on foot and escorted by English-speaking Christian guides (many of them Coptic), they visited the Holy Sepulcher, the Via Dolorosa, David's Tomb, King Solomon's Temple, and the Dome of the Rock. Again, McCracken noted Bible verses in her diary alongside her descriptions of contemporaneous sites.

Holling C. and Lucille Holling thrilled at the narrow streets, full of all kinds of life: Jews, Arabs, Armenians, Christians, and Turks bartering together. They were entranced by the Mosque of Omar, and McCracken gave rich descriptions of the Jews praying at the Wailing Wall "with reddish beard and long stiff curl hanging in front of each ear."[118] Lillian McCracken was at pains to outline how much of the money behind the Zionist cause came from the United States and how many of the Jewish settlers were American.[119] In McQueen's view, the return of the Jews to Palestine was part of a divine millennial plan in which the United States played a central role.[120]

Nevertheless, these observations simultaneously reflected a broader disquiet, noted by even the skeptical Charles Ladd: "Fezes are everywhere in evidence," he wrote. "Christians were scarce—and this is the birthplace of Christianity!"[121] This was not quite the land the students had been taught to imagine. The Hollings and McCracken were disappointed at the "modern churches with tinsel & candles etc etc."[122] The "grim hills" and "dirty children and dirty streets" were unsettling.[123] "Our Bible illusions are having a jolt," the Hollings admitted.[124] Ladd was equally succinct: "Without any desire to be irreverent, I have the impression that much we saw was fake."[125] As the *Binnacle* acknowledged, it was difficult to fit "the Jerusalem of today into the conception of the Holy City gained from Bible teachings since childhood."[126]

Like so many American visitors before them, the passengers on the *Ryndam* worked hard to insert the continued presence of the biblical past into the modern-day landscape. Acknowledging the newness of much they had seen, McCracken consoled herself that "the mountains & the valleys are the same," and "the flowers of the fields, the houses of the people and the

FIGURE 6.6. Cruise members photographing locals in Palestine. In Walter Conger Harris, *Photographs of the First University World Cruise* (New York: University Travel Association, 1927), no. 494a.

immortal [costumes] remain the same."[127] Lucille Holling, too, imagined that the Arab women in Nazareth were "filling their water jugs and carrying them on their heads, just like Mary."[128] When cast as unchanging in this way, the landscape and its peoples not only worked to bolster American faith by serving as a "living diorama"—twelve cruise members were baptized in the Jordan during the *Ryndam*'s short stop at Haifa—but they also stood as evidence of the United States' national destiny of bringing improvement and salvation abroad (fig. 6.6).[129]

THE BATTLEFIELDS OF THE WESTERN FRONT

For the students on the Floating University, Palestine was not the only stopping place from which their nation's global destiny was fashioned. Since the end of World War I, the battlefields and cemeteries of the western front had become a popular site for American visitors to France.[130] In fact, in October 1926, when the *Ryndam* had just left Los Angeles, the *Binnacle* had carried news that the American Legion would, for its 1927 annual convention in September, undertake en masse a "pilgrimage [*sic*]" to these sites, billed as the "largest peacetime trans-Atlantic movement ever conceived."[131] The passengers on the Floating University were just some of the tens of thousands of Americans who would travel that year in reverence to the graves of their nation's dead.[132]

As the ship approached the port of Le Havre on March 14, the war and the US role in it were highlighted in the shipwide lecture. McCracken recorded a set of statistics in her diary: "5,000,000 lived in war area; 50% were killed or driven out" and "1,400,000 [French] were killed, 243,000,000 maimed, 30% shipping destroyed, [debt] eventually 315,000,000,000 [gold francs]."[133] She also noted the details of France's postwar reconstruction. In five years, "90% of factories were rebuilt, 50% livestock, 94% of mines restored. All done by means of unlimited credit." This, however, had placed France in a crippling financial position, unable even to pay the interest on its debt to the United States. "France and all of Europe think USA took advantage," McCracken wrote, evidently unprepared to pass judgment herself.[134]

The first official activity the following day was a trip to the places the conflict had already made familiar: Belleau Wood, the Marne, Oise-Asne, and Château-Thierry.[135] All were sites, *The Student Magellan* later recorded, "where an American heart skips a beat as the tragedies of nine years ago are relived in these historic spots."[136] The journey by automobile traced a passage from the everyday life and commerce of Paris, along "well-paved, tree-lined highways," to a countryside that for Ladd grew "harder in appearance" as the group approached the battlefields.[137] From the motorcade, he saw villages "where scarcely a house had a wall intact; and churches with their roofs and belfries shot away." A good percentage of the *Ryndam* students, however, chose to skip the trip, because they had heard that "no trenches, shell-holes, etc, remain[ed] to tell the tale"; in this they reflected a growing disinterest in battlefield tourism among Americans visiting Europe.[138]

The mood among the students was somber and reverential as the American cemeteries at Belleau Wood came into view. At "the foot of a hill rising abruptly back" and "laid out in shrubs and flowers & grass" was how McCracken described thousands of "white crosses—many unnamed," marking the spot where "<u>our boys</u> lie" (fig. 6.7).[139] The cruise members uncovered their heads and walked, silently and slowly, among the "hallowed graves" before making their way on foot up a winding path to the top of the hill, where an American flag flew from atop a tall flagpole.[140] It was "an inspiring spectacle," wrote *The Student Magellan,* and impressed on the group "the fact that America had been in the war, that American men and boys had been killed in this spot."[141] If these scenes raised the specter of the United States as a player in European politics, the trenches, filled with water and bridged over with boards; the machine gun pits; and the quotidian remnants of life and death in the form of cooking utensils and bits of cartridge,

FIGURE 6.7. The American cemetery at Oise-Aisne, Seringes-et-Nesles, France. In Walter Conger Harris, *Photographs of the First University World Cruise* (New York: University Travel Association, 1927), no. 805.

the odd shoe or a battered helmet pierced by a flying bit of steel, brought home to the students the human and individual reality of the conflict.[142]

The burial site of Quentin Roosevelt, son of former president Theodore Roosevelt, put a name to the anonymous dead. A pilot in the 95th Aero Squadron, he had been shot down and killed by German forces on July 14, 1918. Almost as soon as the war ended, his solitary grave in a field near Chamery had become a significant stop for Americans visiting the battlefields, with Mrs. Roosevelt and her son Theodore Jr. making, in January 1919, what had already come to be called a pilgrimage.[143] As the youngest son of a combative ex-president, Quentin's death inspired a "cult of remembrance." Poems, cartoons, and postcards depicting the grave site circulated well into the 1920s; airfields were named for him; and twisted metal from his plane was displayed in a hotel in nearby Château-Thierry as an object of veneration. Surrounded by a white oak fence, the grave became one of the most visited—and photographed—sites on the western front.[144] On that cloudy day in March 1927, Charles Ladd and his fellow students "stood reverently with bared heads, about the little fence that railed in the grave" and recited the story that was also part of the legend: "the Germans buried him on the spot his plane had fallen, with full military honors."[145]

Other war-related stops were on the students' itinerary—the Armistice car, the tombs of the unknown soldiers in Paris and Brussels, and the Peace Palace in Den Haag—but it was the visit to the American cemeteries that made concrete the US involvement in the war and the human costs of that involvement.[146] If in the biblical sites of Palestine the students found an ancient origin for their expanding nation, at the battlefields and cemeteries of the western front they paid homage to the sites where that nation had so decisively entered the European stage. The battlefields, of course, were conveniently close to another site that by the 1920s had been made if not sacred then certainly essential for visiting Americans in Europe.

THE CITY OF LIGHTS

So eager were many of the *Ryndam*'s passengers to get to Paris that at least eighty-seven of them had left the ship when it docked in southern European ports and traveled overland in advance of their classmates.[147] DeWitt Reddick and his friends rushed to the station on the evening the ship docked in Le Havre and caught the first train they could. "We got the fever" was how he put it.[148]

After checking into their hotels, they were out on the town, and they headed straight to Montmartre. Reddick checked off the names of places already made famous in American culture: the Moulin Rouge, "with its big red windmill turning steadily in the flaring electric sign over the entrance"; L'Inferno, the "front of which was the huge head of a devil"; Heaven, "the entrance of which was decorated with the forms of angels"; and Neant, where "[you] have the pleasure of drinking your wine from cups shaped like human skulls."[149] But Reddick was unimpressed. These were obviously places "made up for tourists." In their quest for hot chocolates, he and his friends ended up in Le Rat Mort, a café and cabaret in the Pigalle area, full of women eager to flirt with the young Americans. When the bill finally came, it was so exorbitant that they resolved to stay for a dance to "[have their] money's worth."[150] James McKenzie, too, proclaimed himself unimpressed by the women of Montmartre. After a delicious meal of snails, he and his roommate ventured out on an "educational tour" but professed their disgust at what they saw. Yet their reaction did not stop them from spending the rest of the evening "walking about the streets observing the people."[151] The Hollings were more amenable to the charms of the Moulin Rouge. "A varied picture of French nudity and gorgeous costumes" was how they described it. Holling had "amusing experiences in the lobby," receiving invitations that provided the appropriate level of titillation.[152]

Perhaps unsurprisingly, most of the students ended up at Zelli's—a late-night club in Montmartre run by an Italian American who well understood the preferences of his fellow countrymen. There, the *Ryndam*'s passengers experienced a little of *le tumulte noir* that in the mid-1920s was sweeping

Paris, led in part by African American musicians and performers seeking opportunity in segregation-free France. The group delighted in the jazz music of "Buddie," "a dark-skinned drummer from the southern part of the United States," before moving onto Chez Josephine Baker, a club run by an African American woman from St. Louis.[153] In 1927, Josephine Baker was at the height of her international fame, thanks to her dances that astutely exploited exoticized and sexualized notions of Black Africa. The Floating University's students greatly enjoyed the strange familiarity of jazz abroad, even as they failed to understand its connection to the Black and anticolonial intellectual and political movements fermenting in Parisian streets at the time.[154] They had little interest in, or engagement with, the "other Americans" in the city—neither the anticolonial activists, nor the businessmen on the "Right Bank," nor the intellectuals on the "Left."[155] Although the Peace Palace in The Hague was on their itinerary, the students did not seem to visit international educational agencies in the city, such as the American University Union or the Cité Universitaire.[156] Rather, they spent their time mixing cultural with recreational tourism in the way that Harvey Levenstein describes.[157] Along with the crowds visiting the nightclubs of Montmartre, Lillian McCracken attended the opera, Lucille Holling went shopping, Charles Ladd visited the Louvre, and the whole cruise was taken on an automobile tour of the sights that ended at the *Pantheon de la Guerre 1914–18*—a vast painting of the war about to be relocated to New York.[158]

But above all, it was the Paris "created by and for the American tourist" that the *Ryndam*'s passengers came to see and experience.[159] From Harry's New York Bar, "with its real American atmosphere," where you could eat "real American food and listen to Bill Henly sing the latest song hits while Bud Shepherd plays the piano," to the American Express office, where you could pick up the gossip of all that happened the night before: a bit like the battlefields, these were places claimed as part of the American story.[160] As Ladd put it, "no American, whether he is a steady businessman or of sporting blood, misses this phase of life in the capital of capitals."[161] It was in it that he, and many of his fellow passengers, found the education they longed to experience, learning firsthand the purchasing power of their nation's economic prosperity and seeking out contact with the cultural touchstones that would carry meaning upon their return home.

ABBOTSFORD AND STRATFORD

From Paris, the Floating University went on to stops in Germany, Denmark, Sweden, and Norway before arriving in Edinburgh, Scotland, on Sunday, April 10. After nearly seven months of traveling, many of the passengers were growing weary. For Tom Johnson, it was a relief "to get back to where English is spoken."[162] The *Ryndam*'s itinerary in the United Kingdom only reinforced this sense of familiarity.

From Edinburgh, open buses took the shivering Americans on a tour of "Sir Walter Scott country."[163] As *The Student Magellan* later recounted, "There were few on the trip who had not at some time in their lives thrilled at the deeds in the Waverly [*sic*] Novels."[164] Published between 1814 and 1832, many of Scott's books presented the romantic themes of Scottish history to readers through vividly developed heroic characters, acute social observation, and engaging prose, while others celebrated medieval chivalric culture. For critic Kenneth McNeil, they gave recognition to the violence and loss attending clashing cultures and described "new and compensatory identities in the overarching narrative of peace and progress." Little wonder, then, that in an age of empire, the novels proved to be an instant success, making Scott the "author of choice for British imperial reading publics, many of whom could trace their lineage to Scotland and the Celtic peripheries, around the globe."[165]

This enthusiasm extended to the United States, where no less than twenty-two towns were named Waverley.[166] Mark Twain (and many commentators since) even connected the role that Walter Scott's chivalric romances played "in making Southern character" with the outbreak of the American Civil War.[167] Americans began visiting "Scott country" during the author's own lifetime, taking their itinerary from his narrative poem, *Lady of the Lake* (1810), and his popularity in the United States continued long after it had abated in Britain.[168] W. E. B. DuBois was one of the many "literary pilgrims" who made the journey to Loch Katrine, only to find the enchantment broken by his fellow countrymen and -women, "loud and strident," who "pushed other people out of the way."[169] Although the carnage of the war dealt a fatal blow to sales of *Ivanhoe* in Great Britain, the novel, with its ideal of manly chivalry and imperial pride, remained popular in the United States, where it was reworked by figures such as Thomas Dixon, the racist advocate for white supremacy in the South.[170] In the 1920s, a trip to Abbotsford, Melrose, and the Scottish Borders was a must for Americans visiting Scotland. Like the *Ryndam*'s passengers, they went looking for direct contact with the places Scott had walked and thought and with the physical relics of his life.[171]

Ladd was not disappointed. Arriving at Abbotsford, Scott's home, he was met at the door by "an aged custodian," who "might have been one of Scott's characters recalled to life for the purpose of relating to the pilgrim who has come to pay homage to the Great Romancer the endless tales current about him." It gave Ladd a "thrill" to hear these tales, and for two hours

FIGURE 6.8. Easter bank holiday, with the Tower of London in the background. In Walter Conger Harris, *Photographs of the First University World Cruise* (New York: University Travel Association, 1927), no. 936.

he marveled at "Sir Walter's very own pipe," his penknife on the much-used reading table, and rooms "preserved much as Scott left them."[172] For Mc-Cracken, it was "a perfect day."[173] Having lost themselves in an imagined past, which for the last century had played a part in the cultural imagination of American racial politics, the *Ryndam*'s passengers returned to Edinburgh and were ready to leave for their final stop in London.[174]

Arriving in Greenwich on Good Friday, they found a city that was closed to locals and visitors alike. "Newspapers even aren't printed," wrote Johnson to his mother, "and if you were starving, I don't think a restaurant would be open for you."[175] But a sightseeing trip in buses took the students through the famous streets of central London and to already familiar stops such as the Tower of London (fig. 6.8), Saint Paul's Cathedral, the Houses of Parliament, and Buckingham Palace. James McKenzie delighted at the thrill of recognition: "When the places were 'introduced' to us, some of us were almost tempted to say, 'haven't we met before?'"[176]

The following day, buses took the students from London to Oxford and then on to Shakespeare's birthplace, Stratford-upon-Avon, a town that since the mid-nineteenth century had been celebrated in guidebooks and travel accounts as a "pilgrimage" place.[177] The students, too, described their visit in overtly religious terms. For McKenzie, it had an "almost hallowed atmosphere," and at times he felt "it was almost sacrilegious to speak louder than a whisper," because "it was in this atmosphere from which came the inspiration that produced what are widely considered the greatest works of literary art ever written in the English language."[178] The names of famous men "penned on the walls and carved in the woodwork" of Shakespeare's home reminded Ladd that he was one of the "millions [who] have made pilgrimage," motivated by the same reverence, to witness the same scenes and experience the same emotions. Echoing the language it had used only a few months before to report the opening of the transatlantic telegraph cable, the *Binnacle* celebrated the town as "the principal literary shrine of the English-speaking peoples."[179] Like the telegraph cable, Shakespeare bound the United States to Britain.[180] The Americans aboard the *Ryndam* came to claim him as one of the wellsprings of their own culture.

Following in the footsteps of so many of their fellow countrymen, in Palestine, Montmartre, Abbotsford, and Stratford (not to mention many other cities not directly discussed above), the *Ryndam* students read US history into the landscape of the ancient and European worlds, finding in these places abroad a genealogy for their own national culture and identity in an age of expanding US power. They sought a sense of embodied connection with an authentic real presence, not only of a place but of a place that was already somehow theirs; a place in which something crucial to their own culture resided. For them, as for so many other white, middle-class travelers from the United States in the 1920s, American belief, American blood, American money, and American speech made these sites different from the other stops along their route, sanctifying them in a way that made visiting them a pilgrimage—a kind of folk experience of the immanence of the nation abroad.[181] It was in these spaces that they wrote their settler nation into the Old World, giving their country an antiquity, and a trajectory, that legitimated its new international position.[182]

"THE WORLD IS A FINE PLACE"

If Professor Lough had wanted to teach his Floating University students to be world-minded, what they learned on the voyage was one version of the meaning of the United States' place in the world.[183] Their westward route provided the context for these lessons. Progressing from New York to Panama, then to Hollywood, and on to Hawaii, as outlined in chapter 5, the *Ryndam*'s passengers first mapped the expansive boundaries of their nation. Then, sailing from Japan to China to Singapore and then the Philippines, they had danced along the networks of American culture, capital, and expertise that helped constitute the US footprint in Southeast Asia. In this context, and in Hong Kong, Java, and India, they encountered the British and Dutch Empires before finally arriving in Europe itself. The sequence of these encounters, and the process of travel, played a role in how those aboard the *Ryndam* sought to order and make sense of the world around them.[184] The mechanisms through which they did this were not only (and perhaps not even principally) the formal curriculum of classes and assessment. It was through shipwide lectures, guidebooks from the library, the *Binnacle*'s reporting, Forum discussions, and even the plays staged by the Planet Players that collective lessons were progressively fashioned.

The passengers on the *Ryndam* expressed a diversity of views about their country's expanding power and cultural status and were far from passive recipients of travel literature. But across the course of the voyage, a widely held understanding of the United States as an imperial power was produced.[185] "If there were many American anti-imperialists aboard before the *Ryndam* left New York last Sep 18, the number had greatly decreased," Professor Douglas C. Ridgley told the *Christian Science Monitor* upon the ship's arrival in London. His colleague, Dean Albert Heckel, was quoted in the same article as saying that the cruise had succeeded in its goals of cultivating "international-mindedness, and a wider tolerance for other countries, other people and their ideas."[186] However, as far as Ridgley was concerned, there was no contradiction in these two positions: learning to be internationalists meant learning the techniques of empire and turning them to his nation's global mission of improvement. "The world is a fine place," he told the *Monitor*, "and with a clearer understanding of its problems and needs, [the United States] can help to make it better."[187]

The Americans had learned to see their country as an animating force in this global-historical drama of peoples and empires. It was a drama that in many ways relied on notions of national cultures that were able to be corrupted and exploited by bad governance or improved and uplifted by an enlightened rule. Those on the Floating University were eager not to be hoodwinked; they were forever on the lookout for the fake, the overpriced, and the commercial.[188] What they wanted was to feel they were encountering something "genuine," whether in Japan, India, Palestine, or Stratford.[189] This true form was then set against their own nation's dynamism and made to serve either as a point of essential difference or as the wellspring of their own contemporary culture.

Holling C. Holling's drawings, which he made continually throughout the voyage, are one expression of this. They reveal his quest for the "native" and the authentic.[190] This vision was not only evident in the Pacific, Asia, and India but also stretched to Europe. In Holland, he drew women in clogs; in Scandinavia, he sketched Vikings; and in England, he imagined Robin Hood. These were the essentialist folk forms of modernist 1920s American design culture. Of all the countries the *Ryndam* visited, only Germany got to be modern. Holling called it the "new industrial republic" and produced not a folk illustration but a Bauhaus-inspired design.[191]

Drawing this distinction between the authentic and inauthentic, the real and the fake, the traditional and the modern was both a form of cultural consumption and a way of classifying the diverse peoples of the world. However, as Ann Stoler has pointed out, classificatory rubrics can point to not just the dominance but also the fragility of colonial societies.[192] In the context of the Floating University, they perhaps evidence what historian Wendy Martin has called "a latent anxiety" about American cultural limitations as well as doubts about the United States' capacity to assume its new role in the world.[193] Although much of the hand-wringing on board the *Ryndam* was focused on the educational legitimacy of the voyage, its claim to a pseudodiplomatic status also meant that questions about its moral character animated these lurking qualms. Could the United States lead? Did it have the necessary character and experience to do so? As the next chapter shows, these questions shadowed the Floating University's students, even as they learned to see the emerging dominance of the United States within an imperial frame.

7

Other Ways of Knowing

When the members of the Floating University awoke on the morning of November 5, they were greeted by an impressive sight. Standing on the Yokohama dock were representatives from the city government, the League of Nations Association of Japan, the Foreign Office, the Friends Service Committee, the Tourist Bureau, Waseda University, the Women's Peace Association, the YMCA, and the Tokyo Chamber of Commerce.[1] This Japanese welcome committee had taken seriously the invitation extended by the University Travel Association to local educational officials to host the cruise. In addition to visits to the Tuscan Steel Plant and the Kawasaki Fukiai Iron Works factory, the committee had also arranged for a reception hosted by the mayor, a Chamber of Commerce luncheon, and a midday party hosted by the president of Tokyo Imperial University. It turned the prospect of five hundred Americans visiting its country into not only an educational but also a diplomatic and commercial showcase.

Professor James E. Lough's educational experiment was premised on the assumption that those aboard the Floating University would gain experiences in and with the world. It was much less concerned with how those who worked on the *Ryndam*, and those who lived in the port cities at which it docked, would experience the traveling Americans. What did the visit of the Floating University mean to those who encountered it from the shore? The lessons of empire that the Americans absorbed were by no means the only meanings the voyage acquired. As with other cultural and economic exchanges that took place on unequal terms, the arrival of the ship was exploited, employed, and manipulated for a variety of ends—not only by the Americans but also by their host communities. Inverting the perspective on the *Ryndam*'s voyage around the world points to the other worlds, multiple mobilities, and alternative systems of authorization with which the Floating

University intersected and to which it was recruited. It also highlights the limitations of its reach and how an awareness of these limits occasionally found its way back to the Americans on board the ship.

CULTURAL DIPLOMACY

Like the Japanese welcoming committee, the German government had also taken the University Travel Association's invitation seriously. It nominated Kurt Wiedenfeld, the professor of economics at Leipzig, and Alfred Weber, the professor of economics and sociology at Heidelberg, as the Floating University's "guest professors." They were to meet the students as part of an educational program that included visits to universities in both Hamburg and Berlin, a tour through the Reichstag, a reception by the mayor of Berlin, and a trip to Potsdam.[2] What did the German government, only recently stabilized after years of inflation and unrest, hope the Floating University's visit would achieve?

The selection of these two professors is revealing. Both had studied in Berlin under Gustav Schmoller, who in the 1890s was a proponent of the historical school of economics. Both were interested in transportation, and both developed spatial analyses of economic activity. Neither had been among the professors who had announced their support for Germany's military actions at the start of World War I by signing the Manifesto of the Ninety-Three. Wiedenfeld's research centered on railways and ports, trade policy, and the importance of Germany's colonial possessions, although after the war he turned to entrepreneurship, serving also as director of the foreign trade office and as the provisional representative of the Weimar government in Moscow in the early 1920s.[3] Weber was perhaps more prominent as a liberal intellectual and has since been remembered as a pioneer of cultural sociology in Germany.[4] The brother of Max Weber, he wrote about patterns of industrial location and the relationship between science, technology, and culture. He was also a figure who engaged with the Deutsche Hochschule für Politik and, named as a recipient of the Rockefeller Foundation grant that the Hochschule received in 1931, was active in shaping the beginnings of international relations in Weimar Germany.

In September 1925, when Wiedenfeld and Weber were appointed to address the visiting American students, German cultural diplomats were working hard to convince the world that the Weimar Republic was a "new Germany," distinct from the old.[5] As the major creditor of Britain and France, the United States, in their view, was a key player in the reparations debate, and they were very conscious of the direct American investments in German companies. At the same time, German scholars were trying to reenter the international scholarly community from which they had been excluded during the war.[6] In this context, the visit of a shipload of US university students and their professors presented an ideal opportunity to foster good relations between the two countries.[7]

The Berlin program had been organized by the Amerika-Institut, a kind of educational support institution opened in 1910 by none other than Lough's former professor, Hugo Münsterberg, for just this purpose. After the war, it took on the role of reviving scientific and cultural exchange with the United States. The thirty-page *Argonauts' Vademecum*, "a short-cut lesson and souvenir" booklet prepared by the Institut for the Floating University students, brought these concerns together. It contained information on the Institut, the German Institute for Foreigners in Berlin, and the Germany Academy of Politics; a letter from the American ambassador; a summary of the cultural attractions of the city of Cassel (Kassel); a section on the development of German airplane travel; and a notice for the centennial anniversary of Beethoven's death, which would be observed on March 26, 1927, during the students' visit.[8] This booklet, which combined culture with recreational attractions, astutely appealed to an American audience seeking experience. Indeed, Elizabeth Lippincott McQueen was one of the passengers who took the opportunity while in Germany to fly in an airplane, traveling from Berlin to Copenhagen.[9]

Exactly what Wiedenfeld and Weber said to the visiting Americans is not entirely clear. Both are named on the Floating University's official faculty list, and they likely delivered the lectures at the university reception in Hamburg (fig. 7.1), at which Lillian McCracken took detailed notes concerning

FIGURE 7.1. Lecture and reception at the University of Hamburg. In Walter Conger Harris, *Photographs of the First University World Cruise* (New York: University Travel Association, 1927), no. 840.

the nature of German reparation payments.[10] But no lectures were held in Berlin. The Amerika-Institut's director told the *Berliner Nachtausgabe* that the Americans were "happy that we have not prepared lectures for them . . . they are the type who wish to discover things for themselves."[11] Other accounts suggest that the students had been far more taken with the nightlife of the capital than with the official program.[12] Holling C. and Lucille Holling managed to see not one but three films during their three-day stay, including the recently released expressionist science-fiction drama *Metropolis*.[13] Charles Ladd had skipped these proceedings altogether, instead flying from Amsterdam to Cologne and then catching a train to Heidelberg before rejoining the cruise in Berlin.[14]

VIEWS FROM THE SHORE

Perhaps unsurprisingly, the *Berliner Nachtausgabe* described the visiting Americans as "Dollarika" who "travel around the world like uncrowned kings," eager for lunch at the hotel and full of "the most incredible American questions." Newspapers in other locations were equally amused or disapproving. The *Philippines Herald* criticized the students' failure to attend the extensive program of official hospitality organized for them by the University of Manila, and Copenhagen's *Extra Bladet* thought they "look[ed] anything but clean and proper."[15] The *China Press* described the students as "world circling rah-rah boys," and as the *Ryndam* approached the Netherlands, accounts of the students' drunkenness in Japan found their way into the pages of the liberal-leaning *Nieuw Rotterdamsche Courant*.[16] Excerpts were quoted widely in other regional and national Dutch newspapers, with the *Amigoe di Curaçao*, a paper issued on the Dutch colony of Curaçao in the Caribbean, running its article under the headline "The Floating University That, Thank God, Will Not Visit Curaçao."[17]

For the Dutch left-wing press, this bad behavior was a sign of more systemically unequal global power relations. *De Tribune*, the paper of the local Communist Party, saw it as hypocrisy: "Workers, who in a rush of drunkenness cause any harm, are locked up for months; the bourgeois newspapers then lament about the 'wickedness' and the 'degeneration' of the people. But the vandalisms of a bunch of 'studying' bourgeois beasts are condoned with the qualification 'that is . . . entertaining.'"[18] *Voorwaarts*, the newspaper of the Dutch Social Democratic Party, was equally cutting: "Thus the little bourgeois sons of America have demonstrated the blessings of Western civilization in the Far East," ran its commentary. "Is it any wonder that the Mongols [the Chinese nationalists] are getting tired of letting themselves be exploited for the benefits of such scum?"[19] For these newspapers on the

Left, five hundred rich Americans treating the port cities of the world as their playground stood as further evidence of the United States' role in extending the international currents of capitalist imperialism.

VIEWS FROM THE SHIP

The voyage acquired a variety of meanings on board the *Ryndam* as well. Among the officers and engineers and firemen and stokers were a few crew members whose own reasons for being on the ship stood out even to the reporters and editors of the *Binnacle*. One of the stewards was Francis Wanrooy, a well-known Dutch painter who had exhibited at the Salon Modern in Brussels and was working his way home. He was initially assigned to waiting tables, but he was so bad at it that the captain gave him the post of cleaner in the library.[20] Dirk Van Dem was a Dutch journalist who had signed on as dishwasher in Bombay (Mumbai).[21] He had set off from Utrecht with the aim of cycling around the world. But he was beset by various misfortunes, including being robbed in Paris and arrested by police in Syria after being mistaken for a German spy. When his bicycle was stolen, he had continued on foot until he got sick and found himself confined for five months to a hospital in India. The *Ryndam* was also his way to get back home. Then there was Theodore F. Kinsella, one of the few Americans among the crew, who was working in the laundry.[22] He had a talent for finding trouble in port, having been beaten up and robbed in Hawaii and struck over the head and given a black eye in Shanghai; finally, he managed to break his leg in a fight in Batavia (Jakarta), where he was left to recover as the *Ryndam* sailed on, probably to the relief of the captain.[23]

As the ship left Los Angeles, the *Binnacle* reported that seven men from the Philippines had joined the crew. In the face of a shortage of seagoing laundrymen, the Holland America Line had been forced to recruit not only "orientalen" but men who had no previous experience "at the domestic art of cleaning and ironing."[24] Leonard B. Aliwanag was one of them.[25] In 1976, Aliwanag was interviewed as part of the Washington State Oral History Program, and his story presents a very different account of the ship and its routes.

Aliwanag was born in the Bohol region of the Visayan Islands in the Philippines in 1902. His family had been caught between colonial regimes. His father had served as a teacher under the Spanish but lost his position when the United States took possession of the islands. Aliwanag had received four years of the mass education program implemented by the Americans, but at age sixteen he decided to launch his own craft onto the currents of the region's new economic power. Lured by the promises of the recruiting agents who came to his hometown, he signed a three-year contract to work on the sugar plantations in Hawaii with the intention of saving up enough money to complete his education in the United States, which, he had heard, was a "Paradis of dollars."[26] But these hopes went unfulfilled. Arriving in Los Angeles on a Japanese ship and met by a labor contractor at the dock, Aliwanag was placed on a farm near Stanton, California, before moving on to stints as a domestic servant and as a waiter in restaurants and hotels on Catalina Island and in Los Angeles. He even acted as a "native" extra in various silent movies in Hollywood. It was during this time in Los Angeles, while walking down Broadway, that Aliwanag saw a sign in a window: "12 Filipinos Wanted to go around the world." Intrigued, he recruited his friends, and together they boarded the SS *Ryndam* in San Pedro Harbor, soon finding out that "so many whites [had] quit because they cannot take the ship."[27]

The students' educational activities aboard the *Ryndam* were clearly not Aliwanag's central concern. His memory of how the Floating University operated had them going to classes onshore. "If we are in Tokyo we stay there one week while the students are attending school at Tokyo University. And we go to Manila, we stay there two weeks and the students attend their schooling in Philippine University" was how he explained the arrangements. Aliwanag was much more focused on how he could make money through the laundry. He soon realized he could make a healthy profit by contracting out the passengers' dry cleaning on a commission basis to contractors in ports. He waited tables too, sometimes sneaking extra ice cream for himself. He liked the students, who frequently tipped him handsomely; to him, they were impossibly rich. He recalled tickets that cost $10,000 and a son of a multimillionaire who got five girls pregnant in Paris. For Aliwanag, the Floating University was a "Scandal Ship." It was this scandalous nature and the subsequent divisions over coeducation upon the *Ryndam*'s return to the United States in 1927 that he named as the reasons that the Holland America Line cut short his contract after only nine months.[28]

In the years following the ship's return, Aliwanag continued working for various shipping lines. He also waited tables in New York and Chicago and moved to Alaska to work in the canneries before finally settling in Seattle. His life had, in many ways, traced the very currents of empire and unequal exchange along which the Floating University had sailed, although his experience of them was quite different to that of the rich Americans above deck. Aliwanag never received the US education of which he had once dreamed, but in a way he did get to go to school in the United States. After World War II he decided to apply for US citizenship, but this required a civics exam. The three-week preparation course he attended was taught by a woman instructor, and Aliwanag was careful to note that she was Japanese.[29] Perhaps he recognized in her another person whose life, a little like his own, had been shaped by movements across oceans in which the United States was a forceful, though by no means the only, power.

Schooled in nationalism and colonialism, the Americans on board the Floating University all too easily missed the other global travelers who could, in the words of historian Engseng Ho, be "found across imperial domains in more innocuous dress as 'trading minorities' and indentured labor."[30] As Aliwanag knew only too well, Japanese steamers crisscrossed the Pacific, carrying all sorts of passengers. In fact, the "Mitsuma Maru" (likely the *Katori Maru*) was tracing much the same route as the *Ryndam*, and it was from one of its American passengers that the *Binnacle* learned that savvy locals in Hong Kong and Shanghai upped their prices by as much as 30 percent to exploit the Floating University's arrival in port.[31] It was in such ships that Japanese, Chinese, Tamil, and Filipino workers made their way not only to Hawaii and the United States but around and between the countries of the Asian and Pacific worlds.

At least some of the small craft that greeted the *Ryndam* in Hong Kong's Kowloon Harbor were likely to have been Indian traders.[32] James McKenzie noted the Hindu proprietors in Hong Kong shops, selling goods made in China, India, and Japan.[33] In fact, one of the founding donors to Hong King University was a Gujarati Parsi, Sir Hormusjee Naorojee Mody, who had made a fortune as a land developer. This same region had long been traversed by Muslim traders, who married locals but remained connected to commercial, religious, and family networks that reached from Malaya, Java (Indonesia), and South Asia to Africa and Arabia.[34] The accounts of those aboard the Floating University contained scant details of the complexities of these diasporic worlds. Although Holling, Ladd, and McKenzie as well as the other *Ryndam* passengers frequently noted the presence of sampans and junks and "coolie" laborers in Asian port cities, they invariably presented them in a picturesque and racialized guise that rendered static the intricate mobilities of a host of voyagers both like and very unlike themselves.

OFF THE SHORE AND ONTO THE DECKS

The *Ryndam* was not sealed off from these other worlds. The sellers and beggars who swarmed around the ship in little boats in Hong Kong, scaling its sides and crowding its waters, were noted by several of the passengers.[35] If these visitors were largely seen as picturesque, the stop in Moji (Kitakyushu), Japan, was more disconcerting. Over the course of fourteen hours, three hundred or so workers, covered in black dust, loaded two thousand tons of coal by hand, hauling baskets from sampans pulled up alongside the ship. The Americans looking on, accustomed to the speed of the machine age, gaped at the slow and physical nature of this process.[36] That many of the workers were women who were paid a paltry wage, some laboring with children strapped to their backs, further disquieted them, upsetting their assumptions not only of gender roles but also of the processes that sustained their global travel.[37]

In several ports, particularly in East Asia, this dissolution of the boundary between ship and shore was a planned part of the official program, with the Floating University hosting several official receptions for local students aboard the *Ryndam*. In Shanghai, the Chinese students were invited to a dinner and took part in a staged debate with the Americans, who were embarrassed by their guests' knowledge of the United States and their own ignorance of China.[38] In Hong Kong, the ship held an open house both of the days it was in port and an official dinner attended by the island's British governor, among other dignitaries.[39] A formal reception on board the *Ryndam* was also held on the first night of its stop in the Dutch East Indies (Indonesia). After a day full of activities in which the American students had toured Buitenzorg (Bogor) and Batavia (Jakarta), local students from the Prinz Hendrik Middle Class School, the Training College, and the Medical High School (many of them from "royal families," noted Vernita Lundquist in the *Binnacle*) came onto the ship and performed Javanese court dances, including the *serimpi* (*srimpi*) and the *wayang wong* dance drama (fig. 7.2).[40]

The Hollings were captivated by the performance but struggled to make sense of what they were seeing. "A dance of postures, a dance of pictures," Holling wrote to his mother; the "dancers hands assume poses like strange exotic orchids with nervously trembling petals," he wrote in his diary. He found the music very difficult to grasp; "five minutes of it makes a savage out of you. It has such percise [*sic*] beat and rythm [*sic*]." He thought there was "something strangely mystical" about the whole performance, describing it as timeless, with "an unreal atmosphere."[41] Holling's drawings show him trying to render on the page what he had seen on the stage, captivated by an art form that appealed to his sense of the visual and the sensual but stretched beyond his comprehension. Although he reached for some of the familiar tropes of white men in the tropics to contain the feelings the Javanese dancers evoked in him, their art form escaped his ability to understand it.

Something about these moments in which the shore came onto the ship seemed to discomfort the Americans, although not in a way they were able to fully articulate. It was one thing to venture, cashed-up and eager for experience, into the streets of foreign port cities. It was another thing alto-

FIGURE 7.2. Javanese students at the STOVIA medical school dancing the *serimpi* (*srimpi*) and the *wayang wong* aboard the SS *Ryndam*. In Walter Conger Harris, *Photographs of the First University World Cruise* (New York: University Travel Association, 1927), no. 319.

gether to have the residents of those port cities breach the boundaries of their home-on-the-ocean.

SPORTS DEFEATS

Equally unsettling to the Americans were the defeats that the Floating University's sports teams kept sustaining. James Howard Marshall was particularly rattled by the soccer match against Egyptian students in Cairo.[42] He had arrived in the country expecting to see "the very ancient glory" of the Pyramids and tombs of the pharaohs. He had not expected to be confronted—and comprehensively defeated—by "the spirit that lies behind modern nationalist Egypt."[43] Back at Haverford College in Pennsylvania, Marshall had been a something of a star at soccer, but he had never played against a team like that fielded by the University of Cairo.[44] It had been embarrassing. They were playing in front of an important audience: the Egyptian prime minister, Adly Pasha; the former prime minister, Zaghlul Pasha; and the US ambassador were all in the crowd (fig. 7.3). But within the first fifteen minutes, it had become clear that the *Ryndam* students were "not

FIGURE 7.3. Officials at the soccer match in Cairo. In Walter Conger Harris, *Photographs of the First University World Cruise* (New York: University Travel Association, 1927), no. 484.

the equals of the fast, accurate and well-coached team of the Egyptian University." The game had been suspended, and the Egyptians had very kindly agreed to divide the teams so that they were more evenly matched—some of James's teammates played on the Egyptian side, and vice versa. But still, the Americans were "outclassed in every department," in the end losing 3–2.[45]

Student bodies in competition had been envisioned by the Floating University as a form of diplomacy—a way to "establish personal friendships and gain for America some friends abroad."[46] At the start of the cruise, the *Binnacle* had boasted of the more than two dozen "college athletes of note" among the student passengers.[47] But the student newspaper—like Marshall—was soon forced to change its tune. Although the "SSU" (for SS *University*) team won at basketball against a Chinese YMCA team in Hong Kong and narrowly defeated the University of the Philippines in a swimming competition, they lost to a scratch soccer team composed of *Ryndam* crew members in Honolulu, were trounced 21–1 by the University of the Philippines in baseball, were "mauled" by Shanghai College in basketball 40–6, and managed only a 6–6 tie in the baseball game against the University of Hawaii.[48]

The *Binnacle*'s reporters came up with various explanations for these results: the Floating University team hadn't had any practice; it was inexperienced; its opponents had played since childhood; the SSU team was not expected to win anyway.[49] But it was unsettling when white bodies in competition with "natives" lost at their own game.[50] The *Binnacle* admitted that a *Ryndam* student said he was "amazed at the ability displayed by peoples whom he expected to be anything but interested in our games and [was] often chagrined when that prowess [was] used to overcome him in a contest."[51] In the face of defeat, the newspaper swiftly framed "Western sports" as a force for spreading "the culture and ideals of western civilization."[52] They were activities that provided the "contact which [drew] Oriental People together," ran one editorial line.[53] Fond of athletics and encouraged by missionaries, Chinese girls were refusing to have their feet bound.[54] Someday, the *Binnacle* hoped, "the yellow man will send his representatives in their strength to compete on equal terms with others in the world's Olympic games and race side by side with men of all nations and strive mightily in honest competition."[55]

Such pronouncements echoed the logic of physical culture propounded by the American YMCA and spread through its overseas branches.[56] Indeed, it was YMCA "physical directors" in New England colleges who invented and popularized team games like basketball and volleyball, which, along with baseball, were thought to be safer and more "scientific" than contact sports.[57] In the United States, these sports were celebrated by the YMCA as a means of creating better and more moral citizens, and in India, China, and Japan they were championed as a means of cultivating the values of democratic citizenship, breaking down caste and religious divisions, and improving the moral and physical hygiene of racial subjects.[58] But this was a logic that relied on a construction of nonwhite bodies as inferior and in need of animation.[59] The Floating University teams' repeated sports defeats upset these assumptions. They provoked anxieties about both racial ordering and the United States' civilizational standing. But these defeats were not the only thing that disrupted the American students' preconceptions of themselves and those they were meeting.

"MERE LIP-SERVICE"

As the *Ryndam* made its way along its westward route, it occasionally dawned on the cruising Americans that although they were out to see the places and peoples of the world, those peoples were also looking back—and not always liking what they saw. It was becoming apparent that the Floating University itself was being viewed by many of the people the Americans were meeting as a proxy for the expanding tentacles of US economic, military, and cultural might, not as a representative of US friendship and goodwill.

In Japan, for example, the prominent industrialist Eiichi Shibusawa had made clear that he thought talk of "Japan-American friendship and fraternity" was "mere lip-service." With its recent introduction of immigration-restriction laws, the United States had "shown in her attitude towards Japan that she is not over-eager for the friendly relations we desire."[60] Dr. C. T. Wang (Wang Zhengtin), former acting premier of the Chinese Republic, one of the five Chinese delegates to the Paris Peace Conference of 1919–20, and in 1926 president of China College at Peking, was even more cutting. "Is China a nation, or is she a market?" he asked Marion Wenger, a University of Michigan student who had managed to gain an interview. The United States and European powers "seemed to regard her as a market" was his answer, but "she wants the rights of a nation," including the right to set tariffs and to govern her own affairs.[61]

When the *Ryndam* arrived in India, reporters for the *Binnacle* were surprised to find the *Times of India* running negative editorials on American business interests in the country and to learn that the Nobel Prize–winning poet Sir Rabindranath Tagore refused to return to the United States because of "the unpleasant souvenirs" of his previous trip.[62] Meanwhile, from Mexico the Associated Press carried news that its president and his parliament were rebelling against "American imperialism" and refusing to abolish the "oil laws" banning foreigners from direct ownership of land or water and vesting all ownership of petroleum in the Mexican state.[63] In the student "prison" at the University in Heidelberg were mocking cartoons not only of Bismarck and the kaiser but also "more recent [ones] of Americans with donkey ears."[64] The stop in the Philippines had made clear the aspirations to independence of the United States' own colony. Just as clearly, the Filipinos were not the only colonized peoples seeking to free themselves from foreign rule.

NATIONALISTS AND COMMUNISTS

Arriving in Port Said, Egypt, Tom Johnson observed that the "feeling of nationalism is in evidence in almost every spot in the world": "Young China [was] breaking out," Java (Indonesia) was "beginning to be self-conscious," and the "people ruled by the English feel just as the Filipinos do, that even though they are better off materially, they would rather have less and go to hell in their own way." Johnson's sympathy was "with the natives as far as their desire for self determination goes," but he did not clarify how this could be reconciled with what he saw as an increasingly interdependent world. "No one can be a dog in the manger any longer" was how he put it, borrowing a phrase used in the 1920s to refer to countries restricting foreign access to resources they were not using. Yet Johnson also knew that "the point where helping to free the world from the dog in the manger attitude leaves off and imperialism begins is not a straight line easy to see."[65]

At the start of 1927, no one was speaking against British imperial rule more clearly than Mahatma Gandhi. Even the Henry J. Allen–influenced *Binnacle* acknowledged that he had "become such an epoch-making figure in the recent history of India that he must be taken into account in all discussions of its modern problems."[66] Although the article in the student paper went on to dismiss "the apostle of non co-operation" as an impractical "dreamer," ten *Ryndam* passengers were interested enough in him to leave the ship at Colombo, Ceylon (Sri Lanka), in order to undertake a massive trip overland by train to Benares (Varanasi) and Agra via Jaffna, Madras (Chennai), and Calcutta (Kolkata). In doing so, they hoped to meet both Gandhi and the nationalist students from the Jaffna Youth Congress he had inspired, whose 1926 meeting had just taken place in Keerimalai.[67] And when they finally found the mahatma, sitting "crossed-legged" on a dais amid "a large gathering of people in a village near Calcutta," he was very different from the "fiery Gandhi [they] had pictured." With a shaven head and dressed only in a loincloth and shawl, his "body was extremely thin," and he "seemed far older than his 57 years." But Dessa M. Skinner Jr. was impressed. Gandhi had welcomed him with a firm handshake and, upon hearing of the Floating University's mission, told the Missourian he hoped the students would "carry back to far-off America a true conception of the problems India is striving to solve."[68]

It was very possibly Skinner, one of the *Binnacle*'s regular reporters, who attempted to do just that, in a remarkable unsigned article that appeared in the student newspaper a few days after the *Ryndam* left Bombay (Mumbai). "Call the Swarajists bolshevists, call them agitators, call them revolutionaries," it began, "but would you look back in your own history books and call the American revolutionists bolshevists and communists?" "No," it continued, "you would call them a suppressed race, fighting for their independence, fighting for high ideals, fighting for a liberty of thought and action that was their birth-right." Although the author thought there were clear arguments against the practicality of "Swaraj" plans for a unified India via self-rule, its proponents were insistent that these plans amounted to far more than Gandhi's leadership and ideals. Rather, the Swaraj were a powerful political party with a strong presence in the major cities of India, making a just case that should have been familiar to Americans.[69]

Schooled in the anticolonial foundations of their own national story, Johnson and Skinner, as well as others on the Floating University, could recognize the national aspirations of the Indians agitating against British rule. They had a harder time seeing as legitimate the Chinese rebellions against the kind of international imperialism the United States itself so strategically practiced.[70] Only a few days before the stop in India, the *Binnacle* had reported that the foreign concession at Hankow (Hangzhou) had been seized by Cantonese nationalists, that foreign businesses had been forced to close, and that all European and American women and children had been evacuated.[71] News of the tensions in China had filled the student paper's pages ever since the *Ryndam*'s scheduled visit to Canton (Guangzhou) and Peking (Beijing) was abandoned due to nationalist agitation. Indeed, when the students had arrived in Hong Kong, they were given a forty-page pamphlet that contested the account produced by the (US-funded) local branch of the YMCA on the "Canton incident" of June 23, 1925. The YMCA account had blamed British troops for the killing of more than fifty Chinese protesters.[72] In contrast, the pamphlet, titled *The Truth*, presented to the US students a pro-foreigner account that emphasized Chinese aggression and British restraint, laying the ultimate blame on Bolsheviks who, in its view, had been "disturbing the minds of the younger and more vocal classes of [Southern] China . . . and nourish[ing] their chauvinism on ill-digested ideas of civic rights and liberties."[73]

Robert C. Story, a student at Willamette University in Oregon, had attempted to make sense of the confusing Chinese political situation for the *Binnacle*'s readers. The nationalists, he explained, had two enemies: the warlords within and the imperialists from without.[74] What Story missed, however, was that the nationalists themselves consisted of an uneasy alliance between Sun Yat-sen's Kuomintang party (KMT) and the Chinese Communist Party (CPC). The forces that had taken Hankow were led by Eugene Chen, who was from the leftist wing of the KMT and willing to work with the CPC. In the *Binnacle*, wire reports from the Associated Press collapsed these divisions, referring to the new government in Hankow simply as "the bolshevist [*sic*] Cantonese government" and pointing to the collaborative as well as competitive nature of European and American presence in the region.[75] The great fear was that the nationalists in China were receiving support from the Soviet government in Russia. A newspaper correspondent who went by the name of Frank America and who joined the *Ryndam* in Constantinople at Allen's invitation, was certain that they were. "Soviet influence is undoubtedly behind the Cantonese," he told the *Binnacle*. "Barodin [*sic*] and other Soviet agitators are pushing the Chinese into war in the hope of bringing about their long-cherished world revolution against capitalism."[76]

The student paper's news items, received via radio, revealed a broader anxiety about the global footprint of communist agitation. In November 1926 and January 1927, the newspaper reported that a "Communistic revolt [had] broke[n] out in various districts in Java," with seven hundred "Batavian communists" later exiled to Noesa (Nusa) Island.[77] In January 1927 it told of "a big Moscow plot, with the objective of causing a communist revolution," that had been unearthed in Poland.[78] In the same month, the US secretary of state was insisting it was "the bolshevists" who were "undertaking the destruction of what they termed American Imperialism in Mexico and Latin America."[79] And in March the *Binnacle* informed the students that an attempted coup by "a few small units of the army, some local communists, and the riff-raff from the streets" had taken place in Lisbon only the week before the *Ryndam*'s arrival there.[80] On board the Floating University, it had become clear that the Western liberal order, of which the United States was rapidly assuming a leading role, was not the only version of internationalism around.

DICTATORS OF THE MEDITERRANEAN

Indeed, Henry Allen argued that it was from bolshevism that Mussolini had saved Italy. And Italy, as the paper pointed out, was only one of several "revolutionary governments of the Mediterranean" that the *Ryndam* would be visiting.[81] In Turkey there was Mustafa Kemal Atatürk, who in controlling the Assembly had turned the country "into a dictatorship under the attractive fiction that it is the 'young Turk republic.'"[82] According to Frank America, Atatürk was "to Turkey what Mussolini is to Italy"—he was improving the country, and he had the best interests of the people at heart.[83] In Portugal, General Óscar Carmona "became president" in a coup d'état, creating a "republic" in which all the ministerial posts, save two, were filled by army officers. Spain was also ruled by an army general (Miguel Primo de Rivera) who had dissolved the parliament and declared martial law. But in Spain, according to the *Binnacle*, King Alfonso XIII had "picked out a good revolutionist" and was "furnishing the brains to the dictator."[84] If Tom Johnson looked at these countries and saw corruption and chaos, the Allen-influenced *Binnacle* editors took a different view.[85] They judged that the "new vigor which characterizes the administration of affairs [had] brought a definite improvement in physical and economic conditions." Perhaps dictators were not so bad after all?

Allen was certainly impressed by Benito Mussolini.[86] In fact, it was he who managed to broker a meeting with the Italian fascist leader after the US ambassador, Henry P. Fletcher, had declared it totally impossible. Having traveled all over Europe, first with the Red Cross and YMCA during the war and then with the Near East Relief Committee in 1923, Allen's international connections were extensive—and wherever he went, he kept a meticulous record of the people he met.[87] Thomas Brown, the *Ryndam*'s Journalism professor and Allen's coeditor on the *Binnacle*, thought Allen had "much more influence everywhere than any private citizen has any right to have."[88]

FIGURE 7.4. Mussolini (*center, with arms crossed*) hosting the Floating University at the Palazzo Chigi in Rome. In Walter Conger Harris, *Photographs of the First University World Cruise* (New York: University Travel Association, 1927), no. 692.

Not only did Allen arrange for the whole cruise to meet Mussolini, but he also had a two-hour private audience with him and stayed on in Rome for an additional two days to attend the opening of the Italian parliament as the leader's guest.[89]

And Allen was by no means the only one on the *Ryndam* fascinated by Mussolini. He and Professor Lough jostled for the place of honor beside him in the cruise photograph at the Palazzo Chigi (fig. 7.4).[90] The *Binnacle* pronounced him "without question the most outstanding public man in the world," and *The Student Magellan* (the *Ryndam*'s student yearbook) later reported the "ill-suppressed excitement" among the entire student body at the prospect of meeting him.[91] The students were in no doubt as to Mussolini's status. His countenance had glared at them from every angle as they walked the streets of Rome. DeWitt Reddick described stores "draping paintings of him in their showcases."[92] "He certainly is a strong looking character" was Charles Gauss's verdict.[93]

Others, Reddick among them, were more skeptical. He thought the Italian people feared Mussolini as much as they respected him, and he believed that his power rested on "a slender thread."[94] With dissenting views in evidence, once again Allen staged a Forum meeting to manufacture a consensus opinion. Some students and staff thought "that bolshevism might be preferable to the condition in which Italy would find herself upon the collapse of Mussolini's government," but Allen declared that "Mussolini is stronger in Italy today than was Napoleon . . . after the close of the French Revolution." In the *Binnacle*'s verdict, it was "the almost unanimous opinion" of the Forum that Italy under Mussolini was "in better condition economically and physically" than it was before he took charge.[95] For at least some aboard the *Ryndam*, communist agitation was sufficiently threatening to justify authoritarian rule. But they struggled to see that the capitalist liberal internationalism against which the communists raged, and which the United States advanced through formal and informal means, was experienced by many not as freedom but as empire.

A DOUBLE STAGE

Why did Portugal's General Carmona welcome a delegation of the deans and select students at the Palacio do Congresso Nacional? Why did Abdul Pasha, the Egyptian prime minister, and members of his cabinet host them and attend their exhibition soccer match? Why did the pope grant them an audience in the Vatican, the sultan of Lahej in Arabia receive them, the president of the Reichstag welcome them, and King Rama VII of Siam (Thailand) entertain them?

Gandhi seemed to offer an answer to these questions when he asked Dessa Skinner to "carry back to far-off America a true conception of the problems India is striving to solve." Those who left accounts of their time on the *Ryndam* seemed to understand the hospitality they had received in just this way: as a dimension of the ship's pseudodiplomatic character, a means of influencing the future leaders of the world's rising power.

But these leaders likely also had an eye on a different set of audiences—not only those in the United States but also those in their local contexts. Here was a chance to participate in the theatrics of international diplomacy, something that had especial political value in circumstances in which their own rule was insecure or seeking legitimation.[96] The Dutch colonial government, for example, regarded the Floating University as an international public relations exercise, and Governor Farrington saw its visit as helpful to his ongoing campaign for Hawaiian statehood.[97] For Mussolini, certainly, the meeting with the cruise members seemed principally a photographic opportunity. Standing with his feet wide apart, left hand on his thigh, he shook hands with all five hundred students, one by one. Reddick thought him to be "like an actor facing his audience."[98] With his "head thrown very high" and arms crossed, he posed for the camera before turning theatrically to give the Roman salute and depart.[99]

Behind the passengers' direct experience of port cities were rich, complex, and dynamic hinterlands of social and political life that rarely appear in their firsthand accounts. From the low-paid or indentured workers who pulled them in rickshaws and swept the streets for them—who sold them goods, hiked the prices of those goods, and hauled coal by hand into the

Ryndam's bunkers, not just in Moji but in Batavia, Bombay, Port Said, Naples, and Algiers—to those at the other end of the social spectrum, like Lim Nee Soon, who turned the camera back on the visiting Americans and used the resulting photograph as part of an advertising campaign directed at improving his export markets in England and the United States, the lives and motivations of those who lived in the port cities of the world were flattened out, made picturesque, or taken for granted by the *Ryndam*'s passengers.[100] Lim Nee Soon, for example, was not only the owner of the rubber factory in Singapore but a former Chinese revolutionary who had founded the Tongmenghui (T'ung Meng Hui) in Singapore and was a close associate of Sun Yat-sen. Not long after the Floating University left Singapore, his son and partner in the rubber business, Lim Chong Pang, and his wife traveled east from Singapore to New York on a different Dutch ship so that they could, in their own words, see "how the other half lives."[101]

The people who hosted the Floating University and the cultures they made resisted classifications of traditional and modern, authentic and corrupt. Making lives within not only global but also local structures that were uneven and unequal, they had long engaged with, refashioned, and contested European and American cultural and commercial exports for a variety of political ends.[102] The journeys of elites such as Lim Chong Pan and indentured workers such as Leonard B. Aliwanag remind us that there were many ways to sail around the world in the 1920s and many ways of making sense of its power disparities.

Those who traveled on the Floating University were far from passive tourists who simply parroted the caricatured portrayals of their guidebooks and lectures. They were eager to see and experience port cities for themselves, and they engaged critically in debates about colonial rule and world order, trying to square for themselves the circle of uplift and self-determination. Many were unsettled when their assumptions about foreign peoples were punctured, and many were startled by the hostility toward the United States they sometimes encountered. But they remained the central characters of a narrative in which the alternative meanings of the Floating University were sidelined. Although other ways of knowing sometimes crept onto the ship, the Floating University's passengers were not really that interested in what the voyage meant to other people. They were much more interested in what they could make of themselves in the world.

◆ ◆ ◆

The *Ryndam* left Greenwich in southeast London on April 19, 1927, with a somewhat diminished company. Forty-two of its passengers (including

James Price, the student president) were staying on to spend the summer in Europe, so they waved goodbye to their *Ryndam* companions from the pier rather than the deck.[103] Second-semester examinations were supposed to take place as the ship sailed across the Atlantic, but the *Binnacle* made no mention of them. Its pages suggest that the students were more occupied with preparations for the farewell costume ball than they were with college work.[104] The ball itself was held on April 23. Tables were removed from the upper dining room, and Jack Eakin, chair of the student organizing committee, arranged for several skits to be performed between dances. A grand march traversed the whole ship, led by Lucille Holling and Dean George E. Howes, who for this evening at least did not have academic work on his mind.[105] Lillian McCracken spent most of the crossing reading and socializing, and Walter Conger Harris, the official photographer, displayed two hundred slides of the trip in the main Assembly Room. Meanwhile, in the *Ryndam*'s library, Miss Alida Stephens begged all students to return their books so they could be packed and counted. Those who wanted to register to secure credits with their home universities were given a last chance to do so.[106] The first-ever Floating University world cruise was drawing to an end. But the fight for its legacy was only just beginning.

8

Assessing the Experiment

Professor James E. Lough put on a brave face as he stepped off the *Ryndam* and onto New Jersey's Hoboken pier on May 2, 1927. A gaggle of reporters waited for him in the bulkhead house, along with a brass band and several hundred of the students' parents and friends.[1] "We had no difficulties" was what Lough told the waiting press. The Floating University had "accomplished what it set out to do"; "[the world] had been used as a laboratory for the study" of all manner of subjects.[2] The students, apparently, "scoffed at reports" that scandal had dogged the voyage.[3] Loaded with souvenirs, they were much more anxious to identify their parents on the pier in the hope of having their customs duties paid than to talk with newspapermen (fig. 8.1).[4] Yet, as passengers returned to their homes across the country, local newspapers unearthed the details that Professor Lough had been unwilling to provide.[5] The matter of the expelled students would not go away, reports of engagements continued to emerge, and some of the young women were eager to complain about the judgmental influence of "the old maids" among the nonstudent "tourists."[6] To complicate things further, now two successor organizations were competing for the legacy of the 1926 cruise and attempting to organize rival Floating Universities that would sail in the fall of 1927. Only a few days after the *Ryndam* returned, it was clear that Lough's bold claims of a difficulty-free voyage did not stand up to scrutiny.

Was it possible for the cruise's organizers to reclaim their "educational experiment" when it had already been widely reported as a failure?[7] Who would decide the conventions for what counted as education in interwar America? Although arguments for its merit were advanced by both its professors and its passengers, ultimately it was the judgment of the press, the rejection of the university world, and the dismissal of the US State

FIGURE 8.1. Family and friends greeting the returning students on the Hoboken, New Jersey, pier. In Walter Conger Harris, *Photographs of the First University World Cruise* (New York: University Travel Association, 1927), no. 986.

Department that decided the fate of the Floating University. Professor Lough's academic innovation did not receive sufficient social recognition to achieve legitimacy.

CONTENTIOUS LESSONS

Sidelining their earlier emphasis on experiment as a pedagogic method, the cruise leaders initially embraced the newspapers' own framing of the voyage as a new form of education. The *Ryndam* trip was "only an initial step," faculty member and former Kansas governor Henry J. Allen told the newspapers, and "like every other initial step, had many faults."[8] The problems with the voyage were, in Dean Albert K. Heckel's words, merely "mistakes . . . in large part due to the novelty of the enterprise." It was, after all, "a pioneer venture."[9] According to this line of thinking, a scientific experiment was never a failure, only an opportunity to disprove or support a hypothesis. Any fault lines in the 1926–27 voyage were opportunities to learn and improve. Or, in Allen's words, "As a result of the [*Ryndam*] experiment, the plans proposed for the next voyage will take advantage of all the errors made in the first effort."[10]

What exactly these lessons were, however, remained a hot point of contention; or, as *Time* magazine put it, the cause of "much confused palaver."[11] Allen had made his views on the subject clear before the *Ryndam* even returned to New York. Having left the still-traveling students in Hamburg, he arrived back in the United States in mid-April and gave several interviews to a willing press, telling the *New York Times* that the *Ryndam* had "demonstrated clearly . . . that the plan of a traveling university was sound" but that women should not be included in future voyages: "foreign nations were not accustomed to liberal American ideas."[12]

Swift to lend his support to this analysis was Charles H. Phelps Jr. of Phelps Bros., the shipping agency that had managed the cruise. In March 1927, he had sent John G. MacVicar, the recently retired principal of the Montclair Academy (an elite private boys' school in New Jersey), to Rome to meet the *Ryndam* and investigate the reports of bad behavior. MacVicar had concluded that "coeducation [was] not practical under cruise conditions" for two reasons. First, it lessened student contacts in foreign countries where coeducation was not common or understood; and second, together with the presence of older passengers on board, it lessened "educational effectiveness," because it created "a loosely knit student body" rather than a cohesive one.[13] This assessment, which drew on contemporary objections to coeducation, subsequently became the official line from the University Travel Association (UTA): it was not romantic distractions that caused the *Ryndam*'s difficulties but rather the challenges of accommodating women during shore excursions and explaining their presence to foreign audiences unused to American ways.[14]

However, in keeping with his Quaker beliefs, Andrew J. McIntosh remained convinced of the virtues of coeducation. Having left the *Ryndam* in Hawaii, his *Floating University* magazine had, since the start of 1927, been featuring extracts from the letters of the still-voyaging students. Unsurprisingly, none of them had a problem with the presence of women on board. "To take a party of several hundred consisting exclusively of boys away from all social activities for eight months would be abnormal," McIntosh wrote in the April issue of his magazine.[15] As the principal organizer of the 1926 *Ryndam* voyage, he said he had thought about organizing a men-only cruise but concluded that it would require "some form of naval or military discipline." Given that this was "against every practical modern plan of development," the only way for the cruise "to be absolutely safe" was to include "groups of woman students and a limited number of older people," though who was in danger and from what was not stated.[16] If the UTA had decided that female students were too associated with the pleasure-loving, unstudious flapper to act as effective ambassadors, McIntosh believed in the potential of their civilizing influence—at least for the men on board.[17] Despite their disagreement, both parties saw traveling American women as bearing responsibility for maintaining cultural and civilizational standards—a responsibility that neither of them expected in the same way of men.

McIntosh's insistence on the virtues of coeducation revealed something else: his very different sense of what lessons could be drawn from the *Ryndam* experiment. "There are troubles on the present trip," but "co-education is not one of them," he told the readers of the progressive journal *School and Society*, one of the most significant educational forums of the day.[18] Cramped living conditions and too many opportunities for spending money during unsupervised shore trips were much more to blame. Acceptance of applications to McIntosh's 1927 coed International University Cruise was to be based not on age or gender but on character. No entrance examination would be required, but evidence of students' serious intent was necessary.[19] Each student would be assigned a faculty adviser to whom they would be responsible. Shore trips were to be carefully arranged and would "fully cover all the time" available. There would be "practically no so-called 'Free time,'" McIntosh wrote, seeing it merely as "an incentive to spend money."[20] The implication was clear: the trouble with the *Ryndam* had been the badly organized shore parties and ill-disciplined students, not the presence of women.

Charles Phelps was outraged at this slight on his firm's conduct, and he responded in *School and Society* with an attack on his rival's credentials. McIntosh was "not an educator and naturally lacks familiarity with a co-educational discussion which has been thrashed out for many years," Phelps declared. McIntosh's letter "was simply propaganda to further his own interests and in the hope of increasing the number of passengers" on his cruise.[21] Academic legitimacy required more measured and disinterested conduct, according to Phelps—who, it must be acknowledged, was no educator himself.[22]

McIntosh was undoubtedly seeking to promote his proposed voyage at the expense of the UTA's men-only cruise, but entangled in this commercial rivalry were competing assessments of the *Ryndam* experiment and what was to be learned from it. Where Phelps and Allen saw distracting and misleading women, McIntosh saw other issues of poor discipline and disorganization. Furthermore, the three men were not the only ones offering explanations for the *Ryndam*'s troubles. An article in the *Harvard Crimson* put it this way:

> [The] "dear old FU" was not nearly as bad as it had been painted, [but] no new venture is ever a 100 per cent success. Discipline was weak, we are told, and there were too many students who were only interested in having a good time; the food they say was not always good, and the ship was crowded; there were divisions of authority and petty squabbling among the leaders which lost the respect of the student body. None of these faults ought to be repeated, and all of them can be remedied.[23]

Although there was agreement that the first Floating University was an experiment, there remained a great deal of dissent as to what its results actually showed.

In the end, neither McIntosh's coeducational International University Cruise nor the men-only UTA voyage had the opportunity to prove which party's analysis was the correct one. Without enough enrollments, both had to call off their 1927 plans in order to better concentrate efforts on recruiting for voyages for 1928.[24] As the dust temporarily settled on their rivalry, a more comprehensive assessment began of exactly what Professor Lough's first pedagogic experiment had tested.

MEASURES OF ASSESSMENT

Douglas C. Ridgley, the *Ryndam*'s professor of geography, addressed the challenge head on in an article for the *Journal of Geography* in early 1928. Like any good scientist, he began with an account of the experiment itself: for 227 days between September 18, 1926, and May 2, 1927, there existed an experimental college whose campus was an ocean liner. Enrolled in the program were 486 students, and 49 professors and instructors comprised the faculty. Ridgley then proceeded to describe what he called the "equipment": on board was a well-appointed library as well as a gymnasium and exercise equipment, and in the regions visited were abundant specimens for botany and zoology, opportunities for language immersion, and social encounters and factory visits for history and economics and politics. All this "compared favorably with the usual college equipment" and provided opportunities that "surpassed that offered in a period of one year of land college."[25]

So far, so scientific. But there was a difficulty. The results of the "educational experiment" had, Ridgley told his readers, been inaccurately recorded:

> If the American newspaper reports along the route of the Cruise had sought as diligently for information about the value of the Cruise to the best students, as they did for information about misdemeanours of the ne'er-do-wells, they would have written front-page news items of utmost interest and value. They would have recorded facts about the College Cruise which would have given their readers an insight into the educational results of an important educational experiment, based upon the attitude which characterised the great majority of the student body.[26]

Rather than the reports of bad behavior, in Ridgley's view, the experiences of these earnest students constituted the real results of the Floating University pedagogic experiment. Consequently, it was these results that should be weighed and assessed. Ridgley proceeded to propose two measures for doing so: students' responses and awarded credits, and he evaluated each in turn.

"The value of this educational experiment to the students who entered into college work with a fine spirit of studentship can be indicated by some of the student activities," Ridgley stated, providing a series of supporting examples. At Cristóbal, Panama, members of one group used their free time to investigate the port facilities for handling freight, writing detailed reports for their teacher. In Egypt, another initiated, planned, and led a side trip for nearly one hundred of their fellow passengers to the Valley of Kings, taking charge of all aspects of the undertaking, which went off without a hitch. Two student teachers from New York made a study of native foods, producing special reports for the ship's graduate seminar. According to Ridgley, diligent students such as these "commonly stated" that their year on the *Ryndam* was "the equivalent of two years in their home college."[27]

He then turned to the question of credits. The Floating University's instructors had "granted credits on the same basis of accomplishment as in their home colleges." Some colleges had "accepted the credits at face value," while others had "granted credits upon satisfactory examinations."[28] Dean George E. Howes's official "Report of Scholastic Work on the University Cruise around the World, for the year 1926–27," written soon after the *Ryndam*'s return, provided more detail.[29] A total of 138 courses across both semesters at sea had been offered by 29 instructors. Aggregating the results, Howes recorded that 400 college-level students had attended classes, of whom 137 (or 35 percent) had either not sought credit, failed, or submitted incomplete work (an additional 40 students had been enrolled in the precollegiate preparatory department). The aggregated marks were mapped onto a bell curve: 16 percent of grades were As; 38 percent Bs; 28 percent Cs; 9 percent Ds; 3 percent incomplete; and 3 percent fails.[30] Howes's report noted explicitly that in the second half of the trip, students who lost interest "decided not to try for credit," which probably influenced the lower number of fails in the second semester. However, "for those who were working," he thought that the results showed that in semester 2, "better work was done under less favorable conditions," explaining why "the work of the year as a whole shows a better result than the work of the first half year." For Howes, this vindicated the Floating University's pedagogical experiment. The final sentence of his report was clear: "The best and most faithful of our students have a better record, that is a higher percentage of A's and B's than is normally represented in college records." For Howes and Ridgley alike, "the experiment [was] a success."[31] Education at sea yielded better results for the best students.

Having assessed these results against his two defined measures, Ridgley completed his article with an eight-point numbered summary of "suggestions." A college cruise was feasible and of high educational value, he concluded; credits could be earned at sea as satisfactorily as on land. Although some subjects are better adapted than others to sea conditions and certain methods should be used to select serious-minded students, a "fair evaluation of the results of the First College Cruise leads to the conclusion that the College Cruise is worthy of systematic and permanent development among educational institutions."[32]

Employing the language of the laboratory, Ridgley sought to reclaim from the newspapers on one hand and the boosters on the other both the experimental and the educational status of the *Ryndam*'s voyage. His measures, applicable to the evaluation of any educational innovation, sprang from an awareness that, as student Robert Smith Crowder of California put it, students on board a floating university are "much the same as students elsewhere." Life on the *Ryndam* was characterized by "the same informal discipline as the average co-educational university" on land.[33] Or, as the editors of the *Binnacle* put it, it was "fully as easy to dodge education [aboard the *Ryndam*] as at home."[34] Some students were diligent, while others were not. This was entirely typical, and on land-based campuses was rarely taken as indicative of educational success or failure. Ridgley set aside questions of coeducation, authority, and shore leave and focused instead on measures that educators still recognize nearly a century later—student feedback and grades.

"GETTING AN EDUCATION"

To Ridgley's two measures, the writer of the *Bookman*'s "Point of View" column added a third.[35] Professor Lough had set out to prove that firsthand experiences gained during travel might be used to teach students to think in world terms, but surely that ability could not be assessed so soon after the voyage. This *Bookman* columnist thought that the longer-term effects of the trip on students' lives held the answer and that they should be followed up "four years hence."[36] The *Harvard Crimson* suggested that the time frame might need to be longer still: any one of the *Ryndam*'s passengers might turn out to "be the leader of the future so needed to promote good will and break down the barriers of nationalism."[37] Had the Floating University experiment proved its hypothesis? It was simply too soon to tell.

Implicitly, this third measure acknowledged the more subversive question inherent in all these assessments. Perhaps, as noted in the *Philadelphia Inquirer* in March 1927, an education did not "consist in the number of things definitely learned" but was rather "a broadening of tastes and a sharpening of the perceptive powers."³⁸ Pearl Heckel put it this way:

> One may <u>read</u> a <u>description</u> of the Taj Mahal, for example, and learn its color and proportions. To gaze on its beauty and be moved by it, is a very different thing, it works a change in one's <u>soul</u>. In other words, although true education received anywhere and by any method is desirable, education obtained while visiting the important places of the world not only broadens the student's interests, stimulates his imagination, sharpens his intellect and it refines his emotions. It means a very great enriching of his personality and life.³⁹

Perhaps, as the *Harvard Crimson* had implied in its coverage of the Tokyo events, students learned in all sorts of ways, and making mistakes and dancing in nightclubs were two of them.⁴⁰ Even Howes's academic report had emphasized that while some of the experiences the students gained in visiting foreign places might be roughly calculated as contributing to the grades he had enumerated, a "great deal of the rest" was "of incalculable value."⁴¹ *The Student Magellan*, the *Ryndam*'s student yearbook, also contrasted what it described as the "measurable part of the work" with that which had "become a part and parcel of our own mental possession or equipment, and [could] not be evaluated." It, too, looked to the long view— the interest in foreign countries stimulated by the cruise would "last [the students] through [their] lives"; and "in the years to come," the "broadening of [their] educational horizon" would prove to be "a most potent factor in the mutual understanding" between them and other peoples.⁴² "For the first time in their lives," wrote Dean Albert Heckel in his own account of the cruise, "many of the students were enjoying the privilege of getting an education rather than merely piling up credits in the registrar's office."⁴³

The students and their parents seemed to agree, if the letters they wrote to the University Travel Association in response to its request for feedback are anything to judge by. Although several mentioned the academic benefits and reported success in securing credits from their home institutions, for most the lasting value of the cruise lay in its wider value.⁴⁴ Raymond Lester's uncle thought that his nephew had left "underweight and soft and indifferent to diet" but returned "interested in things that not only pertain to his physical self but is ambitious mentally and alive and wide awake to the present and for the future."⁴⁵ Brewster Bingham described the cruise as having "had a great awakening effect": "I sometimes felt as if I had always been dreaming before," he wrote, "and that here, for the first time, the realities of life were being presented before me."⁴⁶ For Wayne Dumont, even the problems of the trip brought benefits, "compel[ling the student] to think of larger things in a larger way than he has ever before."[47]

These glowing testimonials were intended to endorse the success of the cruise, but in citing the "awakening" effects of direct experience, they also alluded to a kind of knowledge acquisition that had potentially dangerous and disruptive associations. By the nineteenth century, "high" culture, understood to be predicated on disinterested, rational contemplation, had become distinguished from "low" culture (and obscenity), which, by contrast, was predicated on more bodily sensations and seen as promoting arousal, appetite, and animation. In the context of democratizing mass industrial and consumerist societies, the potential of this mode of knowing to threaten the foundations of civility was never far beneath discussion of the misconduct of American youth.[48] The extent and visibility of queer and permissive sexual cultures in interwar cities like New York, London, and Paris only heightened it.[49] On this view, the moral panic that surrounded the rumored sexual antics on board the Floating University was both an expression of the gendered meaning of travel and, more fundamentally, a recognition of the challenge to the epistemic and social order that the ship's claims for embodied knowledge presented. It underlay traditionalists' reaction against the perceived hedonism of college youth; what Christian Gauss, dean of the college of Princeton University, called "the general obscuring of the college's original purpose and function" and its conversion into "a kind of glorified playground."[50]

If the awakenings of student bodies aboard the *Ryndam* were covered extensively in the pages of the national press and raised red flags for anxious university administrators, very little attention was given to the lessons in empire that so many of the Floating University's passengers absorbed. The ways they made sense of their nation's place in the world, as expressed in their journals and letters, were neither reflected in the claims for the voyage made by Andrew McIntosh and the University Travel Association (UTA) nor advanced in the newspapers' coverage, both of which instead spoke of international understanding and goodwill. Perhaps this was in part because race relations and imperialism underpinned both the emergent field of international relations and the ways the students came to understand the interwar world order.[51] Bodies and brains, however, are not so easily separated. Governing empire and its racialized others meant governing the bodily passions of colonizers and colonized alike. Acknowledging to domestic audiences the imperial lessons of the Floating University's voyage—and, indeed, the sleeping on decks, the loosening of clothing, and the hardening of attitudes that many passengers reported—perhaps also invoked anxieties about the capacities and (incapacities) of American youth that were better avoided.[52]

Of course, there was one other measure against which the 1926–27 Floating University cruise was being assessed, and that was its financial viability. Charles Phelps quite frankly admitted that the UTA was "a business operated for profit," and an account of McIntosh's International University Cruise asserted that the *Ryndam*'s voyage had cleared between $200,000 and $300,000 in profit for the organizers and the shipping company.[53] Certainly, the Holland America Line was quick to sign a new contract for 1927 with the UTA, and there was no shortage of faculty members willing to teach on the successor voyages. No one from the press seemed to mind particularly much that these cruises were relatively expensive, profit-making enterprises. This was how many bold new educational ventures began. One day, the Floating University would carry an endowment, predicted the writers of the *Harvard Crimson*, and take students from all nations, but in the meantime, it should be wished all possible success.[54] Yet these were arguments that, in the wake of the domestic newspapers' reporting on the one hand and the growing skepticism of university leaders on the other, were never going to get much purchase. The Floating University would struggle to shake its reputation as "a scandal ship."[55]

UNIVERSITY DISTRUST

Professor Lough, meanwhile, was facing a more immediate dilemma: he had been sacked. As per the terms of his leave of absence, he had made some efforts to secure another position, albeit with the UTA, as the educational director for the 1927 cruise.[56] However, with the successor voyage looking increasingly unlikely and his twelve-month leave coming to an end, Lough decided to return to his old employer and report he'd been unable to find a new job. On August 12, 1927, he presented himself at NYU's Washington Square campus, only to find that not only did his old department no longer exist, but the university had "no assignment to offer him."[57] The budget and schedule for the forthcoming academic year had already been drawn up, and his name did not appear on it.

These matters were the subject of "intensive discussion" at NYU's Executive Committee meeting of early October. Led by Chancellor Elmer Ellsworth Brown, the decision of the committee was unanimous. It decided that "nothing short of complete severance of Professor Lough's connection with the University is acceptable in its interests."[58] After twenty-six years of service, he was to be dismissed from employment at New York University.

Lough was informed of this decision and given the chance to offer his resignation, but he refused to do so.[59] Finally, on November 21, 1927, the NYU
Council unanimously resolved to terminate his employment. The bursar
was told to pay him his salary up until the end of the month.[60]

Terminating the employment of a tenured professor was a drastic measure. It reflected the broader retreat from educational travel that NYU
was in the process of undertaking. At the same moment that the Executive Committee was deciding to sack Lough, his successor as director of
the Extension Division, Rufus Smith, was canceling all the summer travel
courses in Europe that Lough had established.[61] The only NYU course
that continued to operate abroad was General Charles H. Sherrill's Paris
program, its classes taught by the College of Fine Arts. Earlier in the year,
Smith had attempted to persuade Sherrill to end it as well. But Sherrill was
adamant that it continue.[62] Indeed, in the summer of 1927, he expanded
NYU's fine arts offerings in Europe, running courses in London and Munich as well as Paris. Neither Smith nor Chancellor Brown could complain
too much, because both programs were guaranteed by local patrons and
had attracted a bequest from the Altman Foundation for $30,000 per year
for five years.[63]

Smith and Harold O. Voorhis, Brown's secretary, remained troubled by
the continuance of Sherrill's overseas offerings. Smith thought the "General" to be "incomparable as a brilliant promoter but lacking in compe-
tence as regards the day-by-day management of an academic enterprise."
There was no way that NYU "could afford to offer credit for work done in
Europe under General Sherrill's personal control." Even if the academic
side could be arranged to the university's satisfaction, Smith was worried
that Sherrill—who had conceived a loathing of travel companies—would
"plunge the University into a really big business venture" involving financial
commitments that it could not afford. Worse still, Sherrill had ambitions to
establish an Overseas Division of the university by taking over the foreign
businesses of a number of American colleges. Such an undertaking, Voorhis
told Chancellor Brown, would only succeed under the wise guidance of a
man having the highest prestige in the academic world." In the hands of anyone else, "it would—like the 'world cruise'—stand the chance of giving New
York University a bad name."[64] NYU wanted nothing to do with the Floating
University it had once agreed to sponsor. When in April 1927 Charles Phelps
wrote to Brown purporting to ask his advice, the response from NYU was
unequivocal.[65] NYU would not be "drawn back in any way or to the slightest
extent," and Phelps received a polite but firm letter from Brown regretting
that he did not find himself able to assist.[66]

NYU was not alone in taking a dim view of the *Ryndam* and its succes-

sors. While Vassar's president, Henry N. MacCracken; Yale-in-China's former president, Edward H. Hume; and even the Institute of International
Education's Stephen Duggan were prepared to assist the UTA in promoting
a second cruise, others in the university world were of a mind with Chancellor Brown.[67] "I am afraid I have not much confidence in the educational
value of a college cruise around the world," wrote Harvard's President A.
Lawrence Lowell in response to Phelps's invitation. "I believe greatly in the
educational value of travel, and in academic instruction, but have very serious doubts whether they can be effectively combined."[68] The dean of Harvard College, Chester N. Greenough, was sure that the essay competitions
Phelps was running were "merely advertising," and the president of Mount
Holyoke "definitely declared that the women's colleges were not in favor of
such co-educational cruises."[69] Writing to Yale's professor of political science to seek his support for the successor voyage, the UTA acknowledged
that the cruise was not yet "recognised [sic] as a legitimate and a necessary part of our educational system."[70] Douglas Ridgley may have been convinced of the force of his scientific evaluation, but many US university and
college presidents were not.

PROFESSOR LOUGH PERSISTS

Although bruised by his treatment at the hands of New York University,
James E. Lough was not prepared to go away quietly. Little more than a
month after the NYU Council had terminated his employment, it received
a summons from the Supreme Court of the State of New York.[71] Lough was
seeking $100,000 in damages on the grounds he had been "illegally dis-
missed."[72] He charged that his employment had been terminated without
due process, that he had not been informed of the charges against him, and
that as a tenured professor, he would have been entitled to not only salary
but a pension upon retirement from the fund for teachers in universities,
colleges, and technical schools endowed by Andrew Carnegie in 1905.[73]

NYU, unsurprisingly, contested these charges.[74] Voorhis claimed that the
university had given Lough twelve months' notice that his services were un-
satisfactory, and the reason had been made clear: he had concealed from the
university his personal business relation as director and stockholder of the
School of Foreign Travel, even as he was hiring the company to conduct the
university's summer student tours.[75] In doing so, he had failed to maintain
the "high standards of efficiency and personal conduct" required under the
university statutes, and the council was within its rights to dismiss him.

Deriding these charges as "slanderous," Lough made a statement to the
press at his attorney's offices. There, he showed reporters the original copy

of the document he had tendered to the court—the report of the special committee of the University's Council that, back in the hopeful days of 1925, had investigated his involvement with the School of Foreign Travel and found no suggestion of wrongdoing.[76] Judge Valente assessed these matters in the more sober surroundings of the New York County Courthouse and found there was a case to be answered. Lough was given permission to examine the records of the university and to interview the defendants. The tables had turned. On June 18, Chancellor Brown, Harold Voorhis, and council member Alexander Lyman would be interviewed by Lough and his attorney before a mediator agreed on by both parties.[77]

THE STATE DEPARTMENT'S SPECIAL AGENT

Press reports of these legal proceedings traveled all the way from New York to Oslo. Laurits Swenson, the US ambassador to Norway, had recently received a letter from Professor Lough and the UTA requesting "special courtesies, including an audience with the sovereigns and leading officials" during the planned 1928 voyage. In view of the news about Lough's lawsuit, the ambassador sought the advice of the State Department "as to the extent to which your Legation should interest itself" in the venture.[78]

It was a good question, not least because it drew the State Department's attention to the fact that Ambassador Swenson was not the only government representative who had received requests from the University Travel Association. Clearly, an investigation was needed. Acting on behalf of the secretary of state, W. R. Castle asked the State Department's chief special agent for New York, R. C. Bannerman, to report on the history, status, and personnel of the UTA, and Bannerman put Special Agent Kinsey on the job.

Kinsey was thorough in his investigations.[79] He read the UTA's publications, collected newspaper clippings, cross-checked against company records, and interviewed Charles H. Phelps Jr., Andrew J. McIntosh, and university authorities at both NYU and the New York City College (the founding institution of the City University of New York, or CUNY). His report for Bannerman was a testament to State Department intelligence gathering. It gave a good summation of the Floating University's history while also making clear Kinsey's own firmly held views as to its legitimacy (or lack thereof) as an educational undertaking.

Agent Kinsey confirmed that Professor Lough was indeed the "father and originator" of the floating university idea and had been attempting to bring it about since 1924.[80] After providing the details of the lawsuit, he reported that it was under the auspices of Lough and the UTA that the 1926 voyage of "the now notorious and ill-fated S.S. RYNDAM" had been made. The UTA

officers were all members of the firm of Phelps Bros., and they intended
to charter the *Ryndam* again for a successor tour that would sail in the fall
of 1928. Whereas the proposed voyage was to be for men only, the original voyage had been a coeducational enterprise, and the "unfortunate and
more or less scandalous manner in which it turned out" was, Kinsey wrote,
"a matter of more or less common knowledge." Its methods of promotion
did not impress him. Although the UTA claimed to be operating with 150
American universities and colleges who had agreed to grant students credit,
Kinsey established that neither NYU nor the City College had ever made
such an agreement. They looked "upon the whole affair with considerable
doubt and misgivings as to its feasibility and possible success." The UTA,
concluded Agent Kinsey, was "in no way a chartered college or regularly
recognized institution of education" but "a steamship ticket agency, selling
tickets and conducting tours abroad." Its claims that the US Departments
of State and Commerce had agreed to cooperate with the voyage could not
be substantiated.[81]

Kinsey's assessment was clear: the UTA presented "ostensibly as an educational enterprise, [but] in reality it appears most obviously as a new style
tourist agency which has adopted the sales method of tendering college instruction en route as bait for patronage from a student clientele." Any recognition from the US government would "be eagerly utilized and capitalized
by these people to gain for themselves abroad exceptional concessions."
Utmost caution from the State Department was fully warranted.[82]

While Kinsey was investigating, the department had also taken the step
of canvassing the opinions of the State Department's Division of Western
European Affairs about the diplomatic implications, and it turned out that
the division was already aware of the letters the UTA was sending to US
ambassadors and had already developed a policy for foreign missions. Its
concern was less with the purported educational character of the voyage,
focusing instead on the likelihood that "the institution may become peren-
nial" and that privileges might continue to be expected on an ongoing basis. Consequently, the division had agreed that foreign missions could offer
only limited assistance.[83] The permanent relations of an educational cruise
should, in its view, "be academic and scholastic, not official."[84]

Bannerman's own position was that the UTA deserved "no countenance
whatever, other than is due any enterprise legally conducted, but for the
personal profit of the promoters."[85] Nelson Trusler Johnson, assistant secretary of state, was inclined to agree, although he conceded that in view of
"the fact that several members of the teaching staff . . . are persons of good
repute and even of moderate distinction in American educational circles,"
some concessions might need to be made.[86]

Two months after sending his letter, Ambassador Swenson in Oslo finally received a reply from his colleagues in the State Department. Diplomatic and consular officers might offer "a certain amount of cooperation" to the UTA's second cruise. However, "no responsibility should be assumed for the success of any entertainments or receptions." Invitations should not be issued, and no formal sponsorship should be given.[87] The cruise organizers might instead make their own relationships with local bodies. Despite the entanglement of US commercial, juridical, cultural, and military power across the world, when it came to the Floating University, in the State Department's view, commerce, education, and diplomacy should be kept separate. Special Agent Kinsey would have been pleased.

THE "HOOFING INSTITUTE" VS. THE "DE LUXE" WORLD CRUISE

As the State Department was deliberating, the nation's newspapers and campus magazines were once again full of announcements for not one but two "floating universities," scheduled to leave in the fall of 1928.

The UTA's men-only College Cruise around the World brought together many leading members of the original voyage. The promotional pamphlet listed Charles F. Thwing, George E. Howes, and Henry J. Allen on the board of governors and Lough and Theodore Phelps as director of education and cruise manager, respectively. The president of this second cruise was to be Elmer W. Smith, head of the English Department at Colgate University. The voyage was to sail with fewer students (350 men were anticipated) on a refitted *Ryndam*, complete with additional freshwater showers, and fans in every room. These upgrades were reflected in the cost, with rooms ranging from $2,500 to $3,700, depending on the cabin.[88]

Meanwhile, the reins of McIntosh's coed Floating University, which was operating under the banner of International University Cruise Inc., had been handed over to Sydney Greenbie, a writer and adult educator who had traveled extensively.[89] McIntosh had originally hired Greenbie as a member of the faculty, but he was asked to take over the organization of the whole venture after McIntosh suddenly fell ill.[90] In contrast to McIntosh, who had explicitly claimed the legacy of the first *Ryndam* cruise, Greenbie sought to shake it off. His Floating University was "a new venture: new in purpose, new in organization, new in students, faculty and administration"; a new institution with "no traditions to guide us on our way."[91] Nevertheless, there were some lines of continuity. Cornelius DuBois, who had served in 1926 as a member of the English faculty, acted as assistant to the president; and Constantine Raises, who had worked in Phelps's travel office on the 1926 voyage, served Greenbie as cruise director. The plan was to set sail on the SS *Aurania* at a cost per person of between $2,500 and $3,600.[92]

In his later account, Greenbie painted a colorful and unflattering picture of the rivalry between the two organizations as they battled each other for enrollments. His competitors spread rumors that he had no ship and no financial backing and sought to poach his professors and students, he said. Greenbie even suspected that someone in his own office was leaking information to his opponents.[93] This vicious competition turned out to be counterproductive for both outfits: once again, neither succeeded in attracting the student numbers necessary to justify chartering a vessel. They did not, however, abandon their respective voyages.

Greenbie sought to make a virtue of necessity: "We would commandeer every available cabin on a westward bound ship, sail as far as we liked, go ashore and stay as long as necessary, pick up a later ship, and so on, around the world."[94] Professors were to each take cases of one hundred books as their travel library; they would come into daily and personal contact with their students; and the courses would have a "definite bearing" on what a student sees and learns and does in the countries visited.[95] Leaving New York in mid-November 1928, Greenbie's group sailed on board the Dollar Line's SS *President Wilson*. His address to students upon departure was triumphant: "We have won; we have a group now of some ninety-four students, both men and women, whereas [the UTA] cruise for men only was cancelled."[96]

But Greenbie was a little preemptive in his celebrations. Although the UTA did have to cancel its charter of the *Ryndam*, it had regrouped and booked the students it had enrolled (about 60) onto the regular round-the-world tourist cruise of the Red Star Line's SS *Belgenland*, sailing east from New York at the end of September on a seven-month trip.[97] Students had the option of joining the College World Tour for the first Grand European Tour part of the voyage only, which would run from September to December 1928, or signing up for the entire "de luxe" world cruise, which would leave New York in mid-December, taking in Cuba, Hawaii, Japan, the Philippines, India, Egypt, and southern Europe, and return mid-1929. Accompanying them were several professors, including Professor Lough and Elmer W. Smith as cruise president. The American Express Company organized the shore excursions, and classes were held on board with the promise of credit transfer to students' home institutions again advertised as an option. The presence of other passengers on board did somewhat dilute the UTA's championing of single-sex education, but the voyage attracted nowhere near the same attention as had its progenitor.[98]

Meanwhile, also proceeding well were Greenbie's itinerant students. Then in Japan they hit a snag. After a stay in the country that was, by all reports, much less eventful than the *Ryndam*'s had been two years before, Greenbie could not find enough berths for the next leg of the trip. So the Floating University split in half, with one party sailing to Java (Indonesia) and the other to Guangzhou (Canton) before reuniting in Singapore. Arrangements for the whole group were then made on the go. As the "advance man," Constantine Raises, together with Greenbie, had the job of organizing it all.[99] Working with a budget of only US$10 per person per day (about $170 a day in 2022 values), he had to book trains and hotels for more than one hundred people, find berths on steamers, organize day trips, sort out meals, pay for visas, charter streetcars, negotiate with the agents at Thomas Cook, and all the while deal with the warring factions emerging among the faculty and the students.[100] In Europe, Raises and Greenbie understandably placed the students in the hands of the International Student Hospitality Association.

In retrospect, this plan was not such a good one. The *Walking Varsity Blister*, a "razz sheet" published secretly by the students, was blistering to say the least, and caught in its crosshairs was Sydney Greenbie.[101] The students dubbed the whole undertaking the "Hoofing Institute" and complained of third-class rail travel, insufficient food, shared rooms, dingy hotels in red-light districts, bedbugs, faculty that abandoned the cruise halfway through it, and a worker at the hotel in Nanking (Nanjing) who tried to sell them opium.[102] Upon his return to the United States, Greenbie published an equally scathing account, although in his view the "torpid intellectual habits and grasping schemes of the faculty" were to blame.[103] The universities had feared that the students would not study en route, but they had "not asked whether professors accepting such a job were in any way qualified to teach anything of value in a world they have seldom before travelled over."[104] In the prose of a former publicist, Greenbie railed against professors who "blame all young people for a host of misdeeds that did not occur, in order to cover up their own inadequacies as teachers and hardening of their intellectual arteries."[105]

What would Andrew McIntosh have made of all this? Having poured his energies and his finances into the 1926 *Ryndam* cruise only to be met with disappointment and betrayal, he did not live to see this successor voyage. Only a few days before the rainy and cheerless November afternoon when the SS *President Wilson* "slipped from its Hoboken pier" and launched Greenbie's "Hoofing Institute" around the world, McIntosh died at Booth Memorial Hospital in Queens of peritonitis.[106] He was sixty-one years of age. If the Floating University had been Professor Lough's idea, it was McIntosh who had made it a reality. Yet by 1928, Professor Lough was unemployed, and his one-time collaborator was being buried in a New York cemetery.

"REMISED, RELEASED, AND FOREVER DISCHARG[ED]"

Lough's case against NYU dragged on for years. Finally, at the beginning of January 1931, it came to trial before the Supreme Court of the State of New York. The city had just experienced an unusual bout of mild winter weather when the parties gathered in the New York County Courthouse in downtown Manhattan before Justice Phoenix Ingraham.[107] On one side sat Professor Lough and his attorney, Abram Tulin. On the other sat Harold Voorhis and New York University's special counsel, Mr. Mooney. Having gone through the process of impaneling a jury, the judge called a brief recess before the trial was to commence. During the break, Mr. Tulin approached Mr. Mooney. Would the university be interested in coming to an amicable settlement? On the prospect of an agreement, the judge adjourned the hearing for one week.[108]

A few days later, Mr. Mooney brought a draft settlement agreement before a specially convened meeting of the New York University Executive Committee. It provided an immediate payment by NYU to Professor Lough of $10,000, plus continuing payment of the sum of $3,000 per year for the six years until his projected retirement in 1936, plus $1,600 per year from 1937 until his death. Excepting these payments, the parties were "remised, released and forever discharg[ed]" from their obligations to each other.[109] It was not quite the $100,000 Lough had originally sought, but it was still a lot of money in Depression-era New York.

Weighing the weakness and strength of the university's position, and estimating the eventualities in the event that NYU should "carry the litigation to the court of last resort," Mr. Mooney thought a settlement on these terms was justified. Perhaps, too, he had examined the minutes of the Executive Committee of April 7, 1925. They recorded that when Chancellor Elmer Ellsworth Brown had presented Lough's proposal to launch a world cruise in the name of the university, he had explicitly stated that "the operation and financial management of the project" would be conducted "by an outside business corporation, the salaries of teachers to be paid out of tuition fees charged by the University, the whole project being planned so as to obviate any possible financial loss to the University."[110] Although Lough had made a profit in the end from NYU's relationship with the School of Foreign Travel, he had also borne the financial risk of something going wrong. And NYU could not claim it had no knowledge of the arrangement.

By 1931, Chancellor Brown was eager to see the end of the dispute. The

Executive Committee authorized the settlement and agreed to Lough's request that the university publish the report of its own 1925 "fact-finding" committee, which had unanimously found "no proof that Dean Lough ever had it in his mind to conceal from the University authorities his connection with the School of Foreign Travel" and cleared him of any wrongdoing.[111] After twenty-six years of employment and three years locked in a legal battle, Lough and NYU finally parted ways.

The university immediately set about banishing its other educational travel ghost. The contracts for General Charles Sherrill's foreign courses in Paris, Berlin, and Munich were due to expire in June, and a special committee led by Fred I. Kent, a New York banker and long-serving council member, had been appointed to investigate them.[112] However, General Sherrill was not prepared to wait for its findings. At the same meeting at which the Executive Committee agreed to settle with Lough, Sherrill demanded a definite answer: would the work abroad be continued or not? A few days later, Kent indicated to Sherrill the university's "disposition to have the foreign program discontinued," whereupon Sherrill indicated his intention to resign, both as a member of the council and as the chair of its Fine Arts Committee. The prospect of losing one of its more rambunctious members was not a deterrent for the council, and at the end of the month it voted to end all of NYU's credit-bearing courses overseas.[113] The chancellor paid tribute to "the services of great interest and value" that General Sherrill had rendered to the university. But he was also clear that the foreign programs should be dissolved in such a way as would "leave [NYU] free of any possible liability."[114] Despite their disagreements, Sherrill and Lough ultimately shared a common fate. After two turbulent decades, NYU's adventure in travel for educational credit was over. Although the NYU Extension Division did run a course called Literary Tour of Great Britain in the 1930s, it took place entirely in a classroom in Washington Square, with readings supplied.[115]

"ILLICIT WOOING OF ALMA MATER BY ALMUS PATER"

By the 1930s, the educational world had grown skeptical about granting credits to travel courses. Although in her 1937 second-edition survey of the study of international relations in the United States, Edith E. Ware noted that "student travel is frequently an extracurricular activity that adopts the laboratory method in the study of international relations," for undergraduates it was a form of study that US colleges and universities were unwilling to recognize.[116] Even the Junior Year Abroad programs, by 1937 run by a handful of (women's) colleges as well as at the University of Delaware and Smith College, operated at the margins of American higher education. As Joan Gore has shown, despite the protections of rigorous student selection, trusted host institutions, and an accompanying American professor, the programs, which in any case attracted little more than twelve hundred students across the entire interwar period, were widely criticized as a frivolous way to travel and not educationally serious endeavors. US universities treated with suspicion the academic rigor of the Cours de Civilisation study-abroad program on which they relied. They viewed them as something undertaken for social standing and private enjoyment, and their interwar reputation as a program for women only exacerbated this sense that they were not academically serious.[117]

The dubious reputation of courses offered by the booming commercial travel industry did not help. Paradoxically, perhaps, it was Sydney Greenbie who articulated this as "the illicit wooing of Alma Mater by Almus Pater of the business world. Nearly every travel agent selling world cruises inserts somewhere a statement about 'faculties' and 'courses,'" he wrote in 1934; the "educational department is now a fixture in the business, while everywhere . . . professors have been converted into travel salesmen."[118] These educational "courses" reached significant numbers of middle-class Americans. Yet regardless of how much they might have been learning about international affairs, this kind of travel was not considered academic. Writing of the Floating University in 1931, the University of Southern California's John Eugene Harley had put it this way: although the idea had "splendid possibilities . . . the difficulty in arranging for regular college or university credit" remained "a formidable obstacle."[119] After briefly coming together for a fling in the early 1920s, Alma Mater had decided to part ways with Almus Pater.

When it came to international education, American universities and colleges were traveling in another direction. Rather than crediting educational travel programs, they set about establishing what the League of Nations' International Institute of Intellectual Co-operation (IIIC) called the "scientific study of international relations." The "main idea," according to the IIIC, was "to study the principal problems of contemporary international life in a spirit of objectivity and from a strictly scientific point of view."[120] While for graduates and academic scholars undertaking research this might necessarily entail travel, for the much larger American undergraduate population it meant enrolling in credit-bearing courses and degree programs taught on home campuses, with syllabi, reading lists, and assessments. For universities, it meant an entirely new discipline of teaching and study. It meant journals, conferences, summer institutes, and new paying audiences for university-sanctioned expertise. In short, it meant the assertion of academic authority over a domain of knowledge that had hitherto been populated by a range of actors, only some of whom were from the academy. In the early stages of disciplinary formation, the emerging field of "international studies" was capacious, absorbing thinkers from diverse knowledge traditions. But by the 1930s, it was increasingly not in the universities' interests to admit other ways of knowing.[121] Henceforth, qualified university professors would be the recognized authorities on how to know the world. The credit-bearing courses they controlled would confer the social and economic benefits of institutionally sanctioned expertise. Although historians of international relations have focused on the ideological approaches and the individual actors who worked to build the new discipline or who were excluded from it, they have given less attention to the shifting institutional and epistemic politics that disciplinary formation represented.[122]

In 1937, Edith E. Ware mapped out the vast number of formal programs in international relations that had emerged in the 582 accredited universities and colleges of the United States.[123] At the undergraduate level, she identified a broad "renaming and rewriting of the descriptions of courses" in a way she thought indicated the influence of world events.[124] Since 1919, courses on contemporary history had emerged, along with units in current affairs, modern political theory, and public opinion, with new subjects in international law as well. Noting that "no one discipline exercise[d] exclusive jurisdiction" over international studies, in the 1935–36 academic year Ware counted 254 institutions offering undergraduate courses in American diplomacy or American foreign relations and 244 in international relations, with these spread across history, political science, and law departments and appearing also in psychology, geography, economics, anthropology, and journalism.[125] Graduate research, too, was booming, with sixty-three doctoral theses accepted in international law and international relations in 1935–36 alone.[126] Many of these theses had been undertaken within the new specialized schools that signaled the increasing self-confidence of the emerging field: the Walter Hines Page School at Johns Hopkins (1924), the Los Angeles University School of International Relations (1924), the School of Public and International Affairs at Princeton (1930), the Fletcher School of Law and Diplomacy at Tufts (1933), the School of Public Affairs and Social Work at Wayne University (1935), the Frank Billings Kellogg Foundation at Carleton College (1937), and the Parker School of International Affairs at Columbia (late 1930s).[127]

The professors who taught in these programs, and the PhD graduates they produced, became a new cadre of experts whose advice was sought by government departments, international organizations, and commercial, regulatory, and even military bodies. They served on industrial relations and trade councils and produced work for the various business research bureaus emerging during this period.[128] Research organizations were also established in the universities themselves, with Ware identifying sixteen that by 1937 were working wholly or in part on international relations.[129]

The universities had much to gain by promoting this way of grounding international knowledge. The full weight of official state sanction, philanthropic support, social prestige, international recognition, and institutional authority was behind it. At the request of the State Department, copies of the first 1934 edition of Ware's volume were distributed to the US embassies and legations across the globe. The Council on Foreign Relations purchased and distributed 25 copies of the book in Europe, the Carnegie Endowment sent 603 copies to libraries and specific individuals, and the American National Committee bought over 300 copies and distributed them according to its members' suggestions. An additional $500 was allotted by the committee for the further distribution of the volume, with $200 given by the World Peace Foundation also for this purpose.[130]

Against such interests, James E. Lough's dream of travel experience as the basis of an education in world affairs did not stand a chance. Although the League of Nations and its IIIC, along with other international organizations directed at student and scholarly cooperation, championed the exchange of knowledge and "mutual contact" as ways to promote the formation of a "universal conscience," the Floating University—which on the face of it shared similar aims—was not recognized by these bodies.[131] Instead, it engaged with lower-status organizations, such as Rotary and the YMCA, which were being pushed to the edges of the emerging academic discipline of international relations. Having lost the endorsement of both American universities and the press, the Floating University did not secure the social and academic authorization required to give it legitimacy, ensuring that the experiences of the *Ryndam*'s passengers were remembered as recreational rather than educational.

WHAT DID LOUGH DO?

Exiled from the university world, Lough nonetheless decided to remain in New York and return to his earlier interests in pedagogy and progressive education. By 1932, he was running the Harriet Melissa Mills Training School for Kindergarten and Primary Teachers, and after 1934 he combined this with service as president of the Scudder School, which offered training in secretarial arts and crafts, social welfare, and community work.[132] A few years later, he was working with Judge Ullrich of the Ridge Foundation to turn the Blue Ridge Brethren School in Washington County, Maryland, into a secular four-year senior college: "one of the first Progressive Education

colleges of America."[133] But this second venture into experimental education did not go well either, and in the summer of 1937 the school ran into
financial trouble and had to be bailed out.[134] Lough's name was not mentioned in the associated legal proceedings, and he continued in his position
at Mills School in New York until at least 1939.

Lough did not, however, give up his commitment to the idea of a floating university. In 1929, the University Travel Association absorbed Andrew
McIntosh's International University cruise, and every year between 1931
and 1936 the newspapers carried announcements for coeducational floating universities, with Lough connected to all of them.[135] But with the effects
of the Great Depression taking a toll, the last voyage to actually sail was
in 1932.[136] As the clouds of another world war closed in on Europe, Lough
continued to pursue his project by lobbying the US Maritime Commission
for the use of a ship at discounted rates.[137] But when the routes of interwar
travel turned into battle zones, his hopes had to be put on hold indefinitely.
Lough retired from his positions in New York and moved with his wife,
Dora, to Los Angeles, where their son Edwin lived.[138]

It was from Los Angeles after the war that, in the context of a new wave
of international enthusiasm, Lough tried once again to relaunch the project
to which he had dedicated so much of his life and reputation. This time
it was to be called the American Floating University, and at age seventy-
five Lough was named as its sponsor and president. Reflecting the nation's
new strategic priorities, the first voyage was to travel to Latin America, and
Constantine Raises, the indefatigable cruise organizer of Greenbie's "Hoofing Institute," was one of those involved.[139] Once again, Lough wrote on
behalf of the University Travel Association to the US Maritime Commission
seeking the use of a suitable vessel, sending along a lavishly produced book
which included course outlines and itineraries.[140] "A ship for a campus—the
world for a laboratory" was the project's motto.[141] Yet this enterprise, too,
like so many of its progenitors, did not eventuate.

It was not until 1952 that American newspapers carried the name of
James Edwin Lough once more. This time it was to note his departure on a
different kind of journey. On June 3, after a bout of pneumonia, he died in
his sleep in Fort Worth, Texas, at the home of his daughter.[142] The Floating
University was both his great achievement and the pivot on which his life
had turned. Developed in the context of the new psychology and the new
educational movements being fertilized at Harvard in the early 1890s, the
idea that animated it was his alone, and he had nurtured it determinedly,
even as it captured the imagination of some and the ire of others, before it
sputtered, then faded from view. Did this mean he had failed? His younger
brother, William, in every way the first beneficiary of Lough's educational

innovations, did not think so. And he did not want Lough's children to think so either. "You are right to feel great pride, as I do, in your father," he wrote to them when he learned of Lough's death.

> Like anyone else who has constructive ideas and the will to make them work, he had to face many difficulties, discouragements, criticisms and jealousies. He did face them throughout his life, in youth as well as in old age, with an unending flow of optimism and persistent courage. He came through to the finish, just as he would have wished, still buoyant and still looking forward, not backward. All of us who loved him are deeply grieved by his death; but for him it was the perfect ending.[143]

The boy from Eaton, Ohio, who had traveled the world reached his final port in Dallas, Texas, in Restland Memorial Park. The site of his grave is not recorded.

9

Thinking with Failure

Is that where the story of the Floating University ends: with the death of its founder in Texas and the demise of his grand plan to make travel experience a credit-bearing part of university education? Was it, at best, a noble idea but an impractical one; a hopeful endeavor that had been co-opted by commercial imperatives; or an educational experiment that had failed? After their brief flirtation in the 1920s, travel experience and accredited education parted ways. In the decades that have followed, the story of the *Ryndam*'s 1926–27 cruise has been neglected by historians of international education, intellectual history, US foreign relations, and maritime history alike. But perhaps this scholarly sidelining says as much about who won the battle to define what counted as authoritative knowledge in the 1920s as it does about the "success" or otherwise of Professor Lough's big idea. Back in 1927, as the Floating University's merits were being discussed in newspapers across the country, a writer for the *Bookman* had suggested that the "experiment" should be judged, not on the basis of contemporary media reports, but rather on its effects on students' lives.[1] A century on from its sailing, how should historians assess the meaning and legacy of the Floating University?

THREE YEARS ON

In December 1929, as Lough's legal case against New York University was still dragging on in the courts, forty members of the first Floating University came together at the Biltmore Hotel. After a dinner of oysters and frozen fruit, they relived the *Ryndam* spirit by dancing until the early hours of the morning. First, however, they established an alumni association. Six months later, it was publishing a newsletter called the *Gangplank*, the stated ambition of which was to "link the past to the present" and carry its readers "back to [their] life and friendships on board the *Ryndam*, and to lead [them] on to renewed and new friendships ashore." The editors had gone to heroic lengths to track down cruise members and find out something of what they had been up to in the three years since the *Ryndam*'s return.[2] Lillian McCracken was back in Colorado supervising music education in Boulder's public schools; DeWitt Reddick had already been appointed Professor of Journalism at the University of Texas; Tom Johnson was lecturing in the English Department at Williams College; and James McKenzie had moved home to Cottonwood Falls, Kansas, where he was working as a bookkeeper for a furniture manufacturer.[3]

For many, the influence of the cruise was already evident. James Price, the Floating University's student president, had undertaken a stint at the Sorbonne in 1927 and then earned a law degree at Stanford before setting sail for Shanghai as legal adviser to four US financial companies—the Raven Trust, the American-Oriental Banking Corporation, the American-Oriental Finance Corporation, and the Asia Realty Company.[4] Mortimer H. Cobb had taken a job with the En Route Travel Service, and Marshall J. Howard was working with Constantine Raises as a cruise manager. Wendell Goddard and Alex Hudson were even running their own round-the-world tutoring tour, teaching ten students as they traveled from port to port via the Dollar Line. Ex-governor Henry Allen, meanwhile, had been elected a US senator from Kansas. Was his success as the *Binnacle*'s editor in chief the "final recommendation that won [him] the distinction of being chosen as Director of Publicity" for Herbert Hoover's presidential campaign? the *Gangplank* wondered.[5]

The publication also carried news of another kind of personal transformation consequent to the *Ryndam*'s voyage. Ten couples had indeed gotten married after meeting on "cupid's ship," with Professor Lough's son Edwin among them. Already, three "cruise babies" had been born to these couples. Their marriages helped knit together a diffuse network of relationships that continued among the *Ryndam* passengers throughout the 1930s. Laura Yaggy, Holling C. and Lucille Holling, and Edith Weir were key figures in this network. Their correspondence recorded exchanges of addresses, snippets of news, photographs of children, and visits to each other's houses. The Hollings led a group of seventeen alumni who met in Chicago several times a year. The couple went on road trip up the coast of the Northwest with Richard Black, canoed in Western Ontario with Edward Sweeny, and kayaked in Canada's northeast with Thomas Brown.[6] Holling wrote to James Lough in 1934, "We have yet to find a member [of the *Ryndam* voyage] who does not date a substantial growth from that trip, and most of them feel that it was the most profitable experience of their lives. . . . It is impossible to calculate the far reaching and beneficial results of your splendid idea."[7] If there was to be another cruise, Holling wanted to be on it. If judged against the *Bookman*'s criteria, there is at least a case to be made that three years after the *Ryndam*'s return, the Floating University was far from the failure the newspapers portrayed.

A FLOTILLA OF SMALL SHIPS

Several of those who had traveled aboard the *Ryndam* were inspired by the model of experiential learning. For the Hollings, the 1926–27 Floating University cruise was particularly transformative. The journey, and the illustrations they had made during it, became an immediate resource for their commercial and artistic production. *Little Folks of Other Lands*, which came out in 1929, drew directly on the experience.[8] Many of the couple's illustrations for this book were taken from sketches they had made aboard the *Ryndam*: Dutch clothing and windmills, Viking ships, Hawaiian canoes, Thai stilt houses and elephants, and Chinese sampans. In fact, a visual culture of the voyage and its many stopover places can be traced throughout Holling's oeuvre, much of it for children. Geographer Hayden Lorimer argues that Holling's intense coloration and figurative-realist style emerged directly from the *Ryndam* cruise.[9]

Featuring rich visual imagery, the children's books for which Holling became famous also gave their young readers an experience of the world that, much like a sea voyage, progressively unfolded along with their stories. Many of his *Ryndam* shipmates saw echoes of their travels in the "World Museum" diorama that he created in the 1930s.[10] Published in newspapers all across the United States, its colorful pictures were designed to be cut out and pasted onto cardboard, then assembled into a three-dimensional scene.[11] This exemplary form of educational play once again brought to children many of the scenes that Holling had first sketched on the *Ryndam* cruise, including in Holland, China, France, and India. Although the Hollings' passion for "other peoples" was figured through a colonial and orientalist lens, Lorimer believes it nonetheless entailed an awareness that there were ways of knowing the world that colonizers could never understand—and that this, too, dated to the *Ryndam*.[12]

Holling C. and Lucille Holling were not the only ones who, in the wake of the 1926–27 cruise, sought to fashion experiences through which their fellow Americans might come to know the world. Douglas C. Ridgley, for example, was immediately inspired to adapt the travel method of the *Ryn-*

dam to American college life. Returning to his post as professor of geography in education at Clark University, during the fall of 1928 he and his wife, Winifred, undertook what the *Gangplank* described as "a 12,000 mile journey around the U.S. to make plans for the Clark University Transcontinental College Field Trip, an outgrowth of their experiences on the University Cruise."[13] In 1933, Ridgley sought to further extend the method of direct observation and investigation in two books intended for schoolchildren. *Home Journeys* and *World Journeys* were based on the activities of four cousins and featured imaginary trips to other parts of the world together with a series of reader exercises.[14]

After traveling in an airplane for the first time on the *Ryndam* voyage, Elizabeth Lippincott McQueen returned to the United States fired with a new passion to combine aeronautics and internationalism.[15] Following her move to the West Coast in 1928, she set about launching the Women's International Association of Aeronautics (WIAA). Using this organization as a platform, in the 1930s McQueen developed a distinctive vision for the international power of women's thought. In the air, she argued, "the boundaries and limitations of earthly life and earthly bodies melted away," and in an adaptation of her Christian Science beliefs, she saw "air-mindedness" as a force that could bring about international peace.[16] For her, reading about women's aeronautical activities in local newspapers, penning aviation-themed poetry, singing aeronautical songs, and meeting women pilots, not to mention the thrill of actually flying, were transformative experiences, and she promoted them through the WIAA.

University of Missouri student Francis Gano Chance had traveled on the *Ryndam* with his parents, and upon their return to Centralia, the father and son expanded the family civil construction company, making a lot of money from an invention called the earth anchor that is now used in the electrical industry (to this day, Centralia hosts its Annual Anchor Festival).[17] In 1936, they began constructing lavish gardens at their family home. Inspired by their trip on the Floating University and by the many botanical gardens they had visited, Francis's father, Albert Bishop Chance, wanted to recreate in his hometown a little bit of what they had seen on their travels. Once completed, visitors entered the gardens through a Japanese torii gateway, discovering, among other attractions, a Moorish arch, Chinese elms, Lombardy poplars, a replica of the Taj Mahal, and a lagoon designed to imitate the place where the infant Moses had been hidden and later discovered within bullrushes.[18] A fountain of youth stood in the northern part of the garden, and in a case inside the Japanese pergola were displayed all the family memorabilia from the Floating University cruise (figs. 9.1 and 9.2). Opened to visitors in 1937, the Chance Gardens gave the citizens of

FIGURE 9.1. F. Gano Chance's photograph of gardens in Japan taken on the 1926–27 cruise. Image courtesy of Garrison Chance.

FIGURE 9.2. The Chance Gardens in Centralia, Missouri, ca. 1937. Image courtesy of the Centralia Historical Society, Missouri.

Centralia, not least the children at the nearby school, an experience of the wonders of the world.[19] Since the 1970s, the Chance family house has been the home of the Centralia Historical Society, and the Gardens are listed on the National Register of Historic Places.

In the lives of other passengers are further suggestions that the Floating University's experiential learning model had a lasting impact. Thomas G. Brown, who had shared the editorship of the *Binnacle* with Henry Allen, went on to lecture on several Mediterranean cruises before returning to work as a journalist for the *New York Herald Tribune*. He later joined the staff of the Brooklyn Public Library.[20] Brown saved his copies of the *Binnacle* his whole life, entrusting them in 1963 to the librarian at his alma mater, Trinity College in Hartford, Connecticut.[21] In 1950 J. Harold Tarbell, the *Ryndam*'s lecturer in international relations who had served as a major in the Air Corps during World War II, launched a Flying College. As professor of economics at Lafayette College, he took forty students on a forty-three-day tour around the world in a four-engine DC-4.[22] And is it too much to think that Creighton C. Hart's career as a stamp collector sprung at least in part from his travels in 1926–27?

AGENTS OF EMPIRE

These were by no means the only paths pursued by the Floating University's alumni. In 1930, the *Gangplank*'s editors revealed that many were also working in industries that were both the product and the engine of their nation's growing global power: electronics, telephonics, air travel, shipping, and tourism.[23] Several were in the hotel business, and no less than eleven former cruise members were involved in banking and insurance—a sector that had not only triggered the interwar global economic crisis but continued to channel American commercial might toward the ends of dollar diplomacy in the decades following. Others would go on to serve in the armed forces or work in the oil industry or as lawyers or for US government agencies at home and abroad.

Brewster Bingham became a missionary in China; Robert S. Farrell Jr. served as the Republican secretary of state in Oregon; and David Inglis became a physicist who worked on the development of the nuclear bomb.[24] After marrying Lucie Bedford, the granddaughter of one of the directors of Standard Oil, Briggs Cunningham II became a competitive racing car driver and sailor, gaining significant fame at Le Mans and Sebring as well as in the World Sportscar Championships.[25] Richard Black (who had been in the Mt. Fuji climbing party) went on to join American explorer Richard E. Byrd's second expedition to Antarctica and became an agent of the US military expansion in the Pacific.[26] After graduating from law school, James Howard Marshall went from college soccer star and Quaker to oil baron and 16 percent owner of Koch Industries, eventually marrying Playboy Playmate and reality television star Anna Nicole Smith.[27]

It is impossible to say that these career choices were directly induced by the world cruise and likely that in many cases they were not. In pursuing them, however, these Floating University alumni were helping maintain the commercial, military, and cultural routes along which the *Ryndam* had sailed. Although the voyage's lessons in empire had received little press coverage in 1926 and 1927, its uneven geographies were reproduced and expanded by its alumni in the decades that followed. Rejected by the world of higher education, the Floating University was nonetheless very much a contributor to the collegiate and social cultures that, in the 1920s and 1930s, helped shape the generation that would go on to lead the postwar world.[28]

THE WORLD OF AUTHORIZED KNOWLEDGE

Perhaps the greatest irony of Professor Lough's voyage was that having experienced firsthand the places and people of the world, several of the Floating University's passengers went on to build careers within the university world of authorized knowledge.[29]

When the Floating University left New York in 1926, Carl Gamer had just been ordained as a Methodist minister. When the ship reached Europe, he decided to remain there to attend the 1927 summer school of the Institute for International Studies in Geneva.[30] Although he initially returned to parish work, Gamer left the ministry in the early 1930s to study international relations, undertaking a PhD in political science at the University of Illinois under the direction of James Wilford Garner, John Fairlie, and the international studies scholar Clarence A. Berdahl.[31] His dissertation focused on the relationship between religion and the state in Germany. Based on the research Gamer had conducted in Berlin during the height of Kristallnacht, it examined the free (not state-supported) churches of American and English origin under National Socialism. Of her husband's PhD studies, his wife, Alice, wrote, "It's a never-ending grind, but I do think it gets one places [in] these days of competition, because so few have PhDs in his field—and yet men are needed in it."[32] After serving as a chaplain in Illinois during World War II, Gamer secured a position as assistant professor of political science at Monmouth College. There, he set up an International Relations Club, led the YMCA group, and continued his involvement in church life.[33] He was a vocal advocate for racial integration, and during the civil rights violence in the early 1960s, he led his Monmouth students in helping rebuild that city's African Methodist Episcopal church.[34]

Marion A. ("Gus") Wenger described the Floating University as the turning point in his life.[35] After completing his degree at the University of Michigan, he initially went into business with his father in Ohio, but in 1931 he returned to the university to undertake a PhD in educational psychology, finishing his doctoral studies at the University of Iowa. After obtaining academic posts at Yale, Chicago, the Samuel S. Fels Research Institute (Ohio), and Antioch College in the 1930s, Wenger worked in research during the war. Then in 1945 he was appointed professor at the University of California, Los Angeles. In focusing on psychophysiology—the relationship between signals received from the body and the brain and mental processes—Wenger's research took up some of the themes that first animated William James and underpinned Lough's original ideas.[36] At the time of his retirement in 1971, he was hailed as one of the three scholars who laid the foundations of this disciplinary field.[37] In 1968–69, he became director of the University of California Study Abroad Program in Hong Kong.

Then there was Lynn Townsend White Jr. After the *Ryndam*'s return, he earned his arts degree at Stanford University and then completed a PhD in medieval history at Princeton.[38] He went on to hold academic posts at both institutions. In 1966, he gave an address to the American Association for the Advancement of Science that changed how the scholarly world thought about the environment.[39] White argued that the ecological crisis (even then clear to scientists) was the product of a Judeo-Christian tradition that, unlike the religions of antiquity and of Asia, drew a hard boundary between humans on the one hand and nature on the other, giving the former dominion over the latter. All of modern Western science, he thought, even in its most secular form, was cast in this matrix. White consequently feared that "more science and more technology [was] not going to get us out of the present ecological crisis." What the West desperately needed was to "find a new religion, or rethink our old one." Although acknowledging the Buddhist tradition, he did not think it likely to be broadly "viable" outside Asia. Instead, he cited the example of Saint Francis of Assisi, whose democratic vision of creation saw "all things animate and inanimate [as] designed for the glorification of their transcendent Creator."[40] Saint Francis, White argued, might become the "patron saint for ecologists." With this, he aroused a "storm of protest" that continues to echo into the twenty-first century.[41] Fundamental to his talk was an understanding that humans were not separate from, but instead deeply embedded in, their environment. Perhaps, if he had been alive, James Edwin Lough might have recognized in White's argument echoes of his own belief that students learned best when their education was connected to their surroundings, experiences, and interests. "We live in a world where all sides are bound together," Dewey had said.[42]

SEMESTER AT SEA

Nor did Lough live to see what was perhaps the greatest testament to his big idea: the postwar revival of the Floating University project. In 1951, the Holland America Line (HAL) announced it was naming one of its newly built liners the SS *Rijndam* (or *Ryndam*) for the interwar ship that had carried Lough's students on their cruise around the world. Reading this news from his home in Bridgeport, Connecticut, former Floating University student Goodwin Stoddard conceived of the idea for another reunion on board the new ship. Securing the backing of HAL's New York general manager, Stoddard located as many of his fellow 1926 voyagers as he could. Hundreds of letters were sent out, press releases were issued to newspapers, and students were encouraged to contact others.

The result was that on April 30, 1952, seventy-five of the original Floating University passengers gathered once again on the Hoboken, New Jersey, pier to board a ship that looked very different from the one they had stepped off twenty-five years before. Cocktails were served in the palm court and dinner was held in the A-deck dining room, with greetings cabled in not only from the directors of the HAL but also from a retired Captain Jan K. Liewen and more than 130 absent friends. Across the country, three other "sub-reunions" were simultaneously taking place in Chicago, St. Louis, and Los Angeles. "Such enthusiasm," thought Stoddard, "was proof enough that our trip left a deep impression on each of us and I think, made us rather unique citizens of this country and the world."[43] Constantine Raises was among those in attendance at the New York gathering, and two years later he organized another reunion, this time in California in honor of Sydney Greenbie's 1928–29 International University Cruise voyage.[44]

Since the first sailing in 1926, Raises had remained a dedicated advocate of the idea of a floating university. He had worked with Lough to relaunch the project after the war, and in the decade that followed he witnessed several groups emerge to champion the concept. The American President Lines ran three luxury "floating university" educational tours in the early 1950s, and a few years later Les Biederman, the president of Northwestern Michigan College, attempted to launch a credit-bearing educational cruise. Holling C. Holling had been working with Lough and Julius W. Butler (a Chicago millionaire land developer) on the idea of a floating school, and a group called Student World-O-Rama was attempting to interest the Ford

Foundation in a similar venture.[45] In 1958, Raises himself pressed the secretary of state, John Foster Dulles, to establish a travel university that would be sent on yearly round-the-world voyages (for more on Raises, see the appendix).[46]

Meanwhile in California, the Whittier Rotary Club was developing its own plans. William T. Hughes, a businessman, and E. Ray Nichols Jr., a professor at Whittier College, were thinking seriously about how they might contribute to international education. Hughes was director of the club's Visiting International Student Activities program, and as a child Nichols had spent a year living in Japan.[47] They, too, had come up with the idea of launching a university that would sail around the world, its passengers studying international problems. According to Raises's version of the story, Hughes got in touch with him sometime in 1958, having read about the 1926 voyage in a newspaper article. The Floating University veteran encouraged the Rotarian to pursue the idea.[48] Hughes contacted Rufus Von Kleinsmid, chancellor and former president of the University of Southern California, who put the men in touch with Edith Weir, his former appointment secretary who had also been the French teacher on board the original *Ryndam*. She was sufficiently impressed with their approach to lend them her personal materials from the 1926–27 cruise, including course guides and advertising booklets.[49]

By 1959, Hughes and Nichols had persuaded Democratic congressmen from California, George Kasem and D. S. Saund, to take up the cause in Washington, and in March 1961 the University of the Seven Seas became an "independent legal entity authorized . . . to conduct a program of higher education."[50] Serving on its board was none other than James Price, the student president from the original *Ryndam*. Two years later, a Floating University was once again on the water. Carrying three hundred students and thirty-eight professors, the University of the Seven Seas sailed in October of 1963 on the MS *Seven Seas*, with the blessing of former president Dwight D. Eisenhower. With words that directly echoed Edith Weir's original 1926 materials, it, too, promised students a "challenging experience in international living and study, using the world as its laboratory."[51]

Over the next few decades, the venture went through several iterations.[52] The University of the Seven Seas sailed again in 1964, but Hughes needed to find a permanent university sponsor. He contacted Chapman College, which agreed to take on its organization and accreditation.[53] The Seven Seas Division was established and a ship under Chapman College's sponsorship sailed in 1965. The following year, the Holland America Line made available a new and bigger vessel—none other than the *Ryndam* II, on which the 1926 students had gathered for their reunion in 1952—and Chapman changed the name of the program to the World Campus Afloat, which ran trips annually until 1970. It was already crediting James E. Lough with being the first to implement the idea.

Just when the costs seemed too much for the small college to bear, Choa-Yung ("C.Y.") Tung, a Hong Kong shipowner, came to the rescue. Tung established Seawise Foundation Ltd. As a nonprofit corporation that would own the Floating University's ship, and from 1971 Chapman College ran its World Campus Afloat aboard Tung's SS *Universe*. When in 1975 the college did have to step away from cruise sponsorship, a new organization, the Institute of Shipboard Education, was formed. Working with Tung's Seawise Foundation and carrying credit from the University of Colorado, Boulder, in 1977 it launched an academic program called Semester at Sea. After program partnerships with University of Pittsburgh's Center for International Studies and then the University of Virginia, in 2016 Colorado State University took over as its academic sponsor.[54] As of 2022, academic credits for Semester at Sea courses were easily transferable to most US universities and colleges.

RECENT ECHOES

Semester at Sea was one of the many proposals for US education abroad that flowered in the decade following the end of World War II.[55] From the Fulbright and Marshall scholarship programs to overseas summer institutes, service initiatives like the Peace Corps, and immersion courses on the Junior Year Abroad model, these offerings took many forms. They were championed by educators and political leaders alike as playing a critical role in fostering cross-cultural relations and international understanding. Far from advancing the "free flow of information," such educational initiatives, as Sam Lebovic has shown, "sought to protect [the American] home market and to expand [its] international control."[56] Universities, however, remained uncertain about the merits of granting academic credit to students undertaking many of these programs.[57] Their proliferation in the 1950s and 1960s spurred a replay of the concerns that in the 1920s had killed off Professor Lough's Floating University: How educational were such overseas initiatives? What exactly were students learning? If travel education was to be respectable and attract US credits, did it not need to be controlled by US institutions?[58]

In the 1960s, the emergence of student campus activism connected to the Civil Rights and anti-Vietnam movements, and the challenge to established institutional authority that it reflected, made the US domestic agenda much more pressing while also creating international diplomatic friction. Reflecting these priorities, Congress chose not to fund the 1966 International Education Act and philanthropic foundations withdrew their support, leading to a rationalization of both government- and private-led study abroad programs.[59] However, as in the 1920s, this did not stop students seeking experiences overseas. The international travel of young Americans expanded rapidly, stimulating the growth of a whole new tourist infrastructure outside the universities.[60] Although more institutions began to set up travel programs in the 1970s and 1980s, it was not until the increasing globalization of higher education in the 1990s that what is now known as international education came to be widely celebrated by the majority of US universities, who now championed it as key to enhancing cross-cultural understanding, developing confidence, and equipping students to work in a global world.[61] In 2018, the Institute of International Education reported that one in ten US undergraduates studied abroad at some point during their degree program; an increase from approximately 75,000 students in 1991–92 to about 325,000 in the space of only fifteen years.[62] Emphasizing the educational virtues of experience, these programs also found a domestic echo in the movement toward including initiatives such as internships and service- and co-operative learning in the undergraduate curriculum.[63] The boom in foreign study programs once again took a diversity of forms, but a new pattern was clearly evident: 95 percent of trips were for a period of one semester or less.[64] Critics of these more recent programs hold that, much like the Floating University, they frequently serve to bolster American identity rather than develop true engagement with other peoples while also attracting those from middle- and upper-class backgrounds.[65] Less often is it noted that they also help fashion US students into international agents of American commerce, culture, and expertise.

No institution has embraced this new era of international education more enthusiastically than NYU. In 2016–17, it had more students studying abroad than any other institution in the United States.[66] However, NYU's approach to educational travel at the start of the twenty-first century suggests it is no keener now to academically authorize the unpredictable nature of experiences gained overseas than it was in the 1920s. NYU's approach has been to develop a network of overseas campuses, where NYU students undertake courses for NYU credit, organized as part of NYU degree programs and taught by NYU-employed faculty. As historian and educationalist William Hoffa pointed out, the relationship of US study abroad to academic credits remains a problematic one.[67]

Educational travel programs are founded on the recognition that direct personal experience can be the basis of learning: immersion in a place, encounters with other people, and practical engagement in and with the world can offer students something that textbooks cannot. However, this argument fundamentally pushes against universities' claim to be authorizers of knowledge about the world. Although institutions like NYU seek to square this circle by maintaining control over their credits through organizing and regulating study abroad and through assessing its outcomes, this attempt at oversight is itself an acknowledgment that academic authority and personal experience pull in opposite directions. These compromises in many ways reflect the terms of the knowledge regime established in the 1920s, in which universities claimed their twentieth-century status as the ultimate credentializers of knowledge. Direct personal experience is an important part of a liberal college education (and a hugely valuable cultural credential), but it remains in tension with the academic authorization of knowledge claims.

THINKING WITH FAILURE

Why, then, does the story of the 1926 Floating University matter? The voyage was pronounced an educational failure when NYU withdrew its academic endorsement and when the US mass media decided it did not measure up to their image of scholarly behavior. It was these educational and print media institutions that drew the boundaries of what counted as educational legitimacy, and it was against their criteria that the pedagogic experiment was judged. Casting the Floating University as a failure has been a way of reasserting the epistemic and social order that the ship's claims for the legitimacy of experiential knowledge challenged. Perhaps this is one of the reasons that academic historians have not attended to the story of the Floating University in the decades since it sailed: for the most part, they have inherited the rules of knowing that cast it onto the heath of memory, folklore, idealism, and scandal.[68] Instead, they have focused on interwar projects that left a more visible mark on the world of universities and politics and have taken as their methods the conventions for warranting and legitimating knowledge that have dominated twentieth-century academia.

Failure in the United States has attracted its historians, and Scott Sandage's original cultural history of the relationship between individual self-worth and economic "success" stands out among them. He traces the development, in the wake of the Civil War, of "success and failure as the two faces of American freedom," arguing that the American dream—a concept that emerged in the early 1930s—"could neither exist nor endure without failure."[69] Another body of work has emerged on empire, planning, and state intervention, examining what Raghav Kishore calls the "fecundity of failure": how apparent failed projects have often been accompanied by a growth in bureaucratic capability, technical reach, and regulatory power.[70] Evaluating "failed" plans or projects within the instrumentalist terms of their ostensible objectives, argues William Bisell, risks "reifying the 'plan' and missing much of the sociocultural landscape in which planning occurs"; it risks missing much of how organizations and sectors (such as higher education) actually work.[71] The French philosopher of science, Georges Canguilhem (whose students included, among others, Derrida, Foucault, Althusser, and Lacan), also alluded to the generative possibilities of failure in his 1978 essay on error. It "is the abnormal which arouses theoretical interest in the normal," Canguilhem argued. "Norms are recognized as such only when they are broken. Functions are revealed only when they fail. Life rises to the consciousness and science of itself only through maladaptation, failure, and pain."[72] For Canguilhem, the experience of failure to fit existing models of the world begins and sustains all scientific inquiry, because it forces an interrogation of those norms.

This book has suggested that attending to the "failure" of Professor Lough's 1926 pedagogic experiment helps reveal the norms governing knowledge claims in the 1920s and the conditions under which they were and are maintained.[73] It examined first, the different bases for warranting knowledge; second, the rival systems of social acknowledgment; and third, the taken-for-granted background assumptions that both constituted the sociocultural landscape of Lough's project and helped determine its fate. Thinking with failure means thinking carefully about how legitimacy was and is produced—the institutions that normalize it and profit by it, the sanctions that reinforce it, and the other ways of being it excludes. Understood in this way, "failures" can open windows on systems and concepts that are otherwise naturalized and normalized. In many ways, this impulse to interrogate judgments about who and what gets counted and the assumptions these judgments embed has long been at the heart of postcolonial, feminist, queer, Black, and First Nations history movements. Might it not also animate our understanding of universities and the knowledge projects they advance? This is not to say that knowledge claims are relative, but rather that they are made legitimate within very specific social environments, and their acceptance—and rejection—has a history and a politics.

If the 1920s were a decade in which regimes that privileged academic and expert knowledge were institutionalized not only in universities but also in the growth of the administrative state, the early decades of the twenty-first century have seen these regimes transformed by the proliferation of linked, highly granulated, and disembodied big data that are increasingly being used for prediction and control. At the same time, personal, embodied, and experiential knowledge is loudly being cited by a host of actors from across the political spectrum who are challenging experts and their long-privileged ways of claiming authority.[74] Who gets to know in this new world? And how is that knowledge certified? How will social recognition be secured?

Should Professor Lough set sail today, he would traverse a world very different from the one he encountered in 1926. Those changes he would be able to mark, not only because of academically authorized scientific expertise but also because of his own direct bodily experience.[75] Walking down the streets of New York City, he would feel warmer temperatures; driving through port city hinterlands, he would witness the effects of resource extraction; and, gazing over the sides of his ship, he would see oceans emptied of marine life but populated instead with desperate migrants and refugees. If human communities are to find ways to operate within a set of assumptions fit for the political, social, and environmental challenges of the twenty-first century, social recognition of both these ways of grounding knowledge, and the connections between them, will be essential.

Acknowledgments

I hope this is a book about universities that is also fun to read. I certainly had fun writing it. Many people have shared in its making, and to them I owe my deepest thanks. First, Roland Wenzlhuemer and his Floating Spaces group at the University of Heidelberg's Asia-Europe Cluster of Excellence, together with an early seminar at the University of Leicester and subsequent conversations with Matt Houlbrook and Erica Hanna, convinced me that there was more to the story of the Floating University than just the high jinks of a Gatsby-esque gap year. Then, an Australian Research Council Discovery Early Career Research Award (DECRA) gave me the gifts of trust and time, enabling me to develop my ideas, follow research leads, visit archives, obtain digital copies, and have conversations with colleagues across the globe. The DECRA also brought me to Sydney, where I now live. That would not have happened if Geoff Sherington had not snooped at my notes in the University of Sydney archives while I was out to lunch and subsequently introduced me to Julia Horne. They have both become trusted mentors, colleagues, collaborators, and friends. Along with Deryck Schreuder, Stephen Garton, Hannah Forsyth, Kate Darian-Smith, James Waghorne, Gwil Croucher, Joel Barnes, and the late Stuart Macintyre, I have been lucky to have them as Australian interlocutors, both on aspects of this project and on the history and politics of universities more broadly.

My first book was on academic networks in the British Empire. Universities, empire, and the social are themes that run through this study too, but here their context has shifted significantly. Several people have helped me navigate these new waters of international history and US foreign relations. I am especially grateful to Jay Sexton. First in Oxford, and now across oceans, he has been a legendary comrade and friend, generous with his ideas, his introductions, and his sociability. The chapter workshops, visits to archives, and the many wonders of Centralia that I experienced during my visit to the University of Missouri have left their mark on this manuscript. Similarly, the intellectual companionship of Katharina Rietzler and Valeska Huber has meant a great deal. Our little reading group began in London and has continued for over a decade, surviving time zones, witnessing the births of multiple children, and encompassing the vicissitudes of personal and professional life. Our ongoing conversation has been one of the great joys of my career, and it shows on so many pages of this book. Paul Kramer also has offered generous and apposite guidance. Clare Corbould has been an absolute godsend, helping me troubleshoot multiple aspects of this project and offering up her wisdom with characteristic humor and grace. I am not sure where I would have been without Kate Fullagar, who has shared her knowledge, read drafts, and sent me several "just checking in" emails when I needed them most. They both, together with Mike McDonald and Yves Rees, provided a hugely helpful close reading of an early version of this manuscript, for which I am enormously grateful. In different ways, Alecia Simmonds, Leigh Boucher, Alison Bashford, and Warwick Anderson all helped me find a way through particularly knotty problems. That their assistance was accompanied by good food, good wine, good friendship, and good gossip only makes me more grateful to them.

I have received the support of several institutions during this project. Its seeds were sown while I was at Brunel University in London, much of it was developed at University of Sydney, and it came to fruition at the University of Technology Sydney (UTS). Along the way, I have benefited from visiting fellowships, at the University of Heidelberg and in New College, Harris Manchester College, and the Rothermere American Institute at the University of Oxford, and from a Griffith Review Varuna writing residency. But institutions are tended by individuals. At UTS, I have been supremely fortunate in my colleagues, both in the social and political studies discipline group and at the Australian Centre for Public History. Their commitment to their vocation is inspiring. I am particularly grateful to Anna Clark for historical chat, institutional comradery, and friendship. The archivists and librarians who have assisted me with my research are too many to name, but their answers to my questions and preparedness to digitize their holdings have been invaluable. The research assistance of Burcu Cevik, Rebecca Crites, Molly Dias, Patrick Flood, Rosemary Hancock, Kirsten Kamphuis, Gabrielle Kemmis, Anna Kent, Yves Rees, and Sander Tetteroo has made manageable what sometimes seemed like a mammoth project. Davy Baas shared his undergraduate dissertation, Hayden Lorimer his ideas and enthusiasm for Holling C. Holling, and Heike Jöns a crucial newspaper snippet and her knowledge of Alfred Weber. Susan Liebich and Laurence Publicover invited me to be part of their edited volume *Reading, Writing and Performing at Sea* for Palgrave Macmillan, and the reviewers of a companion article for *Diplomatic History* pushed me in all the right directions. Tim Mennel and Susannah Engstrom at the University of Chicago Press have been encouraging and patient from the start. I'm grateful as well to freelance copyeditor Sandra Hazel. Together with the reports of the two anonymous readers of the manuscript, their time and attention have improved my work immensely.

I offer this book up from the middle of things. It has carried me across continents, between institutions, and through major life events. Throughout it all, Frances Flanagan has been a wise and dear friend whose intellectual imagination and insight and commitment to embeddedness I deeply admire. Frances, it is one of the great blessings of my life to owe you debts I can never repay. Mum, you may not live to see this book in print, and I'm sure that much of what I do has seemed a mystery to you; but your life has been one of service to education and its institutions, and I have never doubted your grounding love. Vita, I sent the manuscript off to the publishers the day before you were born, and every day since I have thought my heart might explode. And Ruth, my partner in marriage: thank you for making my life larger, my conversation richer, my bookcase fuller. You outbid all rivals on eBay, read all the books on Wittgenstein, and flew to New York and Copenhagen and Berlin. This book is better because of you, and so am I. As I sail my own little boat upon the seas of life, I am fortunate indeed to have you all as my companions.

APPENDIX

Chasing Constantine Raises

Shortly before his death in San Francisco in 1984, Constantine Raises met Paul Liebhardt, a photographer, author, and one-time teacher in the Semester at Sea study abroad program. As Liebhardt listened, Raises told his own version of the Floating University story. It went something like this:

One night in the New York winter of February 1925, six men met on a ship moored on the East River at the southeastern tip of the Bronx. A professor, a ship's captain, a diplomat, a newspaper editor, and a Quaker former yacht broker were brought together for a meal aboard the New York Maritime Academy's training ship, the (SS) *Newport*, by a Greek refugee named Constantine Raises.

Raises first met the professor on a hot summer's day five years earlier. The American was traveling with a party of his students on a tour of the cultural and classical sites of Greece and Rome, and they had made the journey out to the suburb of Zografou to visit the University of Athens, where Raises was a student. Raises knew a bit about Americans, having learned English as a boy at the American School at Smyrna. Smyrna (now known as Izmir, Turkey) was a city located on the Aegean cost of Anatolia. It was home to a large Greek community, and under the Ottomans it had been a significant port and financial center. Raises's importer-exporter father regularly took him on trips around the Mediterranean. Thinking an English education would be an asset to a prospective trader, he had enrolled his son in the American School, and it was there that Constantine had also met US Consul George Horton. The touring American professor was called James Lough. Impressed with Raises's fluency in English, Lough hired him on the spot to serve as his party's translator and guide. He met up with him on subsequent tours as well until the summer of 1922, when Raises left Athens for his hometown of Smyrna and his family business.

But 1922 was a bad time for him to be returning home. The Greek army had landed in Smyrna in 1919, beginning the conflict now known as the Greco-Turkish War, which was fought in the western and northwestern parts of Anatolia in the wake of the defeat of the Ottoman Empire. After initial victories won by the Greek forces, the conflict reversed course, and the Turkish army recaptured Smyrna in early September 1922. Four days later, a fire broke out that destroyed the Greek and Armenian sections of the city. Tens of thousands died in the blaze. Many more had been killed earlier in the war, and many were to perish later. Between twenty-five thousand and one hundred thousand Greek and Armenian men were deported to Anatolia, where many lost their lives.[1]

Raises managed to escape this fate, very possibly with the assistance of George Horton, who reportedly spent the last hours before his own evacuation signing passes granting the protection of the United States to their recipients. Separated from his family and living in a refugee camp like so many others from his country, he searched for ways to make it to America. Despite the new US restrictions on immigration, he somehow managed to arrive in New York in late 1922. Then Raises contacted his old friend Professor Lough, who helped him find a clerical job on the *New York World* newspaper, edited at the time by renowned reporter Herbert Swope.

But Raises was not suited to a desk job. He longed to travel, so in 1924 he took a position as a purser on the Dollar Line's SS *President Garfield*. Next, he became an aide to Captain Felix Riesenberg, commander of the New York Maritime Academy's training ship, the *Newport*, in 1923 and 1924. Riesenberg was also a prolific author of books on maritime literature, and Raises helped him with research and translation of materials. On his voyages with Riesenberg, the Greek from Smyrna saw firsthand the effect of shipboard education on the young cadets. Upon his return to New York, he contacted Professor Lough, whose own attempts to launch a Floating University had already been reported in the press. At the time, Lough was trying to purchase the SS *President Arthur* from the United States Shipping Board. As the original purpose of the Floating University had been to encourage the creation of a naval reserve and a merchant marine, Raises connected him with Riesenberg.

It was Riesenberg who in early 1925 hosted the dinner party on board the *Newport,* but all the men present were there because of their connection to Raises. All, that is, except Andrew J. McIntosh, a wealthy Quaker, retired shipping broker, and trustee of the New York Maritime Academy. He had an interest in internationalism, so Riesenberg invited him to the gathering, thinking he might be eager to support the Floating University project. Perhaps Raises thought that Horton, who had only recently returned to the

United States, would himself be interested in its internationalist aspects. At the time, he was writing his book, *The Blight of Asia*, which would tell the story of the 1922 occupation of Smyrna, the torching of the city, and the killing and expulsion of its Greek and Armenian citizens.

Enthused about the idea of the Floating University, McIntosh handed over a check for $25,000 at the dinner, much to Lough's surprise. Together, they formed the University Travel Association, with McIntosh as president, Lough as director of educational affairs, and Raises in charge of the itinerary. Their aim was to launch a voyage that would begin in September 1925. Lough managed to obtain a charter from the New York Department of Education that gave him permission to operate a university on a ship, and he persuaded New York University to sponsor the project. Herbert Swope wrote a publicity-generating piece in the *New York World*, and the Holland America Line offered the use of one of its ships—the SS *Ryndam*, at the time sitting idle in Rotterdam—for a token fee. Although not enough students signed up for a cruise in 1925 as initially planned, the Floating University became a reality in 1926, when five hundred students sailed aboard the *Ryndam*, accompanied by Professor Lough, Andrew J. McIntosh, and Constantine Raises.

◆　◆　◆

This origin account was put to paper by Liebhardt, who published it in 1998 in *Steamboat Bill* magazine.[2] It now also appears in the biographical note prefacing the collection of Constantine Raises's papers held by the University of Colorado, Boulder, and in several accounts across the internet.[3]

Some aspects of Raises's story do match those found elsewhere. In early 1925, Lough *was* publishing notices in the newspapers trying to drum up sufficient interest to enable him to purchase the SS *President Arthur*, and these touted the benefits of his Floating University for the merchant marine. In mid-1925, McIntosh *did* join with Lough to play a major role in the organization of the successful 1926–27 Floating University cruise. The ship they sailed on *was* owned by the Holland America Line, and Constantine Raises *was* a member of that voyage.

Nonetheless, it is very unlikely that Professor James E. Lough went to Greece in 1920. The first record of his arrival or departure from New York by ship is in 1924, when he sailed with a party of students to Europe for the summer on the SS *Orduna*. The early 1920s was a turbulent time in Greek history, 1920 particularly so, and Lough's own account of the origins of the Floating University suggests that the NYU summer tours did not start up until 1923 because of the unsettled postwar conditions in Europe.[4] Neither did the Holland America Line lend the *Ryndam* for a token fee. The contract signed between HAL and Phelps Bros. states clearly that the SS *Rijndam* (*Ryndam*) would be chartered for $500,000, the first installment of which was paid on August 13, 1926.[5]

Finally, Constantine Raises did not immigrate to the United States in 1922 after fleeing the Smyrna fire. The passport (issued September 1, 1926) that bears his visas for the 1926–27 cruise indicates that he had indeed been born in Smyrna on April 13, 1900. It lists his occupation as secretary/teacher and notes his address as 17 Washington Place, Mount Vernon, New York.[6] But the only Constantine Raises born in Smyrna around 1900 who appears in the US immigration records entered Ellis Island aboard the SS *Alice*, arriving from Patras, Greece, on December 26, 1908.[7] He was eight years old, and his name was given as "Constantinos Raissis."[8] In February 1919, this same person, his name now altered to "Constantine Raises" (occupation: mariner; birthplace: Smyrna), submitted a petition for naturalization as a US citizen. He had migrated, the application stated, on the SS *Alice*, entered New York on December 26, 1908, and had resided continuously in the United States since that time. From 1919 to 1921, a "C. Raises" of Greek nationality appears on the crew lists of a number of vessels exiting and entering the Port of New York.[9]

By 1921, however, things had changed for this Constantine Raises. His application for naturalization had been approved, and when in 1922 (age: 21; residence: Mount Vernon) he appeared on the lists of passengers entering New York, it was this time as a US citizen, naturalized by the US District Court—Southern District of New York on June 18, 1921. The great fire of Smyrna began on September 13, 1922, and burned for nearly ten days. But in June 1922, "C. Raises" (age: 22; naturalized) had been in New York and applied for a Seaman's Protection Certificate to work as a purser aboard the SS *Philadelphia*. He is recorded as returning to New York on the SS *Cameronia*, which arrived from Naples on August 25.[10]

It seems relatively clear, then, that the Constantine Raises who left New York as a member of the Floating University in 1926 was the Constantinos Raissis who entered New York as a child in 1908. He was not a student at the University of Athens in 1920. He did not meet Professor Lough and act as his tour guide there. He did not flee Smyrna as fire engulfed that city in September 1922.[11]

◆ ◆ ◆

What, then, does this mean for the story about the dinner on the *Newport* that Constantine Raises told Paul Liebhardt in San Francisco in 1984? Here, the archival trail goes cold. The official records of the 1926–27 Floating University have mostly disappeared. The overview to the Constantine A. Raises Collection at the University of Colorado, Boulder, notes that Raises himself had presented this material to the University of the Seven Seas, after which it "may have been permanently lost."[12] The Semester at Sea program confirms that the early records do not exist. The Riesenberg archives in San Francisco contain little more than drafts of books on naval adventure, none of which bears evidence of a Greek translator. Of the books Riesenberg published in the 1920s that I managed to find, none mentions Raises in the acknowledgments. I have failed to find Andrew J. McIntosh's papers and similarly had no success in my search for the records of the diplomat George Horton, though of course these records may appear.

When did Raises begin to tell this version of his life? In late 1920s New York, after Horton's book on Smyrna had received so much attention, had Americans made their own assumptions about him? Or perhaps it was only after Lough's death in 1952, by which time all the other leaders of the original cruise had also died, that the *Newport* story emerged. By then, Raises was in his early fifties and running his own travel agency while working with Bill Hughes to relaunch the Floating University. And by then, after the horrors of the Holocaust, the Nuremberg trials had introduced the world to the concepts of genocide and crimes against humanity, Senator J. William Fulbright had just launched his international scholarship exchange program, and the United States was seizing a new and more interventionist global role. Perhaps an origin myth invoking one man's survival of an earlier catastrophe and linking it to an American innovation in international education fit the times as well as Raises's personal purposes? Much of the story he told Liebhardt is plausible, and it is very possible that the dinner on the *Newport* did happen. Only, how would we know? What forms of warrant would be seen as sufficient to overturn Raises's firsthand account, and which systems of social acknowledgment would legitimate them?

Archival Information

Allen Papers	MSS 50781 Henry Justin Allen Papers, Manuscript Division, Library of Congress.
Archieven van de Holland-Amerika Lijn (HAL)	Holland America Line Archives, Stadsarchief, Rotterdam.
Diary of Lillian McCracken	A/M 132 Diary of Lillian McCracken, 1926–1927, Schlesinger Library, Radcliffe Institute, Harvard University.
Gauss Collection	A3637 Charles E. Gauss Jr. Collection, Archives and Regional History Collections, Western Michigan University, Kalamazoo.
Heckel Papers	C3481 Albert Kerr Heckel Papers, the State Historical Society of Missouri, Columbia.
Holling Papers	1012 Holling Clancy Holling Papers, University Archives, University of California Los Angeles.
Johnson Papers	MSA 441 Thomas H. Johnson Papers, Vermont Historical Society, Barre.
Lough Family Papers	FL887 Lough Family Papers, Cincinnati Historical Society.
Meetings of the Council	RG 2.1.1 Meetings of the Council, Elmer Holmes Bobst Library, New York University Archives.
NARA	National Archives and Records Administration, College Park, Maryland.

Office of
the President

RG 3.0.4 Office of the President, Elmer Ellsworth Brown Administration, Administration Files, Elmer Holmes Bobst Library, New York University Archives.

Office of the
Vice President
and Secretary

RG 4.0.1 Office of the Vice President and Secretary (Harold O. Voorhis), Administrative Subject Files, Elmer Holmes Bobst Library, New York University Archives.

Raises Collection

Constantine A. Raises Collection, University of Colorado Boulder Libraries, Rare and Distinctive Collections Repository.

Reddick Papers

3G454 Reddick (DeWitt C.) Papers, 1927–1980, Dolph Briscoe Center for American History, the University of Texas at Austin.

Semester at
Sea Archives

Institute for Shipboard Education in conjunction with Colorado State University, Semester at Sea Archives, Fort Collins, Colorado.

Thwing Papers

1DD6 Papers of Charles F. Thwing, Case Western University Archives, Kelvin Smith Library, Cleveland.

Walker Papers

DC 2524 Guy Morrison Walker Papers, Archives of DePauw University and Indiana United Methodism, Greencastle, Indiana.

Notes

INTRODUCTION

1   *Binnacle* (University Travel Association), September 21, 1926, box 48, folder 4,
     1DD6 Thwing Papers; Charles E. Benson et al., *Psychology for Teachers* (Boston:
     Ginn, 1926), 89; "Floating University Sails," *Hartford Courant*, September 19, 1926.
2   The pamphlet was this one: *College Cruise around the World Eight Months*, 1926–
     27, H Subject Files/Cruises, New York University Archives.
3   *College Cruise around the World Eight Months*, 1926–27.
4   Brief mentions appear in John Eugene Harley, *International Understanding:
     Agencies Educating for a New World* (Stanford, CA: Stanford University Press,
     1931); Paul Liebhardt and Judy Rogers, *Discovery: The Adventure of Shipboard
     Education* (Olympia, WA: William and Allen, 1985); Paul Liebhardt, "The History
     of Shipboard Education," *Steamboat Bill* 55, no. 3 (1998): 173–86; Woodrow C.
     Whitten, "Floating Campus," *Improving College and University Teaching* 17, no. 4
     (1969): 283–86; Joan Elias Gore, "Discourse and Traditional Belief: An Analysis
     of American Undergraduate Study Abroad" (PhD diss., University of London,
     2000), 197–99; and William Hoffa, *A History of US Study Abroad: Beginnings to
     1965* (Carlisle, PA: Forum on Education Abroad, 2007), 86–96. In addition, the
     1926 voyage is widely cited as part of the history of Semester at Sea. See Institute
     for Shipboard Education in conjunction with Colorado State University, Semester
     at Sea, "Semester at Sea History," 2021, archived copy, April 26, 2021, Internet Ar-
     chive Wayback Machine, https://web.archive.org/web/20210426001218/https://
     www.semesteratsea.org/contact/our-history/.
5   For the role of interwar collegiate culture in shaping the generation that would go
     on to lead the postwar world, see Robert D. Dean, *Imperial Brotherhood: Gender
     and the Making of Cold War Foreign Policy* (Amherst: University of Massachusetts
     Press, 2001); Tamson Pietsch, "Commercial Travel and College Culture: The
     1920s Transatlantic Student Market and the Foundations of Mass Tourism," *Diplo-
     matic History* 43, no. 1 (2019): 83–106.
6   Overviews of the "new international history" include Erez Manela, "Interna-

tional Society as a Historical Subject," *Diplomatic History* 44, no. 2 (April 2020): 184–209; David Thelan, "The Nation and Beyond: Transnational Perspectives on United States History," *Journal of American History* 86, no. 3 (1999): 965–75; Daniel Laqua, ed., *Internationalism Reconfigured: Transnational Ideas and Movements between the World Wars* (London: I. B. Tauris, 2011); Glenda Sluga and Patricia Clavin, eds., *Internationalisms: A Twentieth-Century History* (Cambridge: Cambridge University Press, 2016).

7   The body of work in this area is now significant. See, e.g., Sebastian Conrad and Dominic Sachsenmaier, *Competing Visions of World Order: Global Moments and Movements, 1880s-1930s* (New York: Palgrave Macmillan, 2007); Daniel Gorman, *The Emergence of International Society in the 1920s* (Cambridge: Cambridge University Press, 2012); Or Rosenboim, *The Emergence of Globalism: Visions of World Order in Britain and the United States, 1939–1950* (Princeton, NJ: Princeton University Press, 2017); Quinn Slobodian, *Globalists: The End of Empire and the Birth of Neoliberalism* (Cambridge, MA: Harvard University Press, 2018); Thomas Cayet, Paul-André Rosental, and Marie Thébaud-Sorger, "How International Organisations Compete: Occupational Safety and Health at the ILO, a Diplomacy of Expertise," *Journal of Modern European History* 7, no. 2 (September 2009): 174–96; "Technological Innovation and Transnational Networks: Europe between the Wars," special issue, *Journal of Modern European History* 6, no. 2 (2008); and Daniel Laqua, "Transnational Intellectual Cooperation, the League of Nations, and the Problem of Order," *Journal of Global History* 6, no. 2 (July 2011): 223–47.

8   Sarah E. Igo, *The Averaged American: Surveys, Citizens, and the Making of a Mass Public* (Cambridge, MA: Harvard University Press, 2008); Daniel Hucker, *Public Opinion and Twentieth-Century Diplomacy: A Global Perspective* (London: Bloomsbury, 2020); Katharina Rietzler, *International Experts, International Citizens: American Philanthropy, International Relations and the Problem of the Public, 1913–1954*, forthcoming.

9   As distinct from histories of US internationalism, US empire, and US diplomacy, in which expertise, knowledge, and culture have received significant attention, although many of these also focus on the post–World War II period. See references in notes 13, 14, and 15. Other indicative works include Michael E. Latham, *Modernization as Ideology: American Social Science and "Nation Building" in the Kennedy Era* (Chapel Hill: University of North Carolina Press, 2000); Jonathan Zimmerman, *Innocents Abroad: American Teachers in the American Century* (Cambridge, MA: Harvard University Press, 2006); Victoria De Grazia, *Irresistible Empire: America's Advance through Twentieth-Century Europe* (Cambridge, MA: Harvard University Press, 2009), 75–129; Michael Adas, *Dominance by Design: Technological Imperatives and America's Civilizing Mission* (Cambridge, MA: Harvard University Press, 2009); Frank A. Ninkovich, *Global Dawn: The Cultural Foundation of American Internationalism, 1865–1890* (Cambridge, MA: Harvard University Press, 2009); Sam Lebovic, *A Righteous Smokescreen: Postwar America and the Politics of Cultural Globalization* (Chicago: University of Chicago Press, 2022).

10 Louis Menand, Paul Reitter, and Chad Wellmon, eds., *The Rise of the Research University: A Sourcebook* (Chicago: University of Chicago Press, 2017), quotation is from pp. 229–30; William Clark, *Academic Charisma and the Origins of the Research University* (Chicago: University of Chicago Press, 2006). Roger Geiger

describes two parallel revolutions, one academic and one collegiate. Roger L. Geiger, *The History of American Higher Education: Learning and Culture from the Founding to World War II* (Princeton, NJ: Princeton University Press, 2015), 365.

11 Laurence R. Veysey, *The Emergence of the American University* (Chicago: University of Chicago Press, 1965), 439–44; John R. Thelin, *A History of American Higher Education* (Baltimore: Johns Hopkins University Press, 2011), 155–205; Martin Trow, "Problems in the Transition from Elite to Mass Higher Education," in *Martin Trow: Twentieth-Century Higher Education; Elite to Mass to Universal*, ed. Michael Burrage (Baltimore: Johns Hopkins University Press, 2010), 88–143. Geiger also discusses the assimilation of proprietary professional schools and the importance of extension lectures, commerce, and business schools and evening classes to the growth of student numbers. See Geiger, *The History of American Higher Education*, 443–45; Joseph K. Kett, *The Pursuit of Knowledge under Difficulties: From Self-Improvement to Adult Education in America, 1750–1990* (Stanford, CA: Stanford University Press, 1994), 269–77.

12 Geiger, *The History of American Higher Education*, 447, 454.

13 David F. Labaree, *A Perfect Mess: The Unlikely Ascendancy of American Higher Education* (Chicago: University of Chicago Press, 2017), 159. On the emergence of the credit system, see Dietrich Gerhard, "The Emergence of the Credit System in American Education Considered as a Problem of Social and Intellectual History," *Bulletin of the American Association of University Professors (1915–1955)* 41, no. 4 (1955): 647–68; Jessica M. Shedd, "The History of the Student Credit Hour," *New Directions for Higher Education* 2003, no. 122 (2003): 5–12.

14 The literature in these fields is extensive. Good overviews include Laura Briggs, *Reproducing Empire: Race, Sex, Science and U.S. Imperialism in Puerto Rico* (Berkeley: University of California Press, 2003); Alfred W. McCoy and Francisco A. Scarano, *The Colonial Crucible: Empire in the Making of the Modern American State* (Madison: University of Wisconsin Press, 2009); Adas, *Dominance by Design*; Anne L. Foster, *Projections of Power: The United States and Europe in Colonial Southeast Asia, 1919–1941* (Durham, NC: Duke University Press, 2010).

15 For general accounts and helpful overviews, see A. G. Hopkins, *American Empire: A Global History* (Princeton, NJ: Princeton University Press, 2018); Daniel Immerwahr, *How to Hide an Empire: A History of the Greater United States* (New York: Farrar, Straus and Giroux, 2019); Paul Alexander Kramer, "Power and Connection: Imperial Histories of the United States in the World," *American Historical Review* 116, no. 5 (2011): 1348–91; McCoy and Scarano, *The Colonial Crucible*. For travel, tourism, and foreign relations, see Christopher Endy, "Travel and World Power: Americans in Europe, 1890–1917," *Diplomatic History* 22, no. 4 (1998): 565–94; Christopher Endy, *Cold War Holidays: American Tourism in France* (Chapel Hill: University of North Carolina Press, 2004); Adria L. Imada, *Aloha America: Hula Circuits through the U.S. Empire* (Durham, NC: Duke University Press, 2012); Julia L. Mickenberg, *American Girls in Red Russia: Chasing the Soviet Dream* (Chicago: University of Chicago Press, 2017). For works on the United States as shaped by global connections, see Kristin L. Hoganson, "Cosmopolitan Domesticity: Importing the American Dream, 1865–1920," *American Historical Review* 107, no. 1 (2002): 55–83; Amy Kaplan, *The Anarchy of Empire in the Making of U.S. Culture* (Cambridge, MA: Harvard University Press, 2005); Mary A. Renda, *Taking Haiti: Military Occupation and the Culture of US Imperialism, 1915–1940*

(Chapel Hill: University of North Carolina Press, 2001); Kristin L. Hoganson, *The Heartland: An American History* (New York: Penguin, 2020); Ian R. Tyrrell, *Transnational Nation: United States History in Global Perspective since 1789* (Basingstoke, UK: Palgrave Macmillan, 2007).

16   See note 17 below. For higher education, international relations, and the Cold War, see Frank A. Ninkovich, *The Diplomacy of Ideas: US Foreign Policy and Cultural Relations, 1938–1950* (Cambridge: Cambridge University Press, 1981); Rebecca S. Lowen, *Creating the Cold War University: The Transformation of Stanford* (Berkeley: University of California Press, 1997); Jamie Nace Cohen-Cole, *The Open Mind: Cold War Politics and the Sciences of Human Nature* (Chicago: University of Chicago Press, 2016); Isaac A. Kamola, *Making the World Global: U.S. Universities and the Production of the Global Imaginary* (Durham, NC: Duke University Press, 2019); Jason M. Colby, "Conscripting Leviathan: Science, Cetaceans, and the Cold War," *Diplomatic History* 44, no. 3 (June 2020): 466–78; Lebovic, *A Righteous Smokescreen.* Work on the interwar period includes Martha Hanna, "French Women and American Men: 'Foreign' Students at the University of Paris, 1915–1925," *French Historical Studies* 22, no. 1 (1999): 87–112; Paul Alexander Kramer, "Is the World Our Campus? International Students and U.S. Global Power in the Long Twentieth Century," *Diplomatic History* 33, no. 5 (2009): 775–806; Whitney Walton, *Internationalism, National Identities, and Study Abroad: France and the United States, 1890–1970* (Stanford, CA: Stanford University Press, 2009).

17   For work on education and US empire, see Liping Bu, *Making the World Like Us: Education, Cultural Expansion, and the American Century* (Westport, CT: Praeger, 2003); Zimmerman, *Innocents Abroad*; Julian Go, *American Empire and the Politics of Meaning: Elite Political Cultures in the Philippines and Puerto Rico during U.S. Colonialism* (Durham, NC: Duke University Press, 2007); A. J. Angulo, *Empire and Education: A History of Greed and Goodwill from the War of 1898 to the War on Terror* (New York: Palgrave Macmillan, 2012); Sarah Steinbock-Pratt, *Educating the Empire: American Teachers and Contested Colonization in the Philippines* (Cambridge: Cambridge University Press, 2019); Foster, *Projections of Power.*

18   For works offering useful overviews of this diverse field, see David Armitage, Alison Bashford, and Sujit Sivasundaram, eds., *Oceanic Histories* (Cambridge: Cambridge University Press, 2018); Daniel Margolies, "Introduction: Oceans Forum," *Diplomatic History* 44, no. 3 (June 2020): 409–12; Martin Dusinberre and Roland Wenzlhuemer, "Being in Transit: Ships and Global Incompatibilities," *Journal of Global History* 11, no. 2 (July 2016): 155–62; Glen O'Hara, "'The Sea Is Swinging into View': Modern British Maritime History in a Globalised World," *English Historical Review* 124, no. 510 (2009): 1109–34; John R. Gillis, "The Blue Humanities," *Humanities* 34, no. 3 (May/June 2013), https://www.neh.gov/humanities/2013/mayjune/feature/the-blue-humanities; David Lambert, Luciana Martins, and Miles Ogborn, "Currents, Visions and Voyage: Historical Geographies of the Sea," *Journal of Historical Geography* 32, no. 3 (2006): 479–93; Bernhard Klein and Gesa Mackenthun, eds., *Sea Changes: Historicizing the Ocean* (London: Routledge, 2004).

19   Iain McCalman, *Darwin's Armada: How Four Voyages to Australasia Won the Battle for Evolution and Changed the World* (Camberwell, Victoria, Australia:

Penguin, 2009); Warwick Anderson, "Hybridity, Race, and Science: The Voyage of the Zaca, 1934–1935," *Isis* 103, no. 2 (June 2012): 229–53; Joanna Radin, "Latent Life: Concepts and Practices of Human Tissue Preservation in the International Biological Program," *Social Studies of Science* 43, no. 4 (August 2013): 484–508. For recent work examining meaning-making at sea, see Laurence Publicover and Susann Liebich, eds., *Shipboard Literary Cultures: Reading, Writing, and Performing at Sea* ([Cham, Switzerland]: Palgrave Macmillan, 2022). For the global history of science, see Sujit Sivasundaram, "Sciences and the Global: On Methods, Questions, and Theory," *Isis* 101, no. 1 (2010): 146–58; Suman Seth, "Colonial History and Postcolonial Science Studies," *Radical History Review* no. 127 (2017): 63–85; James Poskett, *Horizons: A Global History of Science* (New York: Viking, 2021).

20 Laurence R. Veysey, "Stability and Experiment in the American Undergraduate Curriculum," in *Content and Context: Essays on College Education*, ed. Carl Kaysen (New York: McGraw-Hill, 1973), 9–14. For other work in the progressive vein, see Patricia Albjerg Graham, *Progressive Education: From Arcady to Academe; A History of the Progressive Education Association, 1919–1955* (New York: Teachers College Press, 1967).

21 "Sea Collegians Startle Japan with Rum Orgy," *Detroit Free Press*, November 6, 1926.

22 "Occidentalism," *Brooklyn Daily Eagle*, December 6, 1926; "Paris Nights Prove More Attractive Than Battlefields to Them," *Times Herald* (Olean, NY), March 16, 1927.

23 Cheryl Misak, *Cambridge Pragmatism: From Peirce and James to Ramsey and Wittgenstein* (Oxford: Oxford University Press, 2016); Morris Dickstein, *The Revival of Pragmatism: New Essays on Social Thought, Law, and Culture* (Durham, NC: Duke University Press, 1998); Steven Shapin and Simon Schaffer, *Leviathan and the Air-Pump: Hobbes, Boyle, and the Experimental Life* (Princeton, NJ: Princeton University Press, 1985); Harry Collins, *Changing Order: Replication and Induction in Scientific Practice* (Chicago: University of Chicago Press, 1985); Stephen Hilgartner, *Science on Stage: Expert Advice as Public Drama* (Stanford, CA: Stanford University Press, 2000).

24 John-Paul A. Ghobrial, "Introduction: Seeing the World Like a Microhistorian," *Past and Present* 242, no. S14 (November 2019): 1–22; Christian G. De Vito and Anne Gerritsen, eds., *Micro-spatial Histories of Global Labour* ([Cham, Switzerland:] Palgrave Macmillan, 2018); Carlo Ginzburg, "Microhistory and Global History," in *The Construction of a Global World, 1400–1800*, ed. Jerry H. Bentley, Sanjay Subrahmanyam, and Merry Wiesner-Hanks, vol. 6 of *Cambridge World History* (Cambridge: Cambridge University Press, 2016), 446–73; Emma Rothschild, *The Inner Life of Empires: An Eighteenth-Century History* (Princeton, NJ: Princeton University Press, 2011); Linda Colley, *The Ordeal of Elizabeth Marsh: A Woman in World History* (New York: Pantheon, 2007); Maxine Berg, "Sea Otters and Iron: A Global Microhistory of Value and Exchange at Nootka Sound, 1774–1792," *Past and Present* 242, no. S14 (November 2019): 50–82.

25 Thomas V. Cohen, "The Macrohistory of Microhistory," *Journal of Medieval and Early Modern Studies* 47, no. 1 (January 2017): 67; Lara Putnam, "The Transnational and the Text-Searchable: Digitized Sources and the Shadows They Cast,"

American Historical Review 71, no. 2 (2016): 377; David Bell, "Questioning the Global Turn: The Case of the French Revolution," *French Historical Studies* 37, no. 1 (2014): 1–24.

26 Special Agent Kinsey to E. C. Bannerman, July 25, 1928, Central Decimal File 1910–29, box 317/032 University Travel Association, RG 59 (Department of State), NARA.

27 Recent and forthcoming works that take up this theme include Jan Stöckmann, *The Architects of Internationalism: Building a Discipline, Designing the World, 1914–1940* (Cambridge: Cambridge University Press, 2022); Rietzler, *International Experts, International Citizens.*

28 E.g., state licensing requirements for accountants. See Geiger, *The History of American Higher Education,* 445.

29 Barbara J. Keys, *Globalizing Sport: National Rivalry and International Community in the 1930s,* Harvard Historical Studies, vol. 152 (Cambridge, MA: Harvard University Press, 2006); Frank Costigliola, *Awkward Dominion: American Political, Economic, and Cultural Relations with Europe, 1919–1933* (Ithaca, NY: Cornell University Press, 1984); Emily S. Rosenberg, *Spreading the American Dream: American Economic and Cultural Expansion, 1890–1945* (New York: Hill and Wang, 1982); Dean, *Imperial Brotherhood.*

30 Su Lin Lewis, *Cities in Motion: Urban Life and Cosmopolitanism in Southeast Asia, 1920–1940* (Cambridge: Cambridge University Press, 2016); Richard Carr and Bradley W. Hart, *The Global 1920s: Politics, Economics and Society* (New York: Routledge, 2016).

31 Igo, *The Averaged American*; Daniel T. Rodgers, *Atlantic Crossings: Social Politics in a Progressive Age* (Cambridge, MA: Harvard University Press, 1998); Andrew Jewett, *Science, Democracy, and the American University: From the Civil War to the Cold War* (Cambridge: Cambridge University Press, 2012); Kevin J. Mumford, *Interzones: Black/White Sex Districts in Chicago and New York in the Early Twentieth Century* (New York: Columbia University Press, 1997).

32 Hoffa, *A History of US Study Abroad*; Konrad H. Jarausch, "American Students in Germany, 1815–1914: The Structure of German and US Matriculants at Göttingen University," in *German Influence on Education in the United States to 1917,* ed. Henry Geitz, Jürgen Heideking, and Jurgen Herbst (Cambridge: Cambridge University Press, 1995), 195–211; Douglas Hart, "Social Class and American Travel to Europe in the Late Nineteenth Century, with Special Attention to Great Britain," *Journal of Social History* (September 2016), 313–40; Emily J. Levine, *Allies and Rivals: German-American Exchange and the Rise of the Research University* (Chicago: University of Chicago Press, 2020).

33 Boyd Henry Bode, *Progressive Education at the Crossroads* (New York: Newson, 1938); Caroline Pratt, *I Learn from Children: An Adventure in Progressive Education.* (New York: Simon and Schuster, 1948); David Allen Kolb and Ronald Eugene Fry, "Toward an Applied Theory of Experiential Learning," in *Theories of Group Process,* ed. C. Cooper (London: John Wiley, 1975), 33–57; David Allen Kolb, *Experiential Learning: Experience as the Source of Learning and Development* (Englewood Cliffs, NJ: Prentice-Hall, 1984); Phyllis Povell, *Montessori Comes to America: The Leadership of Maria Montessori and Nancy McCormick Rambusch* (Lanham, MD: University Press of America, 2009); Rita Kramer, *Maria Montessori: A Biography* (New York: Diversion Books, 2017); Thomas Stehlik, *Waldorf*

Schools and the History of Steiner Education: An International View of 100 Years (Cham, Switzerland: Springer, 2019); Barnard College, "Reacting to the Past," 2021, https://reacting.barnard.edu/.

34 Liebhardt, "The History of Shipboard Education"; Biographical Note, Raises Collection.

35 Eric Ketelaar, "Tacit Narratives: The Meanings of Archives," *Archival Science* 1, no. 2 (June 2001): 131–41; Rodney G. S. Carter, "Of Things Said and Unsaid: Power, Archival Silences, and Power in Silence," *Archivaria* 61 (2006): 215–33; R. Roque and K. Wagner, eds., *Engaging Colonial Knowledge: Reading European Archives in World History* (Basingstoke, UK: Palgrave Macmillan, 2012); Michelle Caswell, "Dusting for Fingerprints," *Journal of Critical Library and Information Studies* 3, no. 1 (2020).

CHAPTER ONE

1 *Binnacle* (University Travel Association), September 17 and 26, 1926, box 48, folder 4, Thwing Papers; Lillian McCracken, September 18, 1926, entry, A/M 132 Diary of Lillian McCracken.

2 James Edwin Lough, n.d., UA III 15.88.10 Harvard College Student Folders, ca. 1890–1995, Harvard University Archives; *Catalogue of Miami University at Oxford, Ohio* (Oxford, OH: Miami University, 1891), Haithi Trust, accessed June 1, 2022, https://hdl.handle.net/2027/uiug.30112111896863.

3 Lough, UA III 15.88.10 Harvard College Student Folders, ca. 1890–1995; William Lough Jr. to the children of his brother James, June 4, 1952, FL887 Lough Family Papers.

4 Lough, UA III 15.88.10 Harvard College Student Folders, ca. 1890–1995; Sheldon M. Stern, "William James and the New Psychology," in *Social Sciences at Harvard, 1860–1920: From Inculcation to the Open Mind*, ed. Paul Buck (Cambridge, MA: Harvard University Press, 1965), 175–222; James E. Lough, "Studies from the Harvard Psychological Laboratory (V): A New Perimeter," *Psychological Review* 3, no. 3 (1896): 282–85.

5 William James, *The Principles of Psychology*, 2 vols. (New York: Henry Holt, 1890); William James, *Psychology: Briefer Course* (New York: Henry Holt, 1892).

6 James, *The Principles of Psychology*, 1:239; James first made this argument in William James, "On Some Omissions of Introspective Psychology," *Mind* 9, no. 33 (1884): 1–26.

7 James, *The Principles of Psychology*, 1:224.

8 Philip P. Wiener, *Dictionary of the History of Ideas: Studies of Selected Pivotal Ideas*, vol. 4 (New York: Scribner, 1973), 27.

9 William James, *Pragmatism: A New Name for Some Old Ways of Thinking* (New York: Longmans, Green, 1907).

10 Quoted in Robert D. Richardson, *William James: In the Maelstrom of American Modernism* (Boston: Houghton Mifflin, 2006), 195.

11 James, *The Principles of Psychology*, 1:107. See also Louis Menand, *The Metaphysical Club: A Story of Ideas in America* (New York: Farrar, Straus and Giroux, 2001), 354.

12 Menand, *The Metaphysical Club*, x, 440.

13 The phrase is John Dewey's, as quoted in Menand, 361.

14 Menand, xi.

15 Merle J. Moskowitz, "Hugo Münsterberg: A Study in the History of Applied Psychology," *American Psychologist* 32, no. 10 (October 1977): 824–42; B. R. Hergenhahn, *An Introduction to the History of Psychology*, 5th ed. (Belmont, CA: Thomson/Wadsworth, 2005), 34. See also Ludy T. Benjamin Jr., "Münsterberg, Hugo (1863–1916)," in *American National Biography* (Oxford University Press, 2000), https://doi.org/10.1093/anb/9780198606697.article.1400431; Kurt Danziger, "Wundt's Theory of Behavior and Volition," in *Wilhelm Wundt and the Making of a Scientific Psychology*, ed. Robert W. Rieber, Path in Psychology (Boston: Springer, 1980), 89–115.

16 Hugo Münsterberg, *Psychology and Industrial Efficiency* (Boston: Houghton Mifflin, 1913), 27.

17 Lough, "Studies from the Harvard Psychological Laboratory (V)"; James E. Lough, "The Intensity of Sensation: An Experimental Essay in Physiological Psychology," 1897, HU 90.398, Harvard University Archives. For a portrait of Lough at this time, see *Portrait of James Edwin Lough*, ca. 1894, box 1, folder 3, C13 Edith Hall Plimpton Papers, 1885–1946, Schlesinger Library, Radcliffe Institute, Harvard University.

18 *Catalogue, Harvard University (1896–97)* (Cambridge, MA: Harvard University, 1896), 100; *Catalogue, Harvard University (1897–98)* (Cambridge, MA: Harvard University, 1897), 349, 385.

19 Ellen Condliffe Langemann, *An Elusive Science: The Troubling History of Education Research* (Chicago: University of Chicago Press, 2002); Lawrence Arthur Cremin, *The Transformation of the School: Progressivism in American Education, 1876–1957* (New York: Alfred A. Knopf, 1961).

20 William James, *Talks to Teachers on Psychology: And to Students on Some of Life's Ideals* (New York: Henry Holt, 1899), 7, 66, 95 (emphasis in the original).

21 John Dewey, "The Reflex Arc Concept in Psychology," *Psychological Review* 3, no. 4 (1896): 357–70.

22 John Dewey, *The School and Society* (Chicago: University of Chicago Press, 1915), 80.

23 "The Tribune," *Cambridge City (IN) Tribune*, August 13, 1896; "Institute Opens," *Richmond (IN) Item*, August 24, 1896. See also Benjamin J. Lough, *The Lough Family in America* (Salt Lake City: Family Heritage, 2002), partly published online, archived copy, May 27, 2022, Internet Archive Wayback Machine, https://web.archive.org/web/20220527045941/https://www.familysearch.org/photos/artifacts/13875205.

24 Folders 15 and 16, M2808.8 James Lough Papers, n.d., William L. Clements Library, University of Michigan Archives; "Lough-Bailey," *Richmond (IN) Item*, July 5, 1900.

25 Jackie Marshall Arnold and Mary-Kate Sableski, "Charles Hubbard Judd (1873–1946): A Leader in Silent and Oral Reading Instruction," in *Shaping the Reading Field: The Impact of Early Reading Pioneers, Scientific Research, and Progressive Ideas*, ed. Susan E. Israel and E. Jennifer Monaghan (Newark, DE: International Reading Association, 2007), 106; "Resigning Professors Accuse Mr. MacCracken," *New York Times*, April 15, 1901.

26 The training of ordinary teachers was seen as the work of the state normal schools.

See 1910 report of Thomas M. Balliet (Dean, School of Pedagogy) in *Report of the Chancellor, 1906/07–1912/13* (New York: New York University, n.d.), 81.

27 *New York University Catalogue, 1903/04* (New York: New York University, 1903), 197; Don C. Charles, "The Emergence of Educational Psychology," in *Historical Foundations of Educational Psychology*, ed. John A. Glover and Royce R. Ronning, Perspectives on Individual Differences (Boston: Springer US, 1987), 32.

28 Presley Downs Stout, as quoted in Raymond A. Katzell, "History of the Department of Psychology at New York University in the Twentieth Century," n.d., H Subject Files/Arts and Sciences, Psychology Department History, New York University Archives.

29 *New York University Catalogue, 1903/04*, 314.

30 James E. Lough, "The New York Academy of Sciences: Section of Anthropology and Psychology," *Journal of Philosophy, Psychology and Scientific Methods* 1, no. 12 (1904): 325–28.

31 *New York University Catalogue, 1903/04*, 325.

32 Dewey, *The School and Society*, 17.

33 James Edwin Lough, n.d., Harvard College Student Folders, ca. 1890–1995, Harvard University Archives.

34 Theodore Francis Jones, *New York University, 1832–1932* (New York: New York University Press, 1933), 182; Thomas Frusciano and Marilyn H. Pettit, *New York University and the City* (New Brunswick, NJ: Rutgers University Press, 1997), 127.

35 Lough, UA III 15.88.10 Harvard College Student Folders, ca. 1890–1995.

36 Address given by Dean Paul A. McGhee, H Subject Files/Continuing Education, Adult Education: Its Beginnings, 1957, New York University Archives; "Annual Report of the Work and Needs of New York University, 1909–1910," in *Report of the Chancellor, 1906/07–1912/13*, 16–17.

37 Copy of a letter from William Lough Jr. to the children of his brother James at the time of his death, June 4, 1952, Lough Family Papers.

38 *Harvard College: Record of the Class of 1894 for the Twenty-Fifth Anniversary* (Cambridge, MA: Crimson Printing, 1914), 145–46. With titles such as "Juries Never Convict Pretty Women" and "Germany's Warped View of Us," Lough's pieces veered toward the popular and even the sensationalist, lacking the assurance and intellectual gravity of commentators such as John Dewey and Hugo Münsterberg.

39 James E. Lough to Chancellor Elmer Ellsworth Brown, December 24, 1913, box 39, folder 6, RG 3.0.4 Office of the President.

40 Address given by Dean Paul A. McGhee, May 4, 1957, H/NYU Continuing Education, Adult Education: Its Beginnings, New York University Archives.

41 Jones, *New York University, 1832–1932*, 198.

42 *Annual Reports of New York University, 1913–1914* (New York: New York University, 1914), 15.

43 *Annual Reports of New York University, 1913–1914*, 16. "The several lines planned by the Director of that Division" are referred to in Report of Dean of Commerce, *Annual Reports of New York University, 1913–1914*, 130.

44 Dewey, *The School and Society*, 69.

45 Erastus W. Bulkley to William H. Lough, December 10, 1913, box 22, folder 15, Office of the President.

46 *Annual Reports of New York University, 1913–1914*, 130.

47   H. W. Stokes, "Future Bankers in University of Wall Street," *New York Tribune*,
     December 6, 1914; Chancellor Elmer Ellsworth Brown to Mr. James H. Post,
     March 9, 1915, box 22, folder 15, Office of the President.

48   James E. Lough to Chancellor Elmer Ellsworth Brown, April 23, 1915, box 39,
     folder 6, Office of the President; NYU Board of Trustees cards, H/NYU Continu-
     ing Education, Adult Education: Its Beginnings, New York University Archives.

49   James E. Lough to James J. Kerr, May 19, 1920, in James Edwin Lough, UA III
     15.88.10 Harvard College Student Folders, ca. 1890–1995, Harvard University
     Archives; Report of the Committee on Summer School Credits, 1915, box 7, RG
     18.0.2 Records of the Office of the Dean, University College of Arts and Science
     (Archibald L. Bouton), New York University Archives; see also correspondence in
     box 39, folder 6, Office of the President.

50   Stokes, "Future Bankers in University of Wall Street." The Extension [Extramu-
     ral] Division was described as the "proving ground for [the] Wall Street division
     of School of Commerce" in Notes on History, Introduction, H/NYU Continuing
     Education, Adult Education: Its Beginnings, 1A, New York University Archives.

51   Charles E. Benson et al., *Psychology for Teachers* (Boston: Ginn, 1926), 177.

52   "Chief of Commerce Bureau Resigns Post," *Evening Star* (Washington, DC), Sep-
     tember 16, 1914. A picture of Dr. E. E. Pratt with a party at the model houses of the
     Krupp factories, 1912, can be found in "Commerce Bulletin," January 10, 1913, box
     30, folder 9, Office of the President; "Sociologists Homeward Bound," *Sun* (New
     York City), August 18, 1912.

53   Edward E. Pratt to Chancellor Elmer Ellsworth Brown, June 26, 1913, Office of the
     President. See also "To Study Social Conditions Abroad," *Monroe (LA) News-
     Star*, June 27, 1913; "Commerce Bulletin," January 10, 1913, box 30, folder 9, Office
     of the President.

54   William Hoffa, *A History of US Study Abroad: Beginnings to 1965* (Carlisle, PA:
     Forum on Education Abroad, 2007), 46.

55   "To Study Social Conditions Abroad," *Monroe (LA) News-Star*, June 27, 1913;
     "Commerce Bulletin," January 10, 1913, box 30, folder 9, Office of the President.

56   "Report of the Chancellor," in *Annual Reports of New York University, 1913–
     1914*, 28.

57   *Garden Cities in Europe*, pamphlet published by the Institute of Educational
     Travel, 1914, box 30, folder 9; and Charles W. Gerstenberg to Chancellor Elmer
     Ellsworth Brown, October 10, 1914, box 30, folder 9, Office of the President.

58   Minutes of the Executive, February 16 and April 20, 1914, box 5, RG 2.1.1 Meetings
     of the Council.

59   Benjamin P. DeWitt to Royal Ransom Miller, March 4, 1915; and Miller to DeWitt,
     March 8, 1915, box 30, folder 9, Office of the President. A class action by the
     students was considered but in the end not pursued. See Minutes of the Executive,
     September 18 and October 20, 1914, box 5, Meetings of the Council.

60   Royal Ransom Miller to Benjamin P. DeWitt, March 8, 1915, box 30, folder 9, Of-
     fice of the President.

61   "Foreign Trade School Starts," *Akron Beacon Journal*, April 15, 1916.

62   See the section "Trouble for Christmas" in chapter 2.

63   Roger L. Geiger, *The History of American Higher Education: Learning and Culture
     from the Founding to World War II* (Princeton, NJ: Princeton University Press,
     2015), 425–26.

64 James E. Lough to Chancellor Elmer Ellsworth Brown, February 22, 1917, box 39, folder 6, Office of the President.

65 In 1921, the Extramural Division began to offer courses in Americanization, the cost of which was borne by the State Department of Education, and in 1922 it also began offering courses in citizenship, in cooperation with the Department of Education. See Board of Trustee cards, H/NYU Continuing Education, Adult Education: Its Beginnings, New York University Archives.

66 Paula S. Fass, *The Damned and the Beautiful: American Youth in the 1920's* (Oxford: Oxford University Press, 1977), 331–43; Warren F. Kuehl and Lynne Dunn, *Keeping the Covenant: American Internationalists and the League of Nations, 1920–1939* (Kent, OH: Kent State University Press, 1997), 65–7.

67 Kuehl and Dunn, *Keeping the Covenant*; Emily S. Rosenberg, *Financial Missionaries to the World: The Politics and Culture of Dollar Diplomacy, 1900–1930* (Durham, NC: Duke University Press, 2004); Erez Manela, *The Wilsonian Moment: Self-Determination and the International Origins of Anticolonial Nationalism* (Oxford: Oxford University Press, 2009); Daniel Gorman, *The Emergence of International Society in the 1920s* (Cambridge: Cambridge University Press, 2012).

68 Arthur Warner, "National Rivalry in Shipping," *Current History* 39, no. 1 (1933): 51; Graham P. Gladden, "Marketing Ocean Travel: Cunard and the White Star Line, 1910–1940," *Journal of Transport History* 35, no. 1 (2014): 71.

69 The report of the transatlantic passenger movement judged the number of third-class passengers arriving at all US and Canadian ports in 1925 to be 186,067. See Sydney E. Morse and John Haskell Kemble, *Report of the Trans-Atlantic Passenger Movement* (New York: [Publisher not identified], 1923). The US Bureau of the Census put the total number of immigrants for all classes in 1925 at 294,315—down from 706,896 in 1924. United States Bureau of the Census, *Historical Statistics of the United States, Colonial Times to 1957; a Statistical Abstract Supplement* (Washington, DC: US Dept. of Commerce, Bureau of the Census, 1960), 56.

70 Tamson Pietsch, "Commercial Travel and College Culture: The 1920s Transatlantic Student Market and the Foundations of Mass Tourism," *Diplomatic History* 43, no. 1 (January 2019): 89.

71 Pietsch, 89.

72 Pietsch, 97; Harvey Levenstein, *Seductive Journey: American Tourists in France from Jefferson to the Jazz Age* (Chicago: University of Chicago Press, 2000), 248.

73 This was in addition to the 195,394 traveling east in ordinary third class (the old steerage). Of course, most of these eastbound passengers also made the return trip home, compared with the one-way westbound steerage ticket. Quoted in Pietsch, "Commercial Travel and College Culture," 88. See Morse and Kemble, *Report of the Trans-Atlantic Passenger Movement*; Eunice Fuller Barnard, "The Swelling Tide of Foreign Travel," *New York Times Magazine*, May 6, 1928. Levenstein suggested that by 1927, 40 percent of those sailing to Europe had gone "Tourist Third"; Levenstein, *Seductive Journey*, 236.

74 *American University Tours* Extension Courses pamphlet, summer 1923, H Subject Files/Study Abroad, General, New York University Archives.

75 Chancellor Elmer Ellsworth Brown to the Secretary of State, Charles Evans Hughes, April 26, 1923, box 313, Name Index 1910–29, RG 59 (Department of State), NARA.

76 "An Idea Takes Root," in *The Student Magellan* (New York: Voelcker Bros., 1927), 5.

77 "European Travel with Credits at New York University," *School and Society* 19, no. 478 (1924): 215; James Edwin Lough, UA III 15.88.10 Harvard College Student Folders, ca. 1890–1995, Harvard University Archives. See also Ship Manifest, *Berengaria*, August 19, 1924, image 0933, "New York Passenger Arrival Lists (Ellis Island), 1892–1924," database with images, Passenger Search, The Statue of Liberty—Ellis Island Foundation Inc., accessed June 1, 2022, https://heritage.statueofliberty.org/.

78 Levenstein, *Seductive Journey*, 242, 248–50.

79 Joyce E. Chaplin, *Round about the Earth: Circumnavigation from Magellan to Orbit* (New York: Simon and Schuster, 2012), 258; see also 281–82.

80 For a brief overview of the tourist/traveler distinction in tourism scholarship and alternative ways of understanding travel, see Levenstein, *Seductive Journey*, ix–xiii.

81 Pietsch, "Commercial Travel and College Culture"; Levenstein, *Seductive Journey*, 236; See NYU Extramural Division pamphlets: *University Tours Europe 1925* and *Advance Announcement 1926 New York Travel Courses*, H Subject Files/Study Abroad, General, New York University Archives.

82 Edward E. Pratt to Chancellor Elmer Ellsworth Brown, January 21 and 29, 1925, box 22, folder 16, Office of the President. See also Edward E. Pratt and Neals Becker to James E. Lough, October 21, 1925, box 22, folder 16, Office of the President.

83 Benson et al., *Psychology for Teachers*, iii.

84 Benson et al., 83, 133.

85 Benson et al., 89.

86 Benson et al., 89.

87 Benson et al., 183, 83.

88 Benson et al., 83, 180–81.

89 Benson et al., 206.

90 Benson et al., 203.

91 Benson et al., 206.

92 "The organization of the University World Cruise came about as a direct result of the success of the summer study tours." See "An Idea Takes Root," in *The Student Magellan*, 5.

93 James E. Lough to Admiral Leigh C. Palmer, February 18, 1924, box 950, folders 130-112, RG 178 (Records of the US Maritime Commission), NARA.

94 Proposal for the Purchase of *SS President Arthur*, March 4, 1924, box 950, folder 112, RG 178 (Records of the US Maritime Commission), NARA.

95 "In working out the proposition," n.d., box 48, folder 3, Thwing Papers.

96 Chaplin, *Round about the Earth*, 263–64; E. Mowbray Tate, *Transpacific Steam: The Story of Steam Navigation from the Pacific Coast of North America to the Far East and the Antipodes, 1867–1941* (New York: Cornwall Books, 1986), 163–65. In the 1920s, sailing on a foreign-owned ship came with another advantage as well—it enabled Americans to escape the strictures of Prohibition.

97 "Floating University Would Cruise World," *Hot Springs (AR) New Era*, February 20, 1923.

98 "A Floating University Sinks," *Guardian* (Manchester), October 6, 1923; "Ocean-Cruising College Strikes Financial Rocks," *Oakland (CA) Tribune*, June 24, 1924.

99   Admiral Leigh C. Palmer [presumed] to J. W. Wadsworth Jr. (Senator), March 26, 1924, box 950, folder 130-112, RG 178 (Records of the US Maritime Commission), NARA.

100 "College Days on Rolling Waves," *Democrat and Chronicle* (Rochester, NY), May 11, 1924; J. Harry Pilbin to Admiral Leigh C. Palmer, March 10, 1924, enclosing James E. Lough to U.S. Shipping Board, "Proposal for the Purchase of the *SS President Arthur*," box 950, folder 130-112, RG 178 (Records of the US Maritime Commission), NARA.

101 "Extension Meet to Open Here on Thursday," *Capital Times* (Madison, WI), January 2, 1924; "Plans Under Way to Give Travel Courses in Extension Work," *Oshkosh (WI) Northwestern*, May 9, 1924.

102 "Floating University to Tour the World," *Nanaimo (BC) Daily News*, May 16, 1924; "Studying by the Mile," *Tampa Bay (FL) Times*, November 23, 1924.

103 "Floating University to Tour the World"; "College Days on Rolling Waves."

104 "Floating University To Tour The World"; "College Days on Rolling Waves."

105 "College Days on Rolling Waves."

106 "Zionists to Run Fleet," *New York Times*, October 10, 1924.

107 "College Days on Rolling Waves"; "Studying by the Mile."

108 Minutes, April 7, 1925, Meetings of the Executive Committee, roll #5 (January 22, 1925–December 15, 1927), Meetings of the Council; Harold O. Voorhis to Prof. Elmer W. Smith, July 16, 1926, box 25, folder 4, RG 4.0.1 Office of the Vice-President and Secretary; Minutes, April 10, 1925, Minutes of the Meetings of the Council, Meetings of the Council.

109 "Around the World S.S. 'University' (18,000 Tons)," 1925, box 48, folder 3, Thwing Papers. A somewhat mixed bag of advantages was advertised, including relieving admission pressures on colleges and fostering support for the US merchant marine, as well as developing an interest among students in foreign affairs.

110 "Around the World S.S. 'University' (18,000 Tons)," 1925, box 48, Thwing Papers.

111 "Students to Tour Europe," *Pittsburgh Daily Post*, May 3, 1925; "First 'Around the World University' to Start in Fall," *Times* (Munster, IN), May 12, 1925; "A College Cruise," n.d. [1925], box 48, folder 3, Thwing Papers. "Three men are especially concerned with a College cruise which is now being planned."

112 Andrew J. McIntosh to J. G. Hun, June 5, 1925, box 48, folder 3, Thwing Papers.

113 R. G. Dun and Co. Report on McIntosh, October 19, 1925, box 22, Office of the President.

114 "College Cruise around The World," bulletin no. 10, March 1926; "College Cruise," En Route Service Inc., n.d.; Approximate Mailing Times, October 20, 1926; and Andrew J. McIntosh to J. G. Hun, June 5, 1925, box 48, folder 3, Thwing Papers; R. G. Dun and Co. Report on McIntosh, October 19, 1925, box 22, Office of the President. R. G. Dun and Co. was a credit reporting agency.

115 Tate, *Transpacific Steam*, 175; "Floating University Would Cruise World"; Andrew J. McIntosh to J. G. Hun, June 5, 1925, box 48, folder 3, Thwing Papers.

116 Charles F. Thwing, *A History of Higher Education in America* (New York: D. Appleton, 1906); Charles F. Thwing, *A History of Education in the United States since the Civil War* (Boston: Houghton Mifflin, 1910).

117 "New Emphases in Education," 1921, box 48, folder 3, Thwing Papers.

118 Mark Frazier Lloyd and Nicholas G. Heavens, "Tuition and Mandated Fees, Room and Board, and Other Educational Costs at Penn," *Penn University Archives and*

Records Center (blog), 2003, archived copy, May 27, 2022, Internet Archive Wayback Machine, https://web.archive.org/web/20220527050224/https://archives .upenn.edu/exhibits/penn-history/tuition/tuition-1920-1929/.

119 *New York Evening Sun*, June 18, 1925; *Waterbury (CT) Democrat*, June 15, 1925, Newspaper Clippings, box 48, folder 3, Thwing Papers.

120 *Cleveland Press*, July 10, 1925, Newspaper Clippings, box 48, folder 2, Thwing Papers.

121 *New York Journal*, June 1, 1925, Newspaper Clippings, box 48, folder 2, Thwing Papers.

122 John R. Thelin, *A History of American Higher Education* (Baltimore: Johns Hopkins University Press, 2011), 211.

123 Thelin, 212; Fass, *The Damned and the Beautiful*.

124 Andrew J. McIntosh to J. G. Hun, June 5, 1925, box 48, folder 3, Thwing Papers.

125 Tate, *Transpacific Steam*, 175–76; Andrew J. McIntosh to J. G. Hun, June 5, 1925; Andrew J. McIntosh to Charles F. Thwing, September 18, 1925, box 48, folder 3, Thwing Papers.

126 Charles F. Thwing to Chancellor Elmer Ellsworth Brown, January 6, 1926, box 22, Office of the President; "European Travel with Credits at New York University," 215.

CHAPTER TWO

1 Minutes, January 7, 1926, roll #5, Meetings of the Council.

2 Minutes, Meeting of the Executive Committee, December 15, 1925, roll #5, Meetings of the Council.

3 Minutes, Meeting of the Executive Committee, December 15, 1925, roll #5, Meetings of the Council. Since 1904, Kingsley had served as council treasurer and Lyman as council secretary. Garvin, the newest member (appointed in 1921), had recently stepped down as judge of the US District Court for East New York.

4 Minutes, Meeting of the Executive Committee, January 6, 1926, roll #5, Meetings of the Council. For Pratt's previous involvement in educational travel with Lough and NYU, see chapter 1.

5 James Abbott to Chancellor Elmer Ellsworth Brown, December 26, 1925, box 22, folder 16, Office of the President.

6 Minutes, Meeting of the Executive Committee, January 6, 1926, roll #5, Meetings of the Council.

7 Edward Ewing Pratt and B. Becker (School of Foreign Travel) to James E. Lough (NYU), October 21, 1925, box 22, folder 16, Office of the President. The university was paid a flat sum of one hundred dollars "per four point course" as well as "the funds necessary to compensate the instructors."

8 Minutes, Meeting of the Executive Committee, January 6, 1926, roll #5, Meetings of the Council.

9 The committee consisted of Marshall S. Brown (dean of faculties), LeRoy E. Kimball (comptroller in charge of finances), Harold Voorhis (secretary), and Frank H. Summer (dean of the Law School). See Minutes, Meeting of the Executive Committee, January 6, 1926, roll #5, Meetings of the Council.

10 Chancellor Elmer Ellsworth Brown to James E. Lough, January 7, 1926, box 22, folder 16, Office of the President; Minutes, Meeting of the Executive, Febru-

ary 16, 1926, roll #5, Meetings of the Council. Voorhis and Brown's involvement is discussed in chapter 1.

11   Minutes, Meeting of the Council, January 7, 1926, roll #5, Meetings of the Council.

12   Memorandum of Action taken by the Council, January 7, 1926, box 22, folder 16, Office of the President; Minutes, Meeting of the Council, January 7, 1926, roll #5, Meetings of the Council.

13   John R. Thelin, *A History of American Higher Education* (Baltimore: Johns Hopkins University Press, 2011), 239.

14   Among Charles Hitchcock Sherrill's works: *Stained Glass Tours in France* (New York: J. Lane, 1908); *Stained Glass Tours in England* (London: John Lane the Bodley Head, 1910); *Stained Glass Tours in Italy* (London: John Lane, 1913); *French Memories of Eighteenth-Century America* (New York: Charles Scribner's Sons, 1915); *Modernizing the Monroe Doctrine* (New York: Houghton Mifflin, 1916); *Have We a Far Eastern Policy?* (New York: Charles Scribner's Sons, 1920); *Prime Ministers and Presidents* (New York: George H. Doran, 1922); *Stained Glass Tours in Spain and Flanders* (London: John Lane the Bodley Head, 1924); "The Purple or the Red: Note," *Social Science Quarterly* 5 (1924): 207; *Stained Glass Tours in Germany, Austria and the Rhinelands* (London: John Lane the Bodley Head, 1927).

15   Pamphlets *Extension Tours in Europe, 1926* and *Summer School Art Courses in Paris*, n.d., H Subject Files/Study Abroad, General, New York University Archives; NYU Secretary [Harold O. Voorhis] to Rufus D. Smith, January 22, 1926, box 22, folder 16, Office of the President.

16   Chancellor Elmer Ellsworth Brown to General Charles H. Sherrill, December 16, 1925, box 22, folder 16, Office of the President.

17   Rufus Smith to University Travel Association, March 10 and 25, 1926, box 25, folder 4, Office of the Vice-President and Secretary.

18   Minutes, Meeting of the Executive Committee, May 26, 1926, roll #5, Meetings of the Council.

19   Theodore Francis Jones, *New York University, 1832–1932* (New York: New York University Press, 1933), 192–209.

20   "The safest opportunity for meeting the needs of the city with least risk to the institution." See Jones, 196; Thomas Frusciano and Marilyn H. Pettit, *New York University and the City* (New Brunswick, NJ: Rutgers University Press, 1997), 151.

21   Jones, *New York University, 1832–1932*, 200.

22   Jones, 201.

23   Jones, 201.

24   Frusciano and Pettit, *New York University and the City*, 153–55.

25   Frusciano and Pettit, 157.

26   Frusciano and Pettit, 167. See also Registrar's Report 1921–22 in *New York University Reports of Officers, 1920–21 and 1921–22* (New York: New York University, 1922), 71.

27   Thomas D. Snyder, ed., *120 Years of American Education: A Statistical Portrait* (Washington, DC: National Center for Education Statistics, 1993), 67–68, 75.

28   Frusciano and Pettit, *New York University and the City*, 175; New York University, *Reports of Officers* (New York: New York University, 1925), 123; Roger L. Geiger, *The History of American Higher Education: Learning and Culture from the Founding*

to *World War II* (Princeton, NJ: Princeton University Press, 2015), 515–16; Thelin, *A History of American Higher Education*, 226.

29 Geiger, *The History of American Higher Education*, 442–43.

30 Roger L. Geiger, *The American College in the Nineteenth Century* (Nashville: Vanderbilt University Press, 2000), 130–37; Helen Lefkowitz Horowitz, *Campus Life: Undergraduate Cultures from the End of the Eighteenth Century to the Present* (Chicago: University of Chicago Press, 1988), 105–6.

31 From 50 percent in 1919 to 31 percent in 1921. See Frusciano and Pettit, *New York University and the City*, 161–63.

32 Quoted in Frusciano and Pettit, 163. See also Ralph Philip Boas, "Who Shall Go to College," *Atlantic Monthly* 130 (1922): 441–48; Geiger, *The American College in the Nineteenth Century*, 132–34.

33 Minutes, Meeting of the Executive Committee, May 26, 1926, roll #5, Meetings of the Council.

34 Some small bequests had been received, but these were not sums likely to make a dent in the university's debt. Minutes, Meeting of the Executive Committee, May 26, 1926, roll #5, Meetings of the Council.

35 Minutes, Meeting of the Executive Committee, May 26, 1926, roll #5, Meetings of the Council.

36 Minutes, Meeting of the Executive Committee, October 14, 1926, exhibit B, roll #5, Meetings of the Council. These two developments were part of the same process and received a good deal of criticism at the time, not least from Thorsten Veblen, whose 1910 book, *The Higher Learning in America*, lambasted universities for becoming businesses.

37 *New York University Catalogue, 1903/04* (New York: New York University, 1903), 204–38.

38 The school was founded on "the belief that through a study of commercial methods and of economic forces one may acquire . . . the technical knowledge and the habits of thought that make for success in business." *New York University Catalogue, 1921/22* (New York: New York University, 1921), 61, 260.

39 Jones, *New York University, 1832–1932*, 206.

40 Jones, 343.

41 Herman Harrell Horne, "The Educational Philosophy of Dean John W. Withers," *Journal of Educational Sociology* 12, no. 9 (1939): 524–33.

42 Withers's report published in Jones, *New York University, 1832–1932*, 346. See also Withers's first report about the reorganization in *New York University Reports of Officers, 1920–21 and 1921–22*, 215.

43 Withers, as quoted in Jones, *New York University, 1832–1932*, 346–47.

44 Establishing the institute as an independent body enabled the School of Education to get around an 1894 agreement with the State of New York that the university would be tax exempt if all instruction in law and pedagogy took place at Washington Square. See Jones, 350–52.

45 Jones, 352–53.

46 Jones, 352.

47 On the transformation of the survey method in this period led by Charles E. Merriam, see Barry D. Karl, *Charles E. Merriam and the Study of Politics* (Chicago: University of Chicago Press, 1974); Mark C. Smith, *Social Science in the Crucible: The American Debate over Objectivity and Purpose, 1918–1941* (Durham, NC: Duke

University Press, 1994), 84–103; Sarah E. Igo, *The Averaged American: Surveys, Citizens, and the Making of a Mass Public* (Cambridge, MA: Harvard University Press, 2008).

48   "Report of the Chancellor 1913–14," in *Annual Reports of New York University, 1913–1914* (New York: New York University, 1914), 15.

49   Thomas Bender, as quoted in Michael Rosenthal, *Nicholas Miraculous: The Amazing Career of the Redoubtable Dr. Nicholas Murray Butler* (New York: Columbia University Press, 2015), 138.

50   Rosenthal, 12.

51   For education, see Ellen Condliffe Langemann, *An Elusive Science: The Troubling History of Education Research* (Chicago: University of Chicago Press, 2002). See also Michael B. Paulsen, *Higher Education: Handbook of Theory and Research* (Dordrecht: Springer Netherlands, 2013).

52   Rosenthal, *Nicholas Miraculous*, 134.

53   Rosenthal, 20.

54   Katharina Rietzler, *International Experts, International Citizens: American Philanthropy, International Relations and the Problem of the Public, 1913–1954*, forthcoming.

55   Geiger, *The American College in the Nineteenth Century*, 141.

56   Geiger, 145.

57   Jessica M. Shedd, "The History of the Student Credit Hour," *New Directions for Higher Education* 2003, no. 122 (2003): 7–9; Clyde Barrow, *Universities and the Capitalist State: Corporate Liberalism and the Reconstruction of American Higher Education, 1894–1928* (Madison: University of Wisconsin Press, 1990).

58   Tom Arnold-Forster, "Democracy and Expertise in the Lippmann-Terman Controversy," *Modern Intellectual History* 16, no. 2 (2019): 3; Daniel T. Rodgers, *Atlantic Crossings: Social Politics in a Progressive Age* (Cambridge, MA: Harvard University Press, 1998), 25–8.

59   For more nuanced interpretations, see Arnold-Forster, "Democracy and Expertise in the Lippmann-Terman Controversy"; Andrew Jewett, *Science, Democracy, and the American University: From the Civil War to the Cold War* (Cambridge: Cambridge University Press, 2012), 141–47; Rosenthal, *Nicholas Miraculous*, 306; Walter Lippmann, *Public Opinion* (New York: Harcourt, Brace, 1922), part 8; Walter Lippmann, *The Phantom Public* (New York: Macmillan, 1925).

60   *New York University Reports of Officers, 1920–21 and 1921–22*, 65. For an example of Brown's interest in internationalism, see Elmer Ellsworth Brown, "Public Schools in the Movement for International Arbitration," *Journal of Education* 66, no. 1 (June 1907): 3–4.

61   Letter from Rufus Smith, March 25, 1926, box 25, folder 4, Office of the Vice-President and Secretary.

62   On the Institute for International Education, see Stephen M. Halpern, "The Institute of International Education: A History" (PhD diss., Columbia University, 1971); Teresa Brawner Bevis and Christopher J. Lucas, *International Students in American Colleges and Universities: A History* (New York: Palgrave Macmillan, 2007), 95–8.

63   Stephan Duggan to Chancellor Elmer Ellsworth Brown, May 14, 1924, box 30, folder 10, Office of the President.

64   On gender, higher education, and travel, see Whitney Walton, *Internationalism,*

National Identities, and Study Abroad: France and the United States, 1890–1970
(Stanford, CA: Stanford University Press, 2009); Joyce Goodman et al., "Travelling Careers: Overseas Migration Patterns in the Professional Lives of Women Attending Girton and Newnham before 1939," *History of Education* 40, no. 2 (March
2011): 179–96; Christine von Oertzen, *Science, Gender, and Internationalism:
Women's Academic Networks, 1917–1955* (New York: Palgrave Macmillan, 2012);
Tanya Fitzgerald and Elizabeth M. Smyth, *Women Educators, Leaders and Activists: Educational Lives and Networks, 1900–1960* (New York: Palgrave Macmillan,
2014); Ludovic Tournés and Giles Scott-Smith, eds., *Global Exchanges: Scholarships and Transnational Circulations in the Modern World* (Oxford: Berghahn,
2011); Anna Cabanel, "'How Excellent . . . for a Woman'? The Fellowship Program
of the International Federation of University Women in the Interwar Period,"
Persona Studies 4, no. 1 (2018): 88–102.

65 Von Oertzen, *Science, Gender, and Internationalism*, 17–19; Emily J. Levine, *Allies
and Rivals: German-American Exchange and the Rise of the Research University*
(Chicago, Illinois: University of Chicago Press, 2020), 82–88.

66 Geiger, *The History of American Higher Education*, 408; Whitney Walton, "Ameri-
can Girls and French Jeunes Filles: Negotiating National Identities in Interwar
France," *Gender and History* 17, no. 2 (2005): 329–30; Dorothy M. Brown, *Setting a
Course: American Women in the 1920s* (Boston: Twayne, 1987).

67 Alys Eve Weinbaum et al., eds., *The Modern Girl around the World: Consump-
tion, Modernity, and Globalization* (Durham, NC: Duke University Press, 2008);
Emily S. Rosenberg, "Consuming Women: Images of Americanization in the
'American Century,'" *Diplomatic History* 23, no. 3 (1999): 479–97; Paula S. Fass,
The Damned and the Beautiful: American Youth in the 1920's (Oxford: Oxford Uni-
versity Press, 1977), 22–25, 51; Walton, "American Girls and French Jeunes Filles."

68 Stephan Duggan to Chancellor Brown, May 14, 1924, box 30, folder 10, Office of
the President.

69 Akira Iriye, *Cultural Internationalism and World Order* (Baltimore: Johns Hopkins
University Press, 1997).

70 Liping Bu, *Making the World Like Us: Education, Cultural Expansion, and the
American Century* (Westport, CT: Praeger, 2003), 51–63, 86–99; von Oertzen,
Science, Gender, and Internationalism; Jehnie I. Reis, "Cultural Internationalism
at the Cité Universitaire: International Education between the First and Second
World Wars," *History of Education* 39, no. 2 (2010): 155–73.

71 Georgina Brewis, *A Social History of Student Volunteering: Britain and Beyond,
1880–1980* (London: Palgrave Macmillan, 2014). For discussion of the post–World
War II period, see Richard Ivan Jobs, *Backpack Ambassadors: How Youth Travel
Integrated Europe* (Chicago: University of Chicago Press, 2017).

72 Quoted in Bu, *Making the World Like Us*, 56–58. For an example of newsletters, see
News Bulletin April 1926, box 30, folder 11, Office of the President.

73 Bu, *Making the World Like Us*, 55, 58.

74 *International Students' Tours under the Auspices of the Institute of International
Education, 1922*, n.d., box 1, Educ 7470.01 Travel as a Means of Education (Misc.
Pamphlets), Monroe C. Gutman Library Special Collections, Harvard Graduate
School of Education.

75 *International Students' Tours under the Auspices of the Institute of International
Education, 1922*.

76 See Walton, *Internationalism, National Identities, and Study Abroad*, 62.

77 Walter Hullihen, "Undergraduate Foreign Study for Credit toward the American Baccalaureate Degree," *Bulletin of the American Association of University Professors (1915–1955)* 10, no. 4 (1924): 16.

78 Joan Elias Gore, "Discourse and Traditional Belief: An Analysis of American Undergraduate Study Abroad" (PhD diss., University of London, 2000), 201; Whitney Walton, "Internationalism and the Junior Year Abroad: American Students in France in the 1920s and 1930s," *Diplomatic History* 29, no. 2 (April 2005): 260.

79 See Hullihen, "Undergraduate Foreign Study for Credit toward the American Baccalaureate Degree"; "General Notes," *Bulletin of the American Association of University Professors (1915–1955)* 12, no. 5 (1926): 290–91.

80 Gore, "Discourse and Traditional Belief," 170.

81 According to Harley, the success of the Junior Year Abroad programs depended on the rigorous selection of students, the willingness of receiving institutions to cooperate, and the right kind of leader. See Harley, *International Understanding*, 41–42.

82 Whitney Walton estimates that approximately one thousand women and two hundred men studied in France on either the Smith College or the University of Delaware program between 1923 and 1939. Walton, "American Girls and French Jeunes Filles," 325.

83 Mary L. Waite, "Notes and News on International Education," *Journal of International Relations* 12, no. 4 (1922): 559. New courses were established after the war at the University of Rome, University of Geneva, and University of Paris. According to Stephen Duggan, in 1923 more than one thousand American teachers and students attended summer courses at foreign universities. "General Announcements (Summer School)," *Bulletin of the American Association of University Professors (1915–1955)* 9, no. 4 (1923): 9–10; Donald J. Cowling et al., "Notes and Reports from Societies and Foundations," *Bulletin of the American Association of University Professors (1915–1955)* 13, no. 5 (1927): 322–23.

84 Bu, *Making the World Like Us*, 52; Walton, "Internationalism and the Junior Year Abroad," 261.

85 Whitney Walton, "National Interests and Cultural Exchange in French and American Educational Travel, 1914–1970," *Journal of Transatlantic Studies* 13, no. 4 (2015): 344–57; David A. Robertson, "International Educational Relations of the United States," *Educational Record* 6 (April 1925): 91–5; Walton, "Internationalism and the Junior Year Abroad," 261.

86 See Tamson Pietsch, "Commercial Travel and College Culture: The 1920s Transatlantic Student Market and the Foundations of Mass Tourism," *Diplomatic History* 43, no. 1 (2019): 83–106.

87 The National Education Council distinguished its own offerings by promising to return any profit to a cooperating university. R. A. Barker to Harvard Secretary F. W. Hunnewell, November 22, 1926, box 239, folder 605, UA I 5.160 President Lowell's Papers, Harvard University Archives.

88 NYU to Edward Ewing Pratt, January 14, 1926, box 22, folder 16, Office of the President; see also "Report of Review Committee to Council Committee on Extramural Department, 13 Jan 1926"; and "Memorandum on Summer Travel Courses," n.d., box 22, folder 16, Office of the President.

89 "Report of Review Committee to Council Committee on Extramural Department, 13 Jan 1926."

90 Secretary [Harold O. Voorhis] to Rufus D. Smith, February 3, 1926, box 22, folder 16, Office of the President; "University Travel Association," box 317/032 University Travel Association, Decimal File 1910–29, RG 59 (Department of State), NARA.

91 Harold O. Voorhis to Alexander Lyman, enclosing Smith's Report on the Extra-mural Division, March 26, 1926, box 25, folder 4, Office of the Vice-President and Secretary.

92 The Extramural Division continued to offer courses that were delivered "outside of the University's buildings to meet community needs" as well as noncredit "cultural" courses. *New York University Reports of Officers, 1920–21 and 1921–22*, 113, 268; Jones, *New York University, 1832–1932*, 347.

93 "Exhibit A: Marshall Brown's Report on Extramural Changes," Minutes, Meeting of the Council, May 26, 1926, roll #5, Meetings of the Council.

94 Cross-reference cards, October 14, 1926, H Subject Files/Continuing Education, Adult Education: Its Beginnings, New York University Archives.

95 "Exhibit A.2: Smith's Report on Extramural Changes," Minutes, Meeting of the Council, May 26, 1926, roll #5, Meetings of the Council.

96 Jones, *New York University, 1832–1932*, 388.

97 *College Cruise around the World*, pamphlet ca. 1926, H Subject Files/Cruises, New York University Archives.

98 Harold O. Voorhis to Prof. Elmer W. Smith, July 16, 1926, box 25, folder 4, Office of the Vice-President and Secretary.

99 Minutes, Meeting of the Council, February 16, 1926, roll #5, Meetings of the Council.

100 Harold O. Voorhis to Prof. Elmer W. Smith (Colgate University), July 16, 1926, box 25, folder 4, Office of the Vice-President and Secretary; Minutes, Meeting of the Executive, February 16, 1926, roll #5, Meetings of the Council; Voorhis to James E. Lough, February 26, 1926, box 22, folder 16, Office of the President.

101 Exhibit A, Minutes, Meeting of the Executive, February 16, 1926, roll #5, Meetings of the Council; Andrew J. McIntosh to Charles F. Thwing, February 17, 1926, box 48, folder 3, Thwing Papers.

102 Andrew J. McIntosh to Charles F. Thwing, February 17, 1926, box 48, folder 3, Thwing Papers.

103 Harold O. Voorhis to Alexander Lyman, March 26, 1926, enclosing Smith's Report on the Extramural Division, box 25, folder 4, Office of the Vice-President and Secretary.

104 Andrew J. McIntosh to Charles F. Thwing, February 17, 1926, box 48, folder 3, Thwing Papers.

105 Report from Rufus Smith to Dean Marshall S. Brown, March 25, 1926; and Rufus Smith to University Travel Association, March 10, 1926, box 25, folder 4, Office of the Vice-President and Secretary.

106 Report from Rufus Smith to Dean Marshall S. Brown, March 25, 1926, box 25, folder 4, Office of the Vice-President and Secretary.

107 University Travel Association to Rufus D. Smith, March 12, 1926, box 25, folder 4, Office of the Vice-President and Secretary.

108 Andrew J. McIntosh to Charles F. Thwing, February 17, 1926, box 48, folder 3,

Thwing Papers; University Travel Association to Rufus D. Smith, March 10, 1926, box 25, folder 4, Office of the Vice-President and Secretary.

109 Minutes, Meeting of the Executive, April 13, 1926, roll #5, Meetings of the Council.

110 Bulletin no. 10, March 1926, box 48, folder 3, Thwing Papers.

111 Agreement between Holland America Line (HAL) and the University Travel Association (UTA), signed March 16, 1926, Directie, 01/Dossiers/Cruises/0831, 318 Archieven van de Holland-Amerika Lijn (HAL); Membership Ticket no. 151, College Cruise around the World, box 48, folder 3, Thwing Papers.

112 "Ryndam Incoming," *Gazette* (Montreal, QC), September 6, 1926.

113 College Cruise around the World, [1926], "H/Cruises"; The College Cruise around the World, 1926–27, box 1, folder 4, Raises Collection.

114 "James Price Named to Go on Student Cruise," *Morning Chronicle* (Manhattan, KS), May 9, 1926.

115 Charles F. Thwing to Andrew J. McIntosh, July 1, 1926, box 48, folder 3, Thwing Papers.

116 College Cruise around the World, [1926], "H/Cruises"; The College Cruise around the World, 1926–27, box 1, folder 4, Raises Collection.

117 Andrew J. McIntosh to Charles F. Thwing, June 10, 1926 (emphasis in the original), box 48, folder 3, Thwing Papers.

118 "8 Months' College Cruise," *Gazette* (Montreal, QC), August 23, 1926.

119 Minutes, Meeting of the Executive, April 13, 1926, roll #5, Meetings of the Council. In his July letter to Colgate University's Elmer Smith, Voorhis wrote that the university's decision to discontinue its sponsorship "was undoubtedly hastened by a lack of confidence in Professor Lough." Harold O. Voorhis to Prof. Elmer W. Smith, July 16, 1926, box 25, folder 4, Office of the Vice-President and Secretary.

120 Minutes, Meeting of the Council, April 26, 1926, roll #5, Meetings of the Council.

CHAPTER THREE

Portions of this chapter are reprinted and adapted by permission from Springer Nature: Tamson Pietsch, "Learning at Sea: Education aboard the 1926–27 Floating University," in *Shipboard Literary Cultures: Reading, Writing, and Performing at Sea*, ed. Laurence Publicover and Susann Liebich ([Cham, Switzerland]: Palgrave Macmillan, 2022), 239–61.

1 *Binnacle* (University Travel Association), September 17, 1926, box 48, folder 4, Thwing Papers.

2 *Binnacle*, September 21, 1926; Charles Ladd, *Around the World at Seventeen* (Rahway, NJ: Quinn and Boden, 1928), 4.

3 *Binnacle*, September 21, 1926; James S. McKenzie, *A Broad Education Abroad: Readin', Writin', and Roamin'* (New York: Vantage Press, 1978), 3.

4 [Pearl Heckel], "A New Educational Project," folder 6, C3481 Heckel Papers.

5 Ladd, *Around the World at Seventeen*, 3–7.

6 *Binnacle* (University Travel Association), January 9, 1927, box 48, folder 4, Thwing Papers; McKenzie, *A Broad Education Abroad*, 3–4, 18–19; Plan of the Transatlantic S.S. *Ryndam*, box 40, folder 1, 1012 Holling Papers.

7 Walter Conger Harris, *Photographs of the First University World Cruise* (New York: University Travel Association, 1927), nos. 627 and 628; "The Ryndam is a well

built little ship," DeWitt Reddick's journal (Early Draft I), folder 1, 3G454 Reddick Papers.

8   Ladd, *Around the World at Seventeen*, 25–26.

9   Ladd, 3–7, 25–26.

10   Charles E. Gauss, Log Book 1926–27, p. 13, A3637 Gauss Collection.

11   Plan of the Transatlantic S.S. *Ryndam*, box 40, folder 1, Holling Papers.

12   Plan of the Transatlantic S.S. *Ryndam*, box 40, folder 1, Holling Papers.

13   Tom Johnson to his mother, September 19, 1926, MSA 441 Johnson Papers.

14   Lillian McCracken, September 18, 1926, Diary of Lillian McCracken.

15   [Pearl Heckel], "A New Educational Project," folder 6, Heckel Papers.

16   *Binnacle* (University Travel Association), September 21, 1926, box 48, folder 4, Thwing Papers.

17   [Pearl Heckel], "A New Educational Project."

18   This article was widely distributed by the United Press news agency. See "Floating College to Carry Students around the World," *Daily Reporter* (Greenfield, IN), June 19, 1925.

19   *Binnacle*, September 23, 1926.

20   En Route Service Inc., College Cruise [ca. 1926], box 48, folder 3, Thwing Papers.

21   *The Panama Canal Record—August 11, 1926 to August 3, 1927*, vol. 20 (Mount Hope, Canal Zone: Panama Canal Press, 1927), 109. James McKenzie records a total of 559 students, "tourists," and faculty, whereas Ridgley put the total number at 538. See McKenzie, *A Broad Education Abroad*, 3; Douglas C. Ridgley, "The First College Cruise around the World: An Educational Experiment," *Journal of Geography* 27, no. 2 (1928): 70.

22   McKenzie, *A Broad Education Abroad*, 3; Douglas C. Ridgley, "The First College Cruise around the World: An Educational Experiment," *Journal of Geography* 27, no. 2 (February 1928): 70–76.

23   These statistics are based on affiliations given in the *Binnacle* (University Travel Association), September 17, 1926, box 48, folder 4, Thwing Papers; McKenzie, *A Broad Education Abroad*. They do not include the preparatory students and are likely to entail a margin of error due to the inability to completely determine who counted as a "tourist." Ridgley later put the number of all enrolled students (including preparatory, college, and "older") at 486. See Ridgley, "The First College Cruise around the World."

24   Ladd, *Around the World at Seventeen*, 3. He was referring to guests at the reception at the Waldorf Astoria. In 1927, tuition, rent and board, and textbooks for one year at the University of Pennsylvania cost $1,215. See Mark Frazier Lloyd and Nicholas G. Heavens, "Tuition and Mandated Fees, Room and Board, and Other Educational Costs at Penn," *Penn University Archives and Records Center* (blog), 2003, archived copy, May 27, 2022, Internet Archive Wayback Machine, https://web.archive.org/web/20220527050224/https://archives.upenn.edu/exhibits/penn-history/tuition/tuition-1920-1929/.

25   McKenzie, *A Broad Education Abroad*, 3.

26   *Binnacle*, September 17, 1926, box 48, folder 4, Thwing Papers. Among the passengers, 306 young men, 57 "girls," and 133 older people were "supplementing their travels with educational offerings of the boat."

27   Ladd, *Around the World at Seventeen*, 26–27.

28 Tom Johnson to his mother, December 2, 1926 (emphasis in the original), Johnson Papers.

29 University Travel Association to W. H. Leonard, June 1, 1927, MS 312 W. E. B. DuBois Papers, Special Collections and University Archives, University of Massachusetts Amherst Libraries.

30 W. H. Leonard to the University Travel Association, June 4, 1927.

31 University Travel Association to W. H. Leonard, June 10, 1927.

32 W. E. B. DuBois to the editor of the *New York Times*, June 24, 1927, MS 312 W. E. B. DuBois Papers, Special Collections and University Archives, University of Massachusetts Amherst Libraries.

33 In 1909, the NAACP demanded "for the Negros as for all others a free and complete education." See Elliott M. Rudwick, "The National Negro Committee Conference of 1909," *Phylon Quarterly* 18, no. 4 (1957): 417.

34 Raymond Wolters, *The New Negro on Campus: Black College Rebellions of the 1920s* (Princeton, NJ: Princeton University Press, 1975); Robert Bruce Slater, "The Blacks Who First Entered the World of White Higher Education," *Journal of Blacks in Higher Education*, no. 4 (1994): 47–56; Roger L. Geiger, *The History of American Higher Education: Learning and Culture from the Founding to World War II* (Princeton, NJ: Princeton University Press, 2015), 467–78.

35 *Binnacle* (University Travel Association), April 10, 1927, box 48, folder 4, Thwing Papers.

36 Agreement between Holland America Line (HAL) and the University Travel Association (UTA), signed March 16, 1926, Directie, 01/Dossiers/Cruises/0831, 318 Archieven van de Holland-Amerika Lijn (HAL).

37 Tom Johnson to his mother, September 20, 1926, Johnson Papers; DeWitt Reddick's journal (Early Draft I), September 21, 1926, folder 1, Reddick Papers. G. Balachandran, *Globalizing Labour? Indian Seafarers and World Shipping, c. 1870–1945* (New Delhi: Oxford University Press, 2012).

38 Davy Baas, "De University World Cruise van 1926–1927: Studentencruise als Grand Tour" (Bachelor's thesis, Leiden University, 2018), 21n8, Leiden University Student Repository. Used with kind permission of the author.

39 Baas, nn79–80.

40 *Binnacle* (University Travel Association), November 5, 1926, box 48, folder 4, Thwing Papers.

41 Agreement between Holland America Line (HAL) and the University Travel Association (UTA), signed March 16, 1926, Directie, 01/Dossiers/Cruises/0831, 318 Archieven van de Holland-Amerika Lijn (HAL).

42 Baas, "De University World Cruise van 1926–1927," 21–22.

43 Ladd, *Around the World at Seventeen*, 33–34.

44 Tamson Pietsch, "Bodies at Sea: Travelling to Australia in the Age of Sail," *Journal of Global History* 11, no. 2 (2016): 209–28.

45 Daniel Allen Butler, *The Age of Cunard: A Transatlantic History 1839–2003* (Annapolis: Lighthouse Press, 2004), 240; *Binnacle*, October 4, 1926, and January 12, 1927, box 48, folder 4, Thwing Papers.

46 Correspondence between Phelps Bros. and Holland America Line New York Agent, October 6–20, 1926, DirectieV, 02/v131.1 (October 1926–April 1927), 318 Archieven van de Holland-Amerika Lijn (HAL).

47 *Binnacle*, January 12, 1927; Letter to Mr. W. Van Doorn, Manager, Holland America Line, October 14, 1926, DirectieV, 02/V131.1 (October 1926–April 1927), 318 Archieven van de Holland-Amerika Lijn (HAL).

48 [Pearl Heckel], "A New Educational Project," folder 6, Heckel Papers.

49 Phelps Bros. to Holland America Line, October 14, 1926, DirectieV, 02/V131.1 (October 1926–April 1927), 318 Archieven van de Holland-Amerika Lijn (HAL).

50 Holland America Line to New York Agent, November 2, 1926, DirectieV, 02/V131.1 (October 1926–April 1927), 318 Archieven van de Holland-Amerika Lijn (HAL). See Jonathan Hyslop, "Steamship Empire: Asian, African and British Sailors in the Merchant Marine c.1880–1945," *Journal of Asian and African Studies* 44, no. 1 (2009): 49–67.

51 *Binnacle* (University Travel Association), October 14, 1926, box 48, folder 4, Thwing Papers. See chapter 7 for the account of Leonard B. Aliwanag, who was one of these laundrymen.

52 *Binnacle*, October 15, 1926.

53 *Binnacle*, January 12, 1927.

54 *Binnacle*, October 27, 1926.

55 See Kris Alexanderson, *Subversive Seas: Anticolonial Networks across the Twentieth-Century Dutch Empire* (Cambridge: Cambridge University Press, 2019); Leon Fink, *Sweatshops at Sea: Merchant Seamen in the World's First Globalized Industry, from 1812 to the Present* (Durham: University of North Carolina Press, 2011); Balachandran, *Globalizing Labour?*

56 Madison Grant, *The Passing of the Great Race; or, The Racial Basis of European History* (New York: Charles Scribner's Sons, 1920); Paul Alexander Kramer, "Is the World Our Campus? International Students and U.S. Global Power in the Long Twentieth Century," *Diplomatic History* 33, no. 5 (2009): 775–806; Tamson Pietsch, "Commercial Travel and College Culture: The 1920s Transatlantic Student Market and the Foundations of Mass Tourism," *Diplomatic History* 43, no. 1 (2019): 83–106; Robert D. Dean, *Imperial Brotherhood: Gender and the Making of Cold War Foreign Policy* (Amherst: University of Massachusetts Press, 2001).

57 Ladd, *Around the World at Seventeen*, 7–8; Tom Johnson to his mother, September 19, 1926, Johnson Papers.

58 *Binnacle* (University Travel Association), September 21, 1926, box 48, folder 4, Thwing Papers.

59 *Binnacle*, September 23, 1926.

60 *Binnacle*, September 21, 1926.

61 *Binnacle*, September 17, 1926, and April 26, 1927.

62 *Binnacle*, September 21, 1926.

63 McKenzie, *A Broad Education Abroad*, 2, 19.

64 Andrew J. McIntosh to Henry J. Allen, March 8, 1927, box C7, MSS 50781 Allen Papers.

65 [Pearl Heckel], "A New Educational Project," folder 6, Heckel Papers.

66 "Astronomy, Navigation and Human Geography," DeWitt Reddick's journal (Early Draft), folder 2, Reddick Papers.

67 McKenzie, *A Broad Education Abroad*, 4.

68 Tom Johnson to his mother, September 19, 1926, Johnson Papers.

69 *Binnacle* (University Travel Association), October 24, 1926, box 48, folder 4, Thwing Papers.

70 *Binnacle*, December 23, 1926. On the disappearance of books from ships' libraries, see Susann Liebich, "A Sea of Fiction: The Libraries of Trans-Pacific Steamships at the Turn of the Twentieth Century," *Library* 20, no. 1 (March 1, 2019): 3–28.

71 *Binnacle*, November 2, 1926.

72 *Binnacle*, November 4, 1926.

73 Charles E. Gauss, Log Book 1926–27, February 14, 1927, and September 19, 1926, Gauss Collection.

74 "Astronomy, Navigation and Human Geography," DeWitt Reddick's journal (Early Draft II), folder 2, Reddick Papers.

75 Holling C. Holling to his mother and siblings, December 23, 1926, box 41, folder 7, Holling Papers.

76 Holling C. Holling to his sister, at sea in the Caribbean, box 41, folder 7, Holling Papers.

77 Holling C. Holling to his mother and siblings, December 23, 1926, box 41, folder 7; Design Class, box 61, folder 13, Holling Papers.

78 DeWitt Reddick's journal (Early Draft I), September 21, 1926, folder 1, Reddick Papers.

79 Charles E. Gauss, Log Book 1926–27, p. 124, Gauss Collection.

80 *Binnacle* (University Travel Association), November 2, 1926, box 48, folder 4, Thwing Papers.

81 *Binnacle*, November 25, 1926, regarding the chairs; McKenzie, *A Broad Education Abroad*, 23, 37.

82 Ladd, *Around the World at Seventeen*, 5. See also Charles E. Gauss, Log Book 1926–27, Gauss Collection.

83 "Astronomy, Navigation and Human Geography," DeWitt Reddick's journal (Early Draft II), folder 2, Reddick Papers.

84 McKenzie, *A Broad Education Abroad*, 19; Orin Raber, "Department of Botany, Preliminary Bulletin," box 48, folder 3, Thwing Papers.

85 Raber, "Department of Botany, Preliminary Bulletin."

86 *Binnacle*, December 17, 1926.

87 *Binnacle*, December 2, 1926; "Santos, José Kabigting (1889–1949)," in "Plant Collectors" (Global Plants), accessed June 1, 2022, https://plants.jstor.org/stable/history/10.5555/al.ap.person.bm000335047. The textbook was possibly Elmer D. Merrill and J. K. Santos, *Pantropic Flora*, publisher unknown, 1926.

88 *Binnacle*, December 16, 1926; McKenzie, *A Broad Education Abroad*, 117.

89 McKenzie, *A Broad Education Abroad*, 118–21.

90 *Binnacle*, March 4, 1927.

91 *Binnacle*, April 21, 1927. See also Richard Drayton, *Nature's Government: Science, Imperial Britain, and the "Improvement" of the World* (New Haven, CT: Yale University Press, 2005); Alfred W Crosby, *Ecological Imperialism: The Biological Expansion of Europe, 900–1900* (Cambridge: Cambridge University Press, 2004).

92 Hazel Gibb Hinman, "The Lives and Works of Holling Clancy Holling" (Master's thesis, University of Redlands, 1958), 65.

93 Holling C. Holling to his mother and siblings, November 4, 1926, box 41, folder 8, Holling Papers.

94 "Art," course outline, box 48, folder 3, Thwing Papers.

95 *Binnacle* (University Travel Association), September 17, 1926, box 48, folder 4,

Thwing Papers; quotations are from "Art," course outline, box 48, folder 3, Thwing Papers.

96 *Binnacle*, October 27, 1926. S. H. Jameson's History of the Near and Far East attracted nearly as many. Dean George E. Howe's Latin and Greek classes were the smallest.

97 Holling C. Holling to his mother and siblings, October 20, 1926, box 41, folder 8; Student List, box 61, folder 13, Holling Papers.

98 Holling C. Holling to his sister, soon after departure from New York, box 41, folder 7, Holling Papers.

99 Holling C. Holling to his mother and siblings, December 23, 1926, box 41, folder 17, Holling Papers.

100 Holling C. Holling to his mother and siblings, December 23, 1926.

101 Design Class: Irene Haines, box 61, folder 13, Holling Papers.

102 *Binnacle* (University Travel Association), December 16, 1926, box 48, folder 4, Thwing Papers; Holling C. Holling to his mother, November 4, 1926, box 41, folder 8, Holling Papers. For Americans' domestic consumption of imported household items, see Kristin L. Hoganson, *Consumers' Imperium: The Global Production of American Domesticity, 1865–1920* (Chapel Hill: University of North Carolina Press, 2007), 13–56.

103 *Binnacle*, November 2, 1926; Course Plan, box 61, folder 13, Holling Papers.

104 Marjorie Reddick, "Reddick, DeWitt Carter," in *Handbook of Texas Online* (Texas State Historical Association), archived copy, May 27, 2022, Internet Archive Wayback Machine, https://web.archive.org/web/20220527050620/https://www.tshaonline.org/handbook/entries/reddick-dewitt-carter.

105 "New School of Journalism," *New York Tribune*, September 20, 1909; "Teach Journalism," *Southwestern Collegian* (Winfield, KS), March 13, 1917.

106 On shipboard newspapers, see Johanna de Schmidt, "'This Strange Little Floating World of Ours': Shipboard Periodicals and Community-Building in the 'Global' Nineteenth Century," *Journal of Global History* 11, no. 2 (2016): 229–50.

107 *Binnacle* (University Travel Association), September 21, 1926; box 48, folder 4, Thwing Papers.

108 "English and Journalism," box 48, folder 3, Thwing Papers.

109 *Binnacle*, September 21, 1926.

110 *Binnacle*, September 21, 1926.

111 The course guide listed Robert C. Elliott from Indiana as the instructor, but it was Thomas G. Brown who eventually sailed. See "English and Journalism" course outline, box 48, folder 3, Thwing Papers; "Name T. G. Brown Boro Library Aide," *Brooklyn Daily Eagle*, December 2, 1937.

112 "Name T. G. Brown Boro Library Aide."

113 *Binnacle*, September 23, 1926.

114 *Binnacle*, November 4 and 25, 1926 (continuing before Manila and Siam and Java); December 3 and 15, 1926.

115 Andrew J. McIntosh to Charles F. Thwing, February 17, 1926, box 48, folder 3, Thwing Papers; Henry J. Allen to Chas. F. Horner, February 15, 1926, C14, Allen Papers.

116 [Pearl Heckel], "A New Educational Project," folder 6, Heckel Papers.

117 *Binnacle* (University Travel Association), October 24 and 29, 1926; December 2, 15, and 16, 1926, box 48, folder 4, Thwing Papers.

118 *Binnacle*, October 30, November 16, and September 21, 1926.

119 *Binnacle*, October 27, 1926.

120 Article for Kansas papers written from Rome, DeWitt Reddick's journal (Early Draft I), folder 1, Reddick Papers.

121 Harris, *Photographs of the First University World Cruise*, no. 146a.

122 *Binnacle* (University Travel Association), October 12, 1926, box 48, folder 4, Thwing Papers.

123 *Binnacle*, October 17, 1926.

124 Female authors included Ellen Day, Clare Ferguson, Carol C. Pierson, Vernita S. Lundquist, and Margaret Johnston.

125 Harris, *Photographs of the First University World Cruise*, no. 991.

126 "'Covering' Honolulu," *Honolulu Star-Bulletin*, October 21, 1926.

127 See, e.g., Laura Coates Yaggy, "At School on the Ryndam in the Caribbean Sea," *Hutchinson (KS) News*, October 16, 1926.

128 See, e.g., Joseph Edmund Woodman on geography in *Binnacle* (University Travel Association), April 23, 1927, box 48, folder 4, Thwing Papers. See also Elizabeth Lippincott McQueen, "Highlights of Pioneer University Cruise," box 2, folder 12, 0055 Library of Aeronautical History, Women's International Association of Aeronautics (WIAA) Records, University of Southern California Libraries Special Collections.

129 By 1926, the emphasis on the "extracurriculum" in American colleges had intensified, but the ideal of student democracy was increasingly being challenged by the rise of specialized study, on the one hand, and universities' desire for control of undergraduate society, on the other. Frederick Rudolph, *The American College and University: A History* (New York: Alfred A. Knopf, 1962), 136; Roger L. Geiger, *The American College in the Nineteenth Century* (Nashville: Vanderbilt University Press, 2000), 14–15.

130 *Binnacle*, September 21 and 17, 1926.

131 McKenzie, *A Broad Education Abroad*, 4.

132 Harris, *Photographs of the First University World Cruise*, nos. 988, 630.

133 Charles E. Gauss, Log Book 1926–27, October 19, 1926, Gauss Collection.

134 *Binnacle* (University Travel Association), November 26, 1926, box 48, folder 4, Thwing Papers.

135 Dina Gusejnova, "Jazz Anxiety and the European Fear of Cultural Change: Towards a Transnational History of a Political Emotion," *Cultural History* 5, no. 1 (2016): 26–50; E. Taylor Atkins, *Blue Nippon: Authenticating Jazz in Japan* (Durham, NC: Duke University Press, 2001), 47–48; E. Taylor Atkins, *Jazz Planet* (Jackson: University Press of Mississippi, 2003), 224–26. For jazz during the Cold War, see Penny M. Von Eschen, *Satchmo Blows Up the World: Jazz Ambassadors Play the Cold War* (Cambridge, MA: Harvard University Press, 2006).

136 *Binnacle* (University Travel Association), November 31 and November 4, 1926, box 48, folder 4, Thwing Papers.

137 *Binnacle*, November 3, 1926.

138 Holling C. Holling to his mother and siblings, December 6, 1926, box 41, folder 8, Holling Papers. See also *Binnacle*, December 9, 1926.

139 *Binnacle*, October 15 and December 24 (Christmas issue), 1926. At least there are no references to them in the *Binnacle*.

140 *Binnacle*, October 15, 1926.

141 McKenzie, *A Broad Education Abroad*, 29; Harris, *Photographs of the First University World Cruise*, nos. 147, 147a, 150, 150a.

142 *Binnacle* (University Travel Association), October 30 and 31 (for report of play), 1926; October 30, 1926; December 4, 1926, box 48, folder 4, Thwing Papers.

143 McKenzie, *A Broad Education Abroad*, 221; Harris, *Photographs of the First University World Cruise*, nos. 979, 149, 313, 314, 350, 764.

144 *Binnacle*, October 31, 1926. For an introduction to student cross-dressing, see Margaret Nash, Danielle C. Mireles, and Amanda Scott-Williams, "'Mattie Matix' and Prodigal Princes: A Brief History of Drag on College Campuses from the Nineteenth Century to the 1940s," in *Rethinking Campus Life: New Perspectives on the History of College Students in the United States*, ed. Christine A. Ogren and Marc A. VanOverbeke (London: Palgrave Macmillan), 61–90.

145 Discussed further in chapters 5 and 6.

146 For the DeMolays and the Masons, see *Binnacle*, October 29 and November 30, 1926; January 28, 1927. For clubs, see Harris, *Photographs of the First University World Cruise*, nos. 416, 979, 989, 990, 992; [Pearl Heckel], "A New Educational Project," folder 6, Heckel Papers.

147 *Binnacle* (University Travel Association), November 26, 1926, box 48, folder 4, Thwing Papers.

148 *Binnacle*, October 15, 1926.

149 Discussed further in chapter 7.

150 *Binnacle*, September 17, 1926.

151 *Binnacle*, September 23, 1926.

152 McKenzie, *A Broad Education Abroad*, 39.

153 *Binnacle*, April 21, 1927.

154 Charles E. Gauss, Log Book 1926–27, April 21, 1927, Gauss Collection.

155 "Art," course outline by Holling C. Holling, box 48, folder 3, Thwing Papers; "Floating College to Sail with Student Body of 450," *New York Times*, September 5, 1926.

156 See chapter 2.

157 Edgar A. Bancroft (US Embassy in Japan) to Secretary of State, July 10, 1925, Central Decimal File 1910–29, box 317/032 University Travel Association, RG 59 (Department of State), NARA.

158 *Binnacle* (University Travel Association), November 5, 1926, box 48, folder 4, Thwing Papers; "Tokyo Program," 1926/27 Excursions and Shore Programs, folder 4, Semester at Sea Archives 1926–1927.

159 See, e.g., the *Binnacle*, March 8, 1927.

160 [Pearl Heckel], "A New Educational Project," folder 6, Heckel Papers; Andrew J. McIntosh to Henry J. Allen, March 8, 1927, box C7, Allen Papers.

161 E.g., an American Express agent called Mr. Nestor traveled ahead of the cruise to arrange the shore trips. *Binnacle*, February 29, 1927.

162 *The Student Magellan* (New York: Voelcker Bros., 1927), 73.

163 Lillian McCracken, December 11, 1926, Diary of Lillian McCracken.

164 Ladd, *Around the World at Seventeen*, 173.

165 "A Party of Students from the American Floating University Visit the Rubber Factory of Messrs. Lim Nee Soon & Sons," *Malayan Saturday Post* (Singapore), December 18, 1926.

166 *Binnacle* (University Travel Association), December 16, 1926, box 48, folder 4, Thwing Papers.

167 See, e.g., the *Binnacle*, October 16 and 17, 1926.

168 HCH and LWH Log Book Journal 1926–27, box 59, folder 4, Holling Papers.

169 McKenzie, *A Broad Education Abroad*, 1.

170 [Pearl Heckel], "A New Educational Project," folder 6, Heckel Papers. For diversity of student experience and interpretations, see chapters 4, 6, and 7.

171 Ladd, *Around the World at Seventeen*, 137.

172 *The Student Magellan*, 47.

173 Ladd, *Around the World at Seventeen*, 138.

174 "Shanghai Program," 1926/27 Excursions and Shore Programs, folder 4, Semester at Sea Archives 1926–1927. The officials who greeted the ship at the wharf included P. K. Chu, H. H. Ling, T. H. Lee, Y. E. Siao, K. T. Woo, T. H. Kuo, Hsi-tao Yuan, C. P. Cheng, C. C. Yu, S. L. Chang, C. H. Kai, King Chu, Francis Zia, M. E. Tisang, and C. P. Hu; Ladd, *Around the World at Seventeen*, 144.

175 Ladd, 144.

176 *Binnacle* (University Travel Association), November 30, 1926, box 48, folder 4, Thwing Papers.

177 *Binnacle*, October 20, 1926.

178 *Binnacle*, October 20, 1926.

179 *Binnacle*, January 16, 1927. On travelers versus tourists, see chapter 6 and Agnieszka Sobocinska and Richard White, "Travel Writing and Tourism," in *The Cambridge History of Travel Writing*, ed. Nandini Das and Tim Youngs (Cambridge: Cambridge University Press, 2019), 565–80.

180 "Tourists or Students?," *Binnacle*, October 24, 1926.

181 *Binnacle*, October 28, 1926, by "One of Them."

182 Harvey Levenstein, *Seductive Journey: American Tourists in France from Jefferson to the Jazz Age* (Chicago: University of Chicago Press, 2000), xi, 237–42, 244, 252; Pietsch, "Commercial Travel and College Culture."

183 *Binnacle* (University Travel Association), January 11, 1927, box 48, folder 4, Thwing Papers. This article marks out three groups: students, passengers, and globe-trotters.

184 *Binnacle*, April 26, 1927.

185 In some cases (e.g., Geography) they had been scheduled slightly earlier. See the *Binnacle*, December 10, 1926.

186 *Binnacle*, December 25, 1926.

187 *Binnacle*, April 26, 1927.

188 See chapter 8 for further discussion of results.

189 *Binnacle*, December 24, 1926.

190 *Binnacle*, December 25, 1926.

191 John R. Thelin, *A History of American Higher Education* (Baltimore: Johns Hopkins University Press, 2011), 211–26.

192 David O. Levine, *The American College and the Culture of Aspiration, 1915–1940* (Ithaca, NY: Cornell University Press, 1988).

193 "On Campus or on Atlantic," clipping in DeWitt Reddick's journal (Early Draft II), folder 2, Reddick Papers.

CHAPTER FOUR

1   For more on H. Dupree Jordan, see *Oglethorpe University Students Yearbook* (Atlanta: Oglethorpe University, 1926), 34.

2 Copies of these draft articles are in DeWitt Reddick's journal (Early Draft I), folder 1, Reddick Papers.

3 "With the Floating University" (from Rome), DeWitt Reddick's journal; *Binnacle* (University Travel Association), January 14, 1927, box 48, folder 4, Thwing Papers.

4 "Geography Girl," *Dayton (OH) Daily News*, September 22, 1926.

5 "Geography Girl."

6 "An Educational Experiment," *Freehold Transcript and Monmouth Inquirer* (Freehold, NJ), September 14, 1926.

7 "Floating University Sails," *Hartford Courant*, September 19, 1926.

8 "Floating College Sails Today with Classes On Board," *Brooklyn Daily Eagle*, September 18, 1926.

9 *Binnacle* (University Travel Association), September 17 and 21 and October 12, 1926, box 48, folder 4, Thwing Papers; letter to the subscribers of the *Binnacle*, November 15, 1926, box 48, folder 4, Thwing Papers.

10 *Binnacle*, September 17, 1926.

11 "Its Campus a Ship's Deck, Its Classrooms in 35 Lands," *Christian Science Monitor*, May 6, 1926.

12 *Binnacle*, September 17, 1926.

13 Kathleen Morgan Drowne and Patrick Huber, *The 1920s* (Westport, CT: Greenwood Press, 2004), 189; Rebekka Hahn, *Mass Media in the 1920s* (Munich: GRIN Verlag, 2008).

14 Including, e.g., the Scripps wire service (United Press) and a news features service (Newspaper Enterprise Association). See Gerald J. Baldasty, "Centralizing Control in Newspaper Chains: EW Scripps and the Newspaper Enterprise Association, 1902–1908," *American Journalism* 18, no. 2 (2001): 13–38; Drowne and Huber, *The 1920s*, 189.

15 "Students Curb Volstead Thirst at Havana Stop," *Detroit Free Press*, September 26, 1926. The *Detroit Free Press* was a Democratic paper that had been opposed to Prohibition. It placed this article next to another on the liquor being smuggled into the country across the Canadian border, 75 percent of it through Detroit. See Paul Finkelman, Martin J. Hershock, and Clifford W. Taylor, *The History of Michigan Law* (Athens, OH: Ohio University Press, 2006), 73–74.

16 *Binnacle* (University Travel Association), September 17, 1926, box 48, folder 4, 1DD6 Thwing Papers.

17 *Binnacle*, September 21, 1926. On models of masculinity, see Gail Bederman, *Manliness and Civilization: A Cultural History of Gender and Race in the United States, 1880–1917* (Chicago: University of Chicago Press, 1996).

18 *Binnacle*, September 21, 1926.

19 *Binnacle*, October 16, 1926.

20 This quote was widely reported, including by the *Detroit Free Press*, the *Washington Post*, and the *New York Times*. See "Ship Students Sober in Havana, Says Dean," *New York Times*, September 26, 1926.

21 "Students Curb Volstead Thirst at Havana Stop."

22 "Students Loyal to Honour System," *Reno (NV) Gazette-Journal*, September 25, 1926.

23 "Floating University's Decks Picture Unique Campus Scene," *Christian Science Monitor*, October 29, 1926.

24 "Floating University's Decks Picture Unique Campus Scene."

25 "Students Go Abroad for Specialized Work," *New York Times*, October 24, 1926.

26 James S. McKenzie, *A Broad Education Abroad: Readin', Writin', and Roamin'* (New York: Vantage Press, 1978), 28.

27 McKenzie, 28.

28 *Binnacle* (University Travel Association), October 12 and 16, 1926, box 48, folder 4, 1DD6 Thwing Papers.

29 [Pearl Heckel], "A New Educational Project," folder 6, Heckel Papers.

30 [Pearl Heckel], "A New Educational Project."

31 [Pearl Heckel], "A New Educational Project." Two students were let off in Los Angeles, but several others were permitted to remain aboard.

32 *Binnacle* (University Travel Association), October 16, 1926, box 48, folder 4, 1DD6 Thwing Papers.

33 [Pearl Heckel], "A New Educational Project."

34 *Binnacle*, October 12, 1926.

35 Richard Black, Ellis Dana, Herbert Brenon, E. E. Haversack, A. S. Barada, Lee Johnson, Stanley Woodard, T. H. Williams, Fred Du Bois, and David Inglis. Walter Conger Harris, *Photographs of the First University World Cruise* (New York: University Travel Association, 1927), no. 526; *Binnacle*, October 15 and 29, 1926.

36 Roger L. Geiger, *The History of American Higher Education: Learning and Culture from the Founding to World War II* (Princeton, NJ: Princeton University Press, 2015), 399.

37 *Binnacle* (University Travel Association), October 27, 1926, box 48, folder 4, 1DD6 Thwing Papers.

38 *Binnacle*, October 15, 1926.

39 *Binnacle*, October 29, 1926.

40 For Holling C. Holling's drawings, see box 73, folder 1; box 138, folders 2–3; box 60, folder 26, Holling Papers.

41 Charles Ladd, *Around the World at Seventeen* (Rahway, NJ: Quinn and Boden, 1928), 65.

42 "Sea Collegians Startle Japan With Rum Orgy," *Detroit Free Press*, November 6, 1926.

43 "Sea Collegians Startle Japan With Rum Orgy."

44 "'Floating University' Skipper Finds Pirate Flag Flying on Mast; Campus Cutups Silent," *Pittsburgh Daily Post*, November 8, 1926; "Denies Wild Drinking by Students Afloat," *New York Times*, November 8, 1926.

45 "The Floating University," *Winona (MN) Daily News*, November 13, 1926.

46 *Binnacle* (University Travel Association), November 15, 1926, box 48, folder 4, 1DD6 Thwing Papers; "U.S. Collegians' Sex Equality Shock to Japan," *Evening News* (Harrisburg, PA), November 6, 1926.

47 "Ryndam Students Expelled after Wild Joy-Ride," *Honolulu Advertiser*, November 20, 1926.

48 "Students Expelled," *Time*, November 29, 1926.

49 [Pearl Heckel], "A New Educational Project," folder 6, Heckel Papers.

50 *Binnacle* (University Travel Association), November 15, 1926, box 48, folder 4, 1DD6 Thwing Papers.

51 Tom Johnson to his mother, November 13, 1926, Johnson Papers; McKenzie, *A Broad Education Abroad*, 77. Diplomatic relations are discussed more generally in chapter 5.

52 *Binnacle*, November 15, 1926.

53 [Pearl Heckel], "A New Educational Project," folder 6, Heckel Papers; *Binnacle*, January 11, 1927.

54 [Pearl Heckel], "A New Educational Project."

55 Joseph R. Taylor to Charles F. Thwing, November 16, 1926, box 48, folder 3, 1DD6 Thwing Papers.

56 Thwing was in fact already back in the United States, having left the ship in Havana to attend Phi Beta Kappa's national conference. See the *Binnacle* (University Travel Association), September 21, 1926, box 48, folder 4, 1DD6 Thwing Papers.

57 "University Ship 'Cans' Eight Boys," *Los Angeles Times*, December 2, 1926.

58 "Their World Tour Cut," *New York Times*, December 2, 1926; "This Steamer Is Collegiate," *Lansing (MI) State Journal*, December 2, 1926.

59 "Some Sober Reflections as December Sets In," *New York Times*, November 28, 1926.

60 Examples include Laura Coates Yaggy, "At School on the Ryndam in the Caribbean Sea," *Hutchinson (KS) News*, October 16, 1926; Margaret B. Lum, "Chatham Girl on World Round Trip," *Chatham (NJ) Press*, December 4, 1926; Douglas C. Ridgley, "College Cruise around the World," *Journal of Geography* 25, no. 9 (1926): 350–51; Douglas C. Ridgley, "Class Work and Shore Trips of Floating University," *Christian Science Monitor*, December 16, 1926.

61 *Binnacle* (University Travel Association), December 1, 1926, box 48, folder 4, 1DD6 Thwing Papers.

62 "Students Invaded Japanese Royal Suite," *New York Times*, December 3, 1926; "Collegiate! Students on Gay Party," *Cincinnati Enquirer*, December 3, 1926.

63 "7 Students Carry Off Image in Tokyo Temple," *Chicago Daily Tribune*, December 3, 1926; "Students Sent Back from Japan," *Time*, December 13, 1926.

64 "Occidentalism," *Brooklyn Daily Eagle*, December 6, 1926.

65 "Student Explains Row on Floating College," *St. Louis Post-Dispatch*, December 5, 1926; *Binnacle* (University Travel Association), November 15, 1926, box 48, folder 4, 1DD6 Thwing Papers; "Nine Students Fired off Ship," *St. Louis Post-Dispatch*, November 16, 1926.

66 Ridgley, "Class Work and Shore Trips of Floating University."

67 Henry Noble MacCracken, "Colleges Grapple with the New Order," *New York Times*, January 2, 1927.

68 MacCracken, "Colleges Grapple with the New Order."

69 [Pearl Heckel], "A New Educational Project," folder 6, Heckel Papers.

70 For instance, *Binnacle* (University Travel Association), January 1, 1927, box 48, folder 4, 1DD6 Thwing Papers.

71 McKenzie, *A Broad Education Abroad*, 129–30; *Binnacle*, December 15, 1926.

72 *Binnacle*, December 31, 1926.

73 Charles E. Gauss, Log Book 1926–27, December 31, 1926, Gauss Collection.

74 Lillian McCracken, "New Year, at Sea," p. 172, Diary of Lillian McCracken.

75 *Binnacle* (University Travel Association), January 2 and January 1, 1927, box 48, folder 4, 1DD6 Thwing Papers.

76 *Binnacle*, January 2, 1927.

77 *Binnacle*, January 2, 1927.

78 *Binnacle*, January 11, 1927.

79 *Binnacle*, January 11, 1927.

80 *Binnacle*, January 11 and 14, 1927.

81 *Binnacle*, January 18, 1927. When the *Ryndam* arrived at the French Riviera and student drunkenness reoccurred, Dean Heckel threatened to take student discipline out of the hands of the Student Council altogether, triggering resignations from some of its members. But many others wholly endorsed an "Advisory" Council approach. See the *Binnacle* (University Travel Association), January 18 and March 8, 1927, box 48, folder 4, 1DD6 Thwing Papers.

82 *Binnacle*, January 14, 1927.

83 *Binnacle*, January 18, 1927.

84 "College Students May Cruise and Study on 'Floating University,'" *Democrat and Chronicle* (Rochester, NY), February 20, 1927.

85 "'Floating University' Bans Girl Students," *Philadelphia Inquirer*, February 21, 1927; "Bar Girls on College Ship," *New York Times*, February 22, 1922; "Girls to Be Barred on Next Cruise of 'Floating University,'" *Democrat and Chronicle* (Rochester, NY), February 21, 1927.

86 "Floating University Divided by Charge Girls Cannot Be Trusted with Boys on Cruise," *Brooklyn Daily Eagle*, February 22, 1927.

87 *Binnacle* (University Travel Association), October 23, 1926, box 48, folder 4, 1DD6 Thwing Papers.

88 Andrew J. McIntosh to Henry J. Allen, March 8, 1927, box C7, Allen Papers.

89 Charles W. Lowack to Holland America Line, July 28 1927, Directie, 01/0831; New York Agent to HAL, August 2, 1926, DirectieV, 02/ v131.1 (October 1926–April 1927), 318 Archieven van de Holland-Amerika Lijn (HAL).

90 *Binnacle*, September 21, 1926; Andrew J. McIntosh to Henry J. Allen, March 8, 1927, box C7, Allen Papers.

91 [Pearl Heckel], "A New Educational Project" (emphasis in the original), folder 6, Heckel Papers.

92 McIntosh to Allen, March 8, 1927.

93 Andrew J. McIntosh to Henry J. Allen, February 26, 1927, Allen Papers.

94 "Coeducation at Sea Disappoints Allen; Too Many 'Floating University' Courtships," *New York Times*, February 24, 1927.

95 John R. Thelin, *A History of American Higher Education* (Baltimore: Johns Hopkins University Press, 2011), 182–83; Geiger, *The History of American Higher Education*, 399.

96 Thelin, *A History of American Higher Education*, 186; Geiger, *The History of American Higher Education*, 404.

97 Madeleine Yue Dong, "Who Is Afraid of the Chinese Modern Girl?," in *The Modern Girl around the World: Consumption, Modernity, and Globalization*, ed. Alys Eve Weinbaum et al. (Durham, NC: Duke University Press, 2008), 201.

98 "Shanghai's Streets," *North China Herald and Supreme Court and Consular Gazette* (Shanghai), November 20, 1926; "[No Title]," trans. Kirsten Kamphuis, *De Indische Courant* (Indonesia), December 21, 1926.

99 Emily S. Rosenberg, "Consuming Women: Images of Americanization in the 'American Century,'" *Diplomatic History* 23, no. 3 (1999): 479–97.

100 *Binnacle* (University Travel Association), January 15, 1927, box 48, folder 4, 1DD6 Thwing Papers.

101 Andrew J. McIntosh to Henry J. Allen, March 8, 1927, box C7, Allen Papers.

102 McIntosh to Allen, March 7, 1927.

103 "'University Afloat': The Study Cruise of the Ryndam," *Observer* (UK), January 23, 1927.

104 "Dr. Butcher to Lead Student Cruise," *New York Times*, March 4, 1927; "Two College Cruises, Plan," *Detroit Free Press*, March 6, 1927; "Floating University on Cunard Liner," *Scranton (PA) Republican*, January 22, 1927.

105 "Two College Cruises, Plan"; "Floating University Is Co-educational," *Heights* (Boston College), March 15, 1927.

106 Andrew J. McIntosh to Henry J. Allen, February 26, 1927, box C7, Allen Papers.

107 "For Men Only," *Lansing (MI) State Journal*, March 2, 1927. The same article was published in the *Battle Creek (MI) Enquirer*, March 9, 1927.

108 "Too Many Extra-curricular Activities," *New York Times*, February 25, 1927.

109 "More Lovemaking Than Study," *Philadelphia Inquirer*, February 25, 1927.

110 "Distractions of Co-education," *Ottawa (ON) Journal*, February 26, 1927.

111 "Distractions of Co-education."

112 "Sanctions Girl Students on Floating University," *Brooklyn Daily Eagle*, February 16, 1927.

113 "Cupid's Culture," *Los Angeles Times*, March 7, 1927.

114 Andrew J. McIntosh, "Why the Floating University Is Co-educational," *School and Society* 25, no. 637 (1927): 320–21.

115 Paula S. Fass, *The Damned and the Beautiful: American Youth in the 1920's* (Oxford: Oxford University Press, 1977), 22–5. See Rise S. Halle, "Is My Daughter Safe at College?," *Good Housekeeping*, September 1929, as quoted in Sydney Greenbie, "Educators beyond Their Depth" (1929), p. 39, folder 22, DC 2524 Walker Papers; Whitney Walton, "American Girls and French Jeunes Filles: Negotiating National Identities in Interwar France," *Gender and History* 17, no. 2 (2005): 325–53.

116 *Binnacle* (University Travel Association), March 14, 1927, box 48, folder 4, 1DD6 Thwing Papers.

117 "Floating University's Classes Thinned by Lure of Paris Cafes," *Tampa (FL) Times*, March 16, 1927.

118 "Ship Students Reported Wed," *Los Angeles Times*, March 16, 1927; "Faculty Oppose Sea Co-education," *New York Times*, March 16, 1927; "Prof, Cupid of Sea University to Graduate 24," *Chicago Daily Tribune*, March 16, 1927.

119 "Faculty Oppose Sea Co-education"; "Ship Students Reported Wed"; "Prof, Cupid of Sea University to Graduate 24."

120 "Wine Given to Floating Coeds for Grape Juice," *Washington Post*, March 17, 1927.

121 "Paris Nights Prove More Attractive Than Battlefields to Them," *Times Herald* (Olean, NY), March 16, 1927.

122 "Floating University's Classes Thinned by Lure of Paris Cafes."

123 "'Night Study' in Paris Empties 'Boat College,'" *Evening Courier* (Camden, NJ), March 16, 1927.

124 "Bubonic Plague Found on 'Floating University,'" *Indiana (PA) Gazette*, March 18, 1927.

125 "Floating University Reaches Rotterdam," *Lansing (MI) State Journal*, March 17, 1927.

126 "No Plague Menace Found on 'Floating University,'" *Indiana (PA) Gazette*, March 19, 1927.

127 "Floating University Has Plague Case," *Daily Capital Journal (Salem, OR)*, March 17,

1927; "Floating University Freed of Quarantine after Disinfection," *Pittsburgh Daily Post*, March 19, 1927; "No Plague Menace Found on 'Floating University.'"

128   "Dirty Work Afloat," *Harvard Crimson*, November 8, 1926; "Good Will to Men," *Harvard Crimson*, May 16, 1927.

129   "Cupid's Culture."

130   Thelin, *A History of American Higher Education*, 211–26; Fass, *The Damned and the Beautiful*; Helen Lefkowitz Horowitz, *Campus Life: Undergraduate Cultures from the End of the Eighteenth Century to the Present* (Chicago: University of Chicago Press, 1988).

131   Geiger, *The History of American Higher Education*, 447, 454.

132   Fass, *The Damned and the Beautiful*, 204–5.

133   "Necking Way 'round World, Ship-College Sheiks Admit," *Courier-Post (Camden, NJ)*, March 24, 1927.

134   "Groups Named for I.U. Revue," *Indianapolis Star*, March 15, 1927.

135   Wilbur E. Sutton, "The Way I Feel About It," *Dayton (OH) Herald*, March 18, 1927; "Occidentalism," *Brooklyn Daily Eagle*, December 6, 1926.

136   "Topics of the Times," *New York Times*, February 25, 1927.

137   See "Ryndam Students Visiting Holland," *Christian Science Monitor*, March 22, 1927; "College Afloat Visits Greece," *Christian Science Monitor*, March 28, 1927; "'Floating University' Entertained at Oslo," *Christian Science Monitor*, April 7, 1927. The paper's take on the "*Ryndam*'s coeducational feature" was that it was "no new thing in Scotland, where the idea of coeducation has existed from the time of the first parish schools." "Ryndam Anchors in Firth of Forth," *Christian Science Monitor*, April 13, 1927.

138   *Binnacle* (University Travel Association), September 21, 1926, box 48, folder 4, 1DD6 Thwing Papers; Ladd, *Around the World at Seventeen*, 4.

139   Tom Arnold-Forster, "Democracy and Expertise in the Lippmann-Terman Controversy," *Modern Intellectual History* 16, no. 2 (2019): 21.

140   *Binnacle*, April 26, 1927.

141   *Binnacle*, April 10, 1927.

142   Tom Johnson to his mother, March 3, 1927, Johnson Papers.

143   Geiger, *The History of American Higher Education*, 447.

144   Quoted in Thelin, *A History of American Higher Education*, 235. See also Geiger, *The History of American Higher Education*, 455–57.

CHAPTER FIVE

1   Lillian McCracken, p. 290, Diary of Lillian McCracken; "Hong Kong Shore Program," folder 4, Semester at Sea Archives 1926–1927.

2   Joyce E. Chaplin, *Round about the Earth: Circumnavigation from Magellan to Orbit* (New York: Simon and Schuster, 2012), 263–64; E. Mowbray Tate, *Transpacific Steam: The Story of Steam Navigation from the Pacific Coast of North America to the Far East and the Antipodes, 1867–1941* (New York: Cornwall Books, 1986), 163–64.

3   Tamson Pietsch, "Bodies at Sea: Travelling to Australia in the Age of Sail," *Journal of Global History* 11, no. 2 (July 2016): 209–28; Lillian McCracken, September 22, 1926, p. 222, Diary of Lillian McCracken.

4   *Binnacle* (University Travel Association), September 23, 1926, box 48, folder 4, 1DD6 Thwing Papers.

5   Natalie J. Ring, *The Problem South: Region, Empire, and the New Liberal State, 1880–1930* (Athens: University of Georgia Press, 2012).

6   *Binnacle*, September 23, 1926.

7   Lillian McCracken, September 23, 1926, p. 223, Diary of Lillian McCracken.

8   Tom Johnson to his mother, September 27, 1926, Johnson Papers.

9   HCH and LWH Log Book Journal, 1926–27, September 23, 1926, box 59, folder 4, Holling Papers.

10   *Binnacle* (University Travel Association), September 23, 1926, box 48, folder 4, 1DD6 Thwing Papers.

11   Noel Maurer and Carlos Yu, *The Big Ditch: How America Took, Built, Ran, and Ultimately Gave Away the Panama Canal* (Princeton, NJ: Princeton University Press, 2010).

12   "We are passing through the lock at Pedro Miguel," DeWitt Reddick's journal (Early Draft I), folder 1, Reddick Papers.

13   "In the center of the car tracks," DeWitt Reddick's journal.

14   Tom Johnson to his mother, September 27, 1926, Johnson Papers; "We are now passing two large dredge boats," DeWitt Reddick's journal (Early Draft I), folder 1, Reddick Papers.

15   E.g., Charles Ladd, *Around the World at Seventeen* (Rahway, NJ: Quinn and Boden, 1928), 22.

16   Tom Johnson to his mother, September 27, 1926, Johnson Papers.

17   *Binnacle* (University Travel Association), October 12, 1926, box 48, folder 4, 1DD6 Thwing Papers.

18   "We are drawing into Honolulu," DeWitt Reddick's journal (Early Draft II), folder 2, Reddick Papers.

19   Paul S. Sutter, "Tropical Conquest and the Rise of the Environmental Management State: The Case of U.S. Sanitary Efforts in Panama," in *Colonial Crucible: Empire in the Making of the Modern American State*, ed. Francisco A. Scarano and Alfred W. McCoy (Madison: University of Wisconsin Press, 2009), 319.

20   HCH and LWH Log Bog Journal, 1926–27, September 28–29, 1926, box 59, folder 4, Holling Papers. On the relationship between US civilizational superiority and the vulnerability of white bodies in the heat, see, e.g., Linda Nash, "Finishing Nature: Harmonizing Bodies and Environments in Late-Nineteenth-Century California," *Environmental History* 8, no. 1 (2003): 25–52.

21   *Binnacle*, October 12 and 15, 1926.

22   *Binnacle*, October 12 and 17, 1926.

23   *Binnacle*, October 15, 1926.

24   Kevin Starr, *Material Dreams: Southern California through the 1920s* (Oxford: Oxford University Press, 1991), 69.

25   Starr, 147.

26   Larry Smith, "Indigenous Urbanity in Los Angeles: 1910s–1930s," UCLA Mapping Indigenous LA, accessed June 1, 2022, https://www.arcgis.com/apps/MapJournal/index.html?appid=385eb4f3432442eab8bcffb19109f92e; Philip J. Deloria, *Indians in Unexpected Places* (Lawrence: University of Kansas Press, 2004); Nicholas G. Rosenthal, *Reimagining Indian Country: Native American Migration and Identity in Twentieth-Century Los Angeles* (Chapel Hill: University of North Carolina Press, 2012); Starr, *Material Dreams*, 223.

27   *Binnacle* (University Travel Association), October 14, 1926, box 48, folder 4, 1DD6 Thwing Papers.

28   *Binnacle*, October 15, 1926.

29   *Binnacle*, October 17, 1926.

30   *Binnacle*, October 15, 1926.

31   *Binnacle*, October 15 and17, 1926.

32   *Binnacle*, October 17, 1926.

33   Now called the Chiefess Kapiolani Elementary School.

34   DeWitt Reddick's journal, October 21, 1928 (Early Draft I), folder 1, Reddick Papers.

35   *Binnacle* (University Travel Association), October 23, 1926, box 48, folder 4, 1DD6 Thwing Papers.

36   *Binnacle*, October 24, 1926.

37   *Binnacle*, October 24, 1926.

38   *Binnacle*, October 28, 1926.

39   *Binnacle*, October 23 and 24, 1926.

40   *Binnacle*, October 23, 1926.

41   *Binnacle*, October 24, 1926.

42   *Binnacle*, October 28, 1926.

43   *Binnacle*, October 23 and 24, 1926.

44   *Binnacle*, October 23, 1926.

45   *Binnacle*, October 24 and 29, 1926.

46   *Binnacle*, October 29 and 30, 1926; Walter Conger Harris, *Photographs of the First University World Cruise* (New York: University Travel Association, 1927), no. 147a. On cross-dressing during World War I, see David A. Boxwell, "The Follies of War: Cross-Dressing and Popular Theatre on the British Front Lines, 1914–18," *Modernism/Modernity* 9, no. 1 (2002): 1–20; Lisa Z. Sigel, "'Best Love': Female Impersonation in the Great War," *Sexualities* 19, nos. 1–2 (February 2016): 98–118.

47   "We are now passing two large dredge boats," DeWitt Reddick's journal (Early Draft I), folder 1, Reddick Papers; James S. McKenzie, *A Broad Education Abroad: Readin', Writin', and Roamin'* (New York: Vantage Press, 1978), 20.

48   In 1926, it was Meriwether Lewis Walker. Michael L. Conniff, *Panama and the United States: The End of the Alliance* (Athens: University of Georgia Press, 2012).

49   Ladd, *Around the World at Seventeen*, 27–28.

50   *Binnacle* (University Travel Association), December 23 and October 28, 1926, box 48, folder 4, 1DD6 Thwing Papers.

51   *Binnacle*, November 25, 1926.

52   McKenzie, *A Broad Education Abroad*, 90–92.

53   *Binnacle*, November 30, 1926.

54   Ladd, *Around the World at Seventeen*, 155.

55   Ladd, 155–56.

56   Ladd, 157.

57   For the US consular service, see the work of Nicole Phelps, "Researching the US Consular Service," Research, *Researching the US Consular Service* (blog), archived copy, May 27, 2022, Internet Archive Wayback Machine, https://web.archive.org/web/20220527050750/https://blog.uvm.edu/nphelps/; Nicole M. Phelps, "One Service, Three Systems, Many Empires: The US Consular Service and the Growth

of US Global Power, 1789–1924," in *Crossing Empires* (Durham, NC: Duke University Press, 2020), 135–58.

58 Andrew J. McIntosh, April 27, 1925, Name Index 1910–29, box 718/250/1/11/05/032 Am 323, RG 59 (Department of State), NARA. Slemp's nephew traveled on board the 1926 *Ryndam*. See the *Gangplank* (*Ryndam* alumni newsletter), May 1930, 1926/27 Reunion in 1952, folder 6, Semester at Sea Archives 1926–1927.

59 Correspondence respecting the University Round-the-World Trip: 1926–1927, 13C/49398, R1081 Registry Files 1919–1927, League of Nations Archives, Geneva, Switzerland.

60 Andrew J. McIntosh, April 27, 1925, Name Index 1910–29, box 718/250/1/1/05/032 Am 323, RG 59 (Department of State), NARA; *Binnacle* (University Travel Association), March 8, 1927, box 48, folder 4, 1DD6 Thwing Papers. See also James E. Lough to the Assistant Secretary of State, April 1, 1929, Decimal File 1910–29, box 317/032 University Travel Association, RG 59 (Department of State), NARA.

61 *Binnacle*, December 15, 1926.

62 "Our Foreign Service," *Binnacle*, March 8, 1927.

63 *Binnacle*, December 15, 1926.

64 *The Student Magellan* (New York: Voelcker Bros., 1927), 57.

65 *The Student Magellan*, 17.

66 Ladd, *Around the World at Seventeen*, 134.

67 Ladd, 29.

68 Maurizio Peleggi, "The Social and Material Life of Colonial Hotels: Comfort Zones as Contact Zones in British Colombo and Singapore, ca. 1870–1930," *Journal of Social History* 46, no. 1 (2012): 124–53.

69 *The Student Magellan*, 23, 31, 37, 51–52, 81, 103, 141; *Binnacle* (University Travel Association), January 18, 1927, box 48, folder 4, 1DD6 Thwing Papers.

70 *Binnacle*, January 2, 1927.

71 HCH and LWH Log Book Journal, 1926–27, November 21, 1926, box 59, folder 4, Holling Papers.

72 Ladd, *Around the World at Seventeen*, 152.

73 *Binnacle*, December 15, 1926.

74 Ladd, *Around the World at Seventeen*, 47.

75 *Binnacle* (University Travel Association), December 15, 1926, box 48, folder 4, 1DD6 Thwing Papers. On the hybridization and creolization of jazz, see Su Lin Lewis, *Cities in Motion: Urban Life and Cosmopolitanism in Southeast Asia, 1920–1940* (Cambridge: Cambridge University Press, 2016); E. Taylor Atkins, *Blue Nippon: Authenticating Jazz in Japan* (Durham, NC: Duke University Press, 2001); William A. Shack, *Harlem in Montmartre: A Paris Jazz Story between the Great Wars*, vol. 4 (Berkeley: University of California Press, 2001); Andrew F. Jones, *Yellow Music: Media Culture and Colonial Modernity in the Chinese Jazz Age* (Durham, NC: Duke University Press, 2001); Penny M. Von Eschen, *Satchmo Blows Up the World: Jazz Ambassadors Play the Cold War* (Cambridge, MA: Harvard University Press, 2006).

76 *Binnacle*, November 15, 1926.

77 Ladd, *Around the World at Seventeen*, 93.

78 "The Cruise of the 'Floating University,'" *Los Angeles Times*, May 9, 1927.

79 "Life on Floating University Much the Same as on Land, Says Robert Smith Crowder of Ryndam," *Decatur (IL) Herald*, May 5, 1927.

80 *Binnacle* (University Travel Association), December 9, 1926, box 48, folder 4, 1DD6 Thwing Papers; Holling C. Holling to his mother and siblings, box 41, folder 8, Holling Papers.

81 Tom Johnson to his mother, December 10, 1926, Johnson Papers; *The Student Magellan*, 69.

82 Irene Haines in McIntosh's magazine, *Floating University: The World Its Campus (1927–28)* (International University Cruise Inc.), February 1927, p. 13, New York Public Library; Laura Coates Yaggy, "At School on the Ryndam in the Caribbean Sea," *Hutchinson (KS) News*, October 16, 1926; Laura Coates Yaggy, "The Charleston Upsets Dignity of Siam's King," *Hutchinson (KS) News*, January 29, 1927. At the 1952 reunion, the king was remembered as having given "the girl a diamond bracelet and the boy a watch." Holland America Line N.A.S.M News, June 1952, 1926/27 Reunion 1952, folder 6, Semester at Sea Archives 1926–1927.

83 *Binnacle* (University Travel Association), December 9, 1926, box 48, folder 4, 1DD6 Thwing Papers; Holling C. Holling to his mother and siblings, December 6, 1926, Holling Papers.

84 *Floating University: The World Its Campus (1927–28)*, March 1927.

85 *Floating University*, February 1927.

86 Ladd, *Around the World at Seventeen*, 146.

87 Ladd, 81.

88 In fact, one of the nicknames for the US Pacific Fleet was "The Standard Oil Navy." *Binnacle* (University Travel Association), December 1, 1926, box 48, folder 4, 1DD6 Thwing Papers. See also Emily S. Rosenberg, *Financial Missionaries to the World: The Politics and Culture of Dollar Diplomacy, 1900–1930* (Durham, NC: Duke University Press, 2004); Brooke L. Blower, "Nation of Outposts: Forts, Factories, Bases, and the Making of American Power," *Diplomatic History* 41, no. 3 (2017): 439–59.

89 On US consumption, see Kristin L. Hoganson, *Consumers' Imperium: The Global Production of American Domesticity, 1865–1920* (Chapel Hill: University of North Carolina Press, 2007); Amy Kaplan, *The Anarchy of Empire in the Making of U.S. Culture* (Cambridge, MA: Harvard University Press, 2005); Christopher Endy, *Cold War Holidays: American Tourism in France* (Chapel Hill: University of North Carolina Press, 2004).

90 *Binnacle* (University Travel Association), December 16, 1926, box 48, folder 4, 1DD6 Thwing Papers.

91 *Binnacle*, January 1, 1927.

92 *Binnacle*, January 13, 1927.

93 *Binnacle*, November 25, 1926, and March 4, 1927.

94 On American expertise abroad, see Daniel T. Rodgers, *Atlantic Crossings: Social Politics in a Progressive Age* (Cambridge, MA: Harvard University Press, 1998); Jonathan Curry-Machado, "'Rich Flames and Hired Tears': Sugar, Sub-imperial Agents and the Cuban Phoenix of Empire," *Journal of Global History* 4, no. 1 (2009): 33–56; Stephen Tuffnell, "Engineering Inter-imperialism: American Miners and the Transformation of Global Mining, 1871–1910," *Journal of Global History* 10, no. 1 (2015): 53–76.

95 *Binnacle*, December 9, 1926.

96   *Binnacle*, December 4, 1926.
97   *Binnacle*, December 2, 1926.
98   *Binnacle*, November 4, 1926.
99   *Binnacle*, October 29, 1926; *Plarr's Lives of the Fellows*, s.v. "Haigh, William Edwin (1878–1961)," 2014, Royal College of Surgeons of England, https://livesonline .rcseng.ac.uk/.
100 *Binnacle*, October 28, 1926.
101 *Binnacle*, December 25, 1926.
102 Ladd, *Around the World at Seventeen*, 281. See also Blower, "Nation of Outposts."
103 Kristin L Hoganson, *The Heartland: An American History* (New York: Penguin, 2020).
104 Ladd, *Around the World at Seventeen*, 92–94.
105 Ladd, 77–78.
106 Tamson Pietsch, "Commercial Travel and College Culture: The 1920s Transatlantic Student Market and the Foundations of Mass Tourism," *Diplomatic History* 43, no. 1 (2019): 83–106. For the relationship between hard and soft power, see Penny Von Eschen, "Duke Ellington Plays Baghdad: Rethinking Hard and Soft Power from the Outside In," in *Contested Democracy: Freedom, Race, and Power in American History*, ed. Manisha Sinha and Penny M. Von Eschen (New York: Columbia University Press, 2007), 279–300.
107 *Binnacle* (University Travel Association), November 4, 1926, box 48, folder 4, 1DD6 Thwing Papers.
108 Ladd, *Around the World at Seventeen*, 138.
109 *Binnacle*, November 21, 1926.
110 Yaggy, "The Charleston Upsets Dignity of Siam's King."
111 Yaggy, 12; Greg Robinson, *The Great Unknown: Japanese American Sketches* (Boulder: University Press of Colorado, 2016), 270; Yasuke Tsurumi, "International Friendship," *Rotarian*, November 1926; Chitoshi Yanaga, "Toward International Understanding," *Far Eastern Quarterly* 15, no. 1 (1955): 130–31; *Asian Perspective*, vols. 8–9 (South Korea: Institute for Far Eastern Studies, Kyung Nam University, 1984); Shore Programs, folder 4, Semester at Sea Archives 1926–1927; *Binnacle*, November 5, 1926; "Tatsunosuke Ueda," in *Prabook* (World Biographical Encyclopedia), accessed June 1, 2022, https://prabook.com/web/tatsunosuke.ueda/3752713.
112 Victor N. Kobayashi, "Japan's Hoashi Riichiro and John Dewey," *Educational Theory* 14, no. 1 (1964): 50–53; Sharon H. Nolte, "Industrial Democracy for Japan: Tanaka Ōdō and John Dewey," *Journal of the History of Ideas* 45, no. 2 (1984): 277–94.
113 Tokyo Official Program, folder 4, Semester at Sea Archives 1926–1927; Harris, *Photographs of the First University World Cruise*, nos. 163, 205, 216.
114 *Binnacle* (University Travel Association), November 16, 1926, box 48, folder 4, 1DD6 Thwing Papers.
115 Lillian McCracken, December 11, 1926, pp. 130–32, Diary of Lillian McCracken.
116 *Binnacle*, November 5, 1926.
117 Ladd, *Around the World at Seventeen*, 119.
118 Ian R. Tyrrell, *Reforming the World: The Creation of America's Moral Empire* (Princeton, NJ: Princeton University Press, 2013). On the American YMCA in Asia, see Jon Thares Davidann, *A World of Crisis and Progress: The American YMCA in Japan, 1890–1930* (Bethlehem, PA: Lehigh University Press, 1998).

119   Harald Fischer-Tiné, "Fitness for Modernity? The YMCA and Physical-Education Schemes in Late-Colonial South Asia (circa 1900–40)," *Modern Asian Studies* 53, no. 2 (2019): 522–24. See also Michael G. Thompson, "Sherwood Eddy, the Missionary Enterprise, and the Rise of Christian Internationalism in 1920s America," *Modern Intellectual History* 12, no. 1 (April 2015): 65–93; Michael Phillipp Brunner, "From Converts to Cooperation: Protestant Internationalism, US Missionaries and Indian Christians and 'Professional' Social Work between Boston and Bombay (c. 1920–1950)," *Journal of Global History* 16, no. 3 (2021): 415–34; Stefan Hübner, "'Uplifting the Weak and Degenerated Races of East Asia': American and Indigenous Views of Sport and Body in Early Twentieth-Century East Asia," in *Race and Racism in Modern East Asia* (Leiden: Brill, 2015), 196–216.

120   Stefan Hübner, "Muscular Christianity and the Western Civilizing Mission: Elwood S. Brown, the YMCA, and the Idea of the Far Eastern Championship Games," *Diplomatic History* 39, no. 3 (2015): 532–57.

121   *Binnacle* (University Travel Association), December 1, 1926, box 48, folder 4, 1DD6 Thwing Papers.

122   On education in the Philippines, see Sarah Steinbock-Pratt, *Educating the Empire: American Teachers and Contested Colonization in the Philippines* (Cambridge: Cambridge University Press, 2019); Julian Go, *American Empire and the Politics of Meaning: Elite Political Cultures in the Philippines and Puerto Rico during U.S. Colonialism* (Durham, NC: Duke University Press, 2007); A. J. Angulo, *Empire and Education: A History of Greed and Goodwill from the War of 1898 to the War on Terror* (New York: Palgrave Macmillan, 2012).

123   On race and hygiene in the Philippines, see Warwick Anderson, *Colonial Pathologies: American Tropical Medicine, Race, and Hygiene in the Philippines, 1898–1921* (Durham, NC: Duke University Press, 2006); Theresa Ventura, "Medicalizing 'Gutom' Hunger, Diet, and Beriberi during the American Period," *Philippine Studies: Historical and Ethnographic Viewpoints* 63, no. 1 (2015): 39–69; René Alexander Orquiza, "Kitchen as Classroom: Domestic Science in Philippine Bureau of Education Magazines, 1906–1932," *Asia Pacific Perspectives* 14, no. 1 (2016): 100–118; Susan K. Harris, *God's Arbiters: Americans and the Philippines, 1898–1902* (Oxford: Oxford University Press, 2011); Kristin L. Hoganson, *Fighting for American Manhood: How Gender Politics Provoked the Spanish-American and Philippine-American Wars* (New Haven, CT: Yale University Press, 1998); Paul Alexander Kramer, *The Blood of Government: Race, Empire, the United States, and the Philippines* (Chapel Hill: University of North Carolina Press, 2006).

124   Angulo, *Empire and Education*; Sutter, "Tropical Conquest and the Rise of the Environmental Management State"; Anne L. Foster, *Projections of Power: The United States and Europe in Colonial Southeast Asia, 1919–1941* (Durham, NC: Duke University Press, 2010); Jessica Wang, "Plants, Insects, and the Biological Management of American Empire: Tropical Agriculture in Early Twentieth-Century Hawai'i," *History and Technology* 35, no. 3 (2019): 203–36; Laura Briggs, *Reproducing Empire: Race, Sex, Science and U.S. Imperialism in Puerto Rico* (Berkeley: University of California Press, 2003); Solsiree del Moral, *Negotiating Empire: The Cultural Politics of Schools in Puerto Rico, 1898–1952* (Madison: University of Wisconsin Press, 2013).

125   Lisandro E. Claudio, "Beyond Colonial Miseducation: Internationalism and Deweyan Pedagogy in the American-Era Philippines," *Philippine Studies: Histori-*

cal and Ethnographic Viewpoints 63, no. 2 (2015): 193–221. For histories of some of these institutions, see Valeska Huber, "International Agendas and Local Manifestations: Universities in Cairo, Beirut and Jerusalem after World War I," *Prospects* 45, no. 1 (2015): 77–93; Betty S. Anderson, *The American University of Beirut: Arab Nationalism and Liberal Education* (Austin: University of Texas Press, 2011); Heather J. Sharkey, *American Evangelicals in Egypt: Missionary Encounters in an Age of Empire* (Princeton, NJ: Princeton University Press, 2015); Ronald Fettes Chapman, *Leonard Wood and Leprosy in the Philippines: The Culion Leper Colony, 1921–1927* (Washington, DC: University Press of America, 1982).

126 Lillian McCracken, November 27, 1926, p. 277 (emphasis in the original), Diary of Lillian McCracken.

127 For the laboratory as a space entangled in complicated networks rather than one sealed off from the world, see Bruno Latour and Steve Woolgar, *Laboratory Life* (Beverly Hills: Sage, 1979).

128 Robert D. Dean, *Imperial Brotherhood: Gender and the Making of Cold War Foreign Policy* (Amherst: University of Massachusetts Press, 2001); Paul Alexander Kramer, "Is the World Our Campus? International Students and U.S. Global Power in the Long Twentieth Century," *Diplomatic History* 33, no. 5 (2009): 775–806; Pietsch, "Commercial Travel and College Culture." On how US power structured the politics of postwar cultural exchange, see Sam Lebovic, *A Righteous Smokescreen: Postwar America and the Politics of Cultural Globalization* (Chicago: University of Chicago Press, 2022).

129 "Empire of Jim Crow" was a phrase used by Condoleezza Rice in a speech at the University of Alabama in October 2005. It has been developed by Nikhil Pal Singh. See Nikhil Pal Singh, "Beyond the 'Empire of Jim Crow': Race and War in Contemporary U.S. Globalism," *Japanese Journal of American Studies* 20 (2009): 89–111; Nikhil Pal Singh, *Race and America's Long War* (Berkeley: University of California Press, 2019).

130 Prices nearly doubled when the *Ryndam* arrived. *Binnacle* (University Travel Association), November 25, 1926, box 48, folder 4, 1DD6 Thwing Papers.

CHAPTER SIX

Portions of this chapter are reprinted and adapted by permission from Springer Nature: Tamson Pietsch, "Learning at Sea: Education aboard the 1926–27 Floating University," in *Shipboard Literary Cultures: Reading, Writing, and Performing at Sea*, ed. Laurence Publicover and Susann Liebich ([Cham, Switzerland]: Palgrave Macmillan, 2022), 239–61.

1 Tom Johnson to his mother, March 10, 1927, Johnson Papers.

2 Tom Johnson to his mother, March 25, 1927.

3 Mark Mazower, *No Enchanted Palace: The End of Empire and the Ideological Origins of the United Nations* (Princeton, NJ: Princeton University Press, 2009).

4 "Student Body on Trip around World," *York (PA) Daily Record*, September 18, 1926.

5 Clothing List, 1926, folder 2, Semester at Sea Archives 1926–1927.

6 Ryan Johnson, "European Cloth and 'Tropical' Skin: Clothing Material and Brit-

ish Ideas of Health and Hygiene in Tropical Climates," *Bulletin of the History of Medicine,* vol. 83, no. 3 (2009): 530–60.

7   Charles Ladd, *Around the World at Seventeen* (Rahway, NJ: Quinn and Boden, 1928), 67; *Binnacle* (University Travel Association), October 30, 1926, box 48, folder 4, 1DD6 Thwing Papers.

8   *Binnacle,* October 30, 1926. On imperial masculinity, adventure, and its remembrance, see M. Jones, "'National Hero and Very Queer Fish': Empire, Sexuality and the British Remembrance of General Gordon, 1918–72," *Twentieth Century British History* 26, no. 2 (2015): 175–202.

9   *Binnacle,* January 2, 1927.

10 "Everywhere we go we've been having a lot of fun." DeWitt Reddick's journal (Early Draft I), folder 1, Reddick Papers.

11 A. G. Hopkins, *American Empire: A Global History* (Princeton, NJ: Princeton University Press, 2018), chaps. 11 and 12.

12 *Binnacle,* November 3, 1926.

13 *Binnacle,* December 3, 1926.

14 Alfred Harmsworth Northcliffe, *My Journey round the World* (London: John Lane, 1923), 157, 161.

15 *Binnacle* (University Travel Association), December 3, 1926, box 48, folder 4, 1DD6 Thwing Papers.

16 James S. McKenzie, *A Broad Education Abroad: Readin', Writin', and Roamin'* (New York: Vantage Press, 1978), 116.

17 *Binnacle,* January 12, 1927.

18 Suggested Booklist [1926], box 48, folder 3, 1DD6 Thwing Papers.

19 *Binnacle,* December 3, 1926.

20 *Bulletin of Yale University—Obituary Records of Graduates of Yale University, Deceased during the Year 1936–1937* (New Haven, CT: Yale University, 1937), 195, http://mssa.library.yale.edu/obituary_record/1925_1952/1936-37.pdf.

21 Fred Elmer Marble, *Marble's round the World Travel-Guide* (New York: Harper and Bros., 1925), vii.

22 Marble, 40, 66, 229.

23 McKenzie, *A Broad Education Abroad,* 1.

24 *The Student Magellan* (New York: Voelcker Bros., 1927), 15.

25 *Binnacle* (University Travel Association), November 2, 1926, box 48, folder 4, 1DD6 Thwing Papers.

26 HCH and LWH Log Book Journal, 1926–27, p. 67, box 59, folder 4, Holling Papers.

27 *Binnacle,* November 25, 1926.

28 *Binnacle,* November 3, 1926.

29 *Binnacle,* November 5, 1926.

30 On antimodernism as an attempt to capture authenticity in the context of capitalist consumer culture, see T. J. Jackson Lears, *No Place of Grace: Antimodernism and the Transformation of American Culture, 1880–1920* (Chicago: University of Chicago Press, 1994.)

31 *Binnacle,* November 16, 1926; Ladd, *Around the World at Seventeen,* 110–20.

32 Lillian McCracken, p. 271, Diary of Lillian McCracken; McKenzie, *A Broad Education Abroad,* 68; Ladd, *Around the World at Seventeen,* 78.

33 McCracken, p. 276.

34 Tom Johnson to his mother, November 13, 1926, Johnson Papers.

35 Johnson to his mother, November 26, 1926.

36 Karl Gerth, *China Made: Consumer Culture and the Creation of the Nation*, vol. 224 (Harvard University Asia Center, 2003), 168; Rana Mitter, *A Bitter Revolution: China's Struggle with the Modern World* (Oxford: Oxford University Press, 2005).

37 Tom Johnson to his mother, November 26, 1926, Johnson Papers.

38 HCH and LWH Log Book Journal, 1926–27, November 15, 1926 (emphasis in the original), box 59, folder 4, Holling Papers.

39 *Binnacle* (University Travel Association), November 16, 1926, box 48, folder 4, 1DD6 Thwing Papers.

40 McKenzie, *A Broad Education Abroad*, 81.

41 McKenzie, 84; HCH and LWH Log Book Journal, 1926–27, November 21, 1926, box 59, folder 4, Holling Papers.

42 McKenzie, *A Broad Education Abroad*, 84.

43 Lillian McCracken, p. 290, Diary of Lillian McCracken.

44 *Binnacle* (University Travel Association), November 25, 126, box 48, folder 4, 1DD6 Thwing Papers. Dean Lough presided, and Deans Howes and Heckel gave speeches emphasizing the "ideals of the Cruise" and "the feeling of friendly curiosity and sympathy felt by the students toward the countries visited."

45 On transimperial collaboration, see Anne L. Foster, *Projections of Power: The United States and Europe in Colonial Southeast Asia, 1919–1941* (Durham, NC: Duke University Press, 2010), 49; Kristin L Hoganson and Jay Sexton, *Crossing Empires: Taking U.S. History into Transimperial Terrain* (Durham, NC: Duke University Press, 2020).

46 McKenzie, *A Broad Education Abroad*, 84.

47 Lillian McCracken, p. 293, Diary of Lillian McCracken.

48 HCH and LWH Log Book Journal, 1926–27, November 16, 1926, Holling Papers. See box 60 for companion drawings.

49 Matthew Hung, "Kowloon Walled City: Heterotopia in a Space of Disappearance," MAS Context, 2013, http://www.mascontext.com/tag/kowloon-walled-city; Greg Girard, Ian Lambot, and Charles Goddard, *City of Darkness: Life in Kowloon Walled City* (Surrey: Watermark, 1993), 95.

50 McKenzie, *A Broad Education Abroad*, 82.

51 Tom Johnson to his mother, November 16, 1926, Johnson Papers.

52 Johnson to his mother, November 16 1926.

53 *Binnacle* (University Travel Association), November 25 and 26, 1926, box 48, folder 4, 1DD6 Thwing Papers.

54 *Binnacle*, November 25 and 26, 1926; "Political affairs in the Philippine Islands," DeWitt Reddick's Journal (Early Draft I), folder 1, Reddick Papers. See also Yoshiko Nagano, *State and Finance in the Philippines, 1898–1941: The Mismanagement of an American Colony* (Singapore: NUS Press, 2015), 181–84.

55 *Binnacle*, November 26, 1926.

56 Ladd, *Around the World at Seventeen*, 154.

57 Lillian McCracken, pp. 102–4 (November 26–28, 1926), Diary of Lillian McCracken.

58 *Binnacle*, November 26, 1926.

59 Ladd, *Around the World at Seventeen*, 155.

60 *Binnacle*, November 30, 1926.

61 *Binnacle* (University Travel Association), December 2, 1926, box 48, folder 4, 1DD6 Thwing Papers; [Pearl Heckel], "A New Educational Project," folder 6, Heckel Papers.

62 HCH and LWH Log Book Journal, 1926–27, November 27–28, 1926, Holling Papers.

63 *Binnacle*, December 1, 1926.

64 *Binnacle*, November 30, 1926; *Binnacle*, December 2, 1926. On the tensions as well as collaborations between religious missionaries and empire, see Andrew Porter, *Religion Versus Empire? British Protestant Missionaries and Overseas Expansion, 1700–1914* (Manchester: Manchester University Press, 2004).

65 *Binnacle*, December 4, 1926.

66 HCH and LWH Log Book Journal, 1926–27, November 27–28, 1926, Holling Papers.

67 *Binnacle* (University Travel Association), December 3, 1926, box 48, folder 4, 1DD6 Thwing Papers.

68 McKenzie, *A Broad Education Abroad*, 53 (emphasis in the original.)

69 HCH and LWH Log Book Journal, 1926–27, November 27–28, 1926, Holling Papers.

70 [Pearl Heckel], "A New Educational Project," folder 6, Heckel Papers.

71 *Binnacle*, December 1, 1926; *Binnacle*, November 30, 1926.

72 Tom Johnson to his mother, 2 December 2, 1926 (emphasis in the original), Johnson Papers.

73 *Binnacle*, December 15, 1926.

74 *The Student Magellan*, 79.

75 *Binnacle*, December 21, 1926.

76 *The Student Magellan*, 79.

77 McKenzie, *A Broad Education Abroad*, 121.

78 Holling C. Holling to his mother and siblings, December 21, 1926, box 41, folder 8, Holling Papers.

79 Tom Johnson to his mother, December 16, 1926, Johnson Papers; Ladd, *Around the World at Seventeen*, 178.

80 Holling C. Holling to his mother and siblings, December 21, 1926.

81 Shore programs 1926, folder 4, Semester at Sea Archives 1926–1927; Holling C. Holling to his mother and siblings, December 21, 1926. On STOVIA, see Hans Pols, *Nurturing Indonesia: Medicine and Decolonisation in the Dutch East Indies* (Cambridge: Cambridge University Press, 2018).

82 Holling C. Holling to his mother and siblings, December 21, 1926.

83 *Binnacle* (University Travel Association), December 21, 1926, box 48, folder 4, 1DD6 Thwing Papers.

84 *Binnacle*, December 21, 1926.

85 *Binnacle*, December 22, 1926.

86 Ladd, *Around the World at Seventeen*, 176–77.

87 *Binnacle*, December 24, 1926.

88 *Binnacle*, December 23, 1926; *Binnacle*, December 24, 1926.

89 *Binnacle* (University Travel Association), December 22, 1926, box 48, folder 4, 1DD6 Thwing Papers.

90 *Binnacle*, December 24, 1926.

91 Northcliffe, *My Journey round the World*, 157.

92 *Binnacle*, December 23, 1926.

93 *Binnacle*, December 25, 1926.

94 *Binnacle*, December 31, 1926.

95 *The Student Magellan*, 93; *Binnacle,* January 9 and 13, 1927.

96 *Binnacle* (University Travel Association), January 13, 1927, box 48, folder 4, 1DD6 Thwing Papers.

97 *The Student Magellan*, 93.

98 *Binnacle*, January 11, 1927.

99 Tom Johnson, dated December 23, 1926, but written December 26 "Sunday Morning," Johnson Papers.

100 *The Student Magellan*, 85; *Binnacle*, March 4, 1927.

101 Robert Vitalis, *White World Order, Black Power Politics: The Birth of American International Relations* (Ithaca, NY: Cornell University Press, 2015), 66. Matthew Jacobson describes the "plaguing-if-quieter-sense-of self-doubt" and highly racialized anxiety underpinning confidence in American superiority. See Matthew Frye Jacobson, *Barbarian Virtues: The United States Encounters Foreign Peoples at Home and Abroad, 1876–1917* (New York: Hill and Wang, 2001), 3.

102 Paul Alexander Kramer, "Power and Connection: Imperial Histories of the United States in the World," *American Historical Review* 116, no. 5 (2011): 1369.

103 Hopkins, *American Empire*, 243; See also Daniel Immerwahr et al., "Roundtable XX-33 on A. G. Hopkins. American Empire: A Global History," H-Diplo (H-Net: Humanities and Social Sciences Online, April 23, 2019), https://networks.h-net .org/node/28443/discussions/4033475/roundtable-xx-33-ag-hopkins-american -empire-global-history.

104 *Binnacle* (University Travel Association), March 4, 1927, box 48, folder 4, 1DD6 Thwing Papers. On interracial marriage, see Kevin J. Mumford, *Interzones: Black/ White Sex Districts in Chicago and New York in the Early Twentieth Century* (New York: Columbia University Press, 1997).

105 *The Student Magellan*, 91.

106 *The Student Magellan*, 91; *Binnacle*, January 13, 1927.

107 *Binnacle*, February 3, 6, and 10, 1927; Harris, *Photographs of the First University World Cruise*, nos. 982, 982a.

108 *Binnacle*, January 19, 1927.

109 Stephanie Stidham Rogers, *Inventing the Holy Land: American Protestant Pilgrimage to Palestine, 1865–1941* (Lanham MD, Lexington Books, 2011), 4.

110 *Binnacle* (University Travel Association), January 19, 1927, box 48, folder 4, 1DD6 Thwing Papers.

111 Rogers, *Inventing the Holy Land*, 1.

112 Rogers, 133.

113 Rogers, 22.

114 Rogers, 4.

115 Tamson Pietsch, "Elizabeth Lippincott McQueen: Thinking International Peace in an Air-Minded Age," in *Women's International Thought: A New History*, ed. Patricia Owens and Katharina Rietzler (Cambridge: Cambridge University Press, 2021), 119–20.

116 Suggested Booklist [1926], box 48, folder 3, 1DD6 Thwing Papers.

117 Lillian McCracken, p. 215 (January 24, 1927), Diary of Lillian McCracken.

118 McCracken, p. 215.

119 McCracken, p. 215.
120 Pietsch, "Elizabeth Lippincott McQueen"; Rogers, *Inventing the Holy Land*, 134.
121 Ladd, *Around the World at Seventeen*, 231; Lillian McCracken, p. 216 (January 15, 1927), Diary of Lillian McCracken.
122 McCracken, p. 215 (January 24, 1927).
123 *Binnacle* (University Travel Association), January 28, 1927, box 48, folder 4, 1DD6 Thwing Papers; Ladd, *Around the World at Seventeen*, 231.
124 HCH and LWH Log Book Journal, 1926–27, January 24, 1927, box 59, folder 4, Holling Papers.
125 Ladd, *Around the World at Seventeen*, 229.
126 *Binnacle*, January 28, 1927.
127 Lillian McCracken, p. 220, Diary of Lillian McCracken.
128 HCH and LWH Log Book Journal, 1926–27, January 26, 1927, box 59, folder 4, Holling Papers.
129 Rogers, *Inventing the Holy Land*, 61; *Binnacle* (University Travel Association), January 28, 1927, box 48, folder 4, 1DD6 Thwing Papers.
130 Harvey Levenstein, *Seductive Journey: American Tourists in France from Jefferson to the Jazz Age* (Chicago: University of Chicago Press, 2000), 225–27.
131 *Binnacle*, October 16, 1926; "The Second AEF," *American Legion Weekly*, February 5, 1926. In fact, the *Ryndam* would be among the ships carrying the American ex-servicemen across the Atlantic. *Binnacle,* February 15, 1927.
132 David William Lloyd, *Battlefield Tourism: Pilgrimage and the Commemoration of the Great War in Britain, Australia and Canada, 1919–1939* (London: A and C Black, 2014); Tony Walter, "War Grave Pilgrimage," in *Pilgrimage in Popular Culture*, ed. Ian Reader and Tony Walter (Basingstoke, UK: Macmillan, 1993), 64–65.
133 Lillian McCracken, p. 71, Diary of Lillian McCracken. For war loans of 1924–25, see Frank Costigliola, *Awkward Dominion: American Political, Economic, and Cultural Relations with Europe, 1919–1933* (Ithaca, NY: Cornell University Press, 1984), 173. Later statistics put the French casualties at 1.35 million and war debt at 4.14 billion francs. See "The French Debt to the United States," in *Editorial Research Reports 1925* (Washington, DC: CQ Press, 1925), 2:327, http://library .cqpress.com/cqresearcher/cqresrre1925061700; Patrice Baubeau, "War Finance (France)," in *1914–1918 Online: International Encyclopedia of the First World War*, ed. Ute Daniel et al. (Berlin: Freie Universität Berlin, 2014), doi:10.15463/ ie1418.10022.
134 Lillian McCracken, p. 71, Diary of Lillian McCracken.
135 McCracken, pp. 73–74; *Binnacle* (University Travel Association), March 26, 1927, box 48, folder 4, 1DD6 Thwing Papers.
136 *The Student Magellan*, 169.
137 McKenzie, *A Broad Education Abroad*, 194; Ladd, *Around the World at Seventeen*, 282.
138 Levenstein, *Seductive Journey*, 271–73.
139 Lillian McCracken, p. 74 (emphasis in the original), Diary of Lillian McCracken.
140 McCracken, p. 74.
141 *The Student Magellan*, 169.
142 McCracken, p. 74; *The Student Magellan*, 169; Ladd, *Around the World at Seventeen*, 281.

143 Elizabeth Borja, "The Grave of Quentin Roosevelt," Smithsonian National Air and Space Museum, July 14, 2018, https://airandspace.si.edu/stories/editorial/grave-quentin-roosevelt; John W Graham, *The Gold Star Mother Pilgrimages of the 1930s: Overseas Grave Visitations by Mothers and Widows of Fallen U.S. World War I Soldiers* (Jefferson, NC: McFarland, 2005), 92.

144 Steven Trout, *On the Battlefield of Memory: The First World War and American Remembrance, 1919–1941* (Tuscaloosa: University of Alabama Press, 2010), 223, 225.

145 Ladd, *Around the World at Seventeen*, 282.

146 Harris, *Photographs of the First University World Cruise*, no. 793.

147 *Binnacle* (University Travel Association), March 11, 1927, box 48, folder 4, 1DD6 Thwing Papers.

148 "Paris," DeWitt Reddick's journal adapted as news stories, folder 3, Reddick Papers.

149 "Paris," Reddick's journal adapted as news stories.

150 "Paris," Reddick's journal adapted as news stories.

151 McKenzie, *A Broad Education Abroad*, 195.

152 HCH and LWH Log Book Journal, 1926–27, March 16, 1927, box 59, folder 4, Holling Papers.

153 *The Student Magellan*, 169. For "le tumulte noir," see William A. Shack, *Harlem in Montmartre: A Paris Jazz Story between the Great Wars*, vol. 4 (Berkeley: University of California Press, 2001), 33, 38.

154 Michael Goebel, *Anti-imperial Metropolis: Interwar Paris and the Seeds of Third World Nationalism* (Cambridge: Cambridge University Press, 2015).

155 Nancy L. Green, *The Other Americans in Paris: Businessmen, Countesses, Wayward Youth, 1880–1941* (Chicago: University of Chicago Press, 2014), 3; Brooke L. Blower, *Becoming Americans in Paris: Transatlantic Politics and Culture between the World Wars* (Oxford: Oxford University Press, 2011); Goebel, *Anti-imperial Metropolis*.

156 These are not on the official program, and they do not appear in any of the surviving travel accounts. Hugh A. Smith, "The American University Union at Paris," *French Review* 3, no. 3 (1930): 161–68.

157 Levenstein, *Seductive Journey*, 237–52.

158 HCH and LWH Log Book Journal, 1926–27, March 16, 1927, box 59, folder 4, Holling Papers; Lillian McCracken, p. 76, Diary of Lillian McCracken. The painting was hung in a complete, uninterrupted circle; visitors descended into a tunnel to emerge right in the middle of it. It was inaugurated by French President Raymond Poincaré less than a month before the end of the war. See Mark Levitch, *"Panthéon de la Guerre": Reconfiguring a Panorama of the Great War* (Columbia: University of Missouri Press, 2006).

159 *The Student Magellan*, 169.

160 Ladd, *Around the World at Seventeen*, 280–81. See also Brooke L. Blower, "Nation of Outposts: Forts, Factories, Bases, and the Making of American Power," *Diplomatic History* 41, no. 3 (2017): 439–59.

161 Ladd, *Around the World at Seventeen*, 283; Green, *The Other Americans in Paris*, 124.

162 Tom Johnson to his mother, April 10, 1927, Thomas H. Johnson Papers.

163 Charles E. Gauss, Log Book 1926–27, April 12, 1927, Gauss Collection.

164 *The Student Magellan*, 201.

165 Kenneth McNeil, "Ballads and Borders," in *The Edinburgh Companion to Sir Walter Scott*, ed. Fiona Robertson (Edinburgh: Edinburgh University Press, 2012), 31.

166 Ann Rigney, *The Afterlives of Walter Scott: Memory on the Move* (Oxford: Oxford University Press, 2012), 1.

167 Mark Twain, *Life on the Mississippi* (1883), quoted in Stuart Kelly, *Scott-Land: The Man Who Invented a Nation* (Edinburgh: Birlinn, 2011).

168 Alastair Durie, "Tourism in Victorian Scotland: The Case of Abbotsford," *Scottish Economic and Social History* 12, no. 1 (1992): 42–54; Allison Lockwood, *Passionate Pilgrims: The American Traveler in Great Britain, 1800–1914* (Madison, NJ: Fairleigh Dickinson University Press, 1981), 70–72.

169 W. E. B. DuBois, "Criteria of Negro Art," *Crisis* 32, no. 6 (1926): 290.

170 Rigney, *The Afterlives of Walter Scott*, 124. Dixon titled the first novel of his trilogy after the famous biblical phrase used in Ivanhoe, "the leopard will not change his spots"; William Pembroke Fetridge, *The American Travellers' Guides* (Boston: Fetridge, 1878).

171 *The Student Magellan*, 201.

172 Ladd, *Around the World at Seventeen*, 307.

173 Lillian McCracken, p. 309 (April 11, 1927), Diary of Lillian McCracken.

174 Up to a quarter of the remaining passengers chose to travel overland via train or even bicycle. McKenzie, *A Broad Education Abroad*, 214; *Binnacle* (University Travel Association), April 10, 1927, box 48, folder 4, 1DD6 Thwing Papers.

175 Tom Johnson to his mother, April 15, 1927, Johnson Papers.

176 McKenzie, *A Broad Education Abroad*, 215.

177 Julia Thomas, *Shakespeare's Shrine: The Bard's Birthplace and the Invention of Stratford-upon-Avon* (Philadelphia: University of Pennsylvania Press, 2012), 123.

178 McKenzie, *A Broad Education Abroad*, 216.

179 *Binnacle* (University Travel Association), April 14, 1927, box 48, folder 4, 1DD6 Thwing Papers; Ladd, *Around the World at Seventeen*, 309.

180 *Binnacle*, January 9, 1927; *Binnacle*, January 11, 1927.

181 Paraphrasing Rogers's definition of pilgrimage. Rogers, *Inventing the Holy Land*, 4. See also Juan Eduardo Campo, "American Pilgrimage Landscapes," *Annals of the American Academy of Political and Social Science* 558 (1998): 40–56; Richard Scriven, "Geographies of Pilgrimage: Meaningful Movements and Embodied Mobilities," *Geography Compass* 8, no. 4 (2014): 249–61; Ruth Harris, *Lourdes: Body and Spirit in the Secular Age* (London: Penguin UK, 2008); Ian Reader, *Pilgrimage in the Marketplace* (New York: Routledge, 2013).

182 For an example of European voyagers framing travel across space as travel through time, see Harriet Guest, *Empire, Barbarism, and Civilisation: Captain Cook, William Hodges and the Return to the Pacific* (Cambridge: Cambridge University Press, 2007).

183 See *Binnacle* (University Travel Association), September 21, 1926, box 48, folder 4, 1DD6 Thwing Papers; "College Days on Rolling Waves," *Democrat and Chronicle* (Rochester, NY), May 11, 1924; "Floating University to Tour the World," *Nanaimo (BC) Daily News*, May 16, 1924.

184 Tamson Pietsch, "A British Sea: Making Sense of Global Space in the Late Nineteenth Century," *Journal of Global History* 5, no. 3 (2010): 423–46.

185 They were far more uncertain about American cultural superiority than Jonathan Zimmerman suggests was usual in the 1920s. See Jonathan Zimmerman, *Innocents*

Abroad: American Teachers in the American Century (Cambridge, MA: Harvard University Press, 2007), 4.

186 "Ryndam Bound for Homeland," *Christian Science Monitor*, April 30, 1927.

187 "Ryndam Bound for Homeland."

188 Lloyd, *Battlefield Tourism*, 28.

189 On travel, tourism, and authenticity literature, see Agnieszka Sobocinska and Richard White, "Travel Writing and Tourism," in *The Cambridge History of Travel Writing*, ed. Nandini Das and Tim Youngs (Cambridge: Cambridge University Press, 2019), 565–80; James Buzard, *The Beaten Track: European Tourism, Literature, and the Ways to "Culture," 1800–1918* (Oxford: Oxford University Press, 1993); Dean MacCannell, *The Tourist: A New Theory of the Leisure Class* (New York: Schocken Books, 1976).

190 On authenticity, modernity, and colonialism in the context of art history, see Sandy Prita Meier and Isabelle Montin, "Authenticity and Its Discontents: Making Modernist Art Histories 'African' and 'Middle Eastern,'" *Multitudes* 53, no. 2 (2013): 77–96; John B. Hertz, "Authenticity, Colonialism, and the Struggle with Modernity," *Journal of Architectural Education* 55, no. 4 (2002): 220–27.

191 *The Student Magellan*, 180–82.

192 Ann Laura Stoler, *Along the Archival Grain: Epistemic Anxieties and Colonial Common Sense* (Princeton, NJ: Princeton University Press, 2008).

193 Wendy Martin, "North American Travel Writing," in *The Cambridge History of Travel Writing*, ed. Nandini Das and Tim Youngs (Cambridge: Cambridge University Press, 2019), 262.

CHAPTER SEVEN

1 Tokyo and Kamakura Shore Program, folder 4, Semester at Sea Archives 1926–1927; *Binnacle* (University Travel Association), November 4, 1926, box 48, folder 4, 1DD6 Thwing Papers.

2 "Professor Alfred Weber Sent to America," *Heidelberger Neueste Nachrichten*, September 9, 1925, newspaper clippings by the Press Department of the Baden state government, GLA 235, no. 4612, Generallandesarchiv, State Archives of Baden-Württemberg; Berlin Shore Program, folder 4, Semester at Sea Archives 1926–1927. Thanks to Katharina Rietzler and Heike Jöns for helpful discussions about Alfred Weber and to Heike in particular for alerting me to this newspaper article.

3 "Kurt Wiedenfeld," s.v. Catalogus Professorum Halensis (Martin Luther University Halle-Wittenberg), accessed June 1, 2022, https://www.catalogus-professorum-halensis.de/wiedenfeldkurt.html.

4 Colin Loader, *Alfred Weber and the Crisis of Culture, 1890–1933* (Basingstoke, UK: Palgrave Macmillan, 2012); Colin Loader, "Free Floating: The Intelligentsia in the Work of Alfred Weber and Karl Mannheim," *German Studies Review* 20, no. 2 (1997): 217–34.

5 The German statesman and Nobel Prize recipient Gustav Stresemann was particularly identified with this phrase. Gustav Stresemann, "Nobel Lecture: The New Germany" (lecture transcript, Oslo University, June 29, 1927), https://www.nobelprize.org/prizes/peace/1926/stresemann/lecture/.

6 See Katharina Rietzler, *International Experts, International Citizens: American*

Philanthropy, International Relations and the Problem of the Public, 1913–1954 (forthcoming), chap. 6; Steven D. Korenblat, "A School for the Republic? Cosmopolitans and Their Enemies at the Deutsche Hochschule für Politik, 1920–1933," *Central European History* 39 (2009): 394–430.

7 For influential accounts of culture as a form of diplomacy in US foreign relations, see Frank A. Ninkovich, *The Diplomacy of Ideas: US Foreign Policy and Cultural Relations, 1938–1950* (Cambridge: Cambridge University Press, 1981); Emily S. Rosenberg, *Spreading the American Dream: American Economic and Cultural Expansion, 1890–1945* (New York: Hill and Wang, 1982); Laura Belmonte, *Selling the American Way: U.S. Propaganda and the Cold War* (Philadelphia: University of Pennsylvania Press, 2008); Justin Hart, *Empire of Ideas: The Origins of Public Diplomacy and the Transformation of U. S. Foreign Policy* (New York: Oxford University Press, 2013).

8 Berlin Shore Program, folder 4, Semester at Sea Archives 1926–1927.

9 Elizabeth Lippincott McQueen, "Highlights of Pioneer University Cruise," box 3, folder 12, 0055 Library of Aeronautical History, Women's International Association of Aeronautics (WIAA) Records, University of Southern California Libraries Special Collections.

10 Lillian McCracken, p. 92, Diary of Lillian McCracken; "College Cruise around the World 1926–1927: Administrative Staff, Faculty and Outline of Courses" (University Travel Association), 331642A, University of Michigan Library.

11 *Binnacle* (University Travel Association), April 2, 1927, box 48, folder 4, 1DD6 Thwing Papers; *The Student Magellan* (New York: Voelcker Bros., 1927), 185.

12 E. Mowbray Tate, *Transpacific Steam: The Story of Steam Navigation from the Pacific Coast of North America to the Far East and the Antipodes, 1867–1941* (New York: Cornwall Books, 1986), 178.

13 HCH and LWH Log Book Journal 1926–27, March 26–31, 1927, box 59, folder 4, Holling Papers.

14 Charles Ladd, *Around the World at Seventeen* (Rahway, NJ: Quinn and Boden, 1928), 290–96.

15 *Binnacle*, April 2, 1927 (from Berliner Nachtausgabe, March 28, 1927); *Binnacle*, April 9, 1927.

16 K. S. Chang, "Ryndam University Boys Have Rotten Time Athletically," *China Press* (Shanghai), November 19, 1926.

17 "The Floating University That, Thank God, Will Not Visit Curaçao," *Amigoe di Curaçao*, March 26, 1927, trans. Kirsten Kamphuis. Other papers in which excerpts were quoted included *Leeuwarder Courant*, February 16, 1927 (a Dutch regional newspaper); *Nieuwsblad van Friesland*, February 18, 1927 (a Dutch regional newspaper); *Het Centrum*, February 21, 1927 (a Dutch national Catholic newspaper); *Het Vaderland*, February 15, 1927 (a Dutch national progressive newspaper); *De Gooi- en Eemlander*, February 16, 1927 (a Dutch regional newspaper).

18 "The Bourgeoisie Is 'Studying,'" *De Tribune* (Amsterdam), February 17, 1927, trans. Kirsten Kamphuis.

19 "Boozing around the World," *Voorwaarts, Sociaal-Democratisch Dagblad* (Rotterdam), February 15, 1927, trans. Kirsten Kamphuis.

20 *Binnacle* (University Travel Association), September 23, 1926, box 48, folder 4, 1DD6 Thwing Papers.

21 *Binnacle*, January 12, 1927.

22 *Binnacle*, October 27, 1926.

23 *Binnacle*, December 21, 1926.

24 Holland America Line to New York Agent, November 2, 1926, DirectieV, 02/v131.1 (October 1926–April 1927), 318 Archieven van de Holland-Amerika Lijn (HAL); *Binnacle*, October 14, 1926.

25 Leonard B. Aliwanag, "Filipino Pioneer: Merchant Marine, Movie Extra and Hotel Worker," oral history interview, August 19, 1976, FIL-KNG76-50cm, Washington State Oral/Aural History Program Interviews, Center for Pacific Northwest Studies, Heritage Resources, Western Washington University, Bellingham.

26 Aliwanag, "Filipino Pioneer."

27 Aliwanag.

28 Aliwanag.

29 Aliwanag.

30 Engseng Ho, "Empire through Diasporic Eyes: A View from the Other Boat," *Comparative Studies in Society and History* 46, no. 2 (2004): 240.

31 *Binnacle* (University Travel Association), November 25, 1926, box 48, folder 4, 1DD6 Thwing Papers.

32 Goolam Vahed, "Passengers, Partnerships, and Promissory Notes: Gujarati Traders in Colonial Natal, 1870–1920," *International Journal of African Historical Studies* 38, no. 3 (2005): 32; Judith M. Brown, *Global South Asians: Introducing the Modern Diaspora* (Cambridge: Cambridge University Press, 2006); G. Balachandran, *Globalizing Labour? Indian Seafarers and World Shipping, c. 1870–1945* (New Delhi: Oxford University Press, 2012); Sujit Sivasundaram, *Waves across the South: A New History of Revolution and Empire* (New York: Harper Collins, 2020). On Dutch shipping and anticolonial networks in the interwar period, see Kris Alexanderson, *Subversive Seas: Anticolonial Networks across the Twentieth-Century Dutch Empire* (Cambridge: Cambridge University Press, 2019).

33 James S. McKenzie, *A Broad Education Abroad: Readin', Writin', and Roamin'* (New York: Vantage Press, 1978), 83.

34 Engseng Ho, *The Graves of Tarim: Genealogy and Mobility across the Indian Ocean* (Berkeley: University of California Press, 2006).

35 See chapter 5 and Lillian McCracken, p. 290, Diary of Lillian McCracken.

36 On the different speeds of modernity, see Valeska Huber, *Channelling Mobilities: Migration and Globalisation in the Suez Canal Region and Beyond, 1869–1914* (Cambridge: Cambridge University Press, 2013).

37 *Binnacle* (University Travel Association), November 15 and 16, 1926, and March 4, 1927, box 48, folder 4, 1DD6 Thwing Papers. This method for coaling the ship was also used at Batavia, Bombay, Port Said, Naples, and Algiers, though it did not attract the same attention—probably because it took place while the passengers were off the ship.

38 Ladd, *Around the World at Seventeen*, 138.

39 *Binnacle*, November 21, 1926; Walter Conger Harris, *Photographs of the First University World Cruise* (New York: University Travel Association, 1927), no. 227.

40 *Binnacle*, December 22, 1926.

41 *Binnacle*, December 22, 1926; HCH and LWH Log Book Journal 1926–27, December 16, 1926, box 59, folder 4, Holling Papers; Holling C. Holling to his mother, December 21, 1926, box 41, folder 8, Holling Papers.

42 The disability studies scholar F. K. Campbell discusses such spaces of encounter as

a "third space" that is strange for all parties. See Fiona Kumari Campbell, *Contours of Ableism: The Production of Disability and Abledness* (London: Palgrave Macmillan UK, 2009). On how mechanisms of bodily comportment were rendered fragile and unstable at sea, see Tamson Pietsch, "Bodies at Sea: Travelling to Australia in the Age of Sail," *Journal of Global History* 11, no. 2 (July 2016): 209–28.

43 Account printed in McIntosh's magazine, *Floating University: The World Its Campus (1927–28)* (International University Cruise Inc.), New York Public Library, March 1927.

44 *The Record of the Class of 1925* (Haverford, PA: Haverford College, 1925), 107.

45 *Binnacle* (University Travel Association), January 8 and February 16 and 18, 1927; February 16, 1927, box 48, folder 4, 1DD6 Thwing Papers.

46 *Binnacle*, September 17, 1926. On sports and "Americanization," see Harald Fischer-Tiné, "Fitness for Modernity? The YMCA and Physical-Education Schemes in Late-Colonial South Asia (circa 1900–40)," *Modern Asian Studies* 53, no. 2 (2019): 512–59; Gerald R. Gems, *The Athletic Crusade: Sport and American Cultural Imperialism* (Omaha: University of Nebraska Press, 2006); Allen Guttmann, *Games and Empires: Modern Sports and Cultural Imperialism*. (New York: Columbia University Press, 1994); Barbara J. Keys, *Globalizing Sport: National Rivalry and International Community in the 1930s*, Harvard Historical Studies, vol. 152 (Cambridge, MA: Harvard University Press, 2006); Thomas W. Zeiler, *Ambassadors in Pinstripes: The Spalding World Baseball Tour and the Birth of the American Empire* (Lanham, MD: Rowman and Littlefield, 2006); Steven W. Pope, "Rethinking Sport, Empire, and American Exceptionalism," *Sport History Review* 38, no. 2 (2007): 92–120; the special issue of *International Journal of the History of Sport* 28 (2011) devoted to American imperialism in the realm of sports.

47 *Binnacle*, September 17 and 23, 1926.

48 *Binnacle*, October 17 and 23, 1926; November 25, 1926; and January 28, 1927; "They Learned Basketball Here, Too!" *China Press* (Shanghai), November 19, 1926; Chang, "Ryndam University Boys Have Rotten Time Athletically"; *The Student Magellan*, 31. The result of the baseball game in Cuba was unrecorded.

49 *Binnacle* (University Travel Association), October 23, 1926, and January 28, 1927, box 48, folder 4, 1DD6 Thwing Papers; *Floating University: The World Its Campus (1927–28)*, March 1927.

50 *Binnacle*, December 1, 1926.

51 *Binnacle*, December 10, 1926; Mark Dyreson, James Anthony Mangan, and Roberta J Park, *Mapping an Empire of American Sport: Expansion, Assimilation, Adaptation and Resistance* (London: Routledge, 2013).

52 *Binnacle*, December 10, 1926; Gems, *The Athletic Crusade*, chaps. 2–4.

53 *Binnacle*, December 10, 1926.

54 *Binnacle*, November 25, 1926.

55 *Binnacle*, December 10, 1926.

56 Fischer-Tiné, "Fitness for Modernity?," 526–29; Clifford Putney, *Muscular Christianity: Manhood and Sports in Protestant America, 1880–1920* (Cambridge, MA: Harvard University Press, 2009), 69–72.

57 Fischer-Tiné, "Fitness for Modernity?," 527.

58 William J. Baker, *Playing with God: Religion and Modern Sport* (Cambridge, MA: Harvard University Press, 2009), 50–55; Andrew D. Morris, *Marrow of the Nation: A History of Sport and Physical Culture in Republican China*, vol. 10 (Berkeley:

University of California Press, 2004); Stefan Hübner, "'Uplifting the Weak and Degenerated Races of East Asia': American and Indigenous Views of Sport and Body in Early Twentieth-Century East Asia," in *Race and Racism in Modern East Asia* (Leiden: Brill, 2015), 196–216.

59 What Harald Fischer-Tiné has called a "somatic Orientalism." Fischer-Tiné, "Fitness for Modernity?," 548.

60 *Binnacle* (University Travel Association), November 4, 1926, box 48, folder 4, 1DD6 Thwing Papers.

61 *Binnacle*, December 2, 1926.

62 *Binnacle*, January 9 and 13, 1927.

63 *Binnacle*, November 30, 1926.

64 Ladd, *Around the World at Seventeen*, 295. In use from 1823 to 1914, the Studentenkarzer was a place where students were incarcerated by the university for disorderly conduct offenses.

65 Johnson to his mother, mid-January 1927, Johnson Papers.

66 *Binnacle* (University Travel Association), January 2, 1927, box 48, folder 4, 1DD6 Thwing Papers.

67 *Binnacle*, December 31, 1926, and January 11, 1927; Rudhramoorthy Cheran, *Pathways of Dissent: Tamil Nationalism in Sri Lanka* (New Delhi: Sage Publications India, 2009).

68 *Binnacle*, January 11, 1927.

69 *Binnacle*, January 13, 1927. The author argued that the Indian nationalists were "trying to put into effect the same principles, and in fact even milder ones than [the United States] used in our own fight" against the British.

70 Ho, "Empire through Diasporic Eyes."

71 *Binnacle*, January 9, 1927.

72 "The Canton Incident," folder 4, Semester at Sea Archives 1926–1927. Paul Kramer argues that US imperialism worked through nationalism. US agencies presented their own crypto-imperial schemes as "radical, modernist breaks with a homogenized Western European 'imperial' past and present characterized by repression, corruption, and decadence." Paul Alexander Kramer, "Power and Connection: Imperial Histories of the United States in the World," *American Historical Review* 116, no. 5 (2011): 1369.

73 "The Canton Incident," folder 4, Semester at Sea Archives 1926–1927.

74 *Binnacle* (University Travel Association), December 3, 1926, box 48, folder 4, 1DD6 Thwing Papers.

75 *Binnacle*, December 1, 1926.

76 Written by "J.I.M.," *Binnacle*, February 3, 1927. Henry Allen later helped "Frank America" get a job running a newspaper in Thailand. Box C17, Allen Papers.

77 *Binnacle*, November 15, 1926, and January 2, 1927.

78 *Binnacle*, January 18, 1927.

79 *Binnacle*, January 14, 1927.

80 *Binnacle*, March 11, 1927.

81 *Binnacle*, March 14, 1927.

82 *Binnacle*, March 11, 1927.

83 *Binnacle*, February 3, 1927.

84 *Binnacle*, March 11 and 14, 1927.

85 Tom Johnson to his mother, March 10, 1927, Johnson Papers.

86 Gian Giacomo Migone, *The United States and Fascist Italy: The Rise of American*

Finance in Europe, trans. Molly Tambor (Cambridge: Cambridge University Press, 2015). See also "Europe's Ill Will, Former Gov. Allen Finds, Due to Error," *Washington Post*, August 17, 1927.

87 Travel diaries, box 4A, MS 883 Allen-Holmes Collection (Henry J. Allen Papers), Kansas State Historical Society, Topeka.

88 Tom Johnson to his mother, March 3, 1927, Johnson Papers.

89 *Binnacle* (University Travel Association), February 26, 1927, box 48, folder 4, 1DD6 Thwing Papers; R. Alton Lee, *Farmers vs. Wage Earners: Organized Labor in Kansas, 1860–1960* (Omaha: University of Nebraska Press, 2005).

90 "Rome—Mussolini," DeWitt Reddick's journal adapted as news stories, folder 3, Reddick Papers; Harris, *Photographs of the First University World Cruise*, no. 262.

91 *Binnacle*, March 26, 1927; *The Student Magellan*, 141.

92 "Rome—Mussolini," Reddick's journal adapted as news stories.

93 Charles E. Gauss, Log Book 1926–27, February 22, 1927, Gauss Collection.

94 "Rome—Mussolini," Reddick's journal adapted as news stories.

95 *Binnacle* (University Travel Association), March 14, 1927, box 48, folder 4, 1DD6 Thwing Papers.

96 Sociologist Ari Adut has argued that the public sphere is "the realm of appearances." Ari Adut, *Reign of Appearances: The Misery and Splendor of the Public Sphere* (Cambridge: Cambridge University Press, 2018), x. See Frank America's description of Turkish, French, and other newspapers carrying reports of the cruise. *Binnacle*, February 3, 1927.

97 "Because this is about the next generation of American intellectuals, this is of the biggest importance, because only a view of the Indies can incite and sustain the well-deserved appreciation!" "[No Title]," *De Indische Courant* (Indonesia), December 21, 1926, trans. Kirsten Kamphuis.

98 "Rome," DeWitt Reddick's journal (Early Draft II), folder 2, Reddick Papers.

99 Tom Johnson to his mother, March 3, 1927, Johnson Papers.

100 Ching-Hwang Yen, *The Overseas Chinese and the 1911 Revolution: With Special Reference to Singapore and Malaya* (Kuala Lumpur: Oxford University Press, 1976); *Binnacle* (University Travel Association), December 10, 1926, box 48, folder 4, 1DD6 Thwing Papers.

101 "Rubber Exporter Here from East," *New York Times*, September 30, 1927.

102 For influential work on the uneven and unequal nature of globalization, see Frederick Cooper, "What Is the Concept of Globalization Good For? An African Historian's Perspective," *African Affairs* 100, no. 399 (2001): 189–213; Frederick Cooper, *Colonialism in Question* (Berkeley: University of California Press, 2005).

103 McKenzie, *A Broad Education Abroad*, 220.

104 *Binnacle* (University Travel Association), April 23, 1927, box 48, folder 4, 1DD6 Thwing Papers.

105 *Binnacle*, April 26, 1927.

106 *Binnacle*, April 23 and 26, 1927.

CHAPTER EIGHT

1 "Floating Co-ed College Back; Liquor Was Biggest Obstacle," *Dothan (AL) Eagle*, May 9, 1927.

2 "First Floating College Docks," *Cornell Daily Sun* (Cornell University), May 2,

1927; "Floating University Back after 'round-World Cruise," *Belvidere (IL) Daily Republican*, May 2, 1927.

3   "Floating University Back after 'round-World Cruise."

4   "Floating University Is Back to New York," *Iola (KS) Daily Register and Evening News*, May 2, 1927.

5   "Members of Floating University Return," *North Adams (MA) Transcript*, May 5, 1927; "Spring Travels Along with Them," *Battle Creek (MI) Enquirer*, May 5, 1927; "Paul Green Will Tell DeMolays of Floating College," *Dispatch* (Moline, IL), May 10, 1927.

6   Imogene Stanley, "Romances Flourish on First Trip of Sea University," *Daily News* (New York), May 3, 1927; "Co-ed of Floating University Tells of Many Gossips," *Palm Beach (FL) Post*, May 3, 1927.

7   "Knowledge Taken from the World Helps," *Huntington (IN) Herald*, May 3, 1927.

8   "Students on Ship School Visit Cafes," *Bee* (Danville, VA), March 18, 1927.

9   Albert K. Heckel, "The enterprise can be pronounced a success" [1927] and Account of the Voyage, p. 5 [1927], folder 6, Heckel Papers.

10   "First Floating College Docks."

11   "Floaters Home," *Time*, May 16, 1927, 28–29.

12   "Floating School Defended by Allen," *New York Times*, April 12, 1927.

13   Charles H. Phelps, "The Floating University," *School and Society* 25, no. 645 (May 7, 1927): 547–48.

14   See chapter 4. For the shifting logics of exclusion, see John R Thelin, *A History of American Higher Education* (Baltimore: Johns Hopkins University Press, 2011), 186; Roger L. Geiger, *The History of American Higher Education: Learning and Culture from the Founding to World War II* (Princeton, NJ: Princeton University Press, 2015), 404.

15   McIntosh's magazine, *Floating University: The World Its Campus (1927–28)* (International University Cruise Inc.), New York Public Library, April 1927.

16   Andrew J. McIntosh, "Why the Floating University Is Co-educational," *School and Society* 25, no. 637 (1927): 320–21.

17   Joan Elias Gore has argued that in the 1920s, the "earlier image of the college woman as serious of purpose, destined to achieve academically and then to serve, gave way to the image of the fun-loving woman pursuing higher education for frivolous reasons." Joan Elias Gore, "Discourse and Traditional Belief: An Analysis of American Undergraduate Study Abroad" (PhD diss., University of London, 2000), 125nn112–13; Alys Eve Weinbaum et al., eds., *The Modern Girl around the World: Consumption, Modernity, and Globalization* (Durham, NC: Duke University Press, 2008).

18   McIntosh, "Why the Floating University Is Co-educational," 320.

19   *Floating University: The World Its Campus (1927–28)*, April 1927.

20   *Floating University: The World Its Campus (1927–28)*, April 1927.

21   Phelps, "The Floating University," 457–58.

22   Tom Arnold-Forster, "Democracy and Expertise in the Lippmann-Terman Controversy," *Modern Intellectual History* 16, no. 2 (2019): 580.

23   "Good Will to Men," *Harvard Crimson*, May 16, 1927.

24   Max Moeller, "Floating University," Hagley Museum and Library, January 22, 2016, archived copy, April 21, 2021, Internet Archive Wayback Machine, https://web.archive.org/web/20210421005826/https://www.hagley.org/fr/about-us/

news/published-collections-world-its-campus; "'University Afloat' Abandons Cruise," *New York Times*, September 13, 1927.

25 Douglas C. Ridgley, "The First College Cruise around the World: An Educational Experiment," *Journal of Geography* 27, no. 2 (1928): 70–72.

26 Ridgley, 72.

27 Ridgley, 73.

28 Ridgley, 75.

29 George Edwin Howes, "Report of Scholastic Work on the University Cruise around the World, for the Year 1926–27," loose-leaf sheet in "College Cruise around the World 1926–1927: Administrative Staff, Faculty and Outline of Courses" (University Travel Association), University of Michigan Library.

30 Howes.

31 Howes; Ridgley, "The First College Cruise around the World," 76.

32 Ridgley, 76.

33 "Life on Floating University Much the Same as on Land, Says Robert Smith Crowder of Ryndam," *Decatur (IL) Herald*, May 5, 1927, 3.

34 *Binnacle* (University Travel Association), December 24, 1926, box 48, folder 4, 1DD6 Thwing Papers.

35 "The Point of View: The Floating University," *Bookman: A Review of Books and Life* 65, no. 4 (June 1927): 369.

36 "The Point of View."

37 "Good Will to Men."

38 "The Floating University Will Try Again," *Philadelphia Inquirer*, March 17, 1927.

39 [Pearl Heckel], "A New Educational Project," folder 6, Heckel Papers (emphasis in the original).

40 "Dirty Work Afloat," *Harvard Crimson*, November 8, 1926.

41 Howes, "Report of Scholastic Work on the University Cruise around the World, for the Year 1926–27."

42 *The Student Magellan* (New York: Voelcker Bros., 1927), 207.

43 Albert K. Heckel, Account of the Voyage, p. 2 [1927], folder 6, Heckel Papers.

44 Robert W. Birdsall (Lafayette College) to James E. Lough, July 6, 1927; R. P. O'Neill to University Travel Association, April 27, 1927; Donald Hambleton to Charles H. Phelps, June 30, 1927, in *The Second Annual College Cruise* (New York: University Travel Association, 1928).

45 George B. Philips to the University Travel Association, July 5, 1927, in *The Second Annual College Cruise*.

46 Brewster Bingham to the University Travel Association, June 8, 1927, in *The Second Annual College Cruise*.

47 Wayne Dumont to Charles H. Phelps, July 5, 1927, in *The Second Annual College Cruise*.

48 Deana Heath, "Obscenity, Censorship, and Modernity," in *A Companion to the History of the Book*, ed. Simon Eliot and Jonathan Rose, 2nd ed. (Hoboken, NJ: John Wiley and Sons, 2019), 801–13; Lynda Nead, *The Female Nude: Art, Obscenity and Sexuality* (London: Routledge, 1992), 24–25; Alison Pease, *Modernism, Mass Culture, and the Aesthetics of Obscenity* (Cambridge: Cambridge University Press, 2000), xii.

49 As a starting point, see George Chauncey, *Gay New York: Gender, Urban Culture, and the Making of the Gay Male World, 1890–1940* (New York: Basic Books, 2008);

Matt Houlbrook, *Queer London: Perils and Pleasures of the Sexual Metropolis, 1918–1957* (Chicago: University of Chicago Press, 2005); Laura Doan, *Disturbing Practices: History, Sexuality, and Women's Experience of Modern War* (Chicago: University of Chicago Press, 2013).

50 Christian Gauss quoted in Paula S. Fass, *The Damned and the Beautiful: American Youth in the 1920s* (Oxford: Oxford University Press, 1977), 46–47. See also Geiger, *The History of American Higher Education*, 546–47.

51 "Ryndam Bound for Homeland," *Christian Science Monitor*, April 30, 1927; Robert Vitalis, *White World Order, Black Power Politics: The Birth of American International Relations* (Ithaca, NY: Cornell University Press, 2015); Mark Mazower, *No Enchanted Palace: The End of Empire and the Ideological Origins of the United Nations* (Princeton, NJ: Princeton University Press, 2009).

52 Wendy Martin, "North American Travel Writing," in *The Cambridge History of Travel Writing*, ed. Nandini Das and Tim Youngs (Cambridge: Cambridge University Press, 2019), 262.

53 Special Agent Kinsey to R. C. Bannerman, July 25, 1928, Central Decimal File 1910–29, box 317/032 University Travel Association, RG 59 (Department of State), NARA; Sydney Greenbie, "Educators beyond Their Depth" (1929), folder 22, Walker Papers.

54 "Good Will to Men."

55 Leonard B. Aliwanag, "Filipino Pioneer: Merchant Marine, Movie Extra and Hotel Worker," oral history interview, August 19, 1976, FIL-KNG76-50 cm, Washington State Oral/Aural History Program Interviews, Center for Pacific Northwest Studies, Heritage Resources, Western Washington University, Bellingham.

56 "The Second Annual College Cruise around the World, 1927–28: Administrative Staff, Faculty and Outline of Courses" (University Travel Association), 331642B, University of Michigan Library.

57 Cross-reference cards, October 25, 1926, H Subject Files/Continuing Education, Adult Education: Its Beginnings, New York University Archives; Minutes of Meeting of the Executive, October 10, 1927, roll #5, Meetings of the Council.

58 Minutes of Meeting of the Executive, October 10, 1927, roll #5, Meetings of the Council.

59 Minutes of Meeting of the Executive, October 24, 1927, roll #5, Meetings of the Council.

60 Harold Voorhis's affidavit, May 22, 1928, #18063/1928 "Lough, James E. vs New York University," New York County Clerk Archives, New York City.

61 Cross-reference cards, February 15, 1927, H/NYU Continuing Education, Adult Education: Its Beginnings, New York University Archives.

62 Harold Voorhis to Chancellor Brown, February 10, 1927, box 64, folder 4, Office of the President.

63 Minutes of Meeting of the Council, February 28, 1927, roll #5, Meetings of the Council.

64 Harold Voorhis to Chancellor Brown, February 10, 1927, box 64, folder 4, Office of the President.

65 Charles H. Phelps to Chancellor Brown, April 4, 1927, box 22, Office of the President.

66 Rufus Smith to Voorhis, April 14, 1927; and Chancellor Brown to Charles H. Phelps, April 19, 1927, box 22, Office of the President.

67 Scholarship notice [1927], box 5, folder 139, MS 807 M. Conover Papers, Manuscripts and Archives, Yale University Library.

68 President A. Lawrence Lowell to Charles H. Phelps, April 1, 1927, box 242, folder 755, UA I 5.160 President Lowell's Papers, Harvard University Archives.

69 Chester N. Greenough to President A. Lawrence Lowell, March 31, 1927, box 242, folder 755, UA I 5.160 President Lowell's Papers. The idea of a Floating University has been received with "well-founded distrust among collect administrators," wrote Greenbie. "The feeling has been that it is a fake institution. . . . Colleges have been afraid that students wouldn't behave, that they couldn't study en route, that co-education would fail." See Greenbie, "Educators beyond Their Depth," pp. 3, 5, folder 22, Walker Papers.

70 University Travel Association to Milton Conover, July 9, 1927, MS 807 M. Conover Papers, Manuscripts and Archives, Yale University Library.

71 Summons, January 3, 1928, #18063/1928 Lough vs NYU.

72 "Lough Says N.Y.U. Knew of His Cruise," *New York Times*, May 24, 1928.

73 For more on the Carnegie pensions, see William Graebner, "The Origins of Retirement in Higher Education: The Carnegie Pension Scheme," *Academe* 65, no. 2 (March 1979): 97–103.

74 Brief for New York University, Defendant, May 22, 1928, #18063/1928 Lough vs NYU.

75 Harold Voorhis's affidavit, May 22, 1928, #18063/1928 Lough vs NYU.

76 "Lough Says N.Y.U. Knew of His Cruise"; "Lough Is Accused of Breaking Faith," *New York Times*, May 23, 1928.

77 Special Term Part One, May 29, 1928, #18063/1928 Lough vs NYU.

78 State Department to Laurits S. Swenson (American Minister, Oslo), replying to a letter from the Ambassador, August 6, 1928, Central Decimal File 1910–29, box 317/032 University Travel Association, RG 59 (Department of State), NARA.

79 Special Agent Kinsey to R. C. Bannerman, July 25, 1928, Central Decimal File 1910–29, box 317/032 University Travel Association, RG 59 (Department of State), NARA.

80 Special Agent Kinsey to R. C. Bannerman, July 25, 1928, Central Decimal File 1910–29, box 317/032 University Travel Association, RG 59 (Department of State), NARA.

81 Special Agent Kinsey to R. C. Bannerman, July 25, 1928, Central Decimal File 1910–29, box 317/032 University Travel Association, RG 59 (Department of State), NARA.

82 Special Agent Kinsey to R. C. Bannerman, July 25, 1928.

83 Division of Western European Affairs to Mr. Rand, January 19, 1928, Central Decimal File 1910–29, box 317/032 University Travel Association, RG 59 (Department of State), NARA.

84 Division of Western European Affairs to Mr. Gilbert, August 1, 1928, Central Decimal File 1910–29, box 317/032 University Travel Association, RG 59 (Department of State), NARA.

85 R. C. Bannerman to Mr. W. R. Castle (Assistant Secretary of State), July 26, 1928, Central Decimal File 1910–29, box 317/032 University Travel Association, RG 59 (Department of State), NARA.

86 Nelson Trusler Johnson for the Secretary of State to Mr. Bannerman, August 4,

1928, Central Decimal File 1910–29, box 317/032 University Travel Association, RG 59 (Department of State), NARA.

87 State Department to Laurits S. Swenson (American Minister, Oslo), August 6, 1928, Central Decimal File 1910–29, box 317/032 University Travel Association, RG 59 (Department of State), NARA.

88 Pamphlet, *The College Cruise around the World* [1928], H Subject Files/Cruises, New York University Archives.

89 See AX567 Sydney and Marjorie Greenbie Papers, 1908–1958, University of Oregon Special Collections.

90 Greenbie, "Educators beyond Their Depth," folder 22, Walker Papers.

91 Greenbie's address to students aboard the SS *President Wilson*, November 8, 1928, box 2, folder 3, Raises Collection.

92 "Around-World 'U' Pupils Bare Ride in Pig Ship," *Chicago Tribune*, May 22, 1929.

93 Greenbie, "Educators beyond Their Depth," pp. 11, 12, folder 22, Walker Papers.

94 Greenbie, p. 13.

95 Greenbie's address to students aboard the SS *President Wilson*, November 8, 1928, box 2, folder 3, Raises Collection; Floating University Faculty and the Course of Instruction, 1928–29, 1928 Ephemera, Raises Collection.

96 Greenbie's address to students aboard the SS *President Wilson*, November 8, 1928, box 2, folder 3, Raises Collection.

97 Belgenland "College World Tour," box 1, Educ 7470.01 Travel as a Means of Education (Misc. Pamphlets), Monroe C. Gutman Library Special Collections, Harvard Graduate School of Education. See also *The College Cruise around the World* [1928], H Subject Files/Cruises, New York University Archives; "Many Notables Are on the Belgenland Trip," *Daily Chronicle* (De Kalb, IL), February 25, 1929; Carroll Willis Ford, "Log Book of the Red Star Line S.S. Belgenland World Cruise, #6368," Division of Rare and Manuscript Collections, Cornell University Library.

98 Belgenland "College World Tour"; "Floating University to Arrive Here on World Liner Belgenland," *China Press* (Shanghai), January 30, 1929.

99 An account of the voyage is in 1929/30 Memorabilia, folder 11, Semester at Sea Archives 1926–1927.

100 Raises's Report on the Straits Settlements; Raises (Calcutta) to Greenbie, February 28, 1929, box 2, folder 2, Raises Collection. See also C. A. Raises, "My Most Unusual Booking," 1928 Ephemera, Raises Collection.

101 *Walking Varsity Blister*, box 2, folder 2, Raises Collection.

102 "Around-World 'U' Pupils Bare Ride in Pig Ship."

103 Greenbie, "Educators beyond Their Depth," p. 2, folder 22, Walker Papers.

104 Greenbie, p. 3.

105 Greenbie, p. 2. Note that another itinerant tour ran in 1929/30. See "1929–30 World Voyage," folder 11, Semester at Sea Archives 1926–1927.

106 Greenbie, "Educators beyond Their Depth," pp. 24, 25, folder 22, Walker Papers; "Andrew J. McIntosh Dies," *New York Times*, October 14, 1928.

107 "Spring Weather Helps, but Poor Still Need Aid," *New York Daily News*, January 6, 1931.

108 Minutes of Meeting of the Executive, January 8, 1931, roll #7, Meetings of the Council.

109 Minutes of Meeting of the Executive, January 8, 1931, roll #7, Meetings of the Council.

110 Minutes of Meeting of the Council, April 7, 1925, roll #5, Meetings of the Council.
111 Minutes of Meeting of the Executive, January 8, 1931, roll #7, Meetings of the Council.
112 Minutes of Meeting of the Council, November 24, 1930, roll #7, Meetings of the Council.
113 Minutes of Meeting of the Council, January 26, 1931, roll #7, Meetings of the Council; Telegrams from General Charles H. Sherrill, 1931, box 90, folder 13, Office of the President. When later that same year the NYU students chose to mark the university's centennial with a musical comedy and revue, the subject chosen by writers Sidney Friedberg and Donald B. Robinson was "Naughtical but Nice." "Two Shows Produced by N.Y.U. Students," *New York Times*, April 19, 1931.
114 Minutes of Meeting of the Council, January 26, 1931, roll #7, Meetings of the Council.
115 "NYU Bulletin, University Extension Division, 1933–34," box 1, folder 3, RG 32.03 Extramural, Extension Division, Division of General Education, New York University Archives.
116 Edith E. Ware, ed., *The Study of International Relations in the United States: Survey for 1937* (New York: Published for the American National Committee on International Intellectual Cooperation by Columbia University Press, 1938), 163. Ware listed several nonprofit agencies designed to encourage student travel, including the Open Road (the travel department of the National Student Federation of America), Bureau of University Travel, Committee on Cultural Relations with Latin America, Pocono Study Tours, Students International Travel Association, and Reconciliation Trips. By 1937, a significant number of scholarships and fellowships also had become available (many managed by the Institute of International Education) to support what was now called the international exchange of US faculty and postgraduate students to work or study in overseas universities. See Ware, 419–38.
117 Gore, "Discourse and Traditional Belief," 38n58; Whitney Walton, "American Girls and French Jeunes Filles: Negotiating National Identities in Interwar France," *Gender and History* vol. 17, no. 2 (2005): 325; Whitney Walton, "Internationalism and the Junior Year Abroad: American Students in France in the 1920s and 1930s," *Diplomatic History* 29, no. 2 (2005): 255–78.
118 Sydney Greenbie, "Learning by Cruising," *American Scholar* 3, no. 3 (1934): 355. Since the first *Ryndam* voyage, wrote Greenbie, "all sorts of travel groups have dubbed themselves or have been dubbed floating universities." Steamship agencies and tourist organizations had filched the title.
119 John Eugene Harley, *International Understanding: Agencies Educating for a New World* (Stanford, CA: Stanford University Press, 1931), 54.
120 "1934–35 Plan of Work, League of Nations International Institute of Intellectual Co-operation," report no. 7, Central Decimal File 1930–39, box 2516/500C 1193/13, RG 59 (Department of State), NARA.
121 E.g., see Vitalis, *White World Order, Black Power Politics*; Patricia Owens and Katharina Rietzler, eds., *Women's International Thought: A New History* (Cambridge: Cambridge University Press, 2021); Patricia Owens, Katharina Rietzler, Kimberly Hutchings, and Sarah C. Dunstan, eds., *Women's International Thought: Towards a New Canon* (Cambridge: Cambridge University Press, 2022).
122 Most recently Jan Stöckmann, *The Architects of Internationalism: Building a Dis-*

cipline, Designing the World, 1914–1940 (Cambridge: Cambridge University Press, 2022), 72–118.

123 Ware, *The Study of International Relations in the United States*; Lucian Ashworth, *A History of International Thought: From the Origins of the Modern State to Academic International Relations* (London: Routledge, 2013), 140–41; Michael Riemens, "International Academic Cooperation on International Relations in the Interwar Period: The International Studies Conference," *Review of International Studies* 37, no. 2 (April 2011): 911–28.

124 Ware, *The Study of International Relations in the United States*, 111, 113.

125 Ware, 113, 117.

126 Ware, 130.

127 Ware, 123–29.

128 Such as the Society of the Advancement of Management, est. 1936 (amalgamation of the Taylor Society and the Society of Industrial Engineers); the National Bureau of Economic Research, est. 1920; the Institute of International Finance, est. 1926 (Investment Bankers Association of America in cooperation with NYU); the US Chamber of Commerce. See Ware, 59–70.

129 Ware, 70.

130 Minutes of the Meeting of the American National Committee on International Cooperation, March 9, 1935, Central Decimal File 1930–39, box 2516/500C 1193/13, RG 59 (Department of State), NARA.

131 "Notes (Summer School)," *Bulletin of the American Association of University Professors (1915–1955)*, May 1927, 323. A handful of students, however, did go on to study at international relations summer schools in Geneva following the voyage. See chapter 9.

132 "Chatham Girls Graduate from Mills School, N.Y.," *Chatham (NY) Press*, June 7, 1935; *Educational Directory 1935: Part III Colleges and Universities*, bulletin 1935, no. 1 (Washington, DC: Government Printing Office, 1934), https://files.eric.ed .gov/fulltext/ED543747.pdf; "Florence Albertini to Graduate from the Scudder School," *Mount Carmel (PA) Item*, May 26, 1939; "Chapter 10 [Lough obituaries]," Lough Family Papers.

133 "College Makes Policy Change," *Daily Mail* (Hagerstown, MD), May 27, 1937.

134 Ch. of Brethren v. Un. Br. B.T. Co., January 10, 1945, Court of Appeals of Maryland, archived copy, May 27, 2022, Internet Archive Wayback Machine, https:// web.archive.org/web/20220527051027/https://casetext.com/case/ch-of -brethren-v-un-br-b-t-co; "Blue Ridge College Purchase, Series 3/23," Digital Archives of the Brethren Historical Library and Archives, Elgin, IL.

135 *Gangplank* (*Ryndam* alumni newsletter), no. 1 (May 1930), box 2, folder 4, Raises Collection.

136 Stephen U. Hopkins to Hon. James A. Farley, January 9, 1937, enclosing Statement on Floating University, box 950, file 130–112, RG 178 (Records of the U.S. Maritime Commission), NARA.

137 William Lough Jr. to Hon. William I Sirovich, October 31, 1938; W. S. Crosley to Admiral Wiley, February 10, 1937; U.S. Shipping Board Merchant Fleet Corporation Inter-office Memorandum, January 28, 1935, box 950, file 130–112, RG 178 (Records of the U.S. Maritime Commission), NARA.

138 William Lough Jr. to the children of his brother James, June 4, 1952; "Chapter 10 [Lough obituaries]," Lough Family Papers.

139 "First Floating College Trip to Latin America," *Chicago Tribune*, June 19, 1947.

140 William Lough Jr. to the U.S. Maritime Commission, November 15, 1944, box 950, file 130–112, RG 178 (Records of the U.S. Maritime Commission), NARA.

141 "American Floating University: Voyages to Latin America [ca. 1944]," box 950, file 130–112, RG 178 (Records of the U.S. Maritime Commission), NARA.

142 "Chapter 10 [Lough obituaries]," Lough Family Papers; Record of Lough, J. E., 1893–94, box 2, Graduate School, UA V 161.272, Harvard University Archives.

143 William Lough Jr. to the children of his brother James, June 4, 1952, Lough Family Papers.

CHAPTER NINE

1 "The Point of View: The Floating University," *Bookman: A Review of Books and Life* 65, no. 4 (1927): 369. See also Woodrow C. Whitten, "Floating Campus," *Improving College and University Teaching* 17, no. 4 (1969): 283–86.

2 *Gangplank* (*Ryndam* alumni newsletter), May 1930, box 2, folder 4, Raises Collection.

3 *Gangplank,* May 1930.

4 *Gangplank,* May 1930.

5 *Gangplank,* May 1930.

6 Holling C. Holling to James E. Lough, 1934, box 59, folder 1, Holling Papers.

7 Holling C. Holling to James E. Lough, 1934.

8 Watty Piper, *Little Folks of Other Lands*, illustrated by Lucille W. and H. C. Holling (New York: Platt and Punk, 1929).

9 Private correspondence with Hayden Lorimer, June 11, 2019.

10 E.g., Mary Ray Eaton [Fraley] to Holling C. Holling, July 19, 1937, box 40, folder 2, Holling Papers. See also Holling C. Holling to J. E. Lough, 1943, box 59, folder 1, Holling Papers.

11 Walt Giersbach, "Hands-on Education, or Building Your Own Museum," *Holling Clancy Holling* (blog), September 11, 2014, archived copy, April 26, 2022, Internet Archive Wayback Machine, https://web.archive.org/web/2021*/https://hollingcholling.blogspot.com/2014/09/hands-on-education-or-building-your-own.html.

12 Holling Clancy Holling, *Paddle-to-the-Sea* (Boston: Houghton Mifflin, 1941).

13 *Gangplank* (newsletter), May 1930, box 2, folder 4, Raises Collection.

14 Douglas C. Ridgley, George F. Howe, and Isabelle K. Hart, *World Journeys* (Bloomington, IL: McKnight and McKnight, 1933); Douglas C. Ridgley, George F. Howe, and Isabelle K. Hart, *Home Journeys* (Bloomington, IL: McKnight and McKnight, 1933).

15 "Highlights of Pioneer University Cruise," box 2, folder 12, 0055 Library of Aeronautical History, Women's International Association of Aeronautics (WIAA) Records, University of Southern California Libraries Special Collections.

16 Tamson Pietsch, "Elizabeth Lippincott McQueen: Thinking International Peace in an Air-Minded Age," in *Women's International Thought: A New History*, ed. Patricia Owens and Katharina Rietzler (Cambridge: Cambridge University Press, 2021), 115–35.

17 "Anchor Festival," Centralia Chamber of Commerce, archived copy, Internet Archive Wayback Machine, April 25, 2021, https://web.archive.org/web/20210425064558/https://www.centraliamochamber.com/anchor-festival.html.

18 Annabel Howard, Ruth Miller, and Maryellen H. McVicker, "Albert Bishop

Chance House and Gardens," 1969, National Register of Historic Places Inventory, Nomination Form, Missouri State Parks, Jefferson City, archived copy, May 27, 2022, Internet Archive Wayback Machine, https://web.archive.org/web/ */https://mostateparks.com/sites/mostateparks/files/Chance%2C%20Albert %20Bishop%2C%20House%20and%20Gardens.pdf.

19 "Centralia Can Now Boast . . . ," *Centralia (MO) Fireside Guard*, June 18, 1937.

20 "Name T. G. Brown Boro Library Aide," *Brooklyn Daily Eagle*, December 2, 1937.

21 "Editor to Give Trinity Record of Ship Newspaper," *Hartford Courant*, June 2, 1963.

22 Jay Pursel, "Lafayette's Flying College," *Lafayette Alumnus*, November 1950.

23 *Gangplank* (newsletter), May 1930, box 2, folder 4, Raises Collection.

24 Nancy Weatherly Sharp et al., *American Legislative Leaders in the West, 1911–1994* (Westport, CT: Greenwood Press), 111; "David R. Inglis, 90: Worked on A-Bomb," *New York Times*, December 8, 1995.

25 Richard Harman, *Cunningham: The Passion, the Cars, the Legacy* (Loughborough, UK: Dalton Watson Fine Books, 2013).

26 "Black, Richard B. Oral History," 1962, Butler Library, Columbia University.

27 "Biographical Note," J. Howard Marshall II Papers, Dolph Briscoe Center for American History, University of Texas at Austin.

28 See Robert D. Dean, *Imperial Brotherhood: Gender and the Making of Cold War Foreign Policy* (Amherst: University of Massachusetts Press, 2001); Tamson Pietsch, "Commercial Travel and College Culture: The 1920s Transatlantic Student Market and the Foundations of Mass Tourism," *Diplomatic History* 43, no. 1 (2019): 83–106.

29 In addition to those discussed here, DeWitt Reddick, Mrs. Frankie G. Merson, and John H. Van Devente Jr. were others who pursued academic careers.

30 *Monmouth College Catalog* (Monmouth, IL: Monmouth College, 1948), 16.

31 Alice Gamer to Holling C. Holling, December 1, 1936, box 40, folder 2, Holling Papers.

32 Alice Gamer to Holling C. Holling, September 25, 1937, emphasis in the original, box 40, folder 2, Holling Papers.

33 Monmouth College, *Ravelings* (Monmouth, IL: Monmouth College, 1951), 58.

34 Jeff Rankin, "College Professor Provided Boost to Struggling Church," *Medium* (blog), April 26, 2018, archived copy, May 27, 2022, Internet Archive Wayback Machine, https://web.archive.org/web/20220527044606/https:// jeffrankin.medium.com/college-professor-provided-boost-to-struggling-church -30f7a333e2c7.

35 J. Gengerelli, D. Lindsley, and G. Mount, "Marion Augustus Wenger, Psychology: Los Angeles," University of California: In Memoriam, 1985, 2011, http://texts.cdlib .org/view?docId=hb4d5nb20m&doc.view=frames&chunk.id=div00173&toc .depth=1&toc.id=.

36 Bruce H. Friedman, "Feelings and the Body: The Jamesian Perspective on Autonomic Specificity of Emotion," *Biological Psychology* 84, no. 3 (July 2010): 383–93.

37 Bernard T. Engel, "Marion A. Wenger: A Eulogy," *Psychophysiology* 20, no. 1 (1983): 116–17.

38 Bert S. Hall, "Lynn Townsend White, Jr. (1907–1987)," *Technology and Culture* 30, no. 1 (1989): 194–213.

39 Lynn White Jr., "The Historical Roots of Our Ecologic Crisis," *Science* 155, no. 3767 (1967): 1203–7.

40 White, 1207.

41 Hall, "Lynn Townsend White, Jr. (1907–1987)," 198.

42 John Dewey, *The School and Society* (Chicago: University of Chicago Press, 1915), 80.

43 "New Ryndam Plays Host at Quarter-Century Dinner," Holland America Line N.A.S.M. News, June 1952, folder 6, Semester at Sea Archives 1926–1927.

44 "New Ryndam Plays Host at Quarter-Century Dinner."

45 "Floating University Visits Fabled Lands," *Boston Globe*, January 6, 1952; "Around the World Student 'Goodwill Cruises' Near Reality," *Battle Creek (MI) Enquirer*, March 14, 1958; Julius W. Butler to Dan R. Collette, March 13, 1958; Holling C. Holling to Mae Noble Rineman, February 14, 1960, box 60, folder 14, Holling Papers.

46 "Suggests Travel University Be Sent Out Yearly," *Gazette* (Cedar Rapids, IA), July 27, 1958; "Floating University Proposed by S. F. Man," *San Francisco News*, March 20, 1958, box 60, folder 14, Holling Papers.

47 "Suggests Travel University Be Sent Out Yearly"; Barry H. Marquardson, "The Origin and Development of Shipboard Education" (Master's thesis, Arizona State University, 1981).

48 Whitten, "Floating Campus."

49 *Binnacle* (University Travel Association), October 12, 1926, box 48, folder 4, 1DD6 Thwing Papers; Holling C. Holling to Mae Noble Rineman, February 14, 1960, box 60, folder 14, Holling Papers.

50 Paul Liebhardt, "The History of Shipboard Education," *Steamboat Bill* 55, no. 3 (1998): 181. See also Whitten, "Floating Campus," 283. In January 1960, Kasem introduced to the US House of Representatives a bill authorizing the Maritime Administration to loan a ship to a new nonprofit corporation "for the purpose of furthering the exchange of cultural, technological, social and economic learning and knowledge for the students of the United States and other nations." The bill was carried through the Senate a month later by Californians Thomas Kuchel and Clair Engle. "Propose Use of Ships as Universities," *Van Nuys (CA) News*, September 17, 1959; "Club Closer to Goal of Floating University," *Los Angeles Times*, January 18, 1960; "Floating University," *Petaluma (CA) Argus-Courier*, February 23, 1960.

51 Quote taken from an advertisement for the 1963 cruise: "Exciting News from the University of the Seven Seas," *Rotarian*, July 1963, 1. See also "A University Sets Sail," *Rotarian*, December 1963, 32–33; E. Ray Nichols, "The University of the Seven Seas," *Improving College and University Teaching* 11, no. 3 (August 1963): 125; "University of the Seven Seas to Sail from NYC in October," *Linden Bark* (Lindenwood College, St. Charles, MO), May 9, 1963.

52 Marquardson, "The Origin and Development of Shipboard Education."

53 World Campus Afloat Association of Colleges and Universities, *Foreign Aft* magazine (Chapman College, Orange, CA, 1963).

54 Marquardson, "The Origin and Development of Shipboard Education," 31; Institute for Shipboard Education in conjunction with Colorado State University, "Semester at Sea History," 2021, archived copy, April 26, 2021, Internet Archive Wayback Machine, https://web.archive.org/web/20210426001218/https://www.semesteratsea.org/contact/our-history/.

55 William Hoffa, *A History of US Study Abroad: Beginnings to 1965* (Carlisle, PA: Forum on Education Abroad, 2007); William W. Hoffa and Stephen C. DePaul, eds., *A History of U.S. Study Abroad, 1965–Present* (Carlisle, PA: Frontiers: The Interdisciplinary Journal of Study Abroad, 2010); Irwin Abrams and Winslow Roper

Hatch, *Study Abroad* (Washington DC: Office of Education, US Department of Health, Education, and Welfare, 1960).

56 Sam Lebovic, *A Righteous Smokescreen: Postwar America and the Politics of Cultural Globalization* (Chicago: University of Chicago Press, 2022), 4; Sam Lebovic, "From War Junk to Educational Exchange: The World War II Origins of the Fulbright Program and the Foundations of American Cultural Globalism, 1945–1950," *Diplomatic History* 37, no. 2 (April 1, 2013): 280–312; Hoffa, *A History of US Study Abroad*, 166–77.

57 Hoffa, *A History of US Study Abroad*, 184a.

58 Hoffa, 236–43; Irwin Abrams quoted in Hoffa, 287.

59 Hoffa, *A History of US Study Abroad*, 271–72; John M. Keller and Maritheresa Frain, "The Impact of Geo-political Events, Globalization, and National Policies on Study Abroad Programming and Participation," in *A History of U.S. Study Abroad, 1965–Present*, ed. William Hoffa and Stephen C. DePaul (Carlisle, PA: Frontiers: The Interdisciplinary Journal of Study Abroad, 2010), 25–29.

60 Sherry Schwarz, "A History of Study Abroad: William W. Hoffa's Fascinating Story about Its Beginnings to 1965," *Transitions Abroad Magazine*, 2007, archived copy, April 25, 2021, Internet Archive Wayback Machine, https://web.archive.org/web/20210425222613/https://www.transitionsabroad.com/publications/studyabroadmagazine/2007Spring/a_history_of_study_abroad.shtml.

61 Hoffa and DePaul, *A History of U.S. Study Abroad, 1965–Present*, 2; Keller and Frain, "The Impact of Geo-political Events, Globalization, and National Policies on Study Abroad Programming and Participation," 39; Joan Elias Gore, "Discourse and Traditional Belief: An Analysis of American Undergraduate Study Abroad' (PhD diss., University of London, 2000), chap. 1.

62 *Open Doors 2018: Report on International Educational Exchange* (New York: Institute of International Education, 2018).

63 There is now a vast literature, as well as several specialist journals, dedicated to this area of educational research. A good starting point is Richard A. Katula and Elizabeth Threnhauser, "Experiential Education in the Undergraduate Curriculum," *Communication Education* 48, no. 3 (1999): 238–55.

64 Todd Giedt, Gigi Gokcek, and Jayati Ghosh, "International Education in the 21st Century: The Importance of Faculty in Developing Study Abroad Research Opportunities," *Frontiers: The Interdisciplinary Journal of Study Abroad* 26, no. 1 (2015): 167–86.

65 In 2008, the American Council on Education found that only 28 percent of study abroad students came from families with an income of less than $50,000. See Elizabeth Stallman et al., "The Diversification of the Student Profile," in *A History of U.S. Study Abroad, 1965–Present*, ed. William W. Hoffa and Stephen C. DePaul (Carlisle, PA: Frontiers: The Interdisciplinary Journal of Study Abroad, 2010): 130.

66 *Open Doors 2018*.

67 Schwarz, "A History of Study Abroad."

68 In some ways the genealogical method, which is otherwise so helpful in revealing the constitution of regimes of knowledge and power across time, works to occlude failure by encouraging historians to look for an unbroken line between past and present. See Michel Foucault, *Language, Counter-memory, Practice: Selected Essays and Interviews* (Ithaca, NY: Cornell University Press, 1977), 139; Cerutti in Roberto Gronda et al., "Histoires Pragmatiques: A Conversation with Simona

Cerutti and Yves Cohen," *European Journal of Pragmatism and American Philosophy* 8, no. 2 (2016), https://doi.org/10.4000/ejpap.654.

69 Scott A. Sandage, *Born Losers: A History of Failure in America* (Cambridge, MA: Harvard University Press, 2009), 18, 277–78.

70 Raghav Kishore, "'Urban Failures': Municipal Governance, Planning and Power in Colonial Delhi, 1863–1910," *Indian Economic and Social History Review* 52, no. 4 (2015): 459. See also Timothy Mitchell, *Rule of Experts: Egypt, Techno-politics, Modernity* (Berkeley: University of California Press, 2002); William Cunningham Bissell, *Urban Design, Chaos, and Colonial Power in Zanzibar* (Bloomington: Indiana University Press, 2011); Raghav Kishore, *The (Un)Governable City: Productive Failure in the Making of Colonial Delhi, 1858–1911* (Hyderabad: Orient BlackSwan, 2020).

71 William Cunningham Bissell, "From Iraq to Katrina and Back: Bureaucratic Planning as Strategic Failure, Fiction, and Fantasy," *Sociology Compass* 2, no. 5 (2008): 1454.

72 Georges Canguilhem, *On the Normal and the Pathological* (Dordrecht: D. Reidel, 1978), 123; Samuel Talcott, "Georges Canguilhem and the Philosophical Problem of Error," *Dialogue* 52, no. 4 (December 2013): 664.

73 For norms and controversies, see Ann Thomson, "L'histoire intellectuelle : Quelles idées, quel contexte ?," *Revue d'histoire moderne et contemporaine* vol. 59-4, no. 5 (2012): 47–63; Harry Collins, *Changing Order: Replication and Induction in Scientific Practice* (Chicago: Chicago University Press, 1985); Ethan Kleinberg, Joan Wallach Scott, and Gary Wilder, "Theses on Theory and History" (Wild On Collective, 2018), archived copy, December 25, 2021, Internet Archive Wayback Machine, https://web.archive.org/web/20211225121852/http://theoryrevolt.com/; Ana Isabel Keilson, "How Should We Know?," *Contemporary European History* 28, no. 2 (May 2019): 252–61.

74 As Karen Barad writes, "We do not obtain knowledge by standing outside of the world; we know because 'we' are *of* the world." Karen Barad, "Posthumanist Performativity: Toward an Understanding of How Matter Comes to Matter," *Signs* 28, no. 3 (Spring 2003): 829.

75 Intergovernmental Panel on Climate Change, *Global Warming of 1.5°C: An IPCC Special Report on the Impacts of Global Warming of 1.5°C above Pre-industrial Levels and Related Global Greenhouse Gas Emission Pathways, in the Context of Strengthening the Global Response to the Threat of Climate Change, Sustainable Development, and Efforts to Eradicate Poverty*, 2018, https://www.ipcc.ch/sr15/.

APPENDIX

1 Giles Milton, *Paradise Lost: Smyrna 1922; The Destruction of Islam's City of Tolerance* (London: Sceptre, 2008); Michelle Tusan, *Smyrna's Ashes: Humanitarianism, Genocide, and the Birth of the Middle East*, Berkeley Series in British Studies (Berkeley: University of California Press, 2012).

2 Paul Liebhardt, "The History of Shipboard Education," *Steamboat Bill* 55, no. 3 (1998): 173–86. The same account also appeared in Paul Liebhardt and Judy Rogers, *Discovery: The Adventure of Shipboard Education* (Olympia, WA: William and Allen, 1985).

3 Biographical Note, Raises Collection. See also Judy Redfield, *That Remarkable Lit-*

tle Lady of Tenafly: Alice Clarke Redfield (Mount Pleasant, SC: Arcadia, 2020), 132; Institute for Shipboard Education in conjunction with Colorado State University, "Semester at Sea History," 2021, archived copy, April 26, 2022, Internet Archive Wayback Machine, https://web.archive.org/web/20210426001218/https://www.semeratsea.org/contact/our-history/.

4   "An Idea Takes Root," in *The Student Magellan* (New York: Voelcker Bros., 1927), 5.

5   Agreement between Holland America Line and the University Travel Association, issued March 16, 1926, Directie, 01/Dossiers/Cruises/0831, 318 Archieven van de Holland-Amerika Lijn (HAL). First installment paid August 13, 1926; see Davy Baas, "De University World Cruise van 1926–1927: Studentencruise als Grand Tour" (Bachelor thesis, Leiden University, 2018), n77, Leiden University Student Repository.

6   Raises's passport, box 1, folder 4, Raises Collection. In 1925, James E. Lough was living in Pelham, Westchester, the neighboring suburb to Mount Vernon. See "New York State Census, 1925," database, FamilySearch, accessed June 1, 2022, http://FamilySearch.org. Records extracted by the genealogy company Ancestry and images digitized by the international nonprofit organization FamilySearch, citing New York State Archives, Albany.

7   Ship manifest, *Alice*, December 26, 1908, image 371, *New York Passenger Arrival Lists (Ellis Island), 1892–1924*, database with images, Passenger Search, The Statue of Liberty—Ellis Island Foundation Inc., accessed June 1, 2022, https://heritage.statueofliberty.org/.

8   He was traveling with his sister, Despina (age 10) and their father, Elias Raissis, a "Taillor" [*sic*] (age 33) who had been to New York before. Their nearest relative in their country of origin was given as Anastassia Raissis of Smyrna, Elias's mother and Constantinos's grandmother.

9   Later that same year, a "C. Raises," age 20 and of Greek nationality, reappears in the New York passenger lists. He was a quartermaster on the crew of the New York and Cuba Mail Steamship Company's SS *Panuco* entering New York from Portugal on August 16. Indeed, a "C. Raises" meeting the same description features on the crew lists of a number of vessels exiting and entering the Port of New York in 1920 and 1921, and on the 1920 Federal Census a "Constantine Raises" (age 20; birthplace Greece; migrated 1908; occupation, mariner) appears as living in New Rochelle.

10 Ship Manifest, *Cameronia*, August 25, 1922, image 132, *New York Passenger Arrival Lists (Ellis Island), 1892–1924*, database with images, Passenger Search, The Statue of Liberty—Ellis Island Foundation Inc., accessed June 1, 2022, https://heritage.statueofliberty.org/.

11 It is possible that Riesenberg captained one of the ships on which Raises worked between 1920 and 1922.

12 Biographical Note, Raises Collection.

Index

Page numbers in italics refer to illustrations.

158, 163; psychology and, 151; racism
and, 138, 145, 148, 152–54, 163; religion,
122, 131, 133, 134, 177; universities and,
132; Urdahl and, 65. *See also* colonialism;
imperialism
End Men, 123
endowments, 44–45, 51, 195
engineering, 25, 28, 33, 45, 48, 118–19
English, Jack, 132
English-Speaking Union, 55
environmental crisis, 14, 217, 224
Excelsior Hotel, 126
experiential education: Dewey and, 8, 11,
15–16, 20–26, 32, 50, 52, 133; Experiential Learning Model, 11; Floating
University and, 72, 77, 86, 138, 212, 215;
Holling C. Holling and, 77–78, 212;
Kolb and, 11; Lough and, 10, 14, 20–22,
31–33, 40, 43, 53, 57, 63, 72, 114, 136, 167,
192, 203, 207, 316; Montessori, 11; shore
program and, 86–89, 133; Steiner, 11;
Thwing and, 71–82; universities and,
8, 11, 222
Experiential Learning Model, 11
expertise: academically authorized, 2, 6,
7, 49–52, 79, 205–06, 223; empire and,
129–32, 164, 221; experience and, 6, 7,
10, 11, 14, 52, 224; faculty and, 49–50, 58;
historians and, 3; universities and, 51–52,
130, 136
expulsions, 101–3, 186
Extra Bladet, 170
Extramural Division (NYU): Brown and,
24–25, 27, 30, 35, 40, 43, 58; Extension
Division, 59, 196, 204; Garvin inquiry
and, 41–43; Lough and, 23–25, 27–28,
30, 32, 35, 40–45, 55, 58; Sherrill and,
40, 43; student travel and, 27–28, 30, 32,
34, 40–44, 58–59

faculty: expertise and, 49–50, 58; Floating
University, 15, 37–38, 60, 61, 63, 65,
66, 73, 74, 81, 91, 98, 100, 107, 112, 146,
169, 190, 195; NYU, 23, 47, 58, 60, 221;
student travel and, 27, 30, 56, 189, 200,
202, 221; World War I and, 45
failure, 170; assessment of voyage and,
6–10, 14, 186–87, 192, 210–24; Brown
and, 24; Lough and, 6, 8, 14, 32, 197,
208, 223; new women and, 38; politics
and, 222–25; positive impact of Floating
University, 210–24; psychology and, 217;
Raises and, 211, 218–19; risk of, 24; Rum

Orgy and, 6, 100–102; scandal and, 8,
106, 114; thinking with, 210–24
Fairlie, John, 216
Farrell, Robert S., Jr., 215
Farrington, Wallace Rider, 122, 183
Fass, Paula, 111
Federal Department of Commerce, 28, 41
Fédération de l'Alliance Française, 55
Field Museum of Natural History, 65
Fish, Grafton B., 34
Fletcher, Henry P., 181
Flint Daily Journal, 102
Floating University: alumni association
of, 210–11; assessment of voyage and,
186–209; cost of, 38; departure of, 71–75,
94–95; diplomacy and, 66, 166, 167, 183,
199–200; experiential education and, 72,
77, 86, 138, 212, 215; faculty, 15, 37–38, 60,
61, 63, 65, 66, 73, 74, 81, 91, 98, 100, 107,
112, 146, 169, 190, 195; failure and, 210–
24; historical obscurity of, 1–2; impact
of, 210–24; imperialism and, 137–66;
institutional life and, 4; internationalism and, 1, 3, 15, 138, 165, 230; laboratory
method and, 5, 17, 32–33, 204, 208, 219;
legitimacy and, 93; negative views of,
170–78; press coverage of, 2, 93–115 (*see
also* press); shipboard education of, 63–
92; shore program and, 86–89, 133; social
recognition and, 94–95; student grades,
192; travel experience and, 116–36 (*see
also* travel experience); universities and,
1, 39, 95, 199; women and, 15 (*see also*
women). *See also* Lough, James Edwin
Floating University magazine, 109, 188
Flying College, 215
football, 38, 85, 124
Ford Foundation, 10, 218–19
Forum Club, 141, 147–48, 150–51, 165, 182
France: Algeria and, 10, 76, 125, 152, 184;
American Expeditionary Forces and, 80;
assessment of voyage and, 212; cabarets
of, 160; imperialism and, 157–61; "just
peace" and, 29; Louvre, 161; Montmartre, 112, 160–61, 164; Moulin Rouge,
160; Paris, 8–9, 29, 44, 55–58, 75–76,
112–14, 131, 158–61, 171–72, 178, 194, 196,
204; as pleasure ground, 30; press and,
112–14; scandal and, 112–14; tours in, 55;
University of Paris, 56, 75; women of,
54, 160
Franck, Harry A., 140
fraternities, 38, 85, 107, 113, 132